Rimbaud

Complete Works, Selected Letters

A Bilingual Edition

Translated with an Introduction and Notes by Wallace Fowlie
Updated, Revised, and with a Foreword by Seth Whidden

The University of Chicago Press | Chicago and London

Until his death in 1998, *Wallace Fowlie* (b. 1909) was professor emeritus of French literature at Duke University. *Seth Whidden* is assistant professor of French at Villanova University, and co-editor in chief of *Parade sauvage,* the scholarly journal of Rimbaud studies.

The University of Chicago Press, Chicago 60637
The University of Chicago Press, Ltd., London
© 1966, 2005 by The University of Chicago
All rights reserved. Published 2005
Printed in the United States of America

14   13   12   4   5

ISBN: 0-226-71976-6 (cloth)
ISBN: 0-226-71977-4 (paper)

Frontispiece: Portrait of Rimbaud, from a lithograph by Picasso. Courtesy M. H. Matarasso.

Library of Congress Cataloging-in-Publication Data

Rimbaud, Arthur, 1854–1891.
   [Works. English & French. 2005]
   Rimbaud : complete works, selected letters : a bilingual edition / translated with an
introduction and notes by Wallace Fowlie ; updated, revised and with a foreword by
Seth Whidden.
      p.   cm.
   Includes bibliographical references and index.
   ISBN 0-226-71976-6 (cloth : alk. paper) — ISBN 0-226-71977-4 (pbk. : alk. paper)
   1. Rimbaud, Arthur, 1854–1891—Translations into English.   2. Rimbaud, Arthur,
1854–1891—Correspondence.   3. Poets, French—19th century—Correspondence.
I. Fowlie, Wallace, 1908–   II. Whidden, Seth Adam, 1969–   III. Title.

PQ2387 .R5A245 2005
841′.8—dc22

                                                                        2005041859

Rimbaud

Complete Works, Selected Letters

Contents

Poésies / Poetry

Poèmes datés de 1871–début 1872 ou dans des lettres de mai ou juin 1871 /
Poems dated 1871–early 1872 or in letters from May or June 1871

Poèmes non datés (fin 1870–début 1872?) /
Undated poems (late 1870–early 1872?)

Album zutique *(fin 1871–début 1872?)* / Album called "zutique" *(end 1871–early 1872?)*

Du temps qu'il était écolier / From His Schoolboy Days

Une saison en enfer (1873) / A Season in Hell (1873)

Illuminations (1872–1874?) / Illuminations (1872–1874?)

Illustrations

Foreword (2005)

BY SETH WHIDDEN

In a letter to Wallace Fowlie in 1965, Henry Miller wrote: "Am amazed too that you are translating [Rimbaud's] 'complete works'! What a task! And how we need this!"[1] An impressive undertaking indeed. Given Rimbaud's taste for neologisms, his juxtaposing of scientific terms with those from nature, and his shattering of traditional French versification—all part of his "dérèglement de *tous les sens*" (derangement of *all the senses*)[2]—Fowlie found that translating Rimbaud was no easy task.[3] In fact, his translation, which was first published in 1966, was the very first translation of all of Rimbaud's poems. To this day, it remains the only side-by-side bilingual edition of his complete works. Of an even greater importance is the simple fact that, in a field of Rimbaud translations that is growing ever more crowded, Fowlie's translations are the most faithful to Rimbaud's original texts.

In addition to its beauty, grace, and utility, Fowlie's edition has taken on something of a life of its own. On the one hand, it bears Picasso's only known sketch of Rimbaud, a gift that Fowlie received from Henri Mata-

---

1. Henry Miller and Wallace Fowlie. *Letters of Henry Miller and Wallace Fowlie (1943–1972)* (New York: Grove Press, 1975), 155.

2. From Rimbaud's letters of 13 and 15 May 1871.

3. See Fowlie's comments concerning his meeting with fellow translator Louise Varèse. Wallace Fowlie, *Rimbaud and Jim Morrison: The Rebel as Poet* (Durham, NC: Duke University Press, 1993), 12.

rasso in 1966;[4] on the other, it made Rimbaud's poetry available to entire generations of sympathetic readers of English. As Fowlie himself recalled:

> In class [in 1966], while waiting for the last few students to take their seats, I casually asked, "Do you recognize the name Jim Morrison?" My students were shocked by my ignorance. "Don't you know the Doors? He's the lead singer." My stock dropped low that morning in my classroom. I had lost favor. To recuperate and to steady my nerves, I held up the letter and said: "Give me a chance! Let me read this letter to you."

> Dear Wallace Fowlie,
>   Just wanted to say thanks for doing the Rimbaud translation. I needed it because I don't read French that easily. . . . I am a rock singer and your book travels around with me.

> The class was quietly attentive by this time, and I said to them, "There is one more sentence, a post-scriptum at the bottom of the page:"

> That Picasso drawing of Rimbaud on the cover is *great*.[5]

The most important scholarly translation of Rimbaud's complete works requires little revision some forty years after it was first published. Nevertheless, Rimbaud readers—scholars and general readers alike—have learned much since this edition first appeared; it seems worthwhile, therefore, to reflect on new information concerning Rimbaud's life and work as well as our constantly evolving interpretations.

Rimbaud's Life

Rimbaud continues to appeal to readers today, for the wonders of his poetry as well as for the turbulent life he led. In France, he clearly remains one of the most-read and best-appreciated poets by the French, nearly all of whom are required to study Rimbaud, some as early as in grade school. Furthermore, he is admired for what he represents—in 1991, one out of five young French people identified with Rimbaud[6]—both within and outside of France. Our attraction to the young rebel-poet is simple; we see

4. For the story of how Fowlie acquired the drawing, see Fowlie, *Rimbaud and Jim Morrison*, 13–14.

5. Fowlie, *Rimbaud and Jim Morrison*, 14–15.

6. "Arthur, entre Morrison et Gainsbourg," *Globe* 56 (April 1991): 84.

him in us, be it for his revolts, for his brash nature, or for leaving poetry after accomplishing so much in so little time. As a result, each time we discover something new about Rimbaud—new insight into his poetry, or a recently uncovered biographical detail—we learn something new about ourselves. Similarly, we learn about him, and ourselves, as our attitudes evolve and taboos of the past slowly turn to matters of course. Most drastically changed since this translation's first edition is our understanding of Rimbaud's relationship with Verlaine and our ability to discuss it in terms of both his biography and his poetic work. Forty years ago, Fowlie wrote of "an enthusiastic, troubled, and at times tragic relationship" and referred to Verlaine as Rimbaud's "friend" but he knew very well—just as we know—that they were much more than traveling partners, close friends, or literary peers; they were all that and more. Their passionate and tormented homosexual relationship—Verlaine once bragged that they made love like tigers[7]—directly led to Verlaine's wife divorcing him, to Verlaine shooting Rimbaud in a Brussels hotel room (which in turn led to Verlaine's incarceration), and to Verlaine's humiliation of being examined for active and passive homosexual acts.[8] Such a relationship necessarily had an impact on the poetry that they wrote while traveling together, and numerous studies have explored the specific influence they had on each other's poetry. While some conclude that Rimbaud was Verlaine's muse and others believe that Verlaine could not even understand—let alone come close to matching—Rimbaud's genius, even more fall somewhere between these two extremes: paying ample attention to Verlaine's debt to

7. The phrase ("Nous avons des amours de tigres!") is attributed to Verlaine by police officer Lombard in his report from 1 August 1873, in which the poet tried to explain how he disliked married life: "[. . .] et, ce disant il montra à sa femme, sa poitrine tatouée et meurtrie de coups de couteau que lui avait appliqués son ami Raimbaud [sic]. Ces deux êtres se battaient et se déchiraient comme des bêtes féroces, pour avoir le plaisir de se raccommoder" ("and, while saying this, he showed his wife his chest, tattooed and covered with knife marks that his friend Raimbaud [sic] gave him. These two beings fought and tore each other apart like ferocious beasts, to then enjoy the pleasure of making up"). Quoted in Auguste Martin, "Verlaine et Rimbaud," *La nouvelle revue française* (February 1943): 212.

8. "En effet, le Juge d'Instruction de Bruxelles ayant ordonné la visite corporelle du prévenu par les docteurs Semal et Vleminckx, ceux-ci firent un rapport en ce sens que Verlaine portait sur sa personne les traces de pédérastie active et passive" ("In fact, the examining magistrate of Brussels ordered the physical examination of the detainee by Doctors Semal and Vleminckx, who reported that Verlaine bore the signs of active and passive pederasty"). See Martin, "Verlaine et Rimbaud," 216; and Françoise Lalande, "L'examen corporel d'un homme de lettres," *Parade sauvage* 2 (April 1985): 97–98.

the young prodigy while still acknowledging Verlaine's individual talents.[9]

Many of the other questions surrounding Rimbaud's life—his participation in the Paris Commune of 1871[10] or his use of slaves in Africa,[11] to name a few—have also been revisited since Fowlie's edition. Rarely, a new discovery about Rimbaud's life unequivocally answers a quandary that had previously gone unsolved; more often, a new theory surfaces, waiting for future biographers to substantiate or refute it.[12] However, with so many biographies already written and with so little available documentation concerning his life in Africa, such finds are increasingly rare. More frequent than new facts are the ways in which those facts are interpreted. As Fowlie's use of the term "friend" indicates, it is only logical that Rimbaud's more recent biographers, with fewer social restrictions, have presented a more accurate—or, to use one of Rimbaud's words, "modern"[13]—account of the life of the *poète maudit* (damned poet).[14] Questions about Rimbaud at the Commune, about African slaves, and about the order of publication of his poems, at one time topics of heated debate, are now largely consid-

9. See Georges Zayed, *La formation littéraire de Verlaine* [1962], rev. ed., Paris: Librairie Nizet, 1970); Henri Peyre, *Rimbaud vu par Verlaine* (Paris: Librairie A.-G. Nizet, 1975); and Paul Schmidt, "Visions of Violence: Rimbaud and Verlaine," in *Homosexualities and French Literature: Cultural Contexts/Critical Texts,* eds. George Stambolian and Elaine Marks (Ithaca, NY: Cornell University Press, 1979), 228–42.

10. Without claiming that he was physically there, Kristin Ross (*The Emergence of Social Space: Rimbaud and the Paris Commune* [Minneapolis: University of Minnesota Press, 1988]) masterfully shows how Rimbaud's work is inextricably linked to the massive socio-historic changes that the Commune brought about. Jean-Jacques Lefrère (*Arthur Rimbaud* [Paris: Librairie Arthème Fayard, 2001], 255–56) has convincingly argued that, even if Rimbaud had gone to Paris, it would have been more for bookstores and reading rooms than for the barricades. As such, his "participation" in the Commune is limited to his poems inspired from it, whether he was in Paris or not. Also see Graham Robb, *Rimbaud: A Biography* (New York: Norton/London: Picador, 2000), 76.

11. See Robb, *Rimbaud: A Biography,* 391.

12. Robb has proposed an interesting theory of how Rimbaud returned from Java after having deserted the Dutch army by assuming the name Edwin Holmes (284).

13. "Il faut être absolument moderne" ("We must be absolutely modern") from "Adieu" ("Farewell") the last poem in *Une saison en enfer (A Season in Hell).*

14. This term comes from Verlaine's study "Les poètes maudits" ("The Damned Poets"), published first in *Lutèce* from 29 March to 5 April 1884 and reprinted in 1888. Within the biographical sketch Verlaine inserted Rimbaud's poems "Voyelles" ("Vowels"), "Oraison du soir" ("Evening Prayer"), "Les assis" ("The Men Who Sit"), "Les effarés" ("The Frightened Ones"), "Les chercheuses de poux" ("The Seekers of Lice"), and "Le bateau ivre" ("The Drunken Boat"). Two years before the publication of poems from *Illuminations,* this study did much to establish the Rimbaud myth (at the time, Rimbaud had abandoned poetry for good and was living in Africa).

ered relatively inconsequential when compared to interpretations of the poems themselves, which have been enjoying a renewed focus.

Rimbaud's Work

Paralleling the increased liberties accorded to biographers, those scholars and general readers who interpret Rimbaud's poetry enjoy a similarly increased freedom, still focusing to a large extent on the general "problem of poetic expression" that Fowlie saw inaugurated by Etiemble's demystifying studies of the early 1950s. Trends during the past forty years of literary criticism—from structuralism to deconstruction, gender studies to cultural studies—have all left their mark on how we read Rimbaud. These critical contributions notwithstanding, the poems are hardly solved once and for all; it is still Rimbaud alone who holds the key to unlocking "Parade" ("Circus").[15] Rather, the texts withstand the tests of time, perhaps even getting better with age, and they are likely to continue to do so as more approaches to reading and interpreting texts come and go.

No previously unknown verse or prose poems of Rimbaud's have been uncovered in the past forty years,[16] but access to original manuscripts and iconographic documents has significantly increased, resulting in a host of books filled with photos and reproductions from Rimbaud's life in both Europe and Africa. In addition, technological advancements have greatly improved the quality of facsimiles, many of which are published for the first time in auction catalogues.[17] However universal and timeless Rim-

15. "J'ai seul la clef de cette parade sauvage" ("I alone have the key of this wild circus"), from *Illuminations (Illuminations); see* "Parade" ("Circus") in this edition.

16. The last time such a find was made public, in 1949, it turned out to be a forgery, that of a lost poem entitled "La chasse spirituelle"; see Bruce Morrissette, *The Great Rimbaud Forgery: The Affair of* La chasse spirituelle (Saint Louis, MO: Washington University, 1956).

17. In March 1998, the Jean Hugues succession attracted such a large public for thirty-five letters and manuscripts by and related to Rimbaud that two entire auction halls were reserved. Both rooms were filled: one for serious bidders, and the other for amateurs who had to settle for following the action on video. Two-thirds of the items were purchased by the Bibliothèque nationale de France, the Bibliothèque littéraire Jacques Doucet, and by the city of Charleville-Mézières. From the collection, the Bibliothèque nationale purchased ten letters between 1871 and 1885, the most important one being the 15 May 1871 letter to Paul Demeny, which fetched the price of three million francs (over $460,000). Another letter addressed to Demeny in 1871, which contained the poems "Les poètes de sept ans," "Les pauvres à l'église," and "Le cœur du pitre" went for 1,200,000F ($183,000). Finally, the letter sent to Ernest Delahaye from Stuttgart in 1875 and detailing (with illustrations) Rimbaud's last meeting with Verlaine, went for 1,100,000F ($168,000). Drouot Richelieu, *Arthur Rimbaud, Paul*

baud's work and its appeal may be, the poems' reception ebbs and flows. Wallace Fowlie's first edition was printed a dozen years after the numerous publications and conferences that commemorated Rimbaud's centenary in 1954. Similarly, this new edition appears a little more than a decade after the one-hundredth anniversary of the poet's death (1891), and in the wake of the sesquicentennial of the poet's birth (1854), two celebrations marked by great groundswells of critical editions, international conferences, and events of all sorts.[18] In addition, Rimbaud's life and writings have inspired

---

Verlaine: Manuscrits et lettres autographes, documents, éditions originales. Succession Jean Hugues, 20 mars 1998 (Paris: Drouot, 1998). Later that year, ten more of Rimbaud's manuscripts, including a draft of *Une saison en enfer (A Season in Hell)*, went on the auction block (see Jean-Jacques Lefrère, "Rimbaud et Lautréamont en salle de ventes," in *La quinzaine littéraire* [16–30 Nov. 1998]: 16–18). More recently, several manuscripts that were previously unknown to scholars came to light at the exhibit of the personal collection of Pierre Berès (Musée Condé, Château de Chantilly, 10 Dec. 2003–8 March 2004). Notable in part since there had been practically no access to the Berès collection since Henry de Bouillane de Lacoste's 1949 *Rimbaud et le problème des* Illuminations (Paris: Mercure de France), the exhibit catalog includes reproductions of the manuscripts of "Génie," "Soir historique," and "Patience" (a second version of "Bannières de mai"). Prior to this exhibit, "Génie" and "Soir historique" were two of the manuscripts that remained completely inaccessible to almost all scholars. Unfortunately, the manuscripts for "Dévotion" and "Démocratie" seem to have disappeared completely. For more information on the whereabouts of Rimbaud's manuscripts, see the notes that accompany each facsimile in Steve Murphy, ed., *Œuvres complètes* (Paris: Honoré Champion, 2002), 4: 498–652.

18. In March of 1991, French Minister of Culture Jack Lang started a chain of poetry: people were invited to write down (or cut out of certain magazines) a poem of Rimbaud's and send it to two people, who would do the same thing to two more people, and so on, each time also sending a copy to a Rimbaud address set up by the government. See "Correspondance poétique," *Globe* 56 (April 1991): 71. During an interview, Lang answered the question "Est-ce que le gouvernement français lit Rimbaud?" ("Does the French government read Rimbaud?") by stating, "Qui dans le gouvernement n'a pas voulu un jour 'changer la vie'? Et si, d'aventure, quelques-uns ne lisent pas Rimbaud, ils vont le lire, je m'en charge. J'ai envoyé à chacun un superbe poème, 'L'éternité,' pour amorcer cette grande chaîne poétique qui va réunir des centaines de milliers de lecteurs d'ici à la fin de l'année" ("Who in the government hasn't wanted to, one day, 'change life'? And if by chance some of them don't read Rimbaud, they're going to read him, I'm going to make sure of that. I've sent each of them a superb poem, 'Eternity,' to begin this great poetry chain, which is going to bring together thousands of readers from now until the end of the year.") "Entretien. Alain Borer: Rimbaud vous démange? Jack Lang: Oui, et c'est ce que j'attends de lui," *Globe* 56 (April 1991): 87. Calling the celebration "Les années Rimbaud" ("The Rimbaud Years"), Lang wanted to avoid a stoic celebration: "[I]l n'y aura pas de centenaire Rimbaud. Nous ne célébrons pas un anniversaire avec tristesse guindée et pompe officielle. Je voudrais que les manifestations organisées soient le signe d'une poésie comme Rimbaud la vivait: un mouvement incessant, une errance, une

numerous works of literature, songs, films, and cultural productions in every medium imaginable.[19] In 1995 Rimbaud's life was brought to the big screen in *Total Eclipse,* a film that received neither critical nor commercial success.[20] Soon after the new Bibliothèque nationale de France (French National Library) was opened to the public in 1996, one of the quays along the Seine River in Paris was officially named "Allée Arthur Rimbaud" in a ceremony on 3 May 1997.

Rimbaud for Today

In closing his prefatory remarks of 1966, Wallace Fowlie stated "our age is one of revolt." Such is, it seems, no longer the case; social and political in-

---

quête inlassable de la liberté. J'ajouterais aussi un appétit pour la modernité, même au prix de ruptures inattendues, et un appétit de découvrir de nouveaux espaces, de nouveaux lieux, d'autres cultures. Je préfère parler des années Rimbaud, dont 1991 marquera le point de départ" ("[T]here will not be a Rimbaud centenary. We will not celebrate an anniversary with stuffy sadness and official pomp. I would like for the organized events to be the sign of poetry the way Rimbaud lived it: an incessant movement, a wandering, a tireless quest for liberty. I should also add an appetite for modernity, even at the cost of unexpected ruptures, and an appetite for discovering new spaces, new places, and other cultures. I prefer talking about Rimbaud years, of which 1991 will mark the starting point.") The year 2004, "Année Rimbaud," was equally filled with cultural and academic events. See Pascal Mateo and Ariane Singer, "Charleville redécouvre Rimbaud," *Le point* 1639 (Feb. 12, 2004): 66.

19. French singers Leo Ferré and Catherine le Forestier are just two who have sung Rimbaud's poems put to music. The long list of musicians who have been inspired by Rimbaud includes, in French: Francis Cabrel, Michel Delpech, Serge Gainsbourg, Gerry Boulet, Patricia Kass, Bernard Lavilliers, and MC Solaar; and in English, Bob Dylan, Van Morrison, and Patti Smith, to name but a few. Ernest Pignon-Ernest's life-size posters, with Rimbaud's face atop a contemporary vagabond body, were seen throughout France in 1978–79 (see Ernest Pignon-Ernest, *Ernest Pignon-Ernest: Intervention-images, 1978–1979* [Paris: Area, 1986]). The poet's residence in Aden was turned into a cultural center and named the Maison Rimbaud (subsequently closed for financial reasons in June 1997). For a more thorough listing of the commemorative events of 1991, see *Globe* 56 (April 1991): 61–88, particularly the fourteen-page program of the year's events stapled between pages 66 and 67.

20. Written and based on the play by Christopher Hampton, directed by Agnieszka Holland, and starring Leonardo DiCaprio as Rimbaud, David Thewlis as Verlaine, and Romane Bohringer as Verlaine's wife Mathilde. For an example of the film's reception, see Janet Maslin, "Rimbaud: Portrait of the Artist as a Young Boor," *The New York Times* (3 November 1995): C14. Another film based on the poet's life is the Italian film *Une stagione all'inferno* (Nelo Risi, 1971). A play based on the two poets' last meeting in Stuttgart in 1875 was performed by Geneva's Théâtre Poétique de l'Orangerie in 1991. Philippe Lüscher, *Rimbaud-Verlaine, Drôle de ménage!* (Lausanne: L'aire, 1991).

justices of today are met more often with apathy than with revolt, just as new media threaten literature's survival. So perhaps we could say that it is precisely in order to remember the importance of revolt that a new generation of readers should read Rimbaud, why they *must* read Rimbaud. While the students involved in the rebellion of May 1968 in France found a slogan in Rimbaud's "Changer la vie" ("Change life"),[21] Rimbaud offers today's readers different motivations to connect with his work. His taste for subversion and his knack for criticism will forever command our attention. The meteoric paths[22] of his life and his career never cease to amaze us. His shattering of the tenets of French versification and the absolute beauty of his poetic expression continue, quite simply, to leave us in awe.[23] For all these reasons and more, Rimbaud's words will always resonate with readers everywhere, every time we need him. At the beginning of a new millennium, in a world that seems as far removed from Wallace Fowlie's 1960s as it is from Arthur Rimbaud's 1860s, Henry Miller's words still ring true: we all need Rimbaud, now more than ever.

A Word on the Text

Following the sale at auction of several manuscripts and the publications of facsimiles of other manuscripts in auction catalogs over the past forty years, the major critical editions of Rimbaud's work—including both of the "most trustworthy editions now available" that Fowlie mentioned—have been replaced. André Rolland de Renéville and Jules Mouquet's edition for Gallimard's "Bibliothèque de la Pléiade" series was replaced in 1972 by a new edition by Antoine Adam; André Guyaux significantly updated and revised Suzanne Bernard's edition for Garnier in 1991. Recently, Alain Borer's *Œuvre-vie* (1991) and Pierre Brunel's "Pochothèque" edition (1999) did away with the traditional groupings that separated verse from prose, presenting Rimbaud's work in its chronological progression and focusing instead on the development of Rimbaud's prosodic trajectory. Fi-

21. The famous phrase was taken from *Une saison en enfer:* "Il a peut-être des secrets pour *changer la vie?*" ("Does he have perhaps secrets for *changing life?*"). See "Délires I: Vierge folle. L'époux infernal" ("Delirium I: The Foolish Virgin. The Infernal Bridegroom") from *Une saison en enfer (A Season in Hell)* in this edition.

22. The term is Stéphane Mallarmé's, who compared Rimbaud to "Éclat, lui, d'un météore" ("Brilliance of a meteor"). Stéphane Mallarmé, *Arthur Rimbaud* (Paris: Jean Daive et fourbis, 1991), 13.

23. It is for these reasons that Ross was right to conclude that "Rimbaud left literature before he even got there" (*The Emergence of Social Space,* 19).

nally, Steve Murphy has undertaken a "pluriversional" project of reprinting all known versions of every one of Rimbaud's poems. The first volume, *Poésies (Poems)*, was published in 1999, and the fourth volume, *Facsimilés*, in 2002, and the remaining two installments—prose poems and correspondence—are sure to be just as invaluable. This present revision of Wallace Fowlie's work draws mainly from the Murphy editions for the text and from others for various points, including Brunel's "Pochothèque" and the Pléiade and Garnier editions.[24]

Of Rimbaud's earliest writings—the poems he wrote for his studies at the Collège de Charleville—this translation includes only those poems written in French, the focus of this edition being a side-by-side presentation of French and English; Rimbaud's Latin verse poems, which earned him several awards, are not included.[25] For the rest of Rimbaud's poetic output, we have kept with the editorial tradition separating verse from prose. Brunel's recent edition prefers to follow the groupings of Rimbaud's verse known to critics as "Recueil Demeny" ("Demeny collection") and "Recueil Verlaine"; the former represents poems Rimbaud gave to his friend Paul Demeny in 1870, and the latter are poems given to and subsequently recopied by Verlaine by the beginning of 1872 (perhaps beginning as early as late 1870).[26]

While there is an argument to be made for following this method of organization, neither collection was compiled by Rimbaud himself; as such, the precise order of the poems within each "recueil" is open to interpretation, as the many French editions of Rimbaud's work suggest. Since Rimbaud wrote, rewrote, and disseminated his poems at different times, an attempt at establishing a chronology in his brief career is a troublesome venture. All readers should bear in mind that, with the exception of *Une saison en enfer (A Season in Hell)*, the only collection that he published, Rimbaud's poems are presented in an order that represents a combination of our best understanding of the poems and the inevitable editorial choices and constraints. Given the lack of certainty of the precise order of Rimbaud's verse poems and our decision to publish only one version of each poem—considering "Les effarés" ("The Frightened Ones"), for example, of which there was a version in both of the "recueils," and six in

24. See the selected bibliography of this edition.

25. For these poems, see Pierre Brunel, "La Pochothèque" (Paris: Le Livre de Poche, 1999), 91–125; the Pléiade edition, 179–90; the *Œuvre-vie*, 31–45; or Mason, vol. 1, 528–38 for the Latin texts, and 277–94 for Mason's translations.

26. For more information on the "Recueil Demeny" and the "Recueil Verlaine," see Murphy, vol. 1, 149–60 and 349–74, respectively.

all—this translation retains the division of verse and prose and presents a chronological ordering within each section (to the extent to which this is possible).

The strength of this grouping—which has been present in nearly all editions and translations of Rimbaud's work—is that it encourages the consideration of how Rimbaud's work explodes the very categories of verse, prose, and free-verse. Since Rimbaud wrote in both verse and prose in 1872 and 1873, readers who are interested more in the contemporaneity of several poems than in their prosodic form (or lack thereof) are invited to consult Brunel's "Pochothèque" edition for a chronological ordering that does not distinguish between verse and prose. Similarly, since our choice of only one version for each poem makes impossible the study of variants between different versions of individual poems, readers wishing to consider these kinds of questions should read Murphy's volume 1, which provides every version of each poem and copious notes.

The nature of the revisions to Fowlie's edition fall into one of two categories: updates and corrections. Most of the changes in this new edition come from the wealth of information that has become available since this volume first went to press; such was the original impetus for this present undertaking, and as such the translations remain largely Fowlie's. With unprecedented access to manuscripts (or facsimiles of manuscripts) comes an unprecedented ability to reproduce accurately Rimbaud's texts; in a bilingual edition that is as faithful to the French as is the present volume, such precision is crucial. As a result of the substantial rewriting and typesetting that both the French and the English texts underwent, there are updates to Fowlie's work on every page, most often in matters of punctuation, but also in capitalization, spelling, and layout. Some of the corrections are of a more substantial variety, including changes to words, phrases, and sometimes entire sentences. These were necessary because of the flawed information that Rimbaud scholars had at their disposal in the 1960s; since greater access to manuscripts and better-quality copies of other manuscripts has led to increased knowledge of Rimbaud's words, on more than one occasion words previously accepted by all critical editions have been proven incorrect. Such new information required changes to the French text and, obviously, to the translation. Other changes evident in the present volume come from translation errors on Fowlie's part; there were precious few in this category. Lastly, typographical and other copyediting errors were corrected, and hopefully not too many new ones were committed.

Acknowledgments

In addition to my reliance on the excellent revised editions of Rimbaud's work listed elsewhere in this volume, I have benefited from the wisdom of teachers, colleagues, and friends, past and present. Wallace Fowlie was kind enough to respond to a letter I wrote him when I was just starting out in graduate school; his kind words have inspired my work throughout these pages, and I can only hope that he would have found my contributions not too intrusive or awkward. Dennis Minahen was the first to explain "je est un autre" to me, after class one day; such was my introduction to Rimbaud. Dennis, along with Ed Ahearn, Alain-Philippe Durand, Steve Murphy, Adrianna Paliyenko, Cat Sama, Gretchen Schultz, and Bill Thomas, instilled in me the confidence that I had something of my own to say. The idea for revising this edition came to me during one of my many moments standing in Jack Iverson's office doorway, and I thank Jack for inviting me in to sit down and discuss it further. Steve Murphy and Jean-Jacques Lefrère have been extremely supportive and generous with their time and thoughts. In Randy Petilos I found an editor with great patience, attention to detail, and an unrelenting desire to make this edition great; he and Kate Frentzel and everyone else at the University of Chicago Press helped make this labor of love fun. This edition's illustrations are the result of the fine work of the Media Technologies & Creative Design team at Villanova University's Falvey Library, and of generous financial support from the Dean's office of Villanova's College of Liberal Arts and Sciences. The Rosman portrait is made possible by Gérard Martin and Alain

Tourneux of the Musée-bibliothèque Arthur Rimbaud in Charleville-Mézières and by the design team of the University of Chicago Press. *Rimbaud, debout,* . . . is part of a private collection and appears courtesy of Pierre Leroy.

In addition to my own family, I am indebted to friends and colleagues—too many to enumerate here—for enduring friendship, hospitality, and comic relief. I cannot thank enough my wife Becky, whose encouragement has picked me up more often than I would care to admit. Lastly, I wish to dedicate the part of this edition that is mine to my children, Carter and Posey, with the hope that they will find something that touches them the way Rimbaud's poetry touches me.

S. W.

Selected Bibliography

A partial listing of works published since 1966

Works by Rimbaud

FRENCH EDITIONS

Lettres de la vie littéraire d'Arthur Rimbaud. Edited by Jean-Marie Carré. Paris: Gallimard, 1991.

Les lettres manuscrites de Rimbaud. Edited by Claude Jeancolas. 4 vols. Paris: Textuel, 1997.

L'œuvre intégrale manuscrite. Edited by Claude Jeancolas. 3 vols. Paris: Textuel, 1997.

Œuvres. Edited by Suzanne Bernard and André Guyaux. Paris: Classiques Garnier-Dunod, 1997.

Œuvres complètes. Edited by Antoine Adam. Bibliothèque de la Pléiade. Paris: Gallimard, 1972.

Œuvres complètes. Edited by Pierre Brunel. Collection "La Pochothèque." Paris: Le Livre de Poche, 1999.

Œuvres complètes. Edition critique avec introduction et notes de Steve Murphy. Vol. 1, *Poésies* (1999); vol. 4, *Fac-similés* (2002). Paris: Honoré Champion.

Œuvre-vie: Edition du centenaire. Edited by Alain Borer. Paris: Arléa, 1991.

TRANSLATIONS

Mason, Wyatt Alexander, trans. *Rimbaud Complete.* 2 vols. New York: Modern Library, 2002–3.

Mathieu, Bertrand, trans. *A Season in Hell. Illuminations.* Brockport, New York: BOA Editions, 1991.

Schmidt, Paul, trans. *Complete Works.* New York: Harper & Row, 1975.

Sorrell, Martin, trans. *Collected Poems.* Oxford: Oxford University Press, 2001.

Secondary Sources

BIOGRAPHIES IN FRENCH

Borer, Alain. *Rimbaud en Abyssinie*. Paris: Seuil, 1984.

Bourguignon, Jean, and Charles Houin. *Vie d'Arthur Rimbaud*. Edited by Michel Drouin. Paris: Editions Payot & Rivages, 1991.

Lefrère, Jean-Jacques. *Arthur Rimbaud*. Paris: Librairie Arthème Fayard, 2001.

Petitfils, Pierre. *Rimbaud*. Paris: Julliard, 1982.

Steinmetz, Jean-Luc. *Arthur Rimbaud. Une question de présence*. Paris: Tallandier, 1991.

BIOGRAPHIES IN ENGLISH

Borer, Alain. *Rimbaud in Abyssinia*. Translated by Rosmarie Waldrop. New York: William Morrow, 1991.

Nicholl, Charles. *Somebody Else: Arthur Rimbaud in Africa 1890–91*. Chicago: University of Chicago Press, 1999.

Petitfils, Pierre. *Rimbaud*. Translated by Alan Sheridan. Charlottesville, Va.: University Press of Virginia, 1987.

Robb, Graham. *Rimbaud: A Biography*. London: Picador/ New York: Norton, 2000.

Steinmetz, Jean-Luc. *Arthur Rimbaud: Presence of an Enigma*. Translated by Jon Graham. New York: Welcome Rain Publishers, 2001.

CRITICAL STUDIES IN FRENCH

Berger, Anne-Emmanuelle. *Le banquet de Rimbaud: Recherches sur l'oralité*. Seyssel: Champ Vallon, 1992.

Brunel, Pierre. Rimbaud: *Rrojets et réalisations*. Paris: Champion, 1983.

Guyaux, André. *Poétique du fragment: Essai sur les* Illuminations *de Rimbaud*. Neuchâtel, Switzerland: Editions de la Baconnière, 1985.

Kittang, Atle. *Discours et jeu: Essai d'analyse des textes d'Arthur Rimbaud*. Bergen, Norway: Universitetsforlaget / Grenoble: PU de Grenoble, 1975.

Murat, Michel. *L'art de Rimbaud*. Paris: José Corti, 2002.

Murphy, Steve. *Le premier Rimbaud ou l'apprentissage de la subversion*. Paris: Editions du CNRS / Lyon: PU de Lyon, 1991.

——, ed. *Rimbaud cent ans après*. Parade sauvage colloque 3 (5–10 Sept. 1991). Charleville-Mézières: Musée-Bibliothèque Arthur Rimbaud, 1992.

Perron, Paul and Sergio Villani, eds. *Lire Rimbaud: Approches critiques*. Preface by Yves Bonnefoy. Toronto: Canadian Scholars' Press, 2000.

CRITICAL STUDIES IN ENGLISH

Ahearn, Edward J. *Rimbaud: Visions and Habitations*. Berkeley: University of California Press, 1983.

Cohn, Robert Greer. *The Poetry of Rimbaud*. Princeton, N.J.: Princeton University Press, 1973. Reprint, Columbia, S.C.: University of South Carolina, 1999.

Lawler, James. *Rimbaud's Theater of the Self*. Cambridge, Mass.: Harvard University Press, 1992.

Little, Roger. *Rimbaud:* Illuminations. London: Grant & Cutler, 1983.

Osmond, Nick. *Arthur Rimbaud:* Illuminations. London: The Athlone P-U of London, 1976.

Ross, Kristin. *The Emergence of Social Space: Rimbaud and the Paris Commune.* Minneapolis: University of Minnesota Press, 1988.

Wing, Nathaniel. *Present Appearances: Aspects of Poetic Structure in Rimbaud's* Illuminations. Romance Monographs 9. University, Miss.: University of Mississippi Press / Romance Monographs, 1974.

SCHOLARLY JOURNALS DEVOTED TO RIMBAUD

Europe, special issue, Paris, June 1991.

Parade sauvage, Charleville-Mézières, Musée-Bibliothèque Arthur Rimbaud, no.1 (oct. 1984)– present.

Rimbaud vivant, Paris, Association des amis de Rimbaud, no. 1 (1973)–present (published as *Études rimbaldiennes* from 1968–).

Sud, special issue: *Arthur Rimbaud: Bruits neufs,* Marseille, September 1991.

ICONOGRAPHY

Album Rimbaud. Edited by Henri Matarasso and Pierre Petitfils. Bibliothèque de la Pléiade, Album 6. Paris: Gallimard, 1967.

Passion Rimbaud: L'album d'une vie. Edited by Claude Jeancolas. Paris: Textuel, 1998.

Introduction (1966)

The Poet's Life

Jean-Nicolas-Arthur Rimbaud was born on October 20, 1854, in Charleville, a city in the Ardennes in northern France. His mother, Vitalie Cuif, came from a family of farmers. His father, Frédéric Rimbaud, was an infantry captain. Rimbaud's earliest school years were spent at the Institution Rossat in Charleville. He began attending the Collège de Charleville in the spring of 1865, in the *classe de 7e*. In October of that year, he entered the *classe de 6e*. At the end of the year he made his first communion. Young Rimbaud learned with such ease and such rapidity that he skipped the *5e classe* and entered the *4e classe* in October, 1866.

He had begun writing at an early age. At thirteen, in 1868, he wrote a letter in Latin hexameters to the imperial prince. In 1869, his Latin poem "Jugurtha" won a first prize at the Concours Académique. His first known French poem, "Les étrennes des orphelins," was composed in the same year.

During 1870, Rimbaud's poetic genius became fully manifest in the twenty-two poems he composed. The young teacher Georges Izambard was Rimbaud's mentor and friend during his last year at the *collège*. The boy's first attempt to attract literary attention was in May, 1870, when he sent a series of poems to Théodore de Banville, for publication in *Le parnasse contemporain*. At graduation, in August, he received many prizes. War

broke out that summer. On the 29th of August, Arthur Rimbaud made his first escape to Paris, by train, and was put into Mazas Prison at the end of the trip because he had not purchased a full ticket. Izambard was instrumental in having him released. Later, on foot, Rimbaud set out for Belgium, an experience which inspired such poems as "Ma bohème," "Le buffet," and "Au Cabaret-Vert."

Early in 1871, Rimbaud spent considerable time in the library of Charleville. *Les assis* is reminiscent of this setting. There was another trip to Paris in February and a return on foot to Charleville. His two letters of May, to Izambard and Izambard's friend, Paul Demeny, are in fact treatises on Rimbaud's conception of poetry. The boy's disposition was strongly anti-religious at this time, testified to in such a poem as "Les premières Communions." In Charleville he enjoyed the company of Bretagne, who had once known Verlaine and who urged Rimbaud to write to Verlaine. After a first exchange of letters, Verlaine invited Rimbaud to Paris. At the end of September, Rimbaud, armed with new poems, including "Le bateau ivre," went to Paris and stayed for a few days with Paul Verlaine and his wife Mathilde.

The next year and a half were very much dominated by Verlaine, by an enthusiastic, troubled, and at times tragic relationship. The two poets were together in Latin Quarter cafés, in gatherings of poets, in intermittent trips to Brussels and London. Verlaine's marriage was threatened by such behavior, and he made efforts to leave Rimbaud and live again with his wife. At times Rimbaud wearied of the quarrels with his friend, and would leave him and return to Charleville. Both Verlaine's mother and Rimbaud's mother tried to intervene.

Rimbaud undoubtedly began writing some of the *Illuminations* in London in 1872, and was engaged in writing *Une saison en enfer* in April, 1873, at his mother's farm in Roche. The definitive break between Verlaine and Rimbaud occurred in Brussels, in July, as the result of a violent quarrel. When Rimbaud said he had decided to leave his friend, Verlaine fired a revolver and wounded Rimbaud in the left wrist. Verlaine was arrested and condemned by the Belgian police court to two years in prison. His arm in a sling, Rimbaud returned to Roche where he completed *Une saison en enfer*. He was nineteen, and his literary work was over, save possibly for some *Illuminations* which he may have written during the next two years.

Une saison en enfer was printed in October, 1873, at Rimbaud's request, by a Brussels printer, and a few copies were distributed to friends in Paris. But Rimbaud almost immediately lost interest in the work. In early 1874, he met the poet Germain Nouveau in Paris and went with him to England.

He gave French lessons in London and in Scotland. After spending part of the winter in Charleville, Rimbaud went to Germany early in 1875; in Stuttgart he saw Verlaine for the last time. Further traveling took him to Switzerland and Italy. By the end of 1875 he was back in Charleville and engaged in studying languages: Spanish, Italian, modern Greek, Arabic, and Dutch.

In Holland, in the spring of 1876, Rimbaud enlisted in the Dutch army and traveled as far as Batavia. He deserted and worked his way back to Europe, reaching Charleville on foot on the last day of the year. In Vienna, in the spring of 1877, he was robbed and expelled from Austria. After traveling through Sweden and Denmark, and making a useless attempt to go to Egypt, he again returned to Charleville where he spent the winter.

In 1878 he worked for a while on the island of Cyprus as a foreman in a stone quarry. After a period of illness in Charleville, he returned to Cyprus in 1880 and from there went to Egypt and finally Aden. There he worked for an export company, dealing principally in coffee. He traveled as buyer for the company and explored the Somalia and Galla countries. He reported to the Société de Géographie on these explorations. In 1887 he sold guns to King Menelik of Choa. His expeditions became more and more dangerous. Menelik cheated him, and Rimbaud's financial losses were heavy. Between 1888 and 1891, Rimbaud worked for a coffee exporter in Harar. In February, 1891, he suffered from a tumor in his right knee. The malady spread and caused him to return to Marseilles in May. His leg was amputated in the Hôpital de la Conception in Marseilles. He returned to Roche to be with his mother and sister, but his condition grew worse. Hoping he would recover in the Mediterranean climate, he returned to Marseilles where he was again hospitalized and where he died on November 10, 1891, at the age of thirty-seven.

History of the Work and Its Publication [27]

Most of Rimbaud's work was written between the ages of sixteen and nineteen, and during those few years he gave little thought to its publication. Soon after this time, within a year or two at the most, he detached himself from all literary activity and never returned to it. The work was quite literally abandoned. In 1873, following the Brussels drama and the break with Verlaine, Rimbaud did publish, on his own initiative, the small

27. For more recent information about the materials mentioned here, see "A Word on the Text" in the foreword accompanying this introduction. —*trans.*

booklet *Une saison en enfer.* But as soon as the work was published and a few copies distributed, he lost all interest and seemed to have forgotten it.

Edited by Paul Verlaine, *Illuminations* were published for the first time by *La vogue* in 1886. This edition was not complete, and it had typographical errors and misreadings which were perpetuated in later editions. In his introduction Verlaine states that the poems were written between 1873 and 1875, during Rimbaud's travels in Belgium, England, and Germany. This dating was contested by Paterne Berrichon in an edition published in 1912 (with a preface by Claudel) and by the important Pléiade edition, of 1946, prepared by Rolland de Renéville and Jules Mouquet. Since that time, the investigations conducted by Bouillane de Lacoste give credence to the original dating suggested by Verlaine, but there is no absolute proof for placing *Illuminations* before or after *Une saison en enfer.*

The first edition of the poems came out in 1891 (the year of Rimbaud's death), edited by L. Genonceaux. It contained four sonnets not written by Rimbaud. This was followed by two more accurate and more carefully prepared editions: one, by Verlaine, in 1895 (Vanier) and the second, by Paterne Berrichon, in 1898 (Mercure de France). The first critical edition, with variant readings, was published by Bouillane de Lacoste in 1939 (Mercure de France). This text has been adopted on the whole by the two most trustworthy editions now available: the Pléiade edition (1946) and the Classiques Garnier (1961) prepared by Suzanne Bernard. *Les stupra,* erotic sonnets, was first published in a private edition in 1923. The prose story, *Un cœur sous une soutane,* was first printed in 1924, with a preface by Aragon and Breton. In Pascal Pia's edition of the *Œuvres Complètes,* in 1931, Rimbaud's poems from the *Album Zutique* were included.

Rimbaud's letters concerning his literary life were first published in various periodicals. In 1931 they were collected and published by Jean-Marie Carré. Many errors were corrected in the Pléiade edition. The letters written in Africa were first published by Paterne Berrichon, the poet's brother-in-law, who took the liberty of making many changes in the texts. The original texts of twenty-eight of these letters (which belong to the Bibliothèque Jacques Doucet) have been accurately reproduced in the Pléiade edition.

Rimbaud's Position Today

The life and the work of Rimbaud have been studied for not much more than half a century. Those facts concerning the poet's biography which are verifiable are not very numerous. At best, all that is available provides merely the sketch of a life in which several important questions are left

unanswered. Despite our ever-increasing familiarity with Rimbaud's writing, it still ranks among the most difficult works in French literature. The poems are the most accessible part of his work. Today most of the poems present few difficulties to a reader trained in the reading of modern poetry, but *Une saison en enfer* is still a troublesome text. Its elliptical outbursts, its seeming contradictions, and the lack of transitions between its various parts force a reader into maximum attentiveness and agility. Moreover, the psychic experience related in *Une saison* is as much that of our age as it is of one adolescent poet. Finally, the prose poems of *Illuminations* are the most difficult to fathom. The experience behind them is so complex that the form into which they are cast had to be equally complex, equally apprehensive of false simplifications and evasive linguistic banalities.

A new era in the understanding of Rimbaud has begun. Heretofore most critical-interpretive studies have exploited poetic data with the usually unavowed intention of advancing a personal psychological theory. Rimbaud's poetic act has been countless times explained in accord with a given psychological or even religious conviction. These monographs are not without value, but they tend to irritate the new reader, the new, impartial reader in search of enlightenment. Etiemble's thesis of gigantic proportions, *Le mythe de Rimbaud,* appearing in 1952–54, denounced the critical method so widely used in turning Rimbaud into this or that mythical figure: angel or demon, Catholic or surrealist, *voyant* or *voyou.* The castigating effect of Etiemble's investigation has been, in part, responsible for initiating a new type of study in which the focus is on the problem of poetic expression.

Rimbaud's art is a poetic language of an exceptional freshness, enrolled in the service of a few very permanent and universal themes. The newness, the novelty of this language is still felt today by the youngest generation of readers. The ultimate lesson, which the art of Rimbaud teaches, states that poetry is one means, among other means, by which life may be changed and renewed. Poetry is one possible stage in a life process. Within the limits of man's fate, the poet's language is able to express his existence although it is not able to create it.

The three major works of Rimbaud, the poems, *Une saison en enfer,* and *Illuminations,* testify to a modern revolt and to that kind of liberation which follows revolt. *Une saison* is a work of interrogation because it is close to the crisis and the disorder. *Illuminations* is more affirmative because it is closer to the resolving of contradictions. In comparison with *Une saison,* of a metaphysical order, *Illuminations* leads us into a very concrete world of rooms and landscapes and cities where the poet attains a

harmonization between desire and reality. "Génie" is the fusion of an ideal being and a human being. This prose poem is both a climactic piece in Rimbaud's art and the apotheosis of a world. In it the poet is engineer showing us the plans of a future universe.

Was he prophet? genius? mythical figure? He was a poet, but no ordinary poet. He was a child expressing himself in the language of a man. "Génie" combines the virile tenderness and the virile vigor of a man.

Our age is one of revolt, and Rimbaud has given, in his literary work and in the example of his life, one of the most vibrant expressions of this revolt. Man's mind is no longer focused on pronouncing the truth or the falseness of a given fact or a given idea. Rather, it is bent on following the direction of an idea. It easily moves back to the origin of an idea, to memories attached to an idea, to very ancient stages and to very recent ones in the history of an idea.

Rimbaud's book seems to us today a dramatic return to consciousness. There was nothing unusual about his life, save that the major events, transpiring while he was a practicing poet, were swift: the interruption of formal study, hatred for his provincial life, his friendship with Verlaine, the discovery that very few people in Paris were interested in him or in his talent, the break with Verlaine, the writing of *Une saison en enfer* and, soon after that, the irrevocable giving up of literature. Revolt, in some form or other, is everywhere manifest in these five years of Rimbaud's life, and yet nothing completely or satisfactorily explains his revolt.

In an almost histrionic way Rimbaud stifled in himself hope, poetry, ambition, love. There was no chance for any gradual development between the joys of childhood (he speaks of so often) and his existence as a man. This existence, because of its closeness to childhood, was judged immediately as false. All trace of illusions disappeared abruptly. In his own words, childhood is defined by Rimbaud as certainty, as a treasure, as something pure and exempt from doubt and falsehood. He recognizes the noblest efforts of man, and names them: love, ambition, poetry, science, religion— but he designates them as vain, as masks concealing a void.

With such a sentence as "la vraie vie est absente," we can feel that Rimbaud's illusions have been destroyed. This is the profound meaning of his most perfect poem, "Mémoire." It is a piece composed of material realities, presented in an Eden-like innocence, which the poet has renounced. Rimbaud believed that his happiness as a child must have existed in some other age, and he was forced, but briefly, to recreate in his art that age of legends peopled by centaurs, fairies, fauns, and angels. Rimbaud's work is a cleavage between himself and a certain past that he faintly evokes.

Poésies

Poetry

1869

1869

Les étrennes des orphelins

I

La chambre est pleine d'ombre; on entend vaguement
De deux enfants le triste et doux chuchotement.
Leur front se penche, encor, alourdi par le rêve,
Sous le long rideau blanc qui tremble et se soulève . . .
—Au dehors les oiseaux se rapprochent frileux;
Leur aile s'engourdit sous le ton gris des cieux;
Et la nouvelle Année, à la suite brumeuse,
Laissant traîner les plis de sa robe neigeuse,
Sourit avec des pleurs, et chante en grelottant . . .

II

Or les petits enfants, sous le rideau flottant,
Parlent bas comme on fait dans une nuit obscure.
Ils écoutent, pensifs, comme un lointain murmure . . .
Ils tressaillent souvent à la claire voix d'or
Du timbre matinal, qui frappe et frappe encor
Son refrain métallique en son globe de verre . . .
—Puis, la chambre est glacée . . . on voit traîner à terre,
Épars autour des lits, des vêtements de deuil:
L'âpre bise d'hiver qui se lamente au seuil
Souffle dans le logis son haleine morose!
On sent, dans tout cela, qu'il manque quelque chose . . .
—Il n'est donc point de mère à ces petits enfants,
De mère au frais sourire, aux regards triomphants?
Elle a donc oublié, le soir, seule et penchée,
D'exciter une flamme à la cendre arrachée,
D'amonceler sur eux la laine et l'édredon
Avant de les quitter en leur criant: pardon.
Elle n'a point prévu la froideur matinale,
Ni bien fermé le seuil à la bise hivernale? . . .
—Le rêve maternel, c'est le tiède tapis,
C'est le nid cotonneux où les enfants tapis,
Comme de beaux oiseaux que balancent les branches,
Dorment leur doux sommeil plein de visions blanches! . . .
—Et là,—c'est comme un nid sans plumes, sans chaleur,
Où les petits ont froid, ne dorment pas, ont peur;
Un nid que doit avoir glacé la bise amère . . .

The Orphans' Gifts (New Year's)

I

The room is full of darkness; indistinctly you hear
The sad soft whispering of two children.
Their heads lean down, still, heavy with dreams,
Under the long white (bed) curtain which trembles and rises . . .
— Outside birds feeling the cold crowd together;
Their wings are numbed under the grey color of the skies;
And the New Year, with her train of fog,
Dragging the folds of her snowy robe,
Smiles through her tears, and, while shivering, sings . . .

II

But the small children, under the swaying curtain,
Speak in low voices as you do on a dark night.
They listen thoughtfully as to a distant murmur . . .
Often they tremble at the clear golden voice
Of the morning bell, which strikes again and again
Its metallic refrain under its glass globe . . .
— Then, the room is icy . . . you see lying on the floor,
Scattered around the beds, mourning clothes:
The bitter wind of winter moaning on the threshold
Blows into the house its sad breath!
You feel, in all this, that something is missing . . .
— Is there then no mother for these small children,
No mother with a fresh smile and triumphant glances?
So she forgot, in the evening, alone and leaning down,
To kindle a flame saved from the ashes,
And to pile over them the wool and the quilt
Before leaving them, and calling out to them: forgive me!
Did she not foresee the cold of the morning,
Did she not close tightly the door on the winter wind? . . .
— A mother's dream is the warm blanket,
The downy nest where children, huddled
Like beautiful birds rocked by the branches,
Sleep their sweet sleep full of white visions! . . .
— And here — it is like a nest without feathers, without warmth,
Where the children are cold and do not sleep and are afraid;
A nest the bitter wind must have frozen . . .

III

Votre cœur l'a compris: — ces enfants sont sans mère.
Plus de mère au logis! — et le père est bien loin! . . .
— Une vieille servante, alors, en a pris soin.
Les petits sont tout seuls en la maison glacée;
Orphelins de quatre ans, voilà qu'en leur pensée
S'éveille, par degrés, un souvenir riant . . .
C'est comme un chapelet qu'on égrène en priant:
— Ah! quel beau matin, que ce matin des étrennes!
Chacun, pendant la nuit, avait rêvé des siennes
Dans quelque songe étrange où l'on voyait joujoux,
Bonbons habillés d'or, étincelants bijoux,
Tourbillonner, danser une danse sonore,
Puis fuir sous les rideaux, puis reparaître encore!
On s'éveillait matin, on se levait joyeux,
La lèvre affriandée, en se frottant les yeux . . .
On allait, les cheveux emmêlés sur la tête,
Les yeux tout rayonnants, comme aux grands jours de fête,
Et les petits pieds nus effleurant le plancher,
Aux portes des parents tout doucement toucher . . .
On entrait! . . . Puis alors les souhaits . . . en chemise,
Les baisers répétés, et la gaîté permise!

IV

Ah! c'était si charmant, ces mots dits tant de fois!
— Mais comme il est changé, le logis d'autrefois:
Un grand feu pétillait, clair, dans la cheminée,
Toute la vieille chambre était illuminée;
Et les reflets vermeils, sortis du grand foyer,
Sur les meubles vernis aimaient à tournoyer . . .
— L'armoire était sans clefs! . . . sans clefs, la grande armoire!
On regardait souvent sa porte brune et noire . . .
Sans clefs! . . . c'était étrange! . . . on rêvait bien des fois
Aux mystères dormant entre ses flancs de bois,
Et l'on croyait ouïr, au fond de la serrure
Béante, un bruit lointain, vague et joyeux murmure . . .
— La chambre des parents est bien vide, aujourd'hui:
Aucun reflet vermeil sous la porte n'a lui;
Il n'est point de parents, de foyer, de clefs prises:
Partant, point de baisers, point de douces surprises!

III

Your heart has understood: — these children are motherless.
No mother in the home! — and the father far away! . . .
—An old servant, then, has taken care of them.
The little ones are all alone in the icy house;
Four-year-old orphans in whose thoughts now
A smiling memory awakens gradually . . .
It is like a rosary you tell as you pray:
—Ah! what a beautiful morning, this New Year's morning!
During the night each had dreamt of his dear ones
In some strange dream when you saw toys,
Candies dressed in gold, sparkling jewels,
Whirling and dancing a sonorous dance,
Then disappearing under curtains, and reappearing!
You awoke in the morning, you got up in a joyous mood,
Your mouth watering, rubbing your eyes . . .
You went, your hair tangled on your head,
Your eyes shining as on holidays,
And your little bare feet grazing the floor,
Softly touching your parents' doors . . .
You went in! . . . And then the good wishes . . . in your nightshirt,
The flood of kisses, and gaiety allowed!

IV

Ah! it was so charming, those words spoken so often!
—But how it has changed, the home we once had:
A big fire crackled brightly in the fireplace,
The old room was all aglow;
And the red reflections, coming from the big hearth,
Like to play over the varnished furniture . . .
—The cupboard had no keys! . . . no keys in the big cupboard!
You often looked at its dark black door . . .
No keys! . . . it was strange! . . . You often wondered
About the mysteries sleeping in its wooden sides,
And you thought you could hear, from the depths of the gaping
Keyhole, a distant noise, a vague joyful murmur . . .
—The parents' room is empty today:
No red reflection shone under the door;
There are no parents, no hearth, no stolen keys:
And therefore no kisses, no sweet surprises!

Oh! que le jour de l'an sera triste pour eux!
—Et, tout pensifs, tandis que de leurs grands yeux bleus
Silencieusement tombe une larme amère,
Ils murmurent: "Quand donc reviendra notre mère?"

. . . .

v

Maintenant, les petits sommeillent tristement:
Vous diriez, à les voir, qu'ils pleurent en dormant,
Tant leurs yeux sont gonflés et leur souffle pénible!
Les tout petits enfants ont le cœur si sensible!
—Mais l'ange des berceaux vient essuyer leurs yeux,
Et dans ce lourd sommeil met un rêve joyeux,
Un rêve si joyeux, que leur lèvre mi-close,
Souriante, semblait murmurer quelque chose . . .
—Ils rêvent que, penchés sur leur petit bras rond,
Doux geste du réveil, ils avancent le front,
Et leur vague regard tout autour d'eux se pose . . .
Ils se croient endormis dans un paradis rose . . .
Au foyer plein d'éclairs chante gaîment le feu . . .
Par la fenêtre on voit là-bas un beau ciel bleu;
La nature s'éveille et de rayons s'enivre . . .
La terre, demi-nue, heureuse de revivre,
A des frissons de joie aux baisers du soleil . . .
Et dans le vieux logis tout est tiède et vermeil:
Les sombres vêtements ne jonchent plus la terre,
La bise sous le seuil a fini par se taire . . .
On dirait qu'une fée a passé dans cela! . . .
—Les enfants, tout joyeux, ont jeté deux cris . . . Là,
Près du lit maternel, sous un beau rayon rose,
Là, sur le grand tapis, resplendit quelque chose . . .
Ce sont des médaillons argentés, noirs et blancs,
De la nacre et du jais aux reflets scintillants;
Des petits cadres noirs, des couronnes de verre,
Ayant trois mots gravés en or: "À NOTRE MÈRE!"

. . . .

Ah! how sad New Year's Day will be for them!
—And pensively, while from their big blue eyes
A bitter tear silently drops,
They murmur: "When will our mother return?"

. . . .

V

Now the children are sleeping sadly:
On seeing them you would say they are crying in their sleep,
So swollen are their eyes and so painful their breathing!
Small children have such sensitive hearts!
—But the angel of cradles comes to wipe their eyes,
And into their heavy sleep puts a happy dream,
So happy a dream that their half-closed lips,
Smiling, seem to murmur something . . .
—They dream that, leaning on their small round arms,
In the sweet gesture of waking up, they raise their heads,
And peer around them . . .
They think they fell asleep in a rose-colored paradise . . .
In the bright hearth, the fire merrily sings . . .
Through the window a beautiful blue sky is visible over yonder;
Nature awakens and is drunk with the rays of light . . .
The earth, half-bare, happy to come alive again,
Stirs with joy under the kisses of the sun . . .
And in the old house everything is warm and red:
The black clothes are no longer spread over the floor,
The wind has at last quieted down under the door . . .
You could say that a fairy had passed through the scene! . . .
—The children, very happy, uttered two cries . . . Here,
Near the mother's bed, under a beautiful rose-colored ray,
Here, on the big rug, something shines . . .
They are silver medallions, black and white,
Mother-of-pearl and jet with glittering lights;
Small black frames, glass wreaths,
With three words engraved in gold: "TO OUR MOTHER!"

. . . .

Première soirée.

I. — Elle était fort déshabillée
Et de grands arbres indiscrets
Aux vitres jetaient leur feuillée
Malinement, tout près, tout près.

Assise sur ma grande chaise,
Mi-nue, elle joignait les mains.
Sur le plancher frissonnaient d'aise
Ses petits pieds si fins, si fins.

— Je regardai, couleur de cire,
Un petit rayon buissonnier
Papillonner dans son sourire
Et sur son sein, — mouche au rosier.

— Je baisai ses fines chevilles.
Elle eut un doux rire brutal
Qui s'égrenait en claires trilles,
Un joli rire de cristal.

Les petits pieds sous la chemise
Se sauvèrent : « Veux-tu finir ! »
— La première audace permise,
Le rire feignait de punir !

— Pauvrets palpitants sous ma lèvre,
Je baisai doucement ses yeux :
— Elle jeta sa tête mièvre
En arrière : « Oh ! c'est encor mieux !..

1870

1870

Sensation

Par les soirs bleus d'été, j'irai dans les sentiers,
Picoté par les blés, fouler l'herbe menue:
Rêveur, j'en sentirai la fraîcheur à mes pieds.
Je laisserai le vent baigner ma tête nue.

Je ne parlerai pas, je ne penserai rien:
Mais l'amour infini me montera dans l'âme,
Et j'irai loin, bien loin, comme un bohémien,
Par la Nature—heureux comme avec une femme.

Soleil et chair [1]

I

Le Soleil, le foyer de tendresse et de vie,
Verse l'amour brûlant à la terre ravie,
Et, quand on est couché sur la vallée, on sent
Que la terre est nubile et déborde de sang;
Que son immense sein, soulevé par une âme,
Est d'amour comme dieu, de chair comme la femme,
Et qu'il renferme, gros de sève et de rayons,
Le grand fourmillement de tous les embryons!

Et tout croît, et tout monte!

                                   —O Vénus, ô Déesse!
Je regrette les temps de l'antique jeunesse,
Des satyres lascifs, des faunes animaux,
Dieux qui mordaient d'amour l'écorce des rameaux
Et dans les nénufars baisaient la Nymphe blonde!
Je regrette les temps où la sève du monde,
L'eau du fleuve, le sang rose des arbres verts
Dans les veines de Pan mettaient un univers!
Où le sol palpitait, vert, sous ses pieds de chèvre;
Où, baisant mollement le clair syrinx, sa lèvre
Modulait sous le ciel le grand hymne d'amour;
Où, debout sur la plaine, il entendait autour

Sensation

In the blue summer evenings, I will go along the paths,
And walk over the short grass, as I am pricked by the wheat:
Daydreaming I will feel the coolness on my feet.
I will let the wind bathe my bare head.

I will not speak, I will have no thoughts:
But infinite love will mount in my soul;
And I will go far, far off, like a gypsy,
Through the countryside—joyous as if with a woman.

Sun and Flesh

I

The Sun, hearth of tenderness and life,
Pours burning love over the delighted earth,
And, when one lies down in the valley, one smells
How the earth is nubile and rich in blood;
How its huge breast, raised by a soul,
Is made of love, like god, and of flesh, like woman,
And how it contains, big with sap and rays of light,
The vast swarming of all embryos!

And everything grows, and everything rises!

                                    —O Venus, O Goddess!
I miss the days of ancient youth,
Of lascivious satyrs, of animal fauns,
Gods who bit, because of love, the bark of boughs
And in the midst of water lilies kissed the blond Nymph!
I miss the time when the world's sap,
The river's water, and the rose blood of green trees
Put a universe into the veins of Pan!
When the earth trembled, green, under his goatfeet;
When, softly kissing the fair Syrinx, his lips
Formed under heaven the great hymn of love;
When, standing on the plain, he heard about him

Répondre à son appel la Nature vivante;
Où les arbres muets, berçant l'oiseau qui chante,
La terre berçant l'homme, et tout l'Océan bleu
Et tous les animaux aimaient, aimaient en Dieu!

Je regrette les temps de la grande Cybèle
Qu'on disait parcourir, gigantesquement belle,
Sur un grand char d'airain, les splendides cités;
Son double sein versait dans les immensités
Le pur ruissellement de la vie infinie.
L'Homme suçait, heureux, sa mamelle bénie,
Comme un petit enfant, jouant sur ses genoux.
—Parce qu'il était fort, l'Homme était chaste et doux.

Misère! Maintenant il dit: Je sais les choses,
Et va, les yeux fermés et les oreilles closes:
—Et pourtant, plus de dieux! plus de dieux! l'Homme est Roi,
L'Homme est Dieu! Mais l'Amour, voilà la grande Foi!
Oh! si l'homme puisait encore à ta mamelle,
Grande mère des dieux et des hommes, Cybèle;
S'il n'avait pas laissé l'immortelle Astarté
Qui jadis, émergeant dans l'immense clarté
Des flots bleus, fleur de chair que la vague parfume,
Montra son nombril rose où vint neiger l'écume,
Et fit chanter, Déesse aux grands yeux noirs vainqueurs,
Le rossignol aux bois et l'amour dans les cœurs!

II

Je crois en toi! je crois en toi! Divine mère,
Aphrodité marine! — Oh! la route est amère
Depuis que l'autre Dieu nous attelle à sa croix;
Chair, Marbre, Fleur, Venus, c'est en toi que je crois!
— Oui l'Homme est triste et laid, triste sous le ciel vaste,
Il a des vêtements, parce qu'il n'est plus chaste,
Parce qu'il a sali son fier buste de dieu,
Et qu'il a rabougri, comme une idole au feu,
Son corps Olympien aux servitudes sales!
Oui, même après la mort, dans les squelettes pâles

Living Nature answer his call;
When the mute trees, cradling the singing bird,
The earth cradling man, and the entire blue Ocean
And all animals loved, loved in God!

I miss the time of great Cybele
Who was said to traverse, gigantically beautiful,
In a great bronze chariot, magnificent cities;
Her two breasts poured into the immense depths
The pure stream of infinite life.
Man sucked joyfully at her blessed nipple,
Like a small child playing on her knees.
—Because he was strong, Man was chaste and gentle.

Woe! Now he says: I comprehend things,
And goes off, with eyes closed and ears closed:
—And yet, no more gods! no more gods! Man is King,
Man is God! But Love is the great Faith!
Oh! if man still drew strength from your nipple,
Great mother of gods and men, Cybele;
If only he had not abandoned immortal Astarte
Who, once, emerging in the immense light
Of blue waves, flower-flesh the wave perfumes,
Showed her rose-colored navel where the foam came snowing,
And—a Goddess with great conquering black eyes—made the
   nightingale
Sing in the woods and love in the hearts!

II

I believe in you! I believe in you! Divine mother,
Aphrodite of the sea!—Oh! the way is bitter
Since the other God harnessed us to his cross;
Flesh, Marble, Flower, Venus, I believe in you!
—Yes, Man is sad and ugly, sad under the vast sky.
He has clothes because he is no longer chaste,
Because he has defiled his proud head of a god,
And bent down, like an idol in the fire,
His Olympian body to base serfdom!
Yes, even after death, in pale skeletons

Il veut vivre, insultant la première beauté!
—Et l'Idole où tu mis tant de virginité,
Où tu divinisas notre argile, la Femme,
Afin que l'Homme pût éclairer sa pauvre âme
Et monter lentement, dans un immense amour,
De la prison terrestre à la beauté du jour,
La Femme ne sait plus même être Courtisane!
—C'est une bonne farce! et le monde ricane
Au nom doux et sacré de la grande Venus!

III

Si les temps revenaient, les temps qui sont venus!
—Car l'Homme a fini! l'Homme a joué tous les rôles!
Au grand jour, fatigué de briser des idoles
Il ressuscitera, libre de tous ses Dieux,
Et, comme il est du ciel, il scrutera les cieux!
L'Idéal, la pensée invincible, éternelle,
Tout le dieu qui vit, sous son argile charnelle,
Montera, montera, brûlera sous son front!
Et quand tu le verras sonder tout l'horizon,
Contempteur des vieux jougs, libre de toute crainte,
Tu viendras lui donner la Rédemption sainte!
—Splendide, radieuse, au sein des grandes mers
Tu surgiras, jetant sur le vaste Univers
L'Amour infini dans un infini sourire!
Le Monde vibrera comme une immense lyre
Dans le frémissement d'un immense baiser:

—Le Monde a soif d'amour: tu viendras l'apaiser.

. . . .

(O! l'Homme a relevé sa tête libre et fière!
Et le rayon soudain de la beauté première
Fait palpiter le dieu dans l'autel de la chair!
Heureux du bien présent, pâle du mal souffert,
L'Homme veut tout sonder,—et savoir! La Pensée,
La cavale longtemps, si longtemps oppressée
S'élance de son front! Elle saura Pourquoi!...
Qu'elle bondisse libre, et l'Homme aura la Foi!

He wishes to live, insulting the original beauty!
—And the Idol in whom you placed such virginity,
In whom you made our clay divine, Woman,
So that Man might illuminate his poor soul
And slowly rise, in boundless love,
From the prison of earth to the beauty of day,
Woman no longer knows even how to be a Courtesan!
—It's a good joke! and the world jeers
At the sweet and sacred name of great Venus!

III

If the times which have passed came back!
—For Man is finished! Man has played all roles!
By day, weary of smashing idols
He will revive, free of all his gods,
And, as he is of heaven, he will scan the skies!
The Ideal, the invincible eternal thought,
The whole god who lives, under his clay of flesh,
Will rise, will rise, and burn under his brow!
And when you see him sounding the whole horizon,
A despiser of old yokes, free from all fear,
You will come and give him holy Redemption!
—Resplendent, radiant, from the bosom of vast oceans
You will rise up, casting over the wide Universe
Infinite Love in its infinite smile!
The World will vibrate like an immense lyre
In the trembling of an immense kiss:

—The World thirsts for love: you will come and slake its thirst.

. . . .

(Oh! Man has raised his free proud head!
And the sudden ray of original beauty
Makes the god tremble in the altar of his flesh!
Happy with the present good, pale from the ill suffered,
Man wills to sound all depths—and know! Thought,
A jade for so long, and oppressed for so long,
Springs from his brow! She will know Why! . . .
Let her leap free, and Man will have Faith!

—Pourquoi l'azur muet et l'espace insondable?
Pourquoi les astres d'or fourmillant comme un sable?
Si l'on montait toujours, que verrait-on là-haut?
Un Pasteur mène-t-il cet immense troupeau
De mondes cheminant dans l'horreur de l'espace?
Et tous ces mondes-là, que l'éther vaste embrasse,
Vibrent-ils aux accents d'une éternelle voix?
—Et l'Homme, peut-il voir? peut-il dire: je crois?
La voix de la pensée est-elle plus qu'un rêve?
Si l'homme naît si tôt, si la vie est si brève,
D'où vient-il? Sombre-t-il dans l'Océan profond
Des Germes, des Fœtus, des Embryons, au fond
De l'immense Creuset d'où la Mère-Nature
Le ressuscitera, vivante créature,
Pour aimer dans la rose, et croître dans les blés? . . .

Nous ne pouvons savoir!—Nous sommes accablés
D'un manteau d'ignorance et d'étroites chimères!
Singes d'hommes tombés de la vulve des mères,
Notre pâle raison nous cache l'infini!
Nous voulons regarder:—le Doute nous punit!
Le doute, morne oiseau, nous frappe de son aile . . .
—Et l'horizon s'enfuit d'une fuite éternelle! . . .

. . . .

Le grand ciel est ouvert! les mystères sont morts
Devant l'Homme, debout, qui croise ses bras forts
Dans l'immense splendeur de la riche nature!
Il chante . . . et le bois chante, et le fleuve murmure
Un chant plein de bonheur qui monte vers le jour! . . .
—C'est la Rédemption! c'est l'amour! c'est l'amour! . . .)

. . . .

IV

Ô splendeur de la chair! ô splendeur idéale!
Ô renouveau d'amour, aurore triomphale
Où, courbant à leurs pieds les Dieux et les Héros
Kallipige la blanche et le petit Eros
Effleureront, couverts de la neige des roses,
Les femmes et les fleurs sous leurs beaux pieds écloses!

—Why the silent sky and the unfathomable space?
Why the golden stars swarming like sand?
If one mounted forever, what would one see up there?
Does a Shepherd drive that huge flock
Of worlds journeying through the horror of space?
And do all those worlds, embraced by the vast ether,
Tremble at the sound of an eternal voice?
—Can Man see? can he say: I believe?
Is the voice of thought more than a dream?
If man is born so soon, if life is so brief,
Whence does he come? Does he sink into the deep Ocean
Of Germs, of Foetuses, of Embryos, to the bottom
Of the huge Crucible where Mother Nature
Will revive him, a living creature,
To love in the rose, and to grow in the wheat? . . .

We cannot know!—We are weighed down
Under a cloak of ignorance and narrow chimeras!
Apes of men, fallen from our mothers' wombs,
Our pale reason hides the infinite from us!
We try to see:—and Doubt punishes us!
Doubt, gloomy bird, strikes us with its wing . . .
—And the horizon rushes off in an eternal flight! . . .

. . . .

The great sky is open! the mysteries are dead
Before erect Man crossing his strong arms
In the vast splendor of rich nature!
He sings . . . and the wood sings, and the river murmurs
A song full of joy which rises toward daylight! . . .
—It is Redemption! it is love! it is love! . . .)

. . . .

IV

O splendor of flesh! O ideal splendor!
O renewal of love, triumphal dawn
When, prostrating Gods and Heroes at their feet
White Callipyge and little Eros,
Covered with the snow of roses,
Will lightly touch women and flowers full-blown under their beautiful feet!

—Ô grande Ariadné, qui jettes tes sanglots
Sur la rive, en voyant fuir là-bas sur les flots
Blanche sous le soleil, la voile de Thésée,
Ô douce vierge enfant qu'une nuit a brisée,
Tais-toi! Sur son char d'or brodé de noirs raisins,
Lysios, promené dans les champs Phrygiens
Par les tigres lascifs et les panthères rousses,
Le long des fleuves bleus rougit les sombres mousses.
Zeus, Taureau, sur son cou berce comme une enfant
Le corps nu d'Europé, qui jette son bras blanc
Au cou nerveux du Dieu frissonnant dans la vague,
Il tourne lentement vers elle son œil vague;
Elle, laisse traîner sa pâle joue en fleur
Au front de Zeus; ses yeux sont fermés; elle meurt
Dans un divin baiser, et le flot qui murmure
De son écume d'or fleurit sa chevelure.
—Entre le laurier rose et le lotus jaseur
Glisse amoureusement le grand Cygne rêveur
Embrassant la Léda des blancheurs de son aile;
—Et tandis que Cypris passe, étrangement belle,
Et, cambrant les rondeurs splendides de ses reins,
Étale fièrement l'or de ses larges seins
Et son ventre neigeux brodé de mousse noire,
—Héraclès, le Dompteur, qui, comme d'une gloire,
Fort, ceint son vaste corps de la peau du lion,
S'avance, front terrible et doux, à l'horizon!

Par la lune d'été vaguement éclairée,
Debout, nue, et rêvant dans sa pâleur dorée
Que tache le flot lourd de ses longs cheveux bleus,
Dans la clairière sombre où la mousse s'étoile,
La Dryade regarde au ciel silencieux . . .
—La blanche Séléné laisse flotter son voile,
Craintive, sur les pieds du bel Endymion,
Et lui jette un baiser dans un pâle rayon . . .
—La Source pleure au loin dans une longue extase . . .
C'est la Nymphe qui rêve, un coude sur son vase,
Au beau jeune homme blanc que son onde a pressé.
—Une brise d'amour dans la nuit a passé,

—O great Ariadne, who pour your sobs
Over the shore, as you see over there on the waves
The white sail of Theseus flying under the sun;
O sweet virgin child whom a night has crushed,
Be silent! On his golden chariot embroidered with black grapes,
Lysios, drawn through the Phrygian fields
By lascivious tigers and russet panthers,
Reddens the dark moss along the blue rivers.
Zeus, the Bull, cradles on his neck like a child
The naked body of Europa, who throws her white arm
Around the God's tensed neck trembling in the wave,
He slowly turns his vague eyes toward her;
She, lets her pale flower cheek rest
On the brow of Zeus; her eyes are closed; she dies
In a divine kiss, and the murmuring wave
Flowers her hair with its golden foam.
—Between the oleander and the blatant lotus
Glides amorously the great dreaming Swan
Embracing Leda with the whiteness of his wing;
—And while Cypris goes by, strangely beautiful,
And, arching the splendid roundness of her back,
Proudly displays the gold of her large breasts
And snowy belly embroidered with black moss,
—Hercules, the Tamer, who, as with a nimbus,
Strongly girds his huge body in a lion skin,
And appears on the horizon, his brow terrible and benign!

Vaguely lit by the summer moon,
Erect, naked, and dreaming in her gilded pallor,
Spotted by the heavy wave of her long blue hair,
In the dark glade where the moss is starred,
The Dryad looks up at the silent sky . . .
—White Selene, timid, lets her veil float
Over the feet of handsome Endymion,
And throws him a kiss in a pale ray . . .
—The Spring far off weeps in a long ecstasy . . .
It is the Nymph, one elbow on her urn, dreaming
Of the handsome white youth her wave pressed against.
—A light wind of love passed in the night,

Et, dans les bois sacrés, dans l'horreur des grands arbres,
Majestueusement debout, les sombres Marbres,
Les Dieux, au front desquels le Bouvreuil fait son nid,
—Les Dieux écoutent l'Homme et le Monde infini!

Ophélie

I

Sur l'onde calme et noire où dorment les étoiles
La blanche Ophélia flotte comme un grand lys,
Flotte très lentement, couchée en ses longs voiles . . .
— On entend dans les bois lointains des hallalis.

Voici plus de mille ans que la triste Ophélie
Passe, fantôme blanc, sur le long fleuve noir;
Voici plus de mille ans que sa douce folie
Murmure sa romance à la brise du soir

Le vent baise ses seins et déploie en corolle
Ses grands voiles bercés mollement par les eaux;
Les saules frissonnants pleurent sur son épaule,
Sur son grand front rêveur s'inclinent les roseaux.

Les nénuphars froissés soupirent autour d'elle;
Elle éveille parfois, dans un aune qui dort,
Quelque nid, d'où s'échappe un petit frisson d'aile:
—Un chant mystérieux tombe des astres d'or

II

Ô pâle Ophélia! belle comme la neige!
Oui, tu mourus, enfant, par un fleuve emporté!
—C'est que les vents tombant des grands monts de Norwège
T'avaient parlé tout bas de l'âpre liberté;

C'est qu'un souffle, tordant ta grande chevelure,
À ton esprit rêveur portait d'étranges bruits;
Que ton cœur écoutait le chant de la Nature
Dans les plaintes de l'arbre et les soupirs des nuits;

And in the sacred wood, in the horror of the great trees,
Majestically erect, the dark Marbles,
The Gods, on whose brows the Bullfinch makes its nest,
—The Gods listen to Man and to the infinite World!

Ophelia

I

On the calm black water where the stars sleep
White Ophelia floats like a great lily;
Floats very slowly, lying in her long veils . . .
—You hear in the distant woods sounds of the kill.

For more than a thousand years sad Ophelia
Has passed, a white phantom, down the long black river;
For more than a thousand years her sweet madness
Has murmured its romance to the evening breeze.

The wind kisses her breasts and unfolds in a wreath
Her great veils softly cradled by the waters;
The trembling willows weep on her shoulder,
Over her wide dreaming brow the reeds bend down.

The ruffled water lilies sigh around her;
At times she awakens, in a sleeping alder,
Some nest, from which escapes a slight rustle of wings;
—A mysterious song falls from the golden stars.

II

O pale Ophelia! beautiful as snow!
Yes, child, you died, carried off by a river!
—Because the winds falling from the great mountains of Norway
Had spoken to you in low voices of bitter freedom;

It was a breath, twisting your great hair,
That bore strange rumors to your dreaming mind;
It was your heart listening to Nature's song
In the complaints of the tree and the sighs of the nights;

C'est que la voix des mers folles, immense râle,
Brisait ton sein d'enfant, trop humain et trop doux;
C'est qu'un matin d'avril, un beau cavalier pâle,
Un pauvre fou, s'assit muet à tes genoux!

Ciel! Amour! Liberté! Quel rêve, ô pauvre Folle!
Tu te fondais à lui comme une neige au feu;
Tes grandes visions étranglaient ta parole
—Et l'Infini terrible effara ton œil bleu!

III

—Et le Poète dit qu'aux rayons des étoiles
Tu viens chercher, la nuit, les fleurs que tu cueillis;
Et qu'il a vu sur l'eau, couchée en ses longs voiles,
La blanche Ophélia flotter, comme un grand lys.

Venus Anadyomène

Comme d'un cercueil vert en fer blanc, une tête
De femme à cheveux bruns fortement pommadés
D'une vieille baignoire émerge, lente et bête,
Avec des déficits assez mal ravaudés;

Puis le col gras et gris, les larges omoplates
Qui saillent; le dos court qui rentre et qui ressort;
Puis les rondeurs des reins semblent prendre l'essor;
La graisse sous la peau paraît en feuilles plates:

L'échine est un peu rouge, et le tout sent un goût
Horrible étrangement; on remarque surtout
Des singularités qu'il faut voir à la loupe . . .

Les reins portent deux mots gravés: CLARA VENUS;
—Et tout ce corps remue et tend sa large croupe
Belle hideusement d'un ulcère à l'anus.

It was the voice of mad seas, a great noise,
That broke your child's heart, too human and too soft;
It was a handsome pale knight, a poor madman
Who one April morning sat mute at your knees!

Heaven! Love! Freedom! What a dream, oh poor mad girl!
You melted to him as snow to a fire;
Your great visions strangled your words
—And fearful Infinity terrified your blue eyes!

III

—And the Poet says that under the rays of the stars
You come at night to look for the flowers you picked;
And that he saw on the water, lying in her long veils,
White Ophelia floating, like a great lily.

Venus Anadyomene

As from a green zinc coffin, a woman's
Head with brown hair heavily pomaded
Emerges slowly and stupidly from an old bathtub,
With bald patches rather badly hidden;

Then the fat gray neck, broad shoulder-blades
Sticking out; a short back which curves in and bulges;
Then the roundness of the buttocks seems to take off;
The fat under the skin appears in slabs:

The spine is a bit red; and the whole thing has a smell
Strangely horrible; you notice especially
Odd details you'd have to see with a magnifying glass . . .

The buttocks bear two engraved words: CLARA VENUS;
—And that whole body moves and extends its broad rump
Hideously beautiful with an ulcer on the anus.

Première soirée

"—Elle était fort déshabillée
Et de grands arbres indiscrets
Aux vitres jetaient leur feuillée
Malinement, tout près, tout près.

Assise sur ma grande chaise,
Mi-nue, elle joignait les mains
Sur le plancher frissonnaient d'aise
Ses petits pieds si fins, si fins.

—Je regardai, couleur de cire,
Un petit rayon buissonnier
Papillonner dans son sourire
Et sur son sein,—mouche au rosier.

—Je baisai ses fines chevilles.
Elle eut un doux rire brutal
Qui s'égrenait en claires trilles,
Un joli rire de cristal.

Les petits pieds sous la chemise
Se sauvèrent: "Veux-tu finir!"
—La première audace permise,
Le rire feignait de punir!

—Pauvrets palpitants sous ma lèvre,
Je baisai doucement ses yeux:
—Elle jeta sa tête mièvre
En arrière: "Oh! c'est encor mieux! . . .

"Monsieur, j'ai deux mots à te dire . . ."
—Je lui jetai le reste au sein
Dans un baiser, qui la fit rire
D'un bon rire qui voulait bien . . .

—Elle était fort déshabillée
Et de grands arbres indiscrets
Aux vitres jetaient leur feuillée
Malinement, tout près, tout près.

The First Evening

"—She had very few clothes on
And big indiscreet trees
Threw their leaves against the panes
Slyly, very close, very close.

Sitting in my big chair,
Half naked, she clasped her hands
Her small feet so delicate, so delicate,
Trembled with pleasure on the floor.

—The color of wax, I watched
A small nervous ray of light
Flutter in her smile
And on her breast—a fly on the rose-bush.

—I kissed her delicate ankles.
Abruptly she laughed. It was soft
And it spread out in clear trills,
A lovely crystal laughter.

Her small feet under the petticoat
Escaped. "Please stop!"
—When the first boldness was permitted,
The laugh pretended to punish!

—Poor things trembling under my lips,
I softly kissed her eyes:
—She threw her sentimental head
Backward: "Oh! that's too much! . . .

"Sir, I have something to say to you . . ."
—What was left I put on her breast
In a kiss, which made her laugh
With a kind laugh that was willing . . .

—She had very few clothes on
And big indiscreet trees
Threw their leaves against the panes
Slyly, very close, very close.

Les reparties de Nina

. . . .

Lui—Ta poitrine sur ma poitrine,
    Hein? nous irions,
Ayant de l'air plein la narine,
    Aux frais rayons

Du bon matin bleu, qui vous baigne
    Du vin de jour? . . .
Quand tout le bois frissonnant saigne
    Muet d'amour

De chaque branche, gouttes vertes,
    Des bourgeons clairs,
On sent dans les choses ouvertes
    Frémir des chairs:

Tu plongerais dans la luzerne
    Ton blanc peignoir,
Rosant à l'air ce bleu qui cerne
    Ton grand œil noir,

Amoureuse de la campagne,
    Semant partout,
Comme une mousse de champagne,
    Ton rire fou:

Riant à moi, brutal d'ivresse,
    Qui te prendrais
Comme cela,—la belle tresse,
    Oh!—qui boirais

Ton goût de framboise et de fraise,
    O chair de fleur!
Riant au vent vif qui te baise
    Comme un voleur;

Nina's Replies

.   .   .   .

He— Your breast on my breast,
  Eh? we would go,
Our nostrils full of air,
  Into the cool rays

Of the good blue morning that bathes you
  With the wine of day? . . .
When all the trembling wood bleeds
  Dumb with love

From every branch, green drops,
  Clear buds,
You feel in opened things
  The quivering of flesh:

You would plunge in the lucerne
  Your white robe
Turning to rose in the air that blue which encircles
  Your great black eyes,

In love with the country,
  Scattering everywhere
Like champagne bubbles
  Your mad laughter:

Laughing at me, who, brutish with drink,
  Would catch you
Like this—your beautiful hair,
  Oh!—who would drink

Your taste of raspberry and strawberry,
  Oh flesh of a flower!
Laughing at the crisp wind kissing you
  Like a thief;

Au rose églantier qui t'embête
    Aimablement:
Riant surtout, ô folle tête,
    À ton amant! . . .

(Dix-sept ans! Tu seras heureuse!
    — Oh! les grands prés,
La grande campagne amoureuse!
    —Dis, viens plus près! . . .)

—Ta poitrine sur ma poitrine,
    Mêlant nos voix,
Lents, nous gagnerions la ravine,
    Puis les grands bois! . . .

Puis, comme une petite morte,
    Le cœur pâmé,
Tu me dirais que je te porte,
    L'œil mi-fermé . . .

Je te porterais, palpitante,
    Dans le sentier:
L'oiseau filerait son andante:
    Au Noisetier . . .

Je te parlerais dans ta bouche:
    J'irais, pressant
Ton corps, comme une enfant qu'on couche,
    Ivre du sang

Qui coule, bleu, sous ta peau blanche
    Aux tons rosés:
Et te parlant la langue franche . . .
    Tiens! . . .—que tu sais . . .

Nos grands bois sentiraient la sève
    Et le soleil
Sablerait d'or fin leur grand rêve
    Vert et vermeil

. . . .

At the wild rose irritating you
    Pleasantly:
Laughing especially, oh madcap,
    At your lover! . . .

(Seventeen! You will be happy!
    — Oh! the great meadows,
The great loving countryside!
    — See here! come closer! . . .)

— Your breast on my breast,
    Mingling our voices,
Slowly, we would reach the ravine,
    Then the big woods! . . .

Then, like a little corpse,
    Your heart swooning,
You would tell me to carry you,
    Your eyes half closed . . .

I would carry you trembling,
    Along the path:
A bird would spin out its andante:
    At the walnut tree . . .

I would speak into your mouth;
    I would move on, pressing
Your body like a child I was putting to bed,
    Drunk with the blood

That flows blue under your white skin
    With rosy tints:
And speaking to you in the frank tongue . . .
    See! . . . — that you understand . . .

Our big woods would smell of sap
    And the sun
Would sprinkle with fine gold their great
    Green and red dream

  . . . .

Le soir? . . . Nous reprendrons la route
    Blanche qui court
Flânant, comme un troupeau qui broute,
    Tout à l'entour

Les bons vergers à l'herbe bleue,
    Aux pommiers tors!
Comme on les sent toute une lieue
    Leurs parfums forts!

Nous regagnerons le village
    Au ciel mi-noir;
Et ça sentira le laitage
    Dans l'air du soir;

Ça sentira l'étable, pleine
    De fumiers chauds,
Pleine d'un lent rhythme d'haleine,
    Et de grands dos

Blanchissant sous quelque lumière;
    Et, tout là-bas,
Une vache fientera, fière,
    À chaque pas . . .

—Les lunettes de la grand'mère
    Et son nez long
Dans son missel; le pot de bière
    Cerclé de plomb,

Moussant entre les larges pipes
    Qui, crânement,
Fument: les effroyables lippes
    Qui, tout fumant,

Happent le jambon aux fourchettes
    Tant, tant et plus:
Le feu qui claire les couchettes
    Et les bahuts:

In the evening? . . . We will take again the white
    Road which winds
Wandering in every direction,
    Like a grazing flock

The good orchards with blue grass,
    And twisted apple trees!
How you smell a league off
    Their strong perfume!

We will get back to the village
    Under a half-black sky;
And it will smell of milking
    In the evening air;

It will smell of the stable, full
    Of warm manure,
Filled with a slow rhythm of breathing,
    And with big backs

Whitening under some light;
    And way over there
A cow dunging proudly
    At each step . . .

— The grandmother's spectacles
    And her long nose
In her missal; the jug of beer
    Circled with pewter,

Foaming among large-bowled pipes
    Which smoke
Jauntily: the terrible thick lips
    Which, while puffing,

Bite up ham with forks
    So much, and even more:
The fire lighting up the bunks
    And the cupboards:

Les fesses luisantes et grasses
    Du gros enfant
Qui fourre, à genoux, dans les tasses,
    Son museau blanc

Frôlé par un mufle qui gronde
    D'un ton gentil,
Et pourlèche la face ronde
    Du cher petit . . .

(Noire, rogue, au bord de sa chaise,
    Affreux profil,
Une vieille devant la braise
    Qui fait du fil;)

Que de choses verrons-nous, chère,
    Dans ces taudis,
Quand la flamme illumine, claire,
    Les carreaux gris! . . .

—Puis, petite et toute nichée
    Dans les lilas
Noirs et frais: la vitre cachée,
    Qui rit là-bas . . .

Tu viendras, tu viendras, je t'aime!
    Ce sera beau.
Tu viendras, n'est-ce pas, et même . . .
Elle—*Et mon bureau?*

« Morts de Quatre-vingt-douze [. . .] »

« . . . Français de soixante-dix, bonapartistes, républicains, souvenez-vous
de vos pères en 92, etc. . . . » —PAUL DE CASSAGNAC *(Le pays)*

Morts de Quatre-vingt-douze et de Quatre-vingt-treize,
Qui, pâles du baiser fort de la liberté,
Calmes, sous vos sabots, brisiez le joug qui pèse
Sur l'âme et sur le front de toute humanité;

The shining fat buttocks
    Of the big baby
Who on his knees sticks
    His white snout into the cups

Rubbed by a muzzle that growls
    With a gentle tone,
And licks the round face
    Of the little dear . . .

(Black, roguish, on the edge of her chair,
    A frightful profile,
An old woman in front of the embers
    Who keeps spinning;)

What things we shall see, my dear,
    In those hovels,
When the fire illumines brightly
    The gray windowpanes! . . .

—Then, small and nestled
    In the black
And cool lilacs: the hidden window,
    Which laughs over there . . .

You will come, you will come! I love you!
    It will be wonderful.
You will come, won't you? and even . . .
She—*And my office?*

"Dead of '92 [. . .]"

> "Frenchmen of '70, Bonapartists, Republicans, remember your fathers
> in '92, etc. . . ." —PAUL DE CASSAGNAC (*Le pays*)

Dead of '92 and '93,
Who, pale from the hard kiss of freedom,
Calm, broke, under your clogs, the yoke which weighs
On the soul and the brow of all humanity;

Hommes extasiés et grands dans la tourmente,
Vous dont les cœurs sautaient d'amour sous les haillons,
O Soldats que la Mort a semés, noble Amante,
Pour les régénérer, dans tous les vieux sillons;

Vous dont le sang lavait toute grandeur salie,
Morts de Valmy, Morts de Fleurus, Morts d'Italie,
Ô million de Christs aux yeux sombres et doux;

Nous vous laissions dormir avec la République,
Nous, courbés sous les rois comme sous une trique:
—Messieurs de Cassagnac nous reparlent de vous!

Les effarés [2]

À Monsieur Jean Aicard

Noirs dans la neige et dans la brume,
Au grand soupirail qui s'allume,
    Leurs culs en rond,

À genoux, cinq petits, — misère!
Regardent le Boulanger faire
    Le lourd pain blond.

Ils voient le fort bras blanc qui tourne
La pâte grise, et qui l'enfourne
    Dans un trou clair:

Ils écoutent le bon pain cuire.
Le boulanger au gras sourire
    Chante un vieil air:

Ils sont blottis, pas un ne bouge
Au souffle du soupirail rouge
    Chaud comme un sein.

Quand, pour quelque médianoche,
Plein de dorures de brioche
    On sort le pain,

Men exalted and noble in the storm,
You whose hearts leapt with love under your rags,
O soldiers whom Death, lofty Mistress, has sown
In all the old furrows, in order to regenerate them;

You whose blood washed every defiled greatness,
You dead of Valmy, of Fleurus, of Italy,
O million Christs with dark soft eyes;

We let you sleep with the Republic,
We, crouching under kings as under a cudgel:
—The gentlemen Cassagnac are speaking again to us about you!

The Frightened Ones

To Monsieur Jean Aicard

Black in the snow and fog,
By the large vent-grating which is lighted up,
    Their behinds in a circle,

On their knees, five children, —poverty!
Watch the Baker making
    Heavy golden bread.

They see the strong white arm kneading
The gray dough, and sticking it
    Into a bright hole:

They listen to the good bread cook.
The baker with a fat smile
    Sings an old tune:

They are nestled down, not one moves
At the fumes of the red vent
    As warm as a breast.

When, for some midnight feast,
All golden like a brioche
    The bread is brought out,

Quand, sous les poutres enfumées
Chantent les croûtes parfumées
    Et les grillons;

Que ce trou chaud souffle la vie;
Ils ont leur âme si ravie
    Sous leurs haillons,

Ils se ressentent si bien vivre,
Les pauvres petits pleins de givre,
    Qu'ils sont là, tous,

Collant leurs petits museaux roses
Au treillage, et disant des choses,
    Entre les trous,

Des chuchotements de prière;
Repliés vers cette lumière
    De ciel rouvert

Si fort, qu'ils crèvent leur culotte
Et que leur lange blanc tremblotte
    Au vent d'hiver.

Roman

I

On n'est pas sérieux, quand on a dix-sept ans.
—Un beau soir, foin des bocks et de la limonade,
Des cafés tapageurs aux lustres éclatants!
—On va sous les tilleuls verts de la promenade

Les tilleuls sentent bon dans les bons soirs de juin!
L'air est parfois si doux, qu'on ferme la paupière;
Le vent chargé de bruits,—la ville n'est pas loin,—
A des parfums de vigne et des parfums de bière . . .

When, under the beams dark with smoke
The sweet-smelling crust sings
          And the crickets;

When that warm hole breathes out life;
Their souls are so happy
          Under their rags,

They feel so renewed with life,
The poor little things covered with frost,
          That they are there, all of them,

Gluing their small pink snouts
To the grating, and saying things,
          Through the holes,

Whispers of prayers;
Crouching before this light
          From heaven opened up again

So hard, that they burst their pants
And their white linen flutters
          In the winter wind.

Novel

I

We aren't serious when we're seventeen.
— One fine evening, to hell with beer and lemonade,
Noisy cafés with their shining lamps!
We walk under the green linden trees of the park

The lindens smell good in the good June evenings!
At times the air is so scented that we close our eyes.
The wind laden with sounds—the town isn't far—
Has the smell of grapevines and beer . . .

II

—Voilà qu'on aperçoit un tout petit chiffon
D'azur sombre, encadré d'une petite branche,
Piqué d'une mauvaise étoile, qui se fond
Avec de doux frissons, petite et toute blanche . . .

Nuit de juin! Dix-sept ans!—On se laisse griser.
La sève est du champagne et vous monte à la tête . . .
On divague; on se sent aux lèvres un baiser
Qui palpite là, comme une petite bête . . .

III

Le cœur fou Robinsonne à travers les romans,
—Lorsque, dans la clarté d'un pale réverbère,
Passe une demoiselle aux petits airs charmants,
Sous l'ombre du faux-col effrayant de son père . . .

Et, comme elle vous trouve immensément naïf,
Tout en faisant trotter ses petites bottines,
Elle se tourne, alerte et d'un mouvement vif . . .
—Sur vos lèvres alors meurent les cavatines . . .

IV

Vous êtes amoureux. Loué jusqu'au mois d'août.
Vous êtes amoureux—Vos sonnets La font rire.
Tous vos amis s'en vont, vous êtes mauvais goût.
—Puis l'adorée, un soir, a daigné vous écrire . . . !

—Ce soir-là, . . . —vous rentrez aux cafés éclatants,
Vous demandez des bocks ou de la limonade . . .
—On n'est pas sérieux, quand on a dix-sept ans
Et qu'on a des tilleuls verts sur la promenade.

II

—There you can see a very small patch
Of dark blue, framed by a little branch,
Pinned up by a naughty star, that melts
In gentle quivers, small and very white . . .

Night in June! Seventeen years old!—We are overcome by it all.
The sap is champagne and goes to our head . . .
We talked a lot and feel a kiss on our lips
Trembling there like a small insect . . .

III

Our wild heart moves through novels like Robinson Crusoe,
—When, in the light of a pale street lamp,
A girl goes by attractive and charming
Under the shadow of her father's terrible collar . . .

And as she finds you incredibly naïve,
While clicking her little boots,
She turns abruptly and in a lively way . . .
—Then *cavatinas* die on your lips . . .

IV

You are in love. Occupied until the month of August.
You are in love.—Your sonnets make Her laugh.
All your friends go off, you are ridiculous.
—Then one evening the girl you worship deigned to write to you . . . !

—That evening, . . . —you return to the bright cafés,
You ask for beer or lemonade . . .
—We're not serious when we are seventeen
And when we have green linden trees in the park.

Rêvé pour l'hiver

À † † † Elle

L'hiver, nous irons dans un petit wagon rose
  Avec des coussins bleus.
Nous serons bien. Un nid de baisers fous repose
  Dans chaque coin moelleux.

Tu fermeras l'œil, pour ne point voir, par la glace,
  Grimacer les ombres des soirs,
Ces monstruosités hargneuses, populace
  De démons noirs et de loups noirs.

Puis tu te sentiras la joue égratignée . . .
Un petit baiser, comme une folle araignée,
  Te courra par le cou . . .

Et tu me diras: "Cherche!", en inclinant la tête;
—Et nous prendrons du temps à trouver cette bête
  — Qui voyage beaucoup . . .

Le buffet

C'est un large buffet sculpté; le chêne sombre,
Très vieux, a pris cet air si bon des vieilles gens;
Le buffet est ouvert, et verse dans son ombre
Comme un flot de vin vieux, des parfums engageants;

Tout plein, c'est un fouillis de vieilles vieilleries,
De linges odorants et jaunes, de chiffons
De femmes ou d'enfants, de dentelles flétries,
De fichus de grand–mère où sont peints des griffons;

—C'est là qu'on trouverait les médaillons, les mèches
De cheveux blancs ou blonds, les portraits, les fleurs sèches
Dont le parfum se mêle à des parfums de fruits.

A Dream for Winter

To † † † Her

In the winter, we will leave in a small pink railway carriage
    With blue cushions.
We will be comfortable. A nest of mad kisses lies
    In each soft corner.

You will close your eyes, in order not to see, through the glass,
    The evening shadows making faces,
Those snarling monstrosities, a populace
    Of black demons and black wolves.

Then you will feel your cheek scratched . . .
A little kiss, like a mad spider,
    Will run around your neck . . .

And you will say to me: "Get it!", as you bend your neck;
—And we will take a long time to find that creature
    —Which travels a great deal . . .

The Cupboard

It is a wide carved cupboard; the dark oak,
Very old, has taken on the pleasant quality of old people;
The cupboard is open, and gives off in its shadow
Delightful odors like a draught of old wine;

Crammed full, it is a jumble of strange old things,
Of sweet-smelling yellow linen, bits of clothing
Of women or children, of faded laces,
Of grandmother kerchiefs embroidered with griffins;

—There you would find medallions, locks
Of white or blond hair, portraits, dried flowers
Whose smell mingles with the smell of fruit.

—Ô buffet du vieux temps, tu sais bien des histoires,
Et tu voudrais conter tes contes, et tu bruis
Quand s'ouvrent lentement tes grandes portes noires.

L'éclatante victoire de Sarrebrück [3]

Remportée aux cris de vive l'Empereur!

(Gravure belge brillamment coloriée, se vend à Charleroi, 35 centimes.)

Au milieu, l'Empereur, dans une apothéose
Bleue et jaune, s'en va, raide, sur son dada
Flamboyant; très heureux,—car il voit tout en rose,
Féroce comme Zeus et doux comme un papa;

En bas, les bons Pioupious qui faisaient la sieste
Près des tambours dorés et des rouges canons,
Se lèvent gentiment. Pitou remet sa veste,
Et, tourné vers le Chef, s'étourdit de grands noms!

À droite, Dumanet, appuyé sur la crosse
De son chassepot, sent frémir sa nuque en brosse,
Et: "Vive l'Empereur!!"—Son voisin reste coi . . .

Un schako surgit, comme un soleil noir . . . —Au centre,
Boquillon rouge et bleu, très naïf, sur son ventre
Se dresse, et,—présentant ses derrières—: "De quoi? . . ."

La maline

Dans la salle à manger brune, que parfumait
Une odeur de vernis et de fruits, à mon aise
Je ramassais un plat de je ne sais quel met
Belge, et je m'épatais dans mon immense chaise.

En mangeant, j'écoutais l'horloge,—heureux et coi.
La cuisine s'ouvrit avec une bouffée
—Et la servante vint, je ne sais pas pourquoi,
Fichu moitié défait, malinement coiffée

—O cupboard of old times, you know many stories,
And you would like to tell your stories, and you murmur
When your big black doors slowly open.

The Dazzling Victory of Sarrebruck

> Won to shouts of Long Live the Emperor!
>
> (Belgian print, brilliantly colored, on sale in Charleroi, 35 centimes.)

In the center, the Emperor, in a blue and yellow
Apotheosis, goes off, stiff, on his flamboyant
Horsie; very happy,—for he sees everything rose-tinted,
Ferocious as Zeus and mild as papa;

Below, the good soldiers who were napping
Near the gilded drums and red cannon,
Get up politely. Pitou puts his jacket back on,
And turning toward the Leader, gets drunk on great names!

On the right, Dumanet, leaning on his Chassepot
Rifle, feels his hair stand up on the nape of his neck,
And: "Long Live the Emperor!!"—His neighbor stays quiet . . .

A shako rises up, like a black sun . . . —In the center,
Boquillon, red and blue, very naïve, on his stomach
Pushes up, and, presenting his backside, asks: "On what?"

The Sly Girl

In the brown dining room, perfumed
With an odor of varnish and fruit, leisurely
I gathered up some Belgian dish
Or other, and spread out in my huge chair.

While I ate, I listened to the clock—happy and quiet.
The kitchen door opened with a gust
—And a servant girl came, I don't know why,
Her neckerchief loose, her hair coyly dressed

Et, tout en promenant son petit doigt tremblant
Sur sa joue, un velours de pêche rose et blanc,
En faisant, de sa lèvre enfantine, une moue,

Elle arrangeait les plats, près de moi, pour m'aiser;
—Puis, comme ça,—bien sûr, pour avoir un baiser,—
Tout bas: "Sens donc: j'ai pris *une* froid sur la joue . . ."

Au Cabaret-Vert

cinq heures du soir

Depuis huit jours, j'avais déchiré mes bottines
Aux cailloux des chemins. J'entrais à Charleroi.
—*Au Cabaret-Vert*: je demandai des tartines
De beurre et du jambon qui fût à moitié froid.

Bienheureux, j'allongeai les jambes sous la table
Verte: je contemplai les sujets très naïfs
De la tapisserie.—Et ce fut adorable,
Quand la fille aux tétons énormes, aux yeux vifs,

—Celle-là, ce n'est pas un baiser qui l'épeure!—
Rieuse, m'apporta des tartines de beurre,
Du jambon tiède, dans un plat colorié,

Du jambon rose et blanc parfumé d'une gousse
D'ail,—et m'emplit la chope immense, avec sa mousse
Que dorait un rayon de soleil arriéré

Le dormeur du val

C'est un trou de verdure où chante une rivière
Accrochant follement aux herbes des haillons
D'argent; où le soleil, de la montagne fière,
Luit: c'est un petit val qui mousse de rayons.

And as she passed her small trembling finger
Over her cheek, a pink and white peach velvet skin,
And pouted with her childish mouth,

She arranged the plates, near me, to put me at ease;
—Then, just like that—to get a kiss, naturally—
Said softly: "Feel there: I've caught a cold on my cheek . . ."

At the Cabaret-Vert

at five in the afternoon

For a week my boots had been torn
By the pebbles on the roads. I was getting into Charleroi.
—*At the Cabaret-Vert*: I asked for bread
And butter, and for ham that would be half chilled.

Happy, I stretched out my legs under the green
Table: I looked at the very naïve subjects
Of the wallpaper.—And it was lovely,
When the girl with huge tits and lively eyes,

—She's not one to be afraid of a kiss!—
Laughing, brought me bread and butter,
Warm ham, in a colored plate,

White and rosy ham flavored with a clove
Of garlic,—and filled my enormous mug, with its foam
Which a late ray of sun turned gold

The Sleeper in the Valley

It is a green hollow where a river sings
Madly catching on the grasses
Silver rags; where the sun shines from the proud mountain:
It is a small valley which bubbles over with rays.

Un soldat jeune, bouche ouverte, tête nue,
Et la nuque baignant dans le frais cresson bleu,
Dort; il est étendu dans l'herbe, sous la nue,
Pâle dans son lit vert où la lumière pleut.

Les pieds dans les glaïeuls, il dort. Souriant comme
Sourirait un enfant malade, il fait une somme:
Nature, berce-le chaudement: il a froid.

Les parfums ne font pas frissonner sa narine;
Il dort dans le soleil, la main sur sa poitrine
Tranquille. Il a deux trous rouges au côté droit.

À la musique

Place de la Gare, à Charleville

Sur la place taillée en mesquines pelouses,
Square où tout est correct, les arbres et les fleurs,
Tous les bourgeois poussifs qu'étranglent les chaleurs
Portent, les jeudis soirs, leurs bêtises jalouses.

—L'orchestre militaire, au milieu du jardin,
Balance ses schakos dans la *Valse des fifres*:
—Autour, aux premiers rangs, parade le gandin;
Le notaire pend à ses breloques à chiffres:

Des rentiers à lorgnons soulignent tous les couacs:
Les gros bureaux bouffis traînent leurs grosses dames
Auprès desquelles vont, officieux cornacs,
Celles dont les volants ont des airs de réclames;

Sur les bancs verts, des clubs d'épiciers retraités
Qui tisonnent le sable avec leur canne à pomme,
Fort sérieusement discutent les traités,
Puis prisent en argent, et reprennent: "En somme! . . ."

A young soldier, his mouth open, his head bare,
And the nape of his neck bathing in the cool blue watercress,
Sleeps; he is stretched out on the grass, under clouds,
Pale on his green bed where the light rains down.

His feet in the gladiolas, he sleeps. Smiling as
A sick child would smile, he is taking a nap:
Nature, cradle him warmly: he is cold.

Odors do not make his nostrils quiver;
He sleeps in the sun, his hand on his breast,
Quieted. There are two red holes in his right side.

To Music

The Station Square, Charleville

On the square, cut up into measly plots of grass,
The square where everything is right, trees and flowers,
All the wheezy bourgeois, choked by the heat,
Bring, Thursday evenings, their jealous stupidities.

—The military band, in the middle of the garden,
Swing their shakos in the *Waltz of the Fifes*:
—Around them, in the first rows, struts the dandy;
The notary hangs from his monogrammed watch-charm:

Private-incomed men in pince-nez point out all the false notes:
Men from huge desks, bloated, drag their fat wives
Near whom, like busy elephant keepers, walk
Women whose flounces resemble public announcements;

On the green benches, clubs of retired grocers
Who poke the sand with their knobbed canes,
Very seriously discuss treaties,
Then take snuff from silver boxes, and continue: "In short!" . . .

Epatant sur son banc les rondeurs de ses reins,
Un bourgeois à boutons clairs, bedaine flamande,
Savoure son onnaing d'où le tabac par brins
Déborde—vous savez, c'est de la contrebande;—

Le long des gazons verts ricanent les voyous;
Et, rendus amoureux par le chant des trombones,
Très naïfs, et fumant des roses, les pioupious
Caressent les bébés pour enjôler les bonnes . . .

—Moi, je suis, débraillé comme un étudiant
Sous les marronniers verts les alertes fillettes:
Elles le savent bien; et tournent en riant,
Vers moi, leurs yeux tout pleins de choses indiscrètes

Je ne dis pas un mot: je regarde toujours
La chair de leurs cous blancs brodés de mèches folles:
Je suis, sous le corsage et les frêles atours,
Le dos divin après la courbe des épaules

J'ai bientôt déniché la bottine, le bas . . .
—Je reconstruis les corps, brûlé de belles fièvres.
Elles me trouvent drôle et se parlent tout bas . . .
—Et je sens les baisers qui me viennent aux lèvres . . .

Bal des pendus

> Au gibet noir, manchot aimable,
> Dansent, dansent les paladins
> Les maigres paladins du diable
> Les squelettes de Saladins.

Messire Belzebuth tire par la cravate
Ses petits pantins noirs grimaçant sur le ciel,
Et, leur claquant au front un revers de savate,
Les fait danser, danser aux sons d'un vieux Noël!

Spreading over his bench the roundness of his buttocks,
A bourgeois with bright buttons, a Flemish paunch,
Savors his onnaing [pipe], from which tobacco in shreds
Hangs out—you know, it is smuggled goods;—

Along the green grass loafers sneer at everyone;
And, made amorous by the song of the trombones,
Very naïve, and smoking pinks, young soldiers
Pat the babies to make up to the nurses . . .

—Dressed as badly as a student, I follow,
Under the green chestnut trees, the lively girls:
They know it, and turn to me, laughing,
Their eyes full of indiscreet things.

I do not say a word: I keep looking
At the flash of their white necks embroidered with stray locks:
I follow, under the bodice and the scanty clothes,
The divine back below the curve of the shoulders.

Soon I have revealed the boot, the stocking . . .
—Burning with fine fevers, I reconstruct the bodies.
They find me silly and speak together in low voices . . .
—And I feel the kisses that come to my lips . . .

Dance of the Hanged Men

> On the black gallows, one-armed fellow,
> The paladins are dancing, dancing
> The thin paladins of the devil
> The skeletons of Saladins.

Sir Beelzebub pulls by the rope
His small black puppets grinning at the sky
And slapping their heads with a backhand blow,
Makes them dance, dance to the sound of an old noel!

Et les pantins choqués enlacent leurs bras grêles:
Comme des orgues noirs, les poitrines à jour
Que serraient autrefois les gentes damoiselles,
Se heurtent longuement dans un hideux amour.

Hurrah! les gais danseurs, qui n'avez plus de panse!
On peut cabrioler, les tréteaux sont si longs!
Hop! qu'on ne sache plus si c'est bataille ou danse!
Belzebuth enragé râcle ses violons!

Ô durs talons, jamais on n'use sa sandale!
Presque tous ont quitté la chemise de peau:
Le reste est peu gênant et se voit sans scandale.
Sur les crânes, la neige applique un blanc chapeau:

Le corbeau fait panache à ces têtes fêlées,
Un morceau de chair tremble à leur maigre menton:
On dirait, tournoyant dans les sombres mêlées,
Des preux, raides, heurtant armures de carton.

Hurrah! la bise siffle au grand bal des squelettes!
Le gibet noir mugit comme un orgue de fer!
Les loups vont répondant des forêts violettes:
À l'horizon, le ciel est d'un rouge d'enfer . . .

Holà, secouez-moi ces capitans funèbres
Qui défilent, sournois, de leurs gros doigts cassés
Un chapelet d'amour sur leurs pâles vertèbres:
Ce n'est pas un moustier ici, les trépassés!

Oh! voilà qu'au milieu de la danse macabre
Bondit dans le ciel rouge un grand squelette fou
Emporté par l'élan, comme un cheval se cabre:
Et, se sentant encor la corde raide au cou,

Crispe ses petits doigts sur son fémur qui craque
Avec des cris pareils à des ricanements,
Et, comme un baladin rentre dans la baraque,
Rebondit dans le bal au chant des ossements.

And the jostled puppets entwine their thin arms:
Like black organ-pipes, their breasts pierced with light
Which once noble ladies pressed,
Struck against one another for a long time in hideous love-making.

Hurrah! You gay dancers who have no more bellies!
You can cavort about, the stages are so long!
Hop! don't try to know whether it is a battle or a dance!
Beelzebub in a rage saws on his fiddles!

Oh the hard heels! one's sandal never wears out!
Almost all have taken off their shirts of skin:
The rest is not embarrassing and can be seen without scandal.
On the skulls, the snow sets a white hat:

The crow is a plume on these cracked heads,
A piece of flesh is loose on their thin chins:
You could say, as they turn about in dark skirmishes,
They are stiff knights clashing cardboard armor.

Hurrah! the breeze whistles in the great ball of skeletons!
The black gallows moans like an iron organ!
Wolves give answer from violet forests:
On the horizon, the sky is a hellish red . . .

Hey! shake those funereal braggarts
Who, surly, with their fat broken fingers, spread
Their beads of love across their pale vertebrae:
You dead, this is no monastery!

Oh! there in the middle of the dance of Death
Leaps into the red sky a great mad skeleton
Carried off by his impetus, like a horse rearing:
And, still feeling the rope tight around his neck,

Clenches his small fingers on his thighbone which cracks
With shouts similar to jeers,
And, like a clown going back into his booth,
Springs back into the dance to the singing of bones.

Au gibet noir, manchot aimable,
Dansent dansent les paladins
Les maigres paladins du diable,
Les squelettes de Saladins.

Le châtiment de Tartufe

Tisonnant, tisonnant son cœur amoureux sous
Sa chaste robe noire, heureux, la main gantée,
Un jour qu'il s'en allait, effroyablement doux,
Jaune, bavant la foi de sa bouche édentée,

Un jour qu'il s'en allait, — "Oremus," — un Méchant
Le prit rudement par son oreille benoîte
Et lui jeta des mots affreux, en arrachant
Sa chaste robe noire autour de sa peau moite!

Châtiment! . . . Ses habits étaient déboutonnés,
Et le long chapelet des péchés pardonnés
S'égrenant dans son cœur, Saint Tartufe était pâle! . . .

Donc, il se confessait, priait, avec un râle!
L'homme se contenta d'emporter ses rabats . . .
— Peuh! Tartufe était nu du haut jusques en bas!

Le forgeron

Palais des Tuileries, vers le 10 août 92

Le bras sur un marteau gigantesque, effrayant
D'ivresse et de grandeur, le front vaste, riant
Comme un clairon d'airain, avec toute sa bouche,
Et prenant ce gros-là dans son regard farouche,
Le Forgeron parlait à Louis Seize, un jour
Que le Peuple était là, se tordant tout autour,
Et sur les lambris d'or traînant sa veste sale.
Or le bon roi, debout sur son ventre, était pâle

On the black gallows, one-armed fellow,
The paladins are dancing dancing
The thin paladins of the devil,
The skeletons of Saladins.

Tartufe's Punishment

Raking, raking his amorous heart under
His chaste black robe, happy, his hand gloved,
One day as he walked along, terribly sweet,
Yellow, drooling piety from his toothless mouth,

One day as he walked along, —"Let us pray," —a Wicked Fellow
Seized him roughly by his blessed ear
And hurled frightful words at him as he tore off
The chaste black robe about his moist skin!

Punishment! . . . His clothes were unbuttoned,
And the long rosary of pardoned sins
Being said in his heart, Saint Tartufe was pale! . . .

So, he confessed, and prayed, with a death rattle!
The man was content to carry off his clerical bands . . .
—Pshaw! Tartufe was naked from top to bottom!

The Blacksmith

Palace of the Tuileries, about August 10, 1792

His arm on a huge hammer, terrible
With drunkenness and size, his brow large, laughing
Like a bronze trumpet, with all of his mouth,
And taking over with his wild gaze that fat man,
The Blacksmith spoke to Louis the Sixteenth, one day
When the People were there, milling about,
And brushing their dirty jackets over the gilded paneling.
Now the good king, upright on his belly, was pale

Pâle comme un vaincu qu'on prend pour le gibet,
Et, soumis comme un chien, jamais ne regimbait
Car ce maraud de forge aux énormes épaules
Lui disait de vieux mots et des choses si drôles,
Que cela l'empoignait au front, comme cela!

"Or, tu sais bien, Monsieur, nous chantions tra la la
Et nous piquions les bœufs vers les sillons des autres:
Le Chanoine au soleil filait des patenôtres
Sur des chapelets clairs grenés de pièces d'or
Le Seigneur, à cheval, passait, sonnant du cor
Et l'un avec la hart, l'autre avec la cravache
Nous fouillaient—Hébétés comme des yeux de vache,
Nos yeux ne pleuraient plus; nous allions, nous allions,
Et quand nous avions mis le pays en sillons,
Quand nous avions laissé dans cette terre noire
Un peu de notre chair . . . nous avions un pourboire
On nous faisait flamber nos taudis dans la nuit
Nos petits y faisaient un gâteau fort bien cuit

. . . "Oh! je ne me plains pas. Je te dis mes bêtises,
C'est entre nous. J'admets que tu me contredises.
Or, n'est-ce pas joyeux de voir, au mois de juin
Dans les granges entrer des voitures de foin
Énormes? De sentir l'odeur de ce qui pousse,
Des vergers quand il pleut un peu, de l'herbe rousse?
De voir des blés, des blés, des épis pleins de grain,
De penser que cela prépare bien du pain? . . .
Oh! plus fort, on irait, au fourneau qui s'allume,
Chanter joyeusement en martelant l'enclume,
Si l'on était certain de pouvoir prendre un peu,
Étant homme, à fin!, de ce que donne Dieu!
—Mais voilà, c'est toujours la même vieille histoire! . . .

"Mais je sais, maintenant! Moi, je ne peux plus croire,
Quand j'ai deux bonnes mains, mon front et mon marteau,
Qu'un homme vienne là, dague sur le manteau,
Et me dise: Mon gars, ensemence ma terre;
Que l'on arrive encor, quand ce serait la guerre,

As pale as the victim you take to the gallows,
And, meek like a dog, made no resistance
For that rascal from the forge with his huge shoulders
Was telling him old phrases and things so strange,
That it took hold of his forelock, just like that!

"Now, Sire, you know how we used to sing tralala
And drive our oxen toward the furrows of others:
The Canon in the sun said his "our Father"
On clear rosaries strung with gold pieces
The Lord passed by on horseback, blowing his horn
And one fellow with the noose, and another with the whip
Lashed us—Bewildered like cows' eyes,
Our eyes did not weep; we went on and on,
And when we had ploughed the countryside,
When we had left in this black soil
Some of our flesh . . . we received a tip
Our hovels were set fire to in the night
Our children made a well-done cake

. . . "Oh! I don't complain. I am telling you my foolishness,
It's between us. I allow you to contradict me.
But isn't it folly to see, in the month of June
Huge hay wagons entering
The barns? To smell the smell of what is growing,
Orchards when it is raining a bit, and hayfields?
To see wheat, and more wheat, ears full of kernels,
And to think that this promises abundant bread? . . .
Oh! stronger we would go to the forge lighting up,
And joyously sing as we hammer on the anvil,
If we were certain of being able to take a bit,
Since we are men, at the end!, of what God gives!
—But that's that! It's always the same old story! . . .

"But now I know! I can no longer believe,
When I have two good hands, and my head and my hammer,
That a man can come here, a dagger under his cloak,
And say to me: Boy, sow my land;
Or that someone else can come, when there's a war,

Me prendre mon garçon comme cela, chez moi!
—Moi, je serais un homme, et toi, tu serais roi,
Tu me dirais: Je veux! . . .—Tu vois bien, c'est stupide.
Tu crois que j'aime voir ta baraque splendide,
Tes officiers dorés, tes mille chenapans,
Tes palsembleu bâtards tournant comme des paons:
Ils ont rempli ton nid de l'odeur de nos filles
Et de petits billets pour nous mettre aux Bastilles
Et nous dirons: C'est bien: les pauvres à genoux!
Nous dorerons ton Louvre en donnant nos gros sous!
Et tu te soûleras, tu feras belle fête
—Et ces Messieurs riront, les reins sur notre tête!

"Non. Ces saletés-là datent de nos papas!
Oh! Le Peuple n'est plus une putain. Trois pas
Et tous, nous avons mis ta Bastille en poussière
Cette bête suait du sang à chaque pierre
Et c'était dégoûtant, la Bastille debout
Avec ses murs lépreux qui nous racontaient tout
Et, toujours, nous tenaient enfermés dans leur ombre!
—Citoyen! citoyen! c'était le passé sombre
Qui croulait, qui râlait, quand nous prîmes la tour!
Nous avions quelque chose au cœur comme l'amour.
Nous avions embrassé nos fils sur nos poitrines.
Et, comme des chevaux, en soufflant des narines
Nous allions, fiers et forts, et ça nous battait là . . .
Nous marchions au soleil, front haut,—comme cela—,
Dans Paris! On venait devant nos vestes sales.
Enfin! Nous nous sentions Hommes! Nous étions pâles,
Sire, nous étions soûls de terribles espoirs:
Et quand nous fûmes là, devant les donjons noirs,
Agitant nos clairons et nos feuilles de chêne,
Les piques à la main; nous n'eûmes pas de haine,
—Nous nous sentions si forts, nous voulions être doux!

. . . .
. . . .

"Et depuis ce jour-là, nous sommes comme fous!
Le tas des ouvriers a monté dans la rue,
Et ces maudits s'en vont, foule toujours accrue

And take my son away, in my own house!
—If I were a man, and you the king,
You would say to me: I want this! . . . —You can see, it is stupid.
You think I like seeing your magnificent barn,
Your gilded officers, your thousand knaves,
Your Od's blood bastards parading like peacocks:
They have filled your nest with the smell of our daughters
And with little letters to put us in Bastilles
And we will say: that's fine; all the poor, kneel down!
We will gild your Louvre by giving you our fat sous!
And you will get drunk, and have a good time
—And these gentlemen will laugh, sitting on our heads!

"No, that filth dates from the time of our fathers!
Oh! The People are no longer whores. Three steps
And all of us have brought your Bastille down to the dust
That beast sweated blood from each stone
And it was disgusting, the Bastille standing
With its leprous walls which told us everything
And still kept us closed up within their shadow!
—Citizen! citizen! it was the dark past
Crumbling, giving its death-rattle, when we took the tower!
We had something like love in our hearts.
We had embraced our sons and held them to our breasts.
And like horses, snorting from the nostrils,
We went out, strong and proud, and our hearts were beating . . .
We marched in the sun, heads high—like this—,
Into Paris! They came to meet us in our dirty clothes.
At last! We felt we were Men! We were pale,
Sire, we were drunk on terrifying hopes:
And when we were there, in front of the black towers,
Waving our bugles and oakleaves,
With pikes in our hands; we had no hate,
—We felt so strong, we wanted to be gentle!

· ·
· ·

"And since that day, we have been like madmen!
The number of workers has increased in the street,
And those wretches go off, in a constantly swelling crowd

De sombres revenants, aux portes des richards.
Moi, je cours avec eux assommer les mouchards:
Et je vais dans Paris, noir, marteau sur l'épaule,
Farouche, à chaque coin balayant quelque drôle,
Et, si tu me riais au nez, je te tuerais!
—Puis, tu peux y compter, tu te feras des frais
Avec tes hommes noirs, qui prennent nos requêtes
Pour se les renvoyer comme sur des raquettes
Et, tout bas, les malins! se disent: "Qu'ils sont sots!"
Pour mitonner des lois, coller de petits pots
Pleins de jolis décrets roses et de droguailles
S'amuser à couper proprement quelques tailles,
Puis se boucher le nez quand nous marchons près d'eux,
—Nos doux représentants qui nous trouvent crasseux!—
Pour ne rien redouter, rien, que les baïonnettes . . . ,
C'est très bien. Foin de leur tabatière à sornettes!
Nous en avons assez, là, de ces cerveaux plats
Et de ces ventres-dieux. Ah! ce sont là les plats
Que tu nous sers, bourgeois, quand nous sommes féroces,
Quand nous brisons déjà les sceptres et les crosses! . . ."

.   .   .   .

Il le prend par le bras, arrache le velours
Des rideaux, et lui montre en bas les larges cours
Où fourmille, où fourmille, où se lève la foule,
La foule épouvantable avec des bruits de houle,
Hurlant comme une chienne, hurlant comme une mer,
Avec ses bâtons forts et ses piques de fer,
Ses tambours, ses grands cris de halles et de bouges,
Tas sombre de haillons saignant de bonnets rouges:
L'Homme, par la fenêtre ouverte, montre tout
Au roi pâle et suant qui chancelle debout,
Malade à regarder cela!
                                        "C'est la Crapule,
Sire. Ça bave aux murs, ça monte, ça pullule:
—Puisqu'ils ne mangent pas, Sire, ce sont des gueux!
Je suis un forgeron: ma femme est avec eux,
Folle! Elle croit trouver du pain aux Tuileries!
—On ne veut pas de nous dans les boulangeries.

Of dark ghosts, at the doors of the rich.
I run along with them to knock out the informers:
And I go through Paris, my face black, hammer on shoulder,
Wild, at each corner sweeping out some fellow,
And if you laughed in my face, I would kill you!
—So, you can count on this: it will cost you plenty
With your men in black, who take our petitions
Only to bat them back and forth as on rackets,
And in low voices (they're cunning!) say to one another: "What fools
    they are!"
To fake laws, and stick bills out of jars
Full of pretty pink decrees and sugar-coated pills
To amuse themselves by cutting down a few sizes,
Then holding their noses when we walk near them,
—Our kind representatives who find us dirty!—
In order to fear nothing, nothing, save bayonets . . . ,
That is fine. Let's get rid of their humbug speeches!
We have had enough of these flat-heads
And these belly-gods. Ah! those are the dishes
You bourgeois serve us, when we are in a frenzy,
When we are already breaking sceptres and croziers! . . ."

. . . .

He takes him by the arm, rips open the velvet
Of the curtains, and shows him down below the large courtyards
Where the mob seethes, seethes about and rises up,
The terrible mob with the sounds of the ocean swell,
Yelling like a bitch, yelling like a sea,
With their stout sticks and their iron pikes,
Their drums, their loud shouts of markets and hovels,
A dark mass of rags bleeding with red caps:
The Man, through the open window, points everything out
To the pale sweating king who reels as he stands,
Sick at watching that!
          "That is the Scum,
Sire. It drools at the walls, it rises and swarms about:
—Since they don't eat, Sire, they are beggars!
I am a blacksmith: my wife is with them,
Mad! She thinks she will find bread in the Tuileries!
—We are not wanted in the bakeries.

J'ai trois petits. Je suis crapule.—Je connais
Des vieilles qui s'en vont pleurant sous leurs bonnets
Parce qu'on leur a pris leur garçon ou leur fille:
C'est la crapule.—Un homme était à la bastille,
Un autre était forçat: et tous deux, citoyens
Honnêtes. Libérés, ils sont comme des chiens:
On les insulte! Alors, ils ont là quelque chose
Qui leur fait mal, allez! C'est terrible, et c'est cause
Que se sentant brisés, que, se sentant damnés,
Ils sont là, maintenant, hurlant sous votre nez!
Crapule.—Là-dedans sont des filles, infâmes
Parce que,—vous saviez que c'est faible, les femmes,—
Messeigneurs de la cour,—que ça veut toujours bien,—
Vous [leur] avez craché sur l'âme, comme rien!
Vos belles, aujourd'hui, sont là. C'est la crapule.

. . . .

"Oh! tous les Malheureux, tous ceux dont le dos brûle
Sous le soleil féroce, et qui vont, et qui vont,
Qui dans ce travail-là sentent crever leur front
Chapeau bas, mes bourgeois! Oh! ceux-là, sont les Hommes!
Nous sommes Ouvriers, Sire! Ouvriers! Nous sommes
Pour les grands temps nouveaux où l'on voudra savoir,
Où l'Homme forgera du matin jusqu'au soir,
Chasseur des grands effets, chasseur des grandes causes,
Où, lentement vainqueur, il domptera les choses
Et montera sur Tout, comme sur un cheval!
Oh! splendides lueurs des forges! Plus de mal,
Plus!—Ce qu'on ne sait pas, c'est peut-être terrible:
Nous saurons!—Nos marteaux en main, passons au crible
Tout ce que nous savons: puis, Frères, en avant!
Nous faisons quelquefois ce grand rêve émouvant
De vivre simplement, ardemment, sans rien dire
De mauvais, travaillant sous l'auguste sourire
D'une femme qu'on aime avec un noble amour:
Et l'on travaillerait fièrement tout le jour,
Écoutant le devoir comme un clairon qui sonne:
Et l'on se sentirait très heureux: et personne,

I have three children. I am scum.—I know
Old women who go about weeping under their bonnets
Because their boy or girl was taken from them:
It is the scum.—One man was in prison
Another was a convict: and both, honest
Citizens. Freed, they are like dogs:
People insult them! So they have here something
That hurts them! It is terrible, and it's the reason
That, feeling themselves broken, feeling themselves damned,
They are here now yelling under your nose!
Scum.—Down there girls, who are infamous
Because,—you knew women are weak,—
Gentlemen of the court,—that they are always willing,—
You spat on their souls, as if that were nothing!
Your girls, today, are down here. They are scum.

. . . .

"Oh! all Wretches, all those whose backs burn
Under the strong sun, and who go, and who go,
Who in this labor feel their heads bursting
Hats off, my bourgeois! Oh! these are Men!
We are Workers, Sire! Workers! We are
For the great new times when men will want to know,
When Man will forge from morning to night,
A hunter of great effects, hunter of great causes,
When, slowly victorious, he will tame things
And mount Everything, as one mounts a horse!
Oh! glorious glare of the forges! No more evil,
No more!—What isn't known is perhaps terrible:
We will know it!—Our hammers in our hands, let us sort out
All that we know: then, Brothers, forward!
Sometimes we have that great moving dream
Of living simply, ardently, without speaking
Any evil, working beneath the solemn smile
Of a woman we love with a noble love:
And we would work proudly all day,
Listening to duty like the sound of a trumpet:
And we would feel happy: and no one,

Oh! personne, surtout, ne vous ferait ployer!
On aurait un fusil au-dessus du foyer . . .

. . . .

"Oh! mais l'air est tout plein d'une odeur de bataille!
Que te disais-je donc? Je suis de la canaille!
Il reste des mouchards et des accapareurs.
Nous sommes libres, nous! nous avons des terreurs
Où nous nous sentons grands, oh! si grands! Tout à l'heure
Je parlais de devoir calme, d'une demeure . . .
Regarde donc le ciel! — C'est trop petit pour nous,
Nous crèverions de chaud, nous serions à genoux!
Regarde donc le ciel! — Je rentre dans la foule
Dans la grande canaille effroyable, qui roule,
Sire, tes vieux canons sur les sales pavés:
— Oh! quand nous serons morts, nous les aurons lavés
— Et si, devant nos cris, devant notre vengeance,
Les pattes des vieux rois mordorés, sur la France
Poussent leurs régiments en habits de gala,
Eh bien, n'est-ce pas, vous tous? Merde à ces chiens-là!"

. . . .

— Il reprit son marteau sur l'épaule.
                              La foule
Près de cet homme-là se sentait l'âme soûle,
Et, dans la grande cour, dans les appartements,
Où Paris haletait avec des hurlements,
Un frisson secoua l'immense populace
Alors, de sa main large et superbe de crasse
Bien que le roi ventru suât, le Forgeron,
Terrible, lui jeta le bonnet rouge au front!

Ma bohème (Fantaisie)

Je m'en allais, les poings dans mes poches crevées;
Mon paletot aussi devenait idéal;
J'allais sous le ciel, Muse! et j'étais ton féal;
Oh! là là! que d'amours splendides j'ai rêvées!

Oh! no one, above all, would make you bend down!
We would have a gun over the hearth . . .

. . . .

"Oh! but the air is full of an odor of battle!
What was I saying to you? I am from the mob!
There remain informers and sharks.
But we are free! we feel terrified
When we feel great!—oh! so great! Just now
I spoke of peaceful duties, of a home . . .
Just look at the sky!—It is too small for us,
We would die of heat, we would be on our knees!
Just look at the sky!—I am going back into the crowd,
Into the huge terrible mob, which is rolling,
Sire, your old cannon over the dirty cobblestones;
—Oh! when we are dead, we will have washed them
—And if, against our cries, against our vengeance,
The claws of old bronzed kings incite
Their regiments in full dress uniforms over France,
Well, isn't it so, all of you? Shit to those dogs!"

. . . .

—He put back his hammer on his shoulder.
                                            The crowd
Near that man felt its soul drunk,
And, in the big courtyard, and in apartments,
Where Paris panted and shouted,
A shudder shook the huge populace.
Then, with his broad hand, superb with dirt,
Although the potbellied king sweated, the Blacksmith,
Frighten, threw his red cap on the king's head!

My Bohemian Life (Fantasy)

I went off, my fists in my torn pockets;
My coat too was becoming ideal;
I walked under the sky, Muse! and I was your vassal;
Oh! oh! what brilliant loves I dreamed of!

Mon unique culotte avait un large trou.
—Petit Poucet rêveur, j'égrenais dans ma course
Des rimes. Mon auberge était à la Grande-Ourse.
—Mes étoiles au ciel avaient un doux frou-frou

Et je les écoutais, assis au bord des routes,
Ces bons soirs de septembre où je sentais des gouttes
De rosée à mon front, comme un vin de vigueur;

Où, rimant au milieu des ombres fantastiques,
Comme des lyres, je tirais les élastiques
De mes souliers blessés, un pied près de mon cœur!

Le mal

Tandis que les crachats rouges de la mitraille
Sifflent tout le jour par l'infini du ciel bleu;
Qu'écarlates ou verts, près du Roi qui les raille,
Croulent les bataillons en masse dans le feu;

Tandis qu'une folie épouvantable, broie
Et fait de cent milliers d'hommes un tas fumant;
—Pauvres morts! dans l'été, dans l'herbe, dans ta joie,
Nature! ô toi qui fis ces hommes saintement! . . —

—Il est un Dieu, qui rit aux nappes damassées
Des autels, à l'encens, aux grands calices d'or;
Qui dans le bercement des hosannah s'endort,

Et se réveille, quand des mères, ramassées
Dans l'angoisse, et pleurant sous leur vieux bonnet noir,
Lui donnent un gros sou lié dans leur mouchoir!

My only pair of trousers had a big hole.
—Tom Thumb in a daze, I sowed rhymes
As I went along. My inn was at the Big Dipper.
—My stars in the sky made a soft rustling sound

And I listened to them, seated on the side of the road,
In those good September evenings when I felt drops
Of dew on my brow, like a strong wine;

Where, rhyming in the midst of fantastic shadows,
Like lyres I plucked the elastics
Of my wounded shoes, one foot near my heart!

Evil

While the red spit of grapeshot
Whistles all day through the endlessness of the blue sky;
While scarlet or green, near the King who mocks them,
Whole battalions collapse in the fire;

While a terrible madness, crushes
And makes of a hundred thousand men a smoking heap;
—Poor dead men! in summer, in the grass, in your joy,
Nature! O you who made these men holy! . . —

—There is a God, who laughs at the damask cloths
Of the altars, at the incense, at the great golden chalices;
Who falls asleep in the lullaby of Hosannas,

And wakes up, when mothers, joined
In anguish, and weeping under their old black bonnets,
Give him a penny tied up in their handkerchiefs!

Rages de Césars

L'Homme pâle, le long des pelouses fleuries,
Chemine, en habit noir, et le cigare aux dents:
L'Homme pâle repense aux fleurs des Tuileries
—Et parfois son œil terne a des regards ardents . . .

Car l'Empereur est soûl de ses vingt ans d'orgie!
Il s'était dit: "Je vais souffler la Liberté
Bien délicatement, ainsi qu'une bougie!"
La Liberté revit! Il se sent éreinté!

Il est pris:—Oh! quel nom sur ses lèvres muettes
Tressaille? Quel regret implacable le mord?
On ne le saura pas. L'Empereur a l'œil mort.

Il repense peut-être au Compère en lunettes . . .
—Et regarde filer de son cigare en feu,
Comme aux soirs de Saint-Cloud, un fin nuage bleu.

Caesars' Rages [4]

The pale Man, along the flowering lawns,
Walks, in a black coat, a cigar between his teeth:
The pale Man thinks back on the flowers of the Tuileries
—And at times his dull eye has burning glances . . .

For the Emperor is drunk on his twenty years' orgy!
He had said to himself: "I will blow out Liberty
Very softly, like a candle!"
Liberty lives again! He feels his back is broken!

He is caught:—Oh! what name trembles
On his mute lips? What implacable remorse plagues him?
We will never know. The Emperor's eye is dead.

He is perhaps thinking of his Accomplice in spectacles . . .
—And watches rising from his burning cigar,
As in the evenings at St. Cloud, thin blue smoke.

Poèmes datés
de 1871–début 1872 ou dans des
lettres de mai ou juin 1871

Poems dated
1871–early 1872 or in
letters from May or June 1871

Le cœur volé[5]

Mon triste cœur bave à la poupe,
Mon cœur couvert de caporal:
Ils y lancent des jets de soupe,
Mon triste cœur bave à la poupe:
Sous les quolibets de la troupe
Qui pousse un rire général,
Mon triste cœur bave à la poupe
Mon cœur couvert de caporal!

Ithyphalliques et pioupiesques,
Leurs quolibets l'ont dépravé!
Au gouvernail on voit des fresques
Ithyphalliques et pioupiesques
Ô flots abracadabrantesques
Prenez mon cœur, qu'il soit lavé:
Ithyphalliques et pioupiesques
Leurs quolibets l'ont dépravé!

Quand ils auront tari leurs chiques
Comment agir, ô cœur volé?
Ce seront des hoquets bachiques
Quand ils auront tari leurs chiques
J'aurai des sursauts stomachiques
Moi, si mon cœur est ravalé:
Quand ils auront tari leurs chiques
Comment agir, ô cœur volé?

Chant de guerre parisien

Le Printemps est évident, car
Du cœur des Propriétés vertes,
Le vol de Thiers et de Picard
Tient ses splendeurs grandes ouvertes!

The Stolen Heart

My sad heart slobbers at the poop,
My heart covered with tobacco-spit:
They spew streams of soup at it,
My sad heart drools at the poop:
Under the jeerings of the soldiers
Who break out laughing,
My sad heart drools at the poop
My heart covered with tobacco-spit!

Ithyphallic and soldierish,
Their jeerings have depraved it!
On the rudder you see frescoes
Ithyphallic and soldierish
O abracadabratic waves
Take my heart, let it be washed:
Ithyphallic and soldierish
Their jeerings have depraved it!

When they have used up their quid
How will I act, O stolen heart?
There will be Bacchic hiccups
When they have used up their quid
I will have stomach retchings
If my heart is degraded:
When they have used up their quid
How will I act, O stolen heart?

Parisian War Song

Spring is in evidence, for
From the heart of green Estates,
The flight of Thiers and Picard
Holds wide open its splendors!

Ô Mai! quels délirants culs-nus!
Sèvres, Meudon, Bagneux, Asnières,
Écoutez donc les bienvenus
Semer les choses printanières!

Ils ont schako, sabre et tam-tam
Non la vieille boîte à bougies
Et des yoles qui n'ont jam, jam . . .
Fendent le lac aux eaux rougies!

Plus que jamais nous bambochons
Quand viennent sur nos tanières
Crouler les jaunes cabochons
Dans des aubes particulières!

Thiers et Picard sont des Eros,
Des enleveurs d'héliotropes,
Au pétrole ils font des Corots:
Voici hannetonner leurs tropes . . .

Ils sont familiers du Grand Truc! . . .
Et couché dans les glaïeuls, Favre
Fait son cillement aqueduc,
Et ses reniflements à poivre!

La Grand ville a le pavé chaud,
Malgré vos douches de pétrole,
Et, décidément, il nous faut
Vous secouer dans votre rôle . . .

Et les Ruraux qui se prélassent
Dans de longs accroupissements,
Entendront des rameaux qui cassent
Parmi les rouges froissements!

O May! what delirious bare asses!
Sèvres, Meudon, Bagneux, Asnières,
Listen to the welcome arrivals
Sowing spring-like things!

They have a shako, a sabre, and a tom-tom
Not the old candle box
And boats that have nev, nev . . .
Cut through the lake of reddened waters!

More than ever we swagger
When yellow heads come
Collapsing over our hideaways
In special dawns!

Thiers and Picard are Cupids,
Thieves of heliotropes,
They paint Corots with gasoline:
Here their tropes are buzzing about . . .

They are friends of the Great What's-His-Name! . . .
And, lying in the gladiolas, Favre
Makes an aqueduct of his tears,
And his peppery sniff!

The Big City has a hot pavement,
In spite of your showers of gasoline,
And decidedly we have to
Shake you up in your roles . . .

And the Rustics who loll about
In long squattings
Will hear boughs breaking
Among red rustlings!

Mes petites amoureuses

Un hydrolat lacrymal lave
    Les cieux vert-chou:
Sous l'arbre tendronnier qui bave,
    Vos caoutchoucs

Blancs de lunes particulières
    Aux pialats ronds,
Entrechoquez vos genouillères
    Mes laiderons!

Nous nous aimions à cette époque,
    Bleu laideron!
On mangeait des œufs à la coque
    Et du mouron!

Un soir, tu me sacras poète,
    Blond laideron:
Descends ici, que je te fouette
    En mon giron;

J'ai dégueulé ta bandoline,
    Noir laideron;
Tu couperais ma mandoline
    Au fil du front

Pouah! mes salives desséchées,
    Roux laideron
Infectent encor les tranchées
    De ton sein rond!

Ô mes petites amoureuses,
    Que je vous hais!
Plaquez de fouffes douloureuses
    Vos tétons laids!

Piétinez mes vieilles terrines
    De sentiment;
—Hop donc! soyez-moi ballerines
    Pour un moment! . . .

My Little Lovers

A lacrymal tincture washes
    The cabbage-green skies:
Under the drooling tree with tender shoots,
    Your raincoats

White with special moons
    With round eyes
Knock together your kneecaps
    My ugly ones!

We loved one another at that time,
    Blue ugly one!
We ate soft boiled eggs
    And chickweed!

One evening you consecrated me poet,
    Blond ugly one:
Come down here, that I can whip you
    On my lap;

I vomited your brilliantine,
    Black ugly one;
You would cut off my mandolin
    On the edge of my brow

Bah! my dried saliva,
    Red-headed ugly one
Still infects the trenches
    Of your round breast!

O my little lovers,
    How I hate you!
Plaster with painful blisters
    Your ugly tits!

Trample on my old pots
    Of sentiment;
—Up now! be ballerinas for me
    For one moment! . . .

Vos omoplates se déboîtent,
       Ô mes amours!
Une étoile à vos reins qui boitent,
       Tournez vos tours!

Et c'est pourtant pour ces éclanches
       Que j'ai rimé!
Je voudrais vous casser les hanches
       D'avoir aimé!

Fade amas d'étoiles ratées,
       Comblez les coins!
—Vous crèverez en Dieu, bâtées
       D'ignobles soins!

Sous les lunes particulières
       Aux pialats ronds,
Entrechoquez vos genouillères,
       Mes laiderons!

Accroupissements

Bien tard, quand il se sent l'estomac écœuré,
Le frère Milotus, un œil à la lucarne
D'où le soleil, clair comme un chaudron récuré,
Lui darde une migraine et fait son regard darne,
Déplace dans les draps son ventre de curé

Il se démène sous sa couverture grise
Et descend, ses genoux à son ventre tremblant,
Effaré comme un vieux qui mangerait sa prise,
Car il lui faut, le poing à l'anse d'un pot blanc,
À ses reins largement retrousser sa chemise!

Or, il s'est accroupi, frileux, les doigts de pied
Repliés, grelottant au clair soleil qui plaque
Des jaunes de brioche aux vitres de papier;
Et le nez du bonhomme où s'allume la laque
Renifle aux rayons, tel qu'un charnel polypier.

. . . .

Your shoulder blades are out of joint,
    O my loves!
A star on your limping backs,
    Turn with your turns!

And yet it is for these mutton shoulders
    That I have made rhymes!
I would like to break your hips
    For having loved!

Insipid pile of stars that have failed,
    Fill the corners!
—You will collapse in God, saddled
    With ignoble cares!

Under special moons
    With round eyes,
Knock together your kneecaps,
    My ugly ones!

Squattings[6]

Very late, when he feels his stomach sicken,
Brother Milotus, an eye on the skylight
When the sun, bright as a scoured cooking-pan,
Darts a migraine at him and blinds his vision,
Moves his curate's belly under the sheets

He stirs about under his grey blanket
And gets out, his knees against his trembling belly,
Terrified like an old man who has eaten his snuff,
Because he has to lift up the folds of his nightshirt
Around his waist, as he takes the handle of a white chamberpot!

Now, he has squatted, cold, his toes
Turned up, shivering in the bright sunlight which daubs
A cake yellow on the paper windowpanes;
And the old man's nose where the crimson catches fire
Sniffs in the rays like a flesh polypary.

. . . .

Le bonhomme mijote au feu, bras tordus, lippe
Au ventre: il sent glisser ses cuisses dans le feu,
Et ses chausses roussir, et s'éteindre sa pipe;
Quelque chose comme un oiseau remue un peu
À son ventre serein comme un monceau de tripe!

Autour, dort un fouillis de meubles abrutis
Dans des haillons de crasse et sur de sales ventres;
Des escabeaux, crapauds étranges, sont blottis
Aux coins noirs: des buffets ont des gueules de chantres
Qu'entrouvre un sommeil plein d'horribles appétits

L'écœurante chaleur gorge la chambre étroite;
Le cerveau du bonhomme est bourré de chiffons:
Il écoute les poils pousser dans sa peau moite,
Et parfois, en hoquets fort gravement bouffons
S'échappe, secouant son escabeau qui boite . . .

. . . .

Et le soir, aux rayons de lune, qui lui font
Aux contours du cul des bavures de lumière,
Une ombre avec détails s'accroupit, sur un fond
De neige rose ainsi qu'une rose trémière . . .
Fantasque, un nez poursuit Venus au ciel profond.

Les poètes de sept ans

Et la Mère, fermant le livre du devoir,
S'en allait satisfaite et très-fière, sans voir,
Dans les yeux bleus et sous le front plein d'éminences
L'âme de son enfant livrée aux répugnances.

Tout le jour il suait d'obéissance; très
Intelligent; pourtant des tics noirs, quelques traits,
Semblaient prouver en lui d'âcres hypocrisies.
Dans l'ombre des couloirs aux tentures moisies,
En passant il tirait la langue, les deux poings
À l'aine, et dans ses yeux fermés voyait des points.

The old man simmers on the fire, his arms twisted, his blubber lip
On his belly: he feels his thighs slipping into the fire,
And his pants getting scorched, and his pipe going out;
Something like a bird stirs a bit
In his serene belly like a pile of tripe!

Round about sleeps a mass of cowering furniture
In rags of grease and over dirty bellies;
Stools, strange toads, are hunched
In dark corners: cupboards have mouths of cantors
Opened by a sleep full of horrible appetites

The sickening heat fills the narrow room;
The old man's brain is stuffed with rags:
He listens to the hairs growing in his moist skin,
And at times, in very seriously clownish hiccoughs
Escapes, shaking his rickety stool. . .

.   .   .   .

And in the evening, in the rays of moonlight which make
Droolings of light on the contours of his buttocks,
A shadow with details crouches, against a background
Of snow pink like a hollyhock. . .
Fantastic, a nose pursues Venus in the deep sky.

Seven-year-old Poets

And the Mother, closing the exercise book,
Went off satisfied and very proud, without seeing,
In the blue eyes and under his brow covered with bumps
The soul of her child given over to repugnance.

All day he sweated obedience; very
Intelligent; yet dark twitchings, a few traits,
Seemed to testify in him to bitter hypocrisy.
In the shadow of the corridors with their moldy hangings,
Passing through he stuck out his tongue, his two fists
In his groin, and in his closed eyes saw spots.

Une porte s'ouvrait sur le soir: à la lampe
On le voyait, là-haut, qui râlait sur la rampe,
Sous un golfe de jour pendant du toit. L'été
Surtout, vaincu, stupide, il était entêté
À se renfermer dans la fraîcheur des latrines:
Il pensait là, tranquille et livrant ses narines.
Quand, lavé des odeurs du jour, le jardinet
Derrière la maison, en hiver, s'illunait,
Gisant au pied d'un mur, enterré dans la marne
Et pour des visions écrasant son œil darne,
Il écoutait grouiller les galeux espaliers.
Pitié! ces enfants seuls étaient ses familiers
Qui, chétifs, fronts nus, œil déteignant sur la joue,
Cachant de maigres doigts jaunes et noirs de boue
Sous des habits puant la foire et tout vieillots,
Conversaient avec la douceur des idiots!
Et si, l'ayant surpris à des pitiés immondes,
La mère s'effrayait; les tendresses, profondes,
De l'enfant se jetaient sur cet étonnement.
C'était bon. Elle avait le bleu regard, — qui ment!

À sept ans, il faisait des romans, sur la vie
Du grand désert, où luit la Liberté ravie,
Forêts, soleils, rios, savanes! —Il s'aidait
De journaux illustrés où, rouge, il regardait
Des Espagnoles rire et des Italiennes.
Quand venait, l'œil brun, folle, en robes d'indiennes,
—Huit ans,—la fille des ouvriers d'à côté,
La petite brutale, et qu'elle avait sauté,
Dans un coin, sur son dos, en secouant ses tresses,
Et qu'il était sous elle, il lui mordait les fesses,
Car elle ne portait jamais de pantalons;
—Et, par elle meurtri des poings et des talons,
Remportait les saveurs de sa peau dans sa chambre.

Il craignait les blafards dimanches de décembre,
Où, pommadé, sur un guéridon d'acajou,
Il lisait une Bible à la tranche vert-chou;
Des rêves l'oppressaient chaque nuit dans l'alcôve.
Il n'aimait pas Dieu; mais les hommes, qu'au soir fauve,

A door opened on to evening: by the lamp
You saw him up there moaning on the stairway,
Under a flood of daylight falling from the roof. In summer
Especially, overcome, stupefied he was bent
On shutting himself up in the coolness of the outhouse:
There he meditated, peacefully, opening his nostrils.
When washed from the day's odors, the small garden
Behind the house, in winter, lit up with the moon,
As he lay at the foot of a wall, buried in clay,
And rubbed his dizzy eyes to bring about visions,
He listened to the mangy espaliers as they seemed to swarm.
Pity! only those children were his friends
Who, sickly, bare-headed, with eyes weeping on their cheeks,
Hiding thin fingers yellow and black with mud
Under worn-out clothes stinking of diarrhea and old,
Talked with the gentleness of idiots!
And if she caught him in actions of filthy pity,
His mother was horrified. The deep tenderness
Of the child forced itself on her surprise.
That was appropriate. She had the blue glance,—that lies!

At seven, he wrote novels about life
In the great desert, where exiled Freedom shines,
Forests, suns, rios, plains!—He was helped
With illustrated newspapers where, blushing, he saw
Spanish and Italian girls laugh.
When the daughter of the workers next door came,
—Eight years old,—brown eyes, wild, in a calico dress,
The little brute, and when in a corner,
She had jumped on his back, shaking her long hair,
And he was under her, he bit her buttocks,
For she never wore panties;
—And, bruised by her fists and heels,
Took back the taste of her flesh to his room.

He feared the grey December Sundays,
When, his hair greased, on a mahogany stool,
He read a Bible with cabbage-green edges.
Dreams oppressed him every night in his small room.
He did not love God; but the men whom, in the brown evening,

Noirs, en blouse, il voyait rentrer dans le faubourg
Où les crieurs, en trois roulements de tambour
Font autour des édits rire et gronder les foules.
—Il rêvait la prairie amoureuse, où des houles
Lumineuses, parfums sains, pubescences d'or,
Font leur remuement calme et prennent leur essor!

Et comme il savourait surtout les sombres choses,
Quand, dans la chambre nue aux persiennes closes,
Haute et bleue, âcrement prise d'humidité,
Il lisait son roman sans cesse médité,
Plein de lourds ciels ocreux et de forêts noyées,
De fleurs de chair aux bois sidérals déployées,
Vertige, écroulements, déroutes et pitié!
—Tandis que se faisait la rumeur du quartier,
En bas,—seul, et couché sur des pièces de toile
Ecrue, et pressentant violemment la voile!

L'orgie parisienne ou Paris se repeuple

O lâches, la voilà! dégorgez dans les gares!
Le soleil expia de ses poumons ardents
Les boulevards qu'un soir comblèrent les Barbares.
Voilà la Cité belle assise à l'occident!

Allez! on préviendra les reflux d'incendie,
Voilà les quais! voilà les boulevards! voilà,
Sur les maisons, l'azur léger qui s'irradie,
Et qu'un soir la rougeur des bombes étoila.

Cachez les palais morts dans des niches de planches!
L'ancien jour effaré rafraîchit vos regards.
Voici le troupeau roux des tordeuses de hanches,
Soyez fous, vous serez drôles, étant hagards!

Tas de chiennes en rut mangeant des cataplasmes,
Le cri des maisons d'or vous réclame. Volez!
Mangez! voici la nuit de joie aux profonds spasmes
Qui descend dans la rue, ô buveurs désolés,

Swarthy, in jackets, he saw going home to their quarters,
Where town criers, with three drum rolls
Make the crowds laugh and roar over edicts.
—He dreamed of an amorous pasture, where shining
Swells, natural perfumes, golden puberties
Move calmly and take flight!

And as he especially savored dark things,
When, in his bare room with closed shutters,
High and blue, sourly covered with humidity,
He read his ceaselessly meditated novel,
Full of heavy ocherous skies and soaked forests,
Of fresh flowers opened in the astral woods,
Dizziness, crumblings, routs and pity!
—While the noise of the neighborhood went on
Down below—alone, and lying on pieces of unbleached
Canvas, and violently announcing a sail!

Parisian Orgy or Paris Is Repopulated [7]

O cowards, here she is! pour out into the stations!
The sun with its burning lungs expiated
The boulevards which the Barbarians filled one evening.
Here is the beautiful City, seated in the west!

Come! We will put off the return of fire,
Here are the quays! and the boulevards! and here,
On the houses, the pale blue which radiates,
And which one evening was starred by the redness of bombs.

Hide the dark palaces in nests of planks!
The ancient terrified day refreshes your glances.
Here is the red-headed troop of hip wrigglers,
Be mad, you will be silly, being wild-eyed!

Pack of bitches in heat, eating poultices,
The cry from the houses of gold calls you. Steal!
Eat! see the night of joy with its deep spasms
Coming down the street, o sad drinkers,

Buvez. Quand la lumière arrive intense et folle
Foulant à vos côtés les luxes ruisselants,
Vous n'allez pas baver, sans geste, sans parole,
Dans vos verres, les yeux perdus aux lointains blancs,

Avalez, pour la Reine aux fesses cascadantes!
Ecoutez l'action des stupides hoquets
Déchirants. Ecoutez, sauter aux nuits ardentes
Les idiots râleux, vieillards, pantins, laquais!

O cœurs de saleté, Bouches épouvantables
Fonctionnez plus fort, bouches de puanteurs!
Un vin pour ces torpeurs ignobles, sur ces tables . . .
Vos ventres sont fondus de hontes, ô Vainqueurs!

Ouvrez votre narine aux superbes nausées,
Trempez de poisons forts les cordes de vos cous,
Sur vos nuques d'enfants baissant ses mains croisées
Le Poète vous dit: ô lâches, soyez fous!

Parce que vous fouillez le ventre de la Femme
Vous craignez d'elle encore une convulsion
Qui crie, asphyxiant votre nichée infâme
Sur sa poitrine, en une horrible pression.

Syphilitiques, fous, rois, pantins, ventriloques,
Qu'est-ce que ça peut faire à la putain Paris,
Vos âmes et vos corps, vos poisons et vos loques?
Elle se secouera de vous, hargneux pourris!

Et quand vous serez bas, geignant sur vos entrailles
Les flancs morts, réclamant votre argent, éperdus,
La rouge courtisane aux seins gros de batailles,
Loin de votre stupeur tordra ses poings ardus!

Quand tes pieds ont dansé si fort dans les colères,
Paris! quand tu reçus tant de coups de couteau,
Quand tu gis, retenant dans tes prunelles claires,
Un peu de la bonté du fauve renouveau,

Drink. When light comes intense and mad
Tanning at your side the streaming luxuries,
Are you not going to drool, with no gesture, with no word,
Into your glasses, your eyes lost in the white distances,

Swallow, for the Queen with the cascading buttocks!
Listen to the action of the stupid tearing
Hiccups. In the burning nights, listen to the panting idiots,
The old men, the puppets, the lackeys leaping about!

O hearts of filth, terrifying Mouths
Work harder, mouths of stench!
Wine for these base torpors, at these tables . . .
Your bellies have melted with shame, o Conquerors!

Open your nostrils to superb nauseas,
Soak the cords of your neck in strong poison,
On the napes of your young necks, placing his crossed hands
The Poet says to you: o cowards, be mad!

Because you search through the womb of Woman
You fear from her another convulsion
That cries out, stifling your infamous perching
On her breast, in a horrible pressure.

Syphilitics, fools, kings, puppets, ventriloquists,
What does Paris the whore care about
Your souls and bodies, your poisons and your rags?
She will shake you off, you rotten scoffers!

And when you are down, moaning on your guts
Your sides dead, calling out for your money, bewildered,
The red courtesan with breasts fat on battles,
Far from your stupor will clench her hardened fists!

When your feet danced so hard in anger,
Paris! when you received so many knife wounds,
When you were stretched out, retaining in your clear eyes,
A little of the goodness of the tawny spring,

O cité douloureuse, ô cité quasi-morte,
La tête et les deux seins jetés vers l'Avenir
Ouvrant sur ta pâleur ses milliards de portes,
Cité que le Passé sombre pourrait bénir:

Corps remagnétisé pour les énormes peines,
Tu rebois donc la vie effroyable! tu sens
Sourdre le flux des vers livides en tes veines,
Et sur ton clair amour rôder les doigts glaçants!

Et ce n'est pas mauvais. Tes vers, tes vers livides
Ne gêneront pas plus ton souffle de Progrès
Que les Stryx n'éteignaient l'œil des Cariatides
Où des pleurs d'or astral tombaient des bleus degrés.

Quoique ce soit affreux de te revoir couverte
Ainsi; quoiqu'on n'ait fait jamais d'une cité
Ulcère plus puant à la Nature verte,
Le Poète te dit: "Splendide est ta Beauté!"

L'orage a sacré ta suprême poésie;
L'immense remuement des forces te secourt;
Ton œuvre bout, la mort gronde, Cité choisie!
Amasse les strideurs au cœur du clairon lourd.

Le Poète prendra le sanglot des Infâmes,
La haine des Forçats, la clameur des maudits:
Et ses rayons d'amour flagelleront les Femmes.
Ses strophes bondiront, voilà! voilà! bandits!

—Société, tout est rétabli: les orgies
Pleurent leur ancien râle aux anciens lupanars:
Et les gaz en délire aux murailles rougies
Flambent sinistrement vers les azurs blafards!

O suffering city, o half-dead city,
Your head and your two breasts pointing toward the Future
Opening to your pallor its million gates,
City whom the dark Past could bless:

Body remagnetized for tremendous pain,
You drink in terrible life once again! You feel
Rising up in your veins the flood of livid worms,[8]
And icy fingers prowling over your clear love!

And this is not harmful. Your worms, your pale worms
Will no more impede your breath of Progress
Than the Stryx extinguished the eyes of the Caryatides,
Where gold astral tears fell from blue heights.

Although it is frightful to see you again covered
Thus; although one has never made of a city
An ulcer more foul-smelling on green nature,
The Poet says to you: "Your Beauty is magnificent!"

The storm consecrated your supreme poetry;
The immense stirring of strength succors you;
Your work boils, death groans, chosen City!
Amass in your heart the blasts of the heavy trumpet.

The Poet will take the sobs of the Infamous,
The hate of the Convicts, the clamor of the damned:
And his rays of love will scourge the Women.
His stanzas will leap forth, this is for you, bandits!

—Society, all is restored: the orgies
Are weeping their ancient sob in the ancient brothels:
And the gaslights in frenzy on the reddened walls
Flare up in sinister fashion toward the pale blue sky!

Les pauvres à l'église

Parqués entre des bancs de chêne, aux coins d'église
Qu'attiédit puamment leur souffle, tous leurs yeux
Vers le chœur ruisselant d'orrie et la maîtrise
Aux vingt gueules gueulant les cantiques pieux;

Comme un parfum de pain humant l'odeur de cire,
Heureux, humiliés comme des chiens battus,
Les Pauvres au bon Dieu, le patron et le sire,
Tendent leurs oremus risibles et têtus.

Aux femmes, c'est bien bon de faire des bancs lisses,
Après les six jours noirs où Dieu les fait souffrir!
Elles bercent, tordus dans d'étranges pelisses,
Des espèces d'enfants qui pleurent à mourir;

Leurs seins crasseux dehors, ces mangeuses de soupe,
Une prière aux yeux et ne priant jamais,
Regardent parader mauvaisement un groupe
De gamines avec leurs chapeaux déformés

Dehors, le froid, la faim, l'homme en ribotte:
C'est bon. Encore une heure; après, les maux sans noms!
— Cependant, alentour, geint, nasille, chuchote
Une collection de vieilles à fanons:

Ces effarés y sont et ces épileptiques
Dont on se détournait hier aux carrefours;
Et, fringalant du nez dans des missels antiques
Ces aveugles qu'un chien introduit dans les cours.

Et tous, bavant la foi mendiante et stupide,
Récitent la complainte infinie à Jésus
Qui rêve en haut, jauni par le vitrail livide,
Loin des maigres mauvais et des méchants pansus,

Loin des senteurs de viande et d'étoffes moisies,
Farce prostrée et sombre aux gestes repoussants;
— Et l'oraison fleurit d'expressions choisies,
Et les mysticités prennent des tons pressants,

The Poor in Church

Parked between oak benches, in corners of the church
Which their breath warms stinkingly, all their eyes
On the chancel dripping with gold, and the choir
With its twenty mouths yelling pious hymns;

Sniffing like the smell of bread the odor of wax,
Happy, humiliated like whipped dogs,
The Poor to the good Lord, their patron and master,
Offer up their ridiculous stubborn prayers.

For the women it is a good thing to wear the benches smooth,
After the six black days when God makes them suffer!
They cradle, wrapped in strange shawls,
Beings like children who cry as if they are dying;

Their dirty breasts uncovered, these eaters of soup,
A prayer in their eyes and never praying,
Watch a group of girls parade
And show off with their hats out of shape

Outside, the cold and hunger and men, on the drunk:
Fine! Another hour; afterward, nameless ills!
—Meanwhile, round about, moans, sniffles and whispers
A collection of old loose-chinned women:

Those terrified ones are here and the epileptics
From whom we turned aside yesterday at the crossroads;
And, sticking their noses into ancient missals
Are those blind led by a dog into the courtyards.

And all, drooling a stupid begging of faith,
Recite an endless complaint to Jesus
Who dreams on high, yellow in a livid stained-glass window,
Far from wicked thin men and from evil pot-bellied men,

Far from the smells of meat and mouldy cloth,
The prostrate somber farce of repulsive gestures;
—And the prayer flowers into choice expressions,
And the mysteries take on accentuated tones,

Quand, des nefs où périt le soleil, plis de soie
Banals, sourires verts, les Dames des quartiers
Distingués, — ô Jésus! — les malades du foie
Font baiser leurs longs doigts jaunes aux bénitiers.

Les sœurs de charité

Le jeune homme dont l'œil est brillant, la peau brune,
Le beau corps de vingt ans qui devrait aller nu,
Et qu'eût, le front cerclé de cuivre, sous la lune
Adoré, dans la Perse un Génie inconnu,

Impétueux avec des douceurs virginales
Et noires, fier de ses premiers entêtements,
Pareil aux jeunes mers, pleurs de nuits estivales
Qui se retournent sur des lits de diamants;

Le jeune homme, devant les laideurs de ce monde
Tressaille dans son cœur largement irrité
Et plein de la blessure éternelle et profonde,
Se prend à désirer sa sœur de charité.

Mais, ô Femme, monceau d'entrailles, pitié douce,
Tu n'es jamais la Sœur de charité, jamais,
Ni regard noir, ni ventre où dort une ombre rousse
Ni doigts légers, ni seins splendidement formés.

Aveugle irréveillée aux immenses prunelles
Tout notre embrassement n'est qu'une question:
C'est toi qui pends à nous, porteuse de mamelles;
Nous te berçons, charmante et grave Passion.

Tes haines, tes torpeurs fixes, tes défaillances
Et les brutalités souffertes autrefois
Tu nous rends tout, ô Nuit pourtant sans malveillances
Comme un excès de sang épanché tous les mois

When, from the naves where the sun dies, banal folds
Of silk, green smiles, Ladies from the correct
Neighborhoods,—oh! Jesus!—those ill with liver trouble
Dip their long yellow fingers in the holy-water basins.

Sisters of Charity

The young man whose eye is bright, whose skin is brown,
The handsome twenty-year-old body that should go naked,
And that, his brow circled with copper, under the moon
Would have been worshipped in Persia by an unknown Genie,

Impetuous with virginal and dark
Softness, proud of his first stubbornness,
Like young seas, tears of summer nights
That turn on beds of diamonds;

The young man, facing the ugliness of this world
Shudders in his heart deeply irritated
And filled with the eternal inner wound,
Begins to desire his sister of charity.

But, o Woman, heap of entrails, sweet pity,
You are never the Sister of charity, never,
Nor the dark glance, nor the belly where sleeps a reddish shadow
Nor light fingers, nor beautifully shaped breasts.

Unawakened blind woman with immense irises
All our embracing is but a question:
It is you who hang on us, bearer of breasts,
We cradle you, charming grave Passion.

Your hates, your fixed torpors, your failings
And your brutalities suffered long ago
You give all back to us, o Night without ill will
Like an excess of blood shed every month

— Quand la femme, portée un instant, l'épouvante,
Amour, appel de vie et chanson d'action
Viennent la Muse verte et la Justice ardente
Le déchirer de leur auguste obsession.

Ah! sans cesse altéré des splendeurs et des calmes,
Délaissé des deux Sœurs implacables, geignant
Avec tendresse après la science aux bras almes
Il porte à la nature en fleur son front saignant.

Mais la noire alchimie et les saintes études
Répugnent au blessé, sombre savant d'orgueil;
Il sent marcher sur lui d'atroces solitudes
Alors, et toujours beau, sans dégoût du cercueil,

Qu'il croie aux vastes fins, Rêves ou Promenades
Immenses, à travers les nuits de Vérité
Et t'appelle en son âme et ses membres malades
O Mort mystérieuse, ô sœur de charité.

L'homme juste[9]

. . . .

Le Juste restait droit sur ses hanches solides:
Un rayon lui dorait l'épaule; des sueurs
Me prirent: "Tu veux voir rutiler les bolides?
Et, debout, écouter bourdonner les flueurs
D'astres lactés, et les essaims d'astéroïdes?

"Par des farces de nuit ton front est épié,
Ô Juste! Il faut gagner un toit. Dis ta prière,
La bouche dans ton drap doucement expié;
Et si quelque égaré choque ton ostiaire,
Dis: Frère, va plus loin, je suis estropié!"

—When woman, carried for a moment, terrifies him,
Love, the call of life and song of action
The green Muse and ardent Justice come
To destroy him with their august obsession.

Ah! endlessly thirsting for splendor and calm,
Abandoned by the two implacable Sisters, moaning
Tenderly for science with benevolent arms
He brings to flowering nature his bleeding forehead.

But black alchemy and sacred studies
Are repulsive to the wounded man, sombre scholar of pride;
He feels terrible solitudes marching toward him
Then, and still handsome, with no disgust for the coffin,

Let him believe in vast purposes, immense Dreams
Or Journeys, through nights of Truth
And let him call you in his soul and sick limbs
O mysterious Death, o sister of charity.

The Just Man

. . . .

The Just Man sat upright on his solid hips:
A ray of light gilded his shoulder; sweat
Came over me: "Do you want to see meteors glow red?
And, standing, hear humming the influence
Of milky stars, and swarms of asteroids?

"In night farces your brow is spied on,
O Just Man! You must find a roof. Say your prayer,
With your mouth in your sheet, after a mild expiation;
And if some lost soul knocks against your bones,
Say: Brother, continue on your way, I am crippled!"

Et le Juste restait debout, dans l'épouvante
Bleuâtre des gazons après le soleil mort:
"Alors, mettrais-tu tes genouillères en vente,
Ô vieillard? Pèlerin sacré! Barde d'Armor!
Pleureur des Oliviers! Main que la pitié gante!

"Barbe de la famille et poing de la cité,
Croyant très doux: ô cœur tombé dans les calices,
Majestés et vertus, amour et cécité,
Juste! plus bête et plus dégoûtant que les lices!
Je suis celui qui souffre et qui s'est révolté!

"Et ça me fait pleurer sur mon ventre, ô stupide,
Et bien rire, l'espoir fameux de ton pardon!
Je suis maudit, tu sais! Je suis soûl, fou, livide,
Ce que tu veux! Mais va te coucher, voyons donc,
Juste! Je ne veux rien à ton cerveau torpide!

"C'est toi le Juste, enfin, le Juste! C'est assez!
C'est vrai que ta tendresse et ta raison sereines
Reniflent dans la nuit comme des cétacés!
Que tu te fais proscrire, et dégoises des thrènes
Sur d'effroyables becs de canne fracassés!

"Et c'est toi l'œil de Dieu! le lâche! quand les plantes
Froides des pieds divins passeraient sur mon cou,
Tu es lâche! Ô ton front qui fourmille de lentes!
Socrates et Jésus, Saints et Justes, dégoût,
Respectez le Maudit suprême aux nuits sanglantes!"

J'avais crié cela sur la terre, et la nuit
Calme et blanche occupait les Cieux pendant ma fièvre
Je relevai mon front: le fantôme avait fui,
Emportant l'ironie atroce de ma lèvre . . .
—Vents nocturnes! venez au Maudit! Parlez-lui!

Cependant que, silencieux sous les pilastres
D'azur, allongeant les comètes et les nœuds
D'univers, remuement énorme sans désastres,
L'ordre, éternel veilleur, rame aux cieux lumineux
Et de sa drague en feu laisse filer des astres!

And the Just Man remained standing, in the bluish
Terror of lawns after the dead sun:
"So, would you put on sale your kneecaps,
Old Man? Holy Pilgrim! Bard of Armorica!
Weeper of Olive Trees! Hand gloved with pity!

"Beard of the family and fist of the city,
Very gentle believer; O heart fallen into chalices,
Majesties and virtues, love and blindness,
Just Man! more stupid and disgusting than hound dogs!
I am the one suffering and who revolted!

"And it makes me weep on my belly, O fool,
And laugh, the famous hope of your pardon!
I am cursed, you know! I am drunk, mad, livid,
Whatever you want! But go lie down, I mean it,
Just Man! I want nothing from your stupid brain!

"You are the Just Man, after all, the Just Man! That's enough!
It is true that your serene tenderness and reason
Blow in the night like whales!
That you have yourself exiled, and yell threnodies
On frightful smashed door-locks!

"And you are the eye of God! the coward! when the cold
Soles of divine feet would trample on my neck,
You are a coward! O your brow teeming with nits!
Socrates and Jesus, Holy and Just, disgusting,
Respect the supreme Accursed One of bloody nights!"

I had cried this over the earth, and the calm
White night filled the Skies during my fever
I raised my brow: the phantom had fled,
Taking with him the terrible irony of my lips . . .
—Night winds! come to the man Cursed! Speak to him!

While, silently under the pillars
Of blue, passing by comets and clusters
Of universes, enormous stirring without disasters,
Order, an eternal watchman, rows in the luminous skies
And from his flaming dragnet lets stars shoot through the air!

Ah qu'il s'en aille, lui, la gorge cravatée
De honte, ruminant toujours mon ennui, doux
Comme le sucre sur la denture gâtée
—Tel que la chienne après l'assaut des fiers toutous,
Léchant son flanc d'où pend une entraille emportée

Qu'il dise charités crasseuses et progrès . . .
—J'exècre tous ces yeux de Chinois [. . .]aines,
[. . .] qui chante: nana, comme un tas d'enfants près
De mourir, idiots doux aux chansons soudaines :
O Justes, nous chierons dans vos ventres de grés

Les premières Communions

I

Vraiment, c'est bête, ces églises des villages
Où quinze laids marmots, encrassant les piliers
Ecoutent, grasseyant les divins babillages,
Un noir grotesque dont fermentent les souliers:
Mais le soleil éveille, à travers des feuillages
Les vieilles couleurs des vitraux irréguliers.

La pierre sent toujours la terre maternelle
Vous verrez des monceaux de ces cailloux terreux
Dans la campagne en rut qui frémit solennelle
Portant près des blés lourds, dans les sentiers ocreux,
Ces arbrisseaux brûlés où bleuit la prunelle,
Des nœuds de mûriers noirs et de rosiers fuireux.

Tous les cent ans on rend ces granges respectables
Par un badigeon d'eau bleue et de lait caillé:
Si des mysticités grotesques sont notables
Près de la Notre-Dame ou du Saint empaillé,
Des mouches sentant bon l'auberge et les étables
Se gorgent de cire au plancher ensoleillé.

Ah let him go off, with his throat wearing a necktie
Of shame, still ruminating on my boredom, sweet
As sugar on bad teeth
—Like the bitch after the assault of the proud doggies,
Licking her flank from which hangs a severed entrail

Let him call for filthy charity and progress. . .
—I execrate all these eyes of Chinese [. . .]ains,
[. . .] which sing: nana, like a ton of children close
To death, sweet idiots in sudden songs:
O Just Men, we will shit in your bellies of stoneware

First Communions

I

Really, it's stupid, these village churches
Where fifteen ugly brats, dirtying the pillars
Listen to a grotesque priest whose shoes stink
As he mouths the divine babble:
But the sun awakens, through the leaves
The old colors of irregular stained-glass.

The stone still smells of the maternal earth
You can see piles of those earth-clotted pebbles
In the aroused countryside which solemnly trembles
Bearing near the heavy wheat, in the ochreous paths,
The burned trees where the plum turns blue,
Tangles of black mulberry and rosebushes covered with cow droppings.

Once every century they make these barns respectable
With a coat of bluing and clabber:
If grotesque mysticities are notable
Near Our Lady or the stuffed saint,
Flies with the strong stench of the inn and stables
Gorge on wax on the sunlit floor.

L'enfant se doit surtout à la maison, famille
Des soins naïfs, des bons travaux abrutissants;
Ils sortent, oubliant que la peau leur fourmille
Où le Prêtre du Christ plaqua ses doigts puissants.
On paie au prêtre un toit ombré d'une charmille
Pour qu'il laisse au soleil tous ces fronts brunissants

Le premier habit noir, le plus beau jour de tartes
Sous le Napoléon ou le Petit Tambour
Quelque enluminure où les Josephs et les Marthes
Tirent la langue avec un excessif amour
Et que joindront, au jour de science, deux cartes,
Ces seuls doux souvenirs lui restent du grand Jour.

Les filles vont toujours à l'église, contentes
De s'entendre appeler garces par les garçons
Qui font du genre après messe ou vêpres chantantes.
Eux qui sont destinés au chic des garnisons
Ils narguent au café les maisons importantes
Blousés neuf, et gueulant d'effroyables chansons.

Cependant le Curé choisit pour les enfances
Des dessins; dans son clos, les vêpres dites, quand
L'air s'emplit du lointain nasillement des danses
Il se sent, en dépit des célestes défenses,
Les doigts de pied ravis et le mollet marquant.

—La Nuit vient, noir pirate aux cieux d'or débarquant.

II

Le Prêtre a distingué parmi les catéchistes,
Congrégés des Faubourgs ou des Riches Quartiers,
Cette petite fille inconnue, aux yeux tristes,
Front jaune. Les parents semblent de doux portiers
"Au grand Jour, le marquant parmi les Catéchistes,
Dieu fera sur ce front neiger ses bénitiers

The child owes a debt especially to the home, family
Simple chores, jobs that wear him out;
They leave, forgetting that their flesh smarts
Where the Priest of Christ laid his powerful fingers.
The Priest is provided with the shaded roof of an arbor
So that he will leave in the sun all the brows turning brown

The first black suit, on the finest day of pastries
Under Napoleon or the Drummer Boy
An engraving where Josephs and Marthas
Stick out their tongues with an excessive love
And which two maps will join on science day,
Only these sweet memories of the great Day will remain for him.

The girls always go to church, happy
To hear themselves called sluts by the boys
Who strut about after mass or sung vespers.
They are headed for the chic of the barracks
And in the cafés jeer at the important houses
In new jackets and bawling unspeakable songs.

Meanwhile the Priest chooses for the young
Some drawings; in his garden, after vespers, when
The air fills with the distant whine of dances
He feels, despite heavenly taboos,
His toes transfigured and his calves keeping tune.

—Night comes, a black pirate disembarking on the golden skies.

II
The Priest has singled out from the catechumens,
Who have come from the Suburbs or the Wealthy Sections,
This strange little girl, with sad eyes,
And sallow. Her parents would seem to be obsequious gatemen
"On the great Day, marking it among the Catechumens,
God will snow down on your brow his holy water fonts

III

La veille du grand Jour, l'enfant se fait malade.
Mieux qu'à l'Eglise haute aux funèbres rumeurs,
D'abord le frisson vient, —le lit n'étant pas fade—
Un frisson surhumain qui retourne: "Je meurs . . ."

Et, comme un vol d'amour fait à ses sœurs stupides,
Elle compte, abattue et les mains sur son cœur,
Les Anges, les Jésus et ses Vierges nitides
Et, calmement, son âme a bu tout son vainqueur.

Adonaï! . . . —Dans les terminaisons latines,
Des cieux moirés de vert baignent les Fronts vermeils
Et, tachés du sang pur des célestes poitrines
De grands linges neigeux tombent sur les soleils!

—Pour ses virginités présentes et futures
Elle mord aux fraîcheurs de ta Rémission,
Mais plus que les lys d'eau, plus que les confitures
Tes pardons sont glacés, ô Reine de Sion!

IV

Puis la Vierge n'est plus que la vierge du livre
Les mystiques élans se cassent quelquefois . . .
Et vient la pauvreté des images, que cuivre
L'ennui, l'enluminure atroce et les vieux bois;

Des curiosités vaguement impudiques
Epouvantent le rêve aux chastes bleuités
Qui s'est surpris autour des célestes tuniques,
Du linge dont Jésus voile ses nudités.

Elle veut, elle veut, pourtant, l'âme en détresse,
Le front dans l'oreiller creusé par les cris sourds
Prolonger les éclairs suprêmes de tendresse,
Et bave . . . —L'ombre emplit les maisons et les cours.

III

On the eve of the great Day, the child makes herself ill.
Stronger than in the high church with its funereal echoes,
At first the shudder comes—the bed not being dull—
A superhuman shudder returning: "I am dying . . ."

And like a theft of love made against her stupid sisters,
She counts, exhausted and with her hands over her breast,
The Angels, the Jesuses, and her dazzling Virgins
And calmly, her soul has drunk in her victor.

Adonai! . . . —In the Latin endings,
Skies shimmering with green bathe the ruddy Brows
And, spotted with the pure blood of heavenly breasts
Great snowy linens fall over the suns!

—For her present and future chastity
She bites into the coolness of your Remission,
But more than water lilies, more than jam
Your forgiveness is icy, o Queen of Zion!

IV

Then the Virgin is only the virgin of the book
Mystical spasms are sometimes broken . . .
And the poverty of images comes, which boredom
Brazens forth, the atrocious engraving and old woodcuts;

Vaguely indecent curiosity
Terrifies her dream with its chaste blue
And is caught around the celestial tunic,
The linen with which Jesus covers his sex.

Yet she wills, she wills, when her soul is distressed,
And her head in the pillow burying her stifled cries
To prolong the supreme bursts of tenderness,
And she drools . . . —Darkness fills houses and courts.

Et l'enfant ne peut plus. Elle s'agite, cambre
Les reins et d'une main ouvre le rideau bleu
Pour amener un peu la fraîcheur de la chambre
Sous le drap, vers son ventre et sa poitrine en feu . . .

V

A son réveil, — minuit, — la fenêtre était blanche.
Devant le sommeil bleu des rideaux illunés,
La vision la prit des candeurs du dimanche,
Elle avait rêvé rouge. Elle saigna du nez.

Et se sentant bien chaste et pleine de faiblesse
Pour savourer en Dieu son amour revenant
Elle eut soif de la nuit où s'exalte et s'abaisse
Le cœur, sous l'œil des cieux doux, en les devinant,

De la nuit, Vierge-Mère impalpable, qui baigne
Tous les jeunes émois de ses silences gris;
Elle eut soif de la nuit forte où le cœur qui saigne
Ecoule sans témoin sa révolte sans cris.

Et faisant la Victime et la petite épouse,
Son étoile la vit, une chandelle aux doigts
Descendre dans la cour où séchait une blouse,
Spectre blanc, et lever les spectres noirs des toits . . .

VI

Elle passa sa nuit sainte dans des latrines.
Vers la chandelle, aux trous du toit coulait l'air blanc,
Et quelque vigne folle aux noirceurs purpurines,
En deçà d'une cour voisine s'écroulant.

La lucarne faisait un cœur de lueur vive
Dans la cour où les cieux bas plaquaient d'ors vermeils
Les vitres; les pavés puant l'eau de lessive
Souffraient l'ombre des murs bondés de noirs sommeils

. . . .

And the child cannot continue. She moves, arches
Her back and with one hand opens the blue curtain
To bring a little cool air from the room
Under the sheet, to her belly and breast on fire . . .

v

On awakening,—midnight,—the window was white.
In front of the blue sleep of the moonlit curtains,
The vision of Sunday's purity overcame her,
She had dreamed red. Her nose bled.

And feeling very chaste and full of weakness
In order to savor in God her returning love
She thirsted for night when the heart rises
And falls, under the eyes of the soft heavens, as it divines their presence,

For the night, impalpable Virgin-Mother, which bathes
All youthful emotions with its grey silence;
She thirsted for the strong night when the heart bleeding
Lets flow without witness its cryless revolt.

And playing the Victim and the little bride,
Her star saw her, with a candle in her hand
Go down into the courtyard, where a jacket was drying,
A white specter, and raise up the black specters of the roofs . . .

VI

She spent her holy night in the outhouse.
Toward the candle the white air flowed into the holes of the roof,
And a wild vine of black purple color,
Within a nearby court fell down.

The window formed a heart of bright light
In the courtyard where low clouds covered the panes
With red gold; the pavements smelling with the water from washing
Suffered the shadow of walls filled with black sleep

. . . .

VII

Qui dira ces langueurs et ces pitiés immondes,
Et ce qu'il lui viendra de haine, ô sales fous
Dont le travail divin déforme encor les mondes,
Quand la lèpre à la fin mangera ce corps doux?

. . . .

VIII

Et quand, ayant rentré tous ses nœuds d'hystéries
Elle verra, sous les tristesses du bonheur,
L'amant rêver au blanc million des Maries,
Au matin de la nuit d'amour, avec douleur:

"Sais-tu que je t'ai fait mourir? J'ai pris ta bouche,
Ton cœur, tout ce qu'on a, tout ce que vous avez;
Et moi, je suis malade: Oh! je veux qu'on me couche
Parmi les Morts des eaux nocturnes abreuvés

"J'étais bien jeune, et Christ a souillé mes haleines
Il me bonda jusqu'à la gorge de dégoûts!
Tu baisais mes cheveux profonds comme les laines
Et je me laissais faire . . . ah! va, c'est bon pour vous,

Hommes! qui songez peu que la plus amoureuse
Est, sous sa conscience aux ignobles terreurs
La plus prostituée et la plus douloureuse,
Et que tous nos élans vers Vous sont des erreurs!

Car ma Communion première est bien passée
Tes baisers, je ne puis jamais les avoir sus:
Et mon cœur et ma chair par ta chair embrassée
Fourmillent du baiser putride de Jésus!

IX

Alors l'âme pourrie et l'âme désolée
Sentiront ruisseler tes malédictions
—Ils auront couché sur ta Haine inviolée,
Echappés, pour la mort, des justes passions.

VII

Who will speak of the languor and filthy compassion,
And the hate that come to her, o prurient fools,
Whose divine labor still deforms our worlds,
When leprosy at the end will devour this sweet body?

. . . .

VIII

And when, after all her knots of hysteria are quieted
She sees, under the sadness of joy,
The lover dreaming of a million white Marys,
In the morning of the night of love, sadly:

"Do you know I caused your death? I took your mouth,
Your heart, everything, everything you have;
And I am sick: Oh! I want you to lay me
Among the Dead who have drunk from the waters of the night

"I was very young, and Christ corrupted my breath
He filled me beyond measure with disgust!
You kissed my hair as profound as wool
And I let you do this . . . ah! this is the way

Of men! of you who do not realize that the girl the most in love
Is, with her consciousness of shameful terrors
The most wanton and the most remorseful,
And that all our impulses toward You are errors!

For my First Communion is now over
I can never have known your kisses:
My heart and my flesh kissed by your flesh
Seethe with the putrified kiss of Jesus!

IX

Then the decayed soul and the malcontent spirit
Will feel your curses rain down
—They will have lain with your inviolate Hate,
Having, for death, escaped from just passions.

Christ! ô Christ, éternel voleur des énergies
Dieu qui pour deux mille ans voues à ta pâleur
Cloués au sol, de honte et de céphalalgies
Ou renversés les fronts des femmes de douleur.

Ce qu'on dit au Poète à propos de fleurs [10]

À Monsieur Théodore de Banville

I

Ainsi, toujours, vers l'azur noir
Où tremble la mer des topazes,
Fonctionneront dans ton soir
Les Lys, ces clystères d'extases!

À notre époque de sagous,
Quand les Plantes sont travailleuses,
Le Lys boira les bleus dégoûts
Dans tes Proses religieuses!

—Le lys de monsieur de Kerdrel,
Le Sonnet de mil huit cent trente,
Le Lys qu'on donne au Ménestrel
Avec l'œillet et l'amarante!

Des lys! Des lys! On n'en voit pas!
Et dans ton Vers, tel que les manches
Des Pécheresses aux doux pas,
Toujours frissonnent ces fleurs blanches!

Toujours, Cher, quand tu prends un bain,
Ta Chemise aux aisselles blondes
Se gonfle aux brises du matin
Sur les myosotis immondes!

L'amour ne passe à tes octrois
Que les Lilas, —o balançoires!
Et les Violettes du Bois,
Crachats sucrés des Nymphes noires! . . .

Christ! O Christ, eternal thief of energy
God who for two thousand years consecrated to your pallor
The brows of women of sorrow, nailed to the ground
Or thrown back with shame and head pains.

What Is Said to the Poet Concerning Flowers

To M. Théodore de Banville

I

Thus, always, toward the black azure,
Where shimmers the sea of topazes,
The Lilies, clysters of ecstasy,
Will function in your evening!

In our age of sago,
When Plants work hard,
The Lily will drink the blue feelings of disgust
From your religious Prose!

—Monsieur de Kerdrel's lily,
The Sonnet of eighteen hundred and thirty
The Lily you give to the Poet
With the pink and the amaranth!

Lilies! Lilies! We can't see any!
And in your Verse, like the sleeves
Of Sinful Women who walk softly,
Those white flowers always tremble!

Always, Dear, when you bathe,
Your shirt with yellow armpits
Swells in the morning breeze
Above the dirty forget-me-nots!

Love lets through at your customs
Only Lilacs—o seesaws!
And Wood Violets,
Sugary spit of black Nymphs! . . .

II

Ô Poètes, quand vous auriez
Les Roses, les Roses soufflées,
Rouges sur tiges de lauriers,
Et de mille octaves enflées!

Quand *Banville* en ferait neiger,
Sanguinolentes, tournoyantes,
Pochant l'œil fou de l'étranger
Aux lectures mal bienveillantes!

De vos forêts et de vos prés,
Ô très-paisibles photographes!
La Flore est diverse à peu près
Comme des bouchons de carafes!

Toujours les végétaux Français,
Hargneux, phtisiques, ridicules,
Où le ventre des chiens bassets
Navigue en paix, aux crépuscules;

Toujours, après d'affreux desseins [11]
De Lotos bleus ou d'Hélianthes,
Estampes roses, sujets saints
Pour de jeunes communiantes!

L'Ode Açoka cadre avec la
Strophe en fenêtre de lorette:
Et de lourds papillons d'éclat
Fientent sur la Pâquerette.

Vieilles verdures, vieux galons!
Ô croquignoles végétales!
Fleurs fantasques des vieux Salons!
—Aux hannetons, pas aux crotales,

Ces poupards végétaux en pleurs
Que Grandville eût mis aux lisières,
Et qu'allaitèrent de couleurs
De méchants astres à visières!

O Poets, if you had
Roses, blown Roses,
Red on laurel stems,
And swollen with a thousand octaves!

If *Banville* made some snow down,
Blood-spotted, whirling,
Blacking the wild eye of the stranger
With his ill-disposed readings!

Concerning your forests and meadows,
O very-peaceful photographers,
The Flora is as diverse
As stoppers on decanters!

Always the French vegetables,
Cross, phthisical, ridiculous,
Where the bellies of basset dogs
Navigate peacefully in the twilight;

Always, after frightful designs
Of blue Lotuses or Sunflowers,
Rose prints, holy subjects
For young girls making their communion!

The Asoke Ode jibes with the
Loretto window stanza:
And heavy brilliant butterflies
Dung on the Daisy.

Old greenery, old stripes!
O vegetable crackers!
Fancy flowers of old Parlors!
—For beetles, not rattlesnakes,

Those crying vegetable dolls
That Grandville would have put in leading-strings,
And those wicked stars with eyeshades
Nursed with colors!

Oui, vos bavures de pipeaux
Font de précieuses glucoses!
—Tas d'œufs frits dans de vieux chapeaux,
Lys, Açokas, Lilas et Roses!...

III

O blanc Chasseur, qui cours sans bas
A travers le Pâtis panique,
Ne peux-tu pas, ne dois-tu pas
Connaître un peu ta botanique?

Tu ferais succéder, je crains,
Aux Grillons roux les Cantharides,
L'or des Rios au bleu des Rhins,
Bref, aux Norwèges les Florides:

Mais, Cher, l'Art n'est plus, maintenant,
—C'est la vérité,—de permettre
À l'Eucalyptus étonnant
Des constrictors d'un hexamètre;

Là!... Comme is les Acajous
Ne servaient, même en nos Guyanes,
Qu'aux cascades des sapajous,
Au lourd délire des lianes!

—En somme, une Fleur, Romarin
Ou Lys, vive ou morte, vaut-elle
Un excrément d'oiseau marin?
Vaut-elle un seul pleur de chandelle?

—Et j'ai dit ce que je voulais!
Toi, même assis là-bas, dans une
Cabane de bambous,—volets
Clos, tentures de perse brune,—

Tu torcherais des floraisons
Dignes d'Oises extravagantes!...
—Poète! ce sont des raisons
Non moins risibles qu'arrogantes!...

Yes! Your droolings from shepherds' pipes
Make precious glucoses!
—Pile of fried eggs in old hats,
Lilies, Asokas, Lilacs and Roses! . . .

III

O white Hunter, who run without stockings
Through the panic Pastures,
Can't you, ought you not
Know your botany a little?

I fear you would make Cantharides
Succeed to red Crickets,
The gold of Rios to the blue of the Rhine,
In short, Floridas to Norways:

But, Dear, Art no longer consists, now,
—It is the truth,—in permitting
The amazing Eucalyptus
Boa-constrictors a hexameter long;

There! . . . As if Mahogany
Served, even in our Guianas,
Only as swings for monkeys
In the heavy maze of creepers!

—In short, is a Flower, Rosemary
Or Lily, alive or dead, worth
The excrement of a sea-bird?
Is it worth one single tear of a candle?

—And I have said what I intended to!
You, even seated over there, in a
Bamboo hut,—shutters
Closed, hangings of brown Persian rugs,—

You would twist flowers
Worthy of extravagant Oise departments! . . .
—Poet! these are reasons
No less laughable than arrogant! . . .

Dis, non les pampas printaniers
Noirs d'épouvantables révoltes,
Mais les tabacs, les cotonniers!
Dis les exotiques récoltes!

Dis, front blanc que Phébus tanna,
De combien de dollars se rente
Pedro Velasquez, Habana;
Incague la mer de Sorrente

Où vont les Cygnes par milliers;
Que tes Strophes soient des réclames
Pour l'abatis des mangliers
Fouillés des hydres et des lames!

Ton quatrain plonge aux bois sanglants
Et revient proposer aux Hommes
Divers sujets de sucres blancs
De pectoraires et de gommes!

Sachons par Toi si les blondeurs
Des Pics neigeux, vers les Tropiques,
Sont ou des insectes pondeurs
Ou des lichens microscopiques!

Trouve, ô Chasseur, nous le voulons,
Quelques garances parfumées
Que la Nature en pantalons
Fasse éclore! — pour nos Armées!

Trouve, aux abords du Bois qui dort,
Les fleurs, pareilles à des mufles,
D'où bavent des pommades d'or
Sur les cheveux sombres des Buffles!

Trouve, aux prés fous, où sur le Bleu
Tremble l'argent des pubescences,
Des Calices pleins d'Œufs de feu
Qui cuisent parmi les essences!

IV

Speak, not of spring pampas,
Black with frightful rebellions,
But of tobacco and cotton plants!
Speak of exotic harvests!

Speak, white face tanned by Phoebus,
Of how many dollars Pedro Velasquez
Of Havana gathers in a year;
Cover with excrement the sea of Sorrento

Where Swans go in thousands;
May your Stanzas be advertisements
For the felling of mangrove trees
Ransacked by hydras and water!

Your quatrain plunges into bloody woods
And returns to propose to Men
Various subjects on white sugar
Coughdrops and rubbers!

Let us know through You if the whiteness
Of snowy Peaks, near the Tropics,
Are insects laying eggs
Or microscopic lichens!

Find, o Hunter, we insist,
A few perfumed madders
Which Nature will cause to bloom
In trousers—for our Armies!

Find, at the edge of the sleeping Wood,
Flowers, resembling snouts,
From which drool golden ointments
On to the dark hair of Buffaloes!

Find, in wild meadows, where on the Blue
The silver of pubescences trembles,
Calyxes full of fiery Eggs
Cooking among essences!

Trouve des Chardons cotonneux
Dont dix ânes aux yeux de braises
Travaillent à filer les nœuds!
Trouve des Fleurs qui soient des chaises!

Oui, trouve au cœur des noirs filons
Des fleurs presque pierres,—fameuses!—
Qui vers leurs durs ovaires blonds
Aient des amygdales gemmeuses!

Sers-nous, ô Farceur, tu le peux,
Sur un plat de vermeil splendide
Des ragoûts de Lys sirupeux
Mordant nos cuillers Alfénide!

v

Quelqu'un dira le grand Amour,
Voleur des Sombres Indulgences:
Mais ni Renan, ni le chat Murr
N'ont vu les Bleus Thyrses immenses!

Toi, fais jouer dans nos torpeurs,
Par les parfums les hystéries;
Exalte-nous vers des candeurs
Plus candides que les Maries . . .

Commerçant! colon! médium!
Ta Rime sourdra, rose ou blanche,
Comme un rayon de sodium,
Comme un caoutchouc qui s'épanche!

De tes noirs Poèmes,—Jongleur!
Blancs, verts, et rouges dioptriques,
Que s'évadent d'étranges fleurs
Et des papillons électriques!

Voilà! c'est le Siècle d'enfer!
Et les poteaux télégraphiques
Vont orner,—lyre aux chants de fer,
Tes omoplates magnifiques!

Find downy Thistles
Whose knots ten donkeys
With burning eyes labor to undo!
Find flowers that are chairs!

Yes, find in the heart of black fissures
Flowers almost stones, —beautiful ones! —
Which, close by their hard blond ovaries,
Have gem-like tonsils!

Serve us, o Joker, you can do this,
On a magnificent vermilion plate
Stews of syrupy Lilies
Which will corrode our Nickel silver spoons!

v

Someone will speak of great Love,
The thief of Somber Indulgences:
But neither Renan nor Murr the cat
Have seen the huge Blue Thyrsuses!

You, enliven in our torpor,
Hysteria by means of perfumes;
Exalt us toward whiteness
More pure than the Marys . . .

Merchant! colonial! medium!
Your Rhyme will rise up, rose or white,
Like a ray of sodium,
Like a bleeding rubber-tree!

From your black Poems, —Juggler!
White, green, and red dioptrics,
Let strange flowers burst forth
And electric butterflies!

There now! it is the Century of hell!
And the telegraph poles
Will embellish, —lyre with iron voice,
Your magnificent shoulder blades!

Surtout, rime une version
Sur le mal des pommes de terre!
—Et, pour la composition
De Poèmes pleins de mystère

Qu'on doive lire de Tréguier
À Paramaribo, rachète
Des Tomes de Monsieur Figuier,
—Illustrés!—chez Monsieur Hachette!

ALCIDE BAVA
A. R.

Les mains de Jeanne-Marie

Jeanne-Marie a des mains fortes,
Mains sombres que l'été tanna,
Mains pâles comme des mains mortes.
—Sont-ce des mains de Juana?

Ont-elles pris les crèmes brunes
Sur les mares des voluptés?
Ont-elles trempé dans des lunes
Aux étangs de sérénités?

Ont-elles bu des cieux barbares,
Calmes sur les genoux charmants?
Ont-elles roulé des cigares
Ou trafiqué des diamants?

Sur les pieds ardents des Madones
Ont-elles fané des fleurs d'or?
C'est le sang noir des belladones
Qui dans leur paume éclate et dort.

Mains chasseresses des diptères
Dont bombinent les bleuisons
Aurorales, vers les nectaires?
Mains décanteuses de poisons?

Above all, put in rhyme a tale
On the potato blight!
—And, for the composition
Of Poems full of mystery

That are to be read from Tréguier
To Paramaribo, buy
Some Volumes of Monsieur Figuier,
Illustrated!—at Monsieur Hachette's!

ALCIDE BAVA
A. R.

The Hands of Jeanne-Marie

Jeanne-Marie has strong hands,
Dark hands the summer tanned,
Hands pale like dead hands.
—Are they the hands of Juana?

Did they get their dark cream color
On pools of voluptuousness?
Have they dipped into moons
In ponds of serenity?

Have they drunk from barbaric skies,
Calm on charming knees?
Have they rolled cigars
Or traded in diamonds?

On the burning feet of Madonnas
Have they tossed golden flowers?
It is the black blood of belladonnas
That bursts and sleeps in their palms.

Are they hands driving the diptera
With which the blueness of dawn
Buzzes, toward the nectars?
Hands decanting poisons?

Oh! quel Rêve les a saisies
Dans les pandiculations?
Un rêve inouï des Asies,
Des Khenghavars ou des Sions?

— Ces mains n'ont pas vendu d'oranges,
Ni bruni sur les pieds des dieux:
Ces mains n'ont pas lavé les langes
Des lourds petits enfants sans yeux.

(Ce ne sont pas mains de cousine
Ni d'ouvrières aux gros fronts
Que brûle, aux bois puant l'usine,
Un soleil ivre de goudrons)

Ce sont des ployeuses[12] d'échines
Des mains qui ne font jamais mal
Plus fatales que des machines,
Plus fortes que tout un cheval!

Remuant comme des fournaises,
Et secouant tous ses frissons
Leur chair chante des Marseillaises
Et jamais les Eleisons!

(Ça serrerait vos cous, ô femmes
Mauvaises, ça broierait vos mains
Femmes nobles, vos mains infâmes
Pleines de blancs et de carmins

L'éclat de ces mains amoureuses
Tourne le crâne des brebis!
Dans leurs phalanges savoureuses
Le grand soleil met un rubis!)

Une tache de populace
Les brunit comme un sein d'hier:
Le dos de ces Mains est la place
Qu'en baisa tout Révolté fier!

Oh! what Dream has held them
In pandiculations?
An extraordinary dream of Asias,
Of Khenghavars or Zions?

—These hands have not sold oranges,
Nor turned brown at the feet of the gods;
These hands have not washed the diapers
Of heavy babies without eyes.

(They are not hands of a cousin
Or of working women with large foreheads
Burned, in woods stinking of a factory,
By a sun drunk on tar)

They are benders of backbones
Hands that do no harm
More fatal than machines,
Stronger than a horse!

Stirring like furnaces,
And shaking off all their tremblings
Their flesh sings Marseillaises
And never Eleisons!

(They would strangle your necks, o evil
Women, they would crush your hands
Noblewomen, your infamous hands
Full of white and carmine

The beauty of those loving hands
Turns the heads of ewes!
On their savory finger-joints
The great sun places a ruby!)

A stain of populace
Turns them brown like a breast of yesterday:
The backs of these Hands are the places
Where every proud Rebel kissed them!

Elles ont pâli, merveilleuses,
Au grand soleil d'amour chargé
Sur le bronze des mitrailleuses
À travers Paris insurgé!

Ah! quelquefois, ô Mains sacrées,
À vos poings, Mains où tremblent nos
Lèvres jamais désenivrées,
Crie une chaîne aux clairs anneaux!

Et c'est un Soubresaut étrange
Dans nos êtres, quand, quelquefois
On veut vous déhâler, Mains d'ange,
En vous faisant saigner les doigts!

They have paled, marvelous,
Under the great sun full of love
On the bronze of machine-guns,
Throughout insurgent Paris!

Ah! sometimes, o sacred Hands,
At your wrists, Hands where tremble our
Never sobered lips,
Cries out a chain of clear links!

And it is a strange Tremor
In our beings, when, at times
They want to remove your sunburn, Hands of an angel,
By making your fingers bleed!

Poemes non datés
(fin 1870 – début 1872?)

Undated poems
(late 1870 – early 1872?)

Les assis[13]

Noirs de loupes, grêlés, les yeux cerclés de bagues
Vertes, leurs doigts boulus crispés à leurs fémurs
Le sinciput plaqué de hargnosités vagues
Comme les floraisons lépreuses des vieux murs;

Ils ont greffé dans des amours épileptiques
Leur fantasque ossature aux grands squelettes noirs
De leurs chaises; leurs pieds aux barreaux rachitiques
S'entrelacent pour les matins et pour les soirs!

Ces vieillards ont toujours fait tresse avec leurs sièges,
Sentant les soleils vifs percaliser leur peau,
Ou, les yeux à la vitre où se fanent les neiges,
Tremblant du tremblement douloureux du crapaud.

Et les Sièges leur ont des bontés: culottée
De brun, la paille cède aux angles de leurs reins;
L'âme des vieux soleils s'allume emmaillottée
Dans ces tresses d'épis où fermentaient les grains.

Et les Assis, genoux aux dents, verts pianistes
Les dix doigts sous leur siège aux rumeurs de tambour
S'écoutent clapoter des barcarolles tristes,
Et leurs caboches vont dans des roulis d'amour.

— Oh! ne les faites pas lever! C'est le naufrage . . .
Ils surgissent, grondant comme des chats gifflés,
Ouvrant lentement leurs omoplates, ô rage!
Tout leur pantalon bouffe à leurs reins boursouflés

Et vous les écoutez, cognant leurs têtes chauves
Aux murs sombres, plaquant et plaquant leurs pieds tors
Et leurs boutons d'habit sont des prunelles fauves
Qui vous accrochent l'œil du fond des corridors!

Puis ils ont une main invisible qui tue:
Au retour, leur regard filtre ce venin noir
Qui charge l'œil souffrant de la chienne battue
Et vous suez pris dans un atroce entonnoir.

The Seated Men

Black with wens, pock-marked, their eyes circled with green
Rings, their swollen fingers clenched on their thighbones
Their skulls caked with vague roughness
Like the leprous flowerings of old walls;

They have grafted in epileptic loves
Their ludicrous bone structure to the large black skeletons
Of their chairs; their feet on the rickety rails
Are entwined mornings and evenings!

These old men have always made one tress with their seats,
Feeling bright suns turn their skin to calico,
Or with their eyes on the windowpane where the snow fades,
Trembling with the painful tremble of the toad.

And the Seats are good to them: worn
Brown, the straw yields to the angles of their buttocks;
The soul of old suns lights up, bound
In those braids of ears where the corn fermented.

And the Seated Men, knees to their teeth, green pianists
Their ten fingers drumming under their seats
Listen to the tapping of sad barcarolles,
And their heads move to the rhythm of love.

—Oh! don't make them get up! It is a shipwreck . . .
They rise up, growling like cats struck,
Slowly spreading their shoulder blades, o rage!
Their trousers puff out at their swollen backsides

And you listen to them, knocking their bald heads
Against the dark walls, stamping and stamping their twisted feet
And the buttons of their coats are the eyes of beasts
Which catch your eyes from the end of the corridors!

Then they have an invisible hand which kills:
Coming back, their eyes filter the black poison
Which floods the suffering eye of the beaten bitch
And you sweat caught in a horrible funnel.

Rassis, les poings noyés dans des manchettes sales
Ils songent à ceux-là qui les ont fait lever
Et, de l'aurore au soir, des grappes d'amygdales
Sous leurs mentons chétifs s'agitent à crever

Quand l'austère sommeil a baissé leurs visières
Ils rêvent sur leur bras de sièges fécondés,
De vrais petits amours de chaises en lisière
Par lesquelles de fiers bureaux seront bordés;

Des fleurs d'encre crachant des pollens en virgule
Les bercent, le long des calices accroupis
Tels qu'au fil des glaïeuls le vol des libellules
—Et leur membre s'agace à des barbes d'épis.

Le bateau ivre

Comme je descendais des Fleuves impassibles,
Je ne me sentis plus guidé par les haleurs:
Des Peaux-rouges criards les avaient pris pour cibles
Les ayant cloués nus aux poteaux de couleurs.

J'étais insoucieux de tous les équipages,
Porteur de blés flamands ou de cotons anglais
Quand avec mes haleurs ont fini ces tapages
Les Fleuves m'ont laissé descendre où je voulais.

Dans les clapotements furieux des marées
Moi l'autre hiver plus sourd que les cerveaux d'enfants
Je courus! Et les Péninsules démarrées
N'ont pas subi tohu-bohus plus triomphants

La tempête a béni mes éveils maritimes
Plus léger qu'un bouchon j'ai dansé sur les flots
Qu'on appelle rouleurs éternels de victimes,
Dix nuits, sans regretter l'œil niais des falots!

Seated again, their fists sunken in soiled cuffs
They think about those who made them get up
And, from dawn to night, bunches of tonsils
Under their meager chins tremble and almost burst

When austere sleep has lowered their lids
They dream, head in arms, of seats made fertile,
Of real little loves of chairs just learning to stand
With which proud desks will be surrounded;

Flowers of ink spitting out pollen like commas
Cradle them, in rows of squatting calyxes
Like the flight of dragonflies along the gladiolas—
And their penises are roused by barbs of wheat.

The Drunken Boat

As I was going down impassive Rivers,
I no longer felt myself guided by haulers:
Yelping redskins had taken them as targets
And had nailed them naked to colored stakes.

I was indifferent to all crews,
The bearer of Flemish wheat or English cottons
When with my haulers this uproar stopped
The Rivers let me go where I wanted.

Into the furious lashing of the tides
More heedless than children's brains the other winter
I ran! And loosened Peninsulas
Have not undergone a more triumphant hubbub

The storm blessed my sea vigils
Lighter than a cork I danced on the waves
That are called eternal rollers of victims,
Ten nights, without missing the stupid eye of the lighthouses!

Plus douce qu'aux enfants la chair des pommes sures
L'eau verte pénétra ma coque de sapin
Et des taches de vins bleus et des vomissures
Me lava, dispersant gouvernail et grappin

Et dès lors, je me suis baigné dans le Poème
De la Mer, infusé d'astres et lactescent,
Dévorant les azurs vers;[14] où, flottaison blême
Et ravie, un noyé pensif parfois descend;

Où, teignant tout à coup les bleuités, délires
Et rhythmes lents sous les rutilements du jour,
Plus fortes que l'alcool, plus vastes que nos lyres
Fermentent les rousseurs amères de l'amour!

Je sais les cieux crevant en éclairs, et les trombes
Et les ressacs et les courants: je sais le soir,
L'Aube exaltée ainsi qu'un peuple de colombes
Et j'ai vu quelquefois ce que l'homme a cru voir!

J'ai vu le soleil bas, taché d'horreurs mystiques,
Illuminant de longs figements violets,
Pareils à des acteurs de drames très-antiques
Les flots roulant au loin leurs frissons de volets!

J'ai rêvé la nuit verte aux neiges éblouies
Baiser montant aux yeux des mers avec lenteurs,
La circulation des sèves inouïes,
Et l'éveil jaune et bleu des phosphores chanteurs!

J'ai suivi, des mois pleins, pareille aux vacheries
Hystériques, la houle à l'assaut des récifs,
Sans songer que les pieds lumineux des Maries
Pussent forcer le mufle aux Océans poussifs!

J'ai heurté, savez-vous, d'incroyables Florides
Mêlant aux fleurs des yeux de panthères à peaux
D'hommes! Des arcs-en-ciel tendus comme des brides
Sous l'horizon des mers, à de glauques troupeaux!

Sweeter than the flesh of hard apples is to children
The green water penetrated my hull of fir
And washed me of spots of blue wine
And vomit, scattering rudder and grappling-hook

And from then on I bathed in the Poem
Of the Sea, infused with stars and lactescent,
Devouring the azure verses; where, like a pale elated
Piece of flotsam, a pensive drowned figure sometimes sinks;

Where, suddenly dyeing the blueness, delirium
And slow rhythms under the streaking of daylight,
Stronger than alcohol, vaster than our lyres
The bitter redness of love ferments!

I know the skies bursting with lightning, and the waterspouts
And the surf and the currents; I know the evening,
And dawn as exalted as a flock of doves
And at times I have seen what man thought he saw!

I have seen the low sun spotted with mystic horrors,
Lighting up, with long violet clots,
Resembling actors of very ancient dramas,
The waves rolling far off their quivering of shutters!

I have dreamed of the green night with dazzled snows
A kiss slowly rising to the eyes of the sea,
The circulation of unknown saps,
And the yellow and blue awakening of singing phosphorus!

I followed during pregnant months the swell,
Like hysterical cows, in its assault on the reefs,
Without dreaming that the luminous feet of the Marys
Could constrain the snout of the wheezing Oceans!

I struck against, you know, unbelievable Floridas
Mingling with flowers panthers' eyes and human
Skin! Rainbows stretched like bridle reins
Under the horizon of the seas to greenish herds!

J'ai vu fermenter les marais énormes, nasses
Où pourrit dans les joncs tout un Léviathan!
Des écroulements d'eaux au milieu des bonaces,
Et les lointains vers les gouffres cataractant!

Glaciers, soleils d'argent, flots nacreux, cieux de braises!
Echouages hideux au fond des golfes bruns
Où les serpents géants dévorés des punaises
Choient, des arbres tordus, avec de noirs parfums!

J'aurais voulu montrer aux enfants ces dorades
Du flot bleu, ces poissons d'or, ces poissons chantants.
—Des écumes de fleurs ont bercé mes dérades
Et d'ineffables vents m'ont ailé par instants.

Parfois, martyr lassé des pôles et des zones,
La mer dont le sanglot faisait mon roulis doux
Montait vers moi ses fleurs d'ombre aux ventouses jaunes
Et je restais, ainsi qu'une femme à genoux . . .

Presque île, ballottant sur mes bords les querelles
Et les fientes d'oiseaux clabaudeurs aux yeux blonds
Et je voguais, lorsqu'à travers mes liens frêles
Des noyés descendaient dormir, à reculons!

Or moi, bateau perdu sous les cheveux des anses,
Jeté par l'ouragan dans l'éther sans oiseau
Moi dont les Monitors et les voiliers des Hanses
N'auraient pas repêché la carcasse ivre d'eau;

Libre, fumant, monté de brumes violettes,
Moi qui trouais le ciel rougeoyant comme un mur,
Qui porte, confiture exquise aux bons poètes
Des lichens de soleil et des morves d'azur,

Qui courais, taché de lunules électriques,
Planche folle, escorté des hippocampes noirs,
Quand les juillets faisaient crouler à coups de triques
Les cieux ultramarins aux ardents entonnoirs;

I have seen enormous swamps ferment, fish-traps
Where a whole Leviathan rots in the rushes!
Avalanches of water in the midst of a calm,
And the distances cataracting toward the abyss!

Glaciers, suns of silver, nacreous waves, skies of embers!
Hideous strands at the end of brown gulfs
Where giant serpents devoured by bedbugs
Fall down from gnarled trees with black scent!

I should have liked to show children those sunfish
Of the blue wave, the fish of gold, the singing fish.
—Foam of flowers rocked my drifting
And ineffable winds winged me at times.

At times a martyr weary of poles and zones,
The sea, whose sob created my gentle roll,
Brought up to me her dark flowers with yellow suckers
And I remained, like a woman on her knees . . .

Resembling an island tossing on my sides the quarrels
And droppings of noisy birds with yellow eyes
And I sailed on, when through my fragile ropes
Drowned men sank backward to sleep!

Now I, a boat lost in the foliage of caves,
Thrown by the storm into the birdless air
I whose water-drunk carcass would not have been rescued
By the Monitors and the Hanseatic sailboats;

Free, smoking, topped with violet fog,
I who pierced the reddening sky like a wall,
Bearing, delicious jam for good poets
Lichens of sunlight and mucus of azure,

Who ran, spotted with small electric moons,
A wild plank, escorted by black seahorses,
When Julys beat down with blows of cudgels
The ultramarine skies with burning funnels;

Moi qui tremblais, sentant geindre à cinquante lieues
Le rut des Behemots et les Maelstroms épais,
Fileur éternel des immobilités bleues
Je regrette l'Europe aux anciens parapets!

J'ai vu des archipels sidéraux! et des îles
Dont les cieux délirants sont ouverts au vogueur:
—Est-ce en ces nuits sans fonds que tu dors et t'exiles,
Million d'oiseaux d'or, ô future Vigueur?—

Mais, vrai, j'ai trop pleuré! Les Aubes sont navrantes
Toute lune est atroce et tout soleil amer:
L'âcre amour m'a gonflé de torpeurs enivrantes
O que ma quille éclate! O que j'aille à la mer!

Si je désire une eau d'Europe, c'est la flache
Noire et froide où vers le crépuscule embaumé
Un enfant accroupi plein de tristesses, lâche
Un bateau frêle comme un papillon de mai.

Je ne puis plus, baigné de vos langueurs, ô lames,
Enlever leur sillage aux porteurs de cotons,
Ni traverser l'orgueil des drapeaux et des flammes,
Ni nager sous les yeux horribles des pontons.

Les chercheuses de poux

Quand le front de l'enfant, plein de rouges tourmentes,
Implore l'essaim blanc des rêves indistincts,
Il vient près de son lit deux grandes sœurs charmantes
Avec de frêles doigts aux ongles argentins.

Elles assoient l'enfant devant une croisée
Grande ouverte où l'air bleu baigne un fouillis de fleurs
Et dans ses lourds cheveux où tombe la rosée
Promènent leurs doigts fins, terribles et charmeurs.

I, who trembled, hearing at fifty leagues off
The moaning of the Behemoths in heat and the thick Maelstroms,
Eternal spinner of the blue immobility
I miss Europe with its ancient parapets!

I have seen sidereal archipelagos! and islands
Whose delirious skies are open to the sea-wanderer:
—Is it in these bottomless nights that you sleep and exile yourself,
Million golden birds, o future Vigor?—

But, in truth, I have wept too much! Dawns are heartbreaking
Every moon is atrocious and every sun bitter.
Acrid love has swollen me with intoxicating torpor
O let my keel burst! O let me go into the sea!

If I want a water of Europe, it is the black
Cold puddle where in the sweet-smelling twilight
A squatting child full of sadness releases
A boat as fragile as a May butterfly.

No longer can I, bathed in your languor, o waves,
Follow in the wake of the cotton boats,
Nor cross through the pride of flags and flames,
Nor swim under the terrible eyes of prison ships.

The Seekers of Lice

When the child's forehead, full of red torments,
Implores the white swarm of indistinct dreams,
There come near his bed two tall charming sisters
With slim fingers that have silvery nails.

They seat the child in front of a wide open
Window where the blue air bathes a mass of flowers
And in his heavy hair where the dew falls
Move their delicate, fearful and enticing fingers.

Il écoute chanter leurs haleines craintives
Qui fleurent de longs miels végétaux et rosés
Et qu'interrompt parfois un sifflement, salives
Reprises sur la lèvre ou désirs de baisers.

Il entend leurs cils noirs battant sous les silences
Parfumés; et leurs doigts électriques et doux
Font crépiter parmi ses grises indolences
Sous leurs ongles royaux la mort des petits poux.

Voilà que monte en lui le vin de la Paresse,
Soupir d'harmonica qui pourrait délirer;
L'enfant se sent, selon la lenteur des caresses
Sourdre et mourir sans cesse un désir de pleurer.

Les douaniers

Ceux qui disent: Cré Nom, ceux qui disent macache,
Soldats, marins, débris d'Empire, retraités
Sont nuls, très nuls, devant les Soldats des Traités
Qui tailladent l'azur frontière à grands coups d'hache

Pipe aux dents, lame en main, profonds, pas embêtés
Quand l'ombre bave aux bois comme un mufle de vache
Ils s'en vont, amenant leurs dogues à l'attache,
Exercer nuitamment leurs terribles gaîtés!

Ils signalent aux lois modernes les faunesses
Ils empoignent les Fausts et les Diavolos
"Pas de ça, les anciens! Déposez les ballots!"

Quand sa sérénité s'approche des jeunesses,
Le Douanier se tient aux appas contrôlés!
Enfer aux Déliquants que sa paume a frôlés!

He listens to the singing of their apprehensive breath
Which smells of long rosy plant honey
And which at times a hiss interrupts, saliva
Caught on the lip or desire for kisses.

He hears their black eyelashes beating in the perfumed
Silence; and their gentle electric fingers
Make in his half-drunken indolence the death of the little lice
Crackle under their royal nails.

Then the wine of Sloth rises in him,
The sigh of an harmonica which could bring on delirium;
The child feels, according to the slowness of the caresses
Surging in him and dying continuously a desire to cry.

The Customs Men

Those who say: In God's Name, those who say not on your life,
Soldiers, sailors, wrecks of the Empire, men pensioned
Are nothing, really nothing, compared with Soldiers of Treaties
Who slash the frontier azure with heavy blows of the ax

A pipe between their teeth, a blade in their hand, deep, not upset
When darkness drools in the woods like a cow's muzzle
They go off, taking their dogs on the leash,
To hold every night their terrible revels!

They report the female fauns to our modern laws
They seize our Fausts and our Devils
"Stop that, you old men! Put down the bundles!"

When his highness approaches young men,
The Customs Man is intent on dutiable attractions!
Hell for the Offenders his palm has frisked!

"L'étoile a pleuré rose [. . .]"

L'étoile a pleuré rose au cœur de tes oreilles,
L'infini roulé blanc de ta nuque à tes reins
La mer a perlé rousse à tes mammes vermeilles
Et l'Homme saigné noir à ton flanc souverain.

Oraison du soir

Je vis assis, tel qu'un ange aux mains d'un barbier,
Empoignant une chope à fortes cannelures,
L'hypogastre et le col cambrés, une Gambier
Aux dents, sous l'air gonflé d'impalpables voilures.

Tels que les excréments chauds d'un vieux colombier,
Mille Rêves en moi font de douces brûlures:
Puis par instants mon cœur triste est comme un aubier
Qu'ensanglante l'or jeune et sombre des coulures.

Puis, quand j'ai ravalé mes rêves avec soin,
Je me tourne, ayant bu trente ou quarante chopes,
Et me recueille, pour lâcher l'âcre besoin:

Doux comme le Seigneur du cèdre et des hysopes,
Je pisse vers les cieux bruns très haut et très loin,
Avec l'assentiment des grands héliotropes.

Tête de faune

Dans la feuillée écrin vert taché d'or
Dans la feuillée incertaine et fleurie
De fleurs splendides où le baiser dort,
Vif et crevant l'exquise broderie,

Un faune effaré montre ses deux yeux
Et mord les fleurs rouges de ses dents blanches:
Brunie et sanglante ainsi qu'un vin vieux
Sa lèvre éclate en rires sous les branches.

"The star wept rose-colored [. . .]"

The star wept rose-colored in the heart of your ears,
The infinite rolled white from your nape to your loins
The sea turned ruddy at your vermilion nipples
And Man bled black on your sovereign flank.

Evening Prayer [15]

I live seated, like an angel in the hands of a barber,
In my fist a strongly fluted mug,
My stomach and neck curved, a Gambier pipe
In my teeth, under the air swollen with impalpable veils of smoke.

Like the warm excrement of an old pigeonhouse,
A Thousand Dreams gently burn inside me:
And at moments my sad heart is like sap-wood
Which the young dark gold of its sweating covers with blood.

Then, when I have carefully swallowed my dreams,
I turn, having drunk thirty or forty mugs,
And collect myself, to relieve the bitter need:

Sweetly as the Lord of the cedar and of hyssops,
I piss toward the dark skies very high and very far,
With the consent of the large heliotropes.

Faun's Head

In the foliage a green jewel box spotted with gold
In the uncertain foliage covered
With magnificent flowers where sleeps the kiss,
Alive and breaking through the exquisite tapestry,

A terrified faun shows his two eyes
And bites the red flowers with his white teeth:
Stained and reddened like old wine
His lips burst in laughter under the branches.

Et quand il a fui—tel qu'un écureuil—
Son rire tremble encore à chaque feuille
Et l'on voit épeuré par un bouvreuil
Le Baiser d'or du Bois, qui se recueille

Voyelles

A noir, E blanc, I rouge, U vert, O bleu: voyelles,
Je dirai quelque jour vos naissances latentes:
A, noir corset velu des mouches éclatantes
Qui bombinent autour des puanteurs cruelles,

Golfes d'ombre; E, candeurs des vapeurs et des tentes,
Lances des glaciers fiers, rois blancs, frissons d'ombelles;
I, pourpres, sang craché, rire des lèvres belles
Dans la colère ou les ivresses pénitentes;

U, cycles, vibrements divins des mers virides,
Paix des pâtis semés d'animaux, paix des rides
Que l'alchimie imprime aux grands fronts studieux;

O, Suprême Clairon plein des strideurs étranges,
Silences traversés des Mondes et des Anges:
—Ô l'Oméga, rayon violet de Ses Yeux!

And when he has fled—like a squirrel—
His laughter still trembles on each leaf
And we can see frightened by a bullfinch
The Golden Kiss of the Wood, as it meditates

Vowels

A black, E white, I red, U green, O blue: vowels,
One day I will tell your latent birth:
A, black hairy corset of shining flies
Which buzz around cruel stench,

Gulfs of darkness; E, whiteness of vapors and tents,
Lances of proud glaciers, white kings, quivering of flowers;
I, purples, spit blood, laughter of beautiful lips
In anger or penitent drunkenness;

U, cycles, divine vibrations of green seas,
Peace of pastures scattered with animals, peace of the wrinkles
Which alchemy prints on heavy studious brows;

O, Supreme Clarion full of strange stridor,
Silences crossed by Worlds and Angels:
—O, the Omega, violet beam from His Eyes!

Album zutique
(fin 1871–début 1872?)

Album called "zutique"
(end 1871–early 1872?) [16]

Sonnet du trou du cul

Obscur et froncé comme un œillet violet
Il respire, humblement tapi parmi la mousse
Humide encor d'amour qui suit la fuite douce
Des Fesses blanches jusqu'au cœur de son ourlet.

Des filaments pareils à des larmes de lait
Ont pleuré, sous le vent cruel qui les repousse,
À travers de petits caillots de marne rousse
Pour s'aller perdre où la pente les appelait.

Mon Rêve s'aboucha souvent à sa ventouse;
Mon âme, du coït matériel jalouse,
En fit son larmier fauve et son nid de sanglots.

C'est l'olive pâmée, et la flûte câline;
C'est le tube où descend la céleste praline:
Chanaan féminin dans les moiteurs enclos!

ALBERT MÉRAT
P.V.-A.R.

Lys

O balançoirs! o lys! clysopompes d'argent!
Dédaigneux des travaux, dédaigneux des famines!
L'Aurore vous emplit d'un amour détergent!
Une douceur de ciel beurre vos étamines!

ARMAND SILVESTRE
A. R.

Vu à Rome

Il est, à Rome, à la Sixtine,
Couverte d'emblèmes chrétiens,
Une cassette écarlatine
Où sèchent des nez fort anciens:

Sonnet to an Asshole

Dark and wrinkled like a deep pink
It breathes, humbly nestled among the moss
Still wet with love that follows the gentle flight
Of the white Buttocks to the heart of its border.

Filaments like tears of milk
Have wept, under the cruel wind pushing them back,
Over small clots of reddish marl
And there lose themselves where the slope called them.

In my Dream my mouth was often placed on its opening;
My soul, jealous of the physical coitus,
Made of it its fawny tear-bottle and its nest of sobs.

It is the fainting olive, and the cajoling flute;
It is the tube where the heavenly praline descends:
A feminine Canaan enclosed in moisture!

ALBERT MÉRAT
P.V.-A.R.

Lily

O swings! o lily! silver instruments for enemas!
Scornful of work, scornful of famines!
Dawn fills you with a detergent love!
A sweetness of heaven butters your stamens!

ARMAND SILVESTRE
A. R.

Seen in Rome

There is, in Rome, in the Sistine,
Covered with Christian emblems,
A scarlet skullcap
Where very ancient noses are drying:

Nez d'ascètes de Thébaïde,
Nez de chanoines du Saint Graal
Où se figea la nuit livide,
Et l'ancien plain-chant sépulcral.

Dans leur sécheresse mystique,
Tous les matins, on introduit
De l'immondice schismatique
Qu'en poudre fine on a réduit.

LÉON DIERX.
A. R.

Fête galante

Rêveur, Scapin
Gratte un lapin
Sous sa capote.

Colombina,
— Que l'on pina! —
—Do, mi,—tapote

L'œil du lapin
Qui tôt, tapin,
Est en ribote. . . .

PAUL VERLAINE
A. R.

"J'occupais un wagon de troisième [. . .]"

J'occupais un wagon de troisième: un vieux prêtre
Sortit son brûle-gueule et mit à la fenêtre,
Vers les brises, son front très calme aux poils pâlis.
Puis ce chrétien, bravant les brocarts impolis,
S'étant tourné, me fit la demande énergique
Et triste en même temps d'une petite chique

Noses of Thebaid ascetics,
Noses of canons of the Holy Grail
In which the pale night coagulated,
And the old sepulchral plain chant.

Into their mystic dryness,
Every morning is introduced
Schismatic filth
Which has been reduced to fine powder.

>   LÉON DIERX.
>   A. R.

Love Feast

Dreaming, Scapin
Scratches a rabbit
Under his cloak.

Colombine,
—Who got laid!—
—Do, mi,—thrums

On the rabbit's eye
Which soon, a drum,
Gets tight. . . .

>   PAUL VERLAINE
>   A. R.

"I occupied a third-class carriage [. . .]"

I occupied a third-class carriage: an old priest
Took out his short pipe and put out of the window,
Toward the breezes, his very calm brow with faded hair.
Then this Christian, defying impolite remarks,
Turning, asked me energetically
And sadly at the same time for a little pinch

De caporal,—ayant été l'aumonier chef
D'un rejeton royal condamné derechef,—
Pour malaxer l'ennui d'un tunnel, sombre veine
Qui s'offre aux voyageurs, près Soissons, ville d'Aisne.

"Je préfère sans doute [. . .]"

Je préfère sans doute, au printemps, la guinguette
Où des marronniers nains bourgeonne la baguette,
Vers la prairie étroite et communale, au mois
De mai. Des jeunes chiens rabroués bien des fois
Viennent près des Buveurs triturer des jacinthes
De plate-bande. Et c'est, jusqu'aux soirs d'hyacinthe,
Sur la table d'ardoise où, l'an dix-sept cent vingt
Un diacre grava son sobriquet latin
Maigre comme une prose à des vitraux d'église
La toux des flacons noirs qui jamais ne les grise.

FRANÇOIS COPPÉE
A. R.

"L'Humanité chaussait [. . .]"

L'Humanité chaussait le vaste enfant Progrès.

LOUIS-XAVIER DE RICARD
A. RIMBAUD.

Conneries—

I. *Jeune goinfre*   II. *Paris*[17]

Casquette   Al. Godillot, Gambier,
De moire,   Galopeau, Volf-Pleyel,
Quéquette   — Ô Robinets! — Menier,
D'ivoire,   — Ô Christs! — Leperdriel!

Of tobacco,—having been the head chaplain
Of a royal scion condemned a second time,—
In order to soften the boredom of a tunnel, a dark vein
Offering itself to travelers, near Soissons, a city of the Aisne.

"Doubtless I prefer [. . .]"

Doubtless I prefer, in the spring, the country café
Where the branches of the dwarf chestnut trees break into leaves,
Toward the narrow common, in the month
Of May. Young dogs scolded many times
Come near the Drinkers to trample on the hyacinths
Of the flower-bed. And there is, until the hyacinth evenings,
On the slate table where, in the year seventeen twenty
A deacon engraved his Latin nickname
Thin as an inscription on church windows
The coughing of black flasks that never makes them drunk.

FRANÇOIS COPPÉE
A. R.

"Humanity was putting shoes on [. . .]"

Humanity was putting shoes on the huge child Progress.

LOUIS-XAVIER DE RICARD
A. RIMBAUD.

Nasty Jokes—

I. Young Glutton

Cap
Of silk,
Prick
Of ivory,

II. Paris

Al. Godillot, Gambier,
Galopeau, Volf-Pleyel,
— O Faucets! — Menier,
— O Christs! — Leperdriel!

Toilette
Très noire,
Paul guette
L'armoire,

Projette
Languette
Sur poire,

S'apprête
Baguette,
Et foire

A. R.

Kinck, Jacob, Bonbonnel!
Veuillot, Tropmann, Augier!
Gill, Mendès, Manuel,
Guido Gonin! — Panier

Des Grâces! L'Hérissé!
Cirages onctueux!
Pains vieux, spiritueux!

Aveugles! — puis, qui sait? —
Sergents de ville, Enghiens
Chez soi! — soyons chrétiens!

A. R.

Conneries 2e Série

I. Cocher ivre

Pouacre
Boit:
Nacre
Voit;

Âcre
Loi,
Fiacre
Choit!

Femme
Tombe:
Lombe

Saigne:
— Clame!
Geigne.

A. R.

Clothes	Kinck, Jacob, Bonbonnel!
Very black,	Veuillot, Tropmann, Augier!
Paul watches	Gill, Mendès, Manuel,
The cupboard,	Guido Gonin! — Panier
Sticks out	Of the Graces! L'Hérissé!
Small tongue	Unctuous waxes!
At pear,	Old loaves of bread, spirits!
Prepares	Blind men! — but, who knows? —
Wand,	Policemen, Enghiens
And diarrhea	In your own home! — let us be christian!
A. R.	A. R.

Nasty Jokes 2nd Series

I. Drunken Coachman

Beast
Drinks:
Mother-of-pearl
Sees;

Bitter
Law,
Cab
Tumbles!

Woman
Falls:
Loin

Bleeds:
— Cry out!
Moan.

     A. R.

Vieux de la vieille!

Aux paysans de l'empereur!
À l'empereur des paysans!
    Au fils de Mars,
    Au glorieux 18 *Mars*
Où le Ciel d'Eugénie a béni les entrailles!

État de siège?

Le pauvre postillon, sous le dais de ferblanc,
Chauffant une engelure énorme sous son gant,
Suit son lourd omnibus parmi la rive gauche,
Et de son aine en flamme écarte la sacoche.
Et tandis que, douce ombre où des gendarmes sont,
L'honnête intérieur regarde au ciel profond
La lune se bercer parmi sa verte ouate,
Malgré l'édit et l'heure encore délicate,
Et que l'omnibus rentre à l'Odéon, impur
Le débauché glapit au carrefour obscur!

     FRANÇOIS COPPÉE
      A. R.

Le balai

C'est un humble balai de chiendent, trop dur
Pour une chambre ou pour la peinture d'un mur.
L'usage en est navrant et ne vaut pas qu'on rie.
Racine prise à quelque ancienne prairie
Son crin inerte sèche: et son manche a blanchi.
Tel un bois d'île à la canicule rougi.
La cordelette semble une tresse gelée.
J'aime de cet objet la saveur désolée
Et j'en voudrais laver tes larges bords de lait,
O Lune où l'esprit de nos Sœurs mortes se plaît.

     F. C.

The Old Man of the Old Woman!

To the peasants of the emperor!
To the emperor of the peasants!
    To the sons of Mars,
     To the glorious 18th of *March!*
When Heaven blessed the womb of Eugénie!

State of Siege?

The poor postilion, under the tin canopy,
Warming a huge chilblain inside his glove,
Follows his heavy omnibus along the left bank,
And from his inflamed groin pushes aside the money bag.
And while, soft shadow where policemen are,
The respectable interior looks at the moon
In the deep sky being rocked in its green cotton wool,
In spite of the edict and the still delicate hour,
And the omnibus returning to the Odeon, a lewd
Rake screams out in the dark square!

      FRANÇOIS COPPÉE
      A. R.

The Brush

It is a humble scrub brush, too rough
For a bedroom or to paint a wall.
Its usage is upsetting and should not make us laugh.
Root torn from some ancient field
Its bristle inert and dry: and its handle has whitened.
Like an island wood reddened by dog-day heat.
The little cord looks like a frozen braid.
I love this object's sad flavor
And with it I wish to wash your large milky borders,
O Moon where the spirit of our dead Sisters like being.

      F. C.

Exil

. . . .

Que l'on s'intéressa souvent, mon cher Conneau! . . .
Plus qu'à l'Oncle Vainqueur, au Petit Ramponneau! . . .
Que tout honnête instinct sort du Peuple débile! . . . .
Hélas!! Et qui a fait tourner mal notre bile! . . . .
Et qu'il nous sied déjà de pousser le verrou
Au Vent que les enfants nomment Bari-barou! . . .

. . . .

Fragment d'une épître en Vers de Napoléon III, 1871.

L'angelot maudit

Toits bleuâtres et portes blanches
Comme en de nocturnes dimanches,

Au bout de la ville sans bruit,
La Rue est blanche, et c'est la nuit.

La Rue a des maisons étranges
Avec des persiennes d'Anges.

Mais, vers une borne, voici
Accourir, mauvais et transi,

Un noir Angelot qui titube
Ayant trop mangé de jujube.

Il fait caca: puis disparaît:
Mais son caca maudit paraît,

Sous la lune sainte qui vaque,
De sang sale un léger cloaque!

      LOUIS RATISBONNE.
        A. RIMBAUD.

Exile

. . . .

That one was often interested, my dear Conneau! . . . .
More than in Uncle Conqueror, than in Little Ramponneau! . . .
That all honest instinct comes from the idiot commoners! . . . .
Alas!! And who made us worry so much! . . . .
And that it is already fitting to lock the door
Against the Wind that the children call Bari-barou! . . .

. . . .

Fragment of an epistle in Verse by Napoleon III, 1871.

The Outcast Cherub

Bluish roofs and white doors
As on nocturnal Sundays,

At the end of the city without noise,
The Street is white, and it is night.

The Street has strange houses
With Angelic shutters.

But toward a stone post, see
Him running, evil and shivering,

A black Cherub staggering
Having eaten too many jujubes.

He makes caca: then disappears:
But his blasted caca appears,

Under the holy moon which is vacant,
A thin cesspool of dirty blood!

   LOUIS RATISBONNE.
    A. RIMBAUD.

« Mais enfin, c' [. . .] » (torn manuscript)

Mais enfin, c'
Qu'ayant p
Je puisse,
Et du mon
Rêver le sé
Le tableau
Des animau
Et, loin du
L'élaborat
D'un *Choler*

"Les soirs d'été [. . .]"

Les soirs d'été, sous l'œil ardent des devantures,
Quand la sève frémit sous les grilles obscures
Irradiant au pied des grêles marronniers,
Hors de ces groupes noirs, joyeux ou casaniers,
Suceurs de brûle-gueule ou baiseurs du cigare,
Dans le kiosque mi-pierre étroit où je m'égare,
—Tandis qu'en haut rougeoie une annonce d'*Ibled,*—
Je songe que l'hiver figera le Filet
D'eau propre qui bruit, apaisant l'onde humaine,
—Et que l'âpre aquilon n'épargne aucune veine

FRANÇOIS COPPÉE.
A. RIMBAUD.

—*Bouts-rimés* (torn manuscript)

lévitiques,
ur fauve *fessier,*
matiques,
enou *grossier,*

"But finally, th[. . .]" (torn manuscript)

But finally, th
That having be
I might be able,
And from my
To dream the se
The painting
Of animal
And, far from
The elaborat
Of a *Choler*

"Summer evenings [. . .]" [18]

Summer evenings, under the burning eye of shop windows,
When the sap trembles under dark gratings
Radiating at the foot of slender chestnut trees,
Outside of those dark groups, joyful men or stay-at-homes,
Suckers of short pipes, or kissers of cigars,
In the narrow half-stone kiosk where I wander,
—While above an *Ibled* advertisement flashes red—
I think that winter will freeze the Trickle
Of clean water that roars, appeasing the human wave,
—And that the bitter north wind will spare no vein

FRANÇOIS COPPÉE.
A. RIMBAUD.

—*Rhymed endings* (torn manuscript)

levitical,
ur wild *buttock,*
matic,
nee *crude,*

apoplectiques,
nassier,
mnastiques,
ux membre d'*acier.*

et peinte en *bile,*
a *sébile*
in,

n fruit d'*Asie,*
saisie,
ve d'*airain.*

    A. R.

"Aux livres de chevet [. . .]"

Aux livres de chevet, livres de l'art serein,
Obermann et Genlis, Ver-vert et le Lutrin,
Blasé de nouveauté grisâtre et saugrenue,
J'espère, la vieillesse étant enfin venue,
Ajouter le Traité du Docteur Venetti.
Je saurai, revenu du public abêti,
Goûter le charme ancien des dessins nécessaires.
Ecrivain et graveur ont doré les misères
Sexuelles: et c'est, n'est-ce pas, cordial:
DR VENETTI, *Traité de l'Amour conjugal.*

    F. COPPÉE
    A. R.

Hypotyposes saturniennes, ex Belmontet

———————

Quel est donc ce mystère impénétrable et sombre?
Pourquoi, sans projeter leur voile blanche, sombre
   Tout jeune esquif royal gréé?

———————

apoplectic,
nassial,
mnastics,
ux member of *steel.*

and painted in *bile,*
a *alms bowl*
in,

n fruit of *Asia,*
seized,
ve of *bronze.*

A. R.

"To the bedside books [. . .]"

To the bedside books, books of serene art,
Obermann and Genlis, Ver-vert and the Lutrin,
Bored with insipid strange novelties,
I hope, old age having come at last,
To add the Treatise of Doctor Venetti.
Disillusioned with the dull public, I will be able
To enjoy the old charm of the indispensable drawings.
Writer and engraver have gilded the sexual
Miseries, and that is heartening, is it not:
Dᴿ VENETTI, *Treatise on Conjugal Love.*

F. COPPÉE
A. R.

Saturnian Hypotyposes, Taken from Belmontet

———————

So what is this dark and impenetrable mystery?
Why, without raising up their white sail, does
Every young royal rigged skiff sink?

———————

159

Renversons la douleur de nos lacrymatoires. ———

. . . .

——— L'amour veut vivre aux dépens de sa sœur,
L'amitié vit aux dépens de son frère.

. . . .

Le sceptre, qu'à peine on révère,   ———
N'est que la croix d'un grand calvaire
Sur le volcan des nations!

———

. . . .

Oh! l'honneur ruisselait sur ta mâle moustache. Belmontet,

—   archétype Parnassien.

Les remembrances du vieillard idiot

Pardon, mon père!
                Jeune, aux foires de campagne,
Je cherchais, non le tir banal où tout coup gagne,
Mais l'endroit plein de cris où les ân[es, le flan]c
Fatigué, déployaient ce long tu[be] sa[ng]lant
—Que je ne comprends pas encore!...
                          [Et puis] ma mère,
Dont la chemise avait une sente[ur amè]re
Quoique fripée au bas et jaune co[mme u]n fruit,
Ma mère qui montait au lit avec [un] bruit
—Fils du travail pourtant,—ma mè[re, a]vec sa cuisse
De femme mûre, avec ses reins très [g]ros où plisse
Le linge, me donna ces chaleurs q[ue] l'on tait!...

Une honte plus crue et plus calme, c'était
Quand ma petite sœur, au retour de la classe,
Ayant usé longtemps ses sabots sur la glace,
Pissait, et regardait s'échapper de sa lèvre
D'en bas serrée et rose, un fil d'urine mièvre!...

Let us upend the grief of our lachrymatories. ———

     . . . .

——— Love tries to live at the expense of its sister,
     Friendship lived at the expense of its brother.

. . . .

The scepter, that we barely revere,   ———
Is but the cross from a great cavalry
On the volcano of nations!

     ———

. . . .

Oh! honor glistened on your manly mustache. Belmontet,

     —   Parnassian archetype.

Memories of the Simple-Minded Old Man

Forgive me, Father!
               Young, at country fairs,
I sought out, not the stupid shooting gallery where every shot wins,
But the place full of shouts where donkeys, their flanks
Tired, displayed that long bloody tube
—Which still I do not understand! . . .
               And then my mother,
Whose nightdress had a sharp odor
Although ragged at the bottom and yellow like a fruit,
My mother who climbed into bed with a noise
—A son of toil just the same,—my mother, with her thigh
Of a mature woman, which her very fat buttocks where the linen
Makes a fold, excited me in a way we don't talk about! . . .

A cruder and calmer shame was
When my little sister, back from school,
Having for a long time worn her sabots on the ice,
Pissed, and watched escape from her lip
Below tight and pink, a delicate thread of urine! . . .

O pardon!
            Je songeais à mon père parfois:
Le soir, le jeu de carte et les mots plus grivois,
Le voisin, et moi qu'on écartait, choses vues . . .
— Car un père est troublant! — et les choses conçues! . . .
Son genou, câlineur parfois; son pantalon
Dont mon doigt désirait ouvrir la fente, . . . — oh! non! —
Pour avoir le bout, gros, noir et dur, de mon père,
Dont la pileuse main me berçait! . . .
                                    Je veux taire
Le pot, l'assiette à manche, entrevue au grenier,
Les almanachs couverts en rouge, et le panier
De charpie, et la Bible, et les lieux, et la bonne,
La Sainte-Vierge et le crucifix . . .
                            Oh! personne
Ne fut si fréquemment troublé, comme étonné!
Et maintenant, que le pardon me soit donné:
Puisque les sens infects m'ont mis de leurs victimes,
Je me confesse de l'aveu des jeunes crimes! . . .

. . . .

Puis! — qu'il me soit permis de parler au Seigneur! —
Pourquoi la puberté tardive et le malheur
Du gland tenace et trop consulté? Pourquoi l'ombre
Si lente au bas du ventre? et ces terreurs sans nombre
Comblant toujours la joie ainsi qu'un gravier noir?
— Moi, j'ai toujours été stupéfait! Quoi savoir?

. . . .

Pardonné? . . .
            Reprenez la chancelière bleue,
Mon père.
            Ô cette enfance! . . . .

. . . .

. . . . — et tirons-nous la queue!.

FRANÇOIS COPPÉE.
A. R.

162

Forgive me!
Some times I thought of my father:
In the evening, the card game and the more rakish words,
The neighbor, and myself they pushed away, things seen . . .
—For a father is disturbing!—and the things imagined! . . .
His knee, at times coaxing; his trousers
Whose fly my finger wanted to open, . . . —oh! no!—
To have the thick, dark hard cock of my father,
Whose hairy hand rocked me! . . .
I will not mention
The pot, the dish with the handle, caught sight of in the attic,
The almanacs covered with red, and the basket
Of lint, and the Bible, and the privies, and the maid,
The Holy Virgin and the crucifix . . .
Oh! no one
Was aroused so often, as if astonished!
And now, may forgiveness be granted me:
Since my infected senses have made me their victim,
I confess and avow my youthful crimes! . . .

.   .   .   .

Then!—let me be allowed to speak to the Lord!—
Why puberty so late and the disgrace
Of my tenacious and too often consulted glans? Why the dark
So slow at the base of my belly? and those numberless terrors
Always burying my joy like black gravel?
—I have always been astounded! What can I know?

.   .   .   .

Forgiven? . . .
Take back the blue hassock,
Father.
O that childhood!   .   .   .   .

.   .   .   .
.   .   .   .   —and let us jack off!.

FRANÇOIS COPPÉE.
A. R.

163

Ressouvenir

Cette année où naquit le Prince impérial
Me laisse un souvenir largement cordial
D'un Paris limpide où des N d'or et de neige
Aux grilles du palais, aux gradins du manège,
Eclatent, tricolorement enrubannés.
Dans le remous public des grands chapeaux fanés,
Des chauds gilets à fleurs, des vieilles redingotes,
Et des chants d'ouvriers anciens dans les gargotes,
Sur des châles jonchés l'Empereur marche, noir
Et propre, avec la Sainte espagnole, le soir.

FRANÇOIS COPPÉE

Remembrance

That year when the imperial Prince was born
Leaves me a generously warm memory
Of a limpid Paris where N's of gold and snow
At the palace gates, on the mounting blocks of the riding school,
Burst forth with tricolored ribbons.
In the public swirl of big faded hats,
Warm flowered vests, old frock-coats,
And songs of old workmen in taverns,
Over strewn shawls the Emperor walks, black
And proper, with the Pious Spanishwoman, in the evening.

FRANÇOIS COPPÉE

D'autres poèmes de la période
dite « zutique » (1871–1872?)

Other poems from the period
called "zutique" (1871–1872?)

"Nos fesses ne sont pas les leurs [. . .]"

Nos fesses ne sont pas les leurs. Souvent j'ai vu
Des gens déboutonnés derrière quelque haie,
Et, dans ces bains sans gêne où l'enfance s'égaie,
J'observais le plan et l'effet de notre cul.

Plus ferme, blême en bien des cas, il est pourvu
De méplats évidents que tapisse la claie
Des poils; pour elles, c'est seulement dans la raie
Charmante que fleurit le long satin touffu.

Une ingéniosité touchante et merveilleuse
Comme l'on ne voit qu'aux anges des saints tableaux
Imite la joue où le sourire se creuse.

Oh! de même être nus, chercher joie et repos,
Le front tourné vers sa portion glorieuse,
Et libres tous les deux murmurer des sanglots?

"Les anciens animaux [. . .]"

Les anciens animaux saillissaient, même en course,
Avec des glands bardés de sang et d'excrément.
Nos pères étalaient leur membre fièrement
Par le pli de la gaine et le grain de la bourse.

Au moyen âge pour la femelle, ange ou pource,
Il fallait un gaillard de solide grément;
Même un Kléber, d'après la culotte qui ment
Peut-être un peu, n'a pas dû manquer de ressource.

D'ailleurs l'homme au plus fier mammifère est égal;
L'énormité de leur membre à tort nous étonne;
Mais une heure stérile a sonné: le cheval

Et le bœuf ont bridé leurs ardeurs, et personne
N'osera plus dresser son orgueil génital
Dans les bosquets où grouille une enfance bouffonne.

"Our backsides are not theirs [. . .]"

Our backsides are not theirs. Often I saw
Men unbuttoned behind some hedge,
And, in those unembarrassed bathings where children frolic,
I observed the form and the function of our ass.

Firmer, in many cases white, it is provided
With obvious planes covered by the screen
Of hairs; for women, it is only in the charming
Furrow that the long tufted satin flowers.

A touching marvelous ingenuity
Such as is seen only on angels of holy pictures
Imitates the cheek where the smile makes a hollow.

Oh! to be naked like that, and look for joy and rest,
Head turned toward companion's glorious part,
And both free murmuring sobs?

"Ancient animals [. . .]"

Ancient animals copulated, even as they ran,
Their glans coated with blood and excrement.
Our fathers proudly displayed their members
By the fold of the sheath and the grain of the balls.

In the middle ages, for the female, angel or sow,
A well hung fellow was needed;
Even a Kléber, according to his breeches, lying
Perhaps a bit, must not have lacked resources.

Moreover, man is equal to the proudest mammal;
The hugeness of their member should not surprise us;
But a sterile hour has struck: the horse

And the ox have bridled their lust, and no one
Will dare again to raise his genital pride
In the woods where playful children are swarming.

Vers pour les lieux

« De ce siège si mal tourné [. . .] »

De ce siège si mal tourné
Qu'il fait s'embrouiller nos entrailles,
Le trou dut être maçonné
Par de véritables canailles.

« Quand le fameux Tropmann [. . .] »

Quand le fameux Tropmann détruisit Henri Kink,
Cet assassin avait dû s'asseoir sur ce siège,
Car le con de Badingue et le con d'Henri V
Sont bien dignes vraiment de cet état de siège.

Verses for Such Places

"Of this seat so poorly made [. . .]"

Of this seat so poorly made
That it ties our entrails in knots,
The hole must have been built
By veritable scoundrels.

"When the famous Tropmann [. . .]"

When the famous Tropmann destroyed Henri Kink,
That assassin must have sat on this seat,
Because Badingue's cunt and Henri V's cunt
Are truly well worthy of this state of siege.

Poèmes datés de, transcrits
ou publiés en 1872

Poems dated, transcribed,
or published in 1872

Comédie de la soif

1. LES PARENTS

Nous sommes tes Grands-Parents
     Les Grands!
Couverts des froides sueurs
De la lune et des verdures.
Nos vins secs avaient du cœur!
Au soleil sans imposture
Que faut-il à l'homme? boire.

MOI: Mourir aux fleuves barbares.

Nous sommes tes Grands-Parents
     Des champs.
L'eau est au fond des osiers:
Vois le courant du fossé
Autour du Château mouillé.
Descendons en nos celliers;
Après, le cidre et le lait.

MOI: Aller où boivent les vaches.

Nous sommes tes Grands-Parents;
     Tiens, prends
Les liqueurs dans nos armoires
Le Thé, le Café, si rares,
Frémissent dans les boulloires.[19]
—Vois les images, les fleurs.
Nous rentrons du cimetière.

MOI: Ah! tarir toutes les urnes!

2. L'ESPRIT

Eternelles Ondines
     Divisez l'eau fine.
Venus, sœur de l'azur,
     Emeus le flot pur.

Comedy of Thirst

1. THE PARENTS

> We are your Grand Parents
> > Grown-ups!
> Covered with the cold sweat
> Of the moon and verdure.
> Our dry wines had life in them!
> In sunlight without deception
> What must a man do? drink.

I: Die in barbarous rivers.

> We are your Grand Parents
> > Of the fields.
> The water is at the roots of the willows:
> See the current of the moat
> Around the wet Castle.
> Let us go down to our cellars;
> Afterward, cider and milk.

I: Go where the cows drink.

> We are your Grand Parents;
> > Here, take
> The liquors in our cupboards
> Tea, Coffee, so rare,
> Hum in the kettles.
> —See the pictures, the flowers.
> We are back from the cemetery.

I: Ah! drink all the urns dry!

2. THE SPIRIT

> Eternal Water Sprites
> > Divide the clear water.
> Venus, sister of azure,
> > Stir up the pure wave.

Juifs errants de Norwège
  Dites-moi la neige.
Anciens exilés chers
  Dites-moi la mer.

MOI: Non, plus ces boissons pures,
  Ces fleurs d'eau pour verres.
Légendes ni figures
  Ne me désaltèrent;

  Chansonnier, ta filleule
  C'est ma soif si folle
Hydre intime sans gueules
  Qui mine et désole.

3. LES AMIS

  Viens, les Vins vont aux plages,
  Et les flots par millions!
  Vois le Bitter sauvage
  Rouler du haut des monts!
  Gagnons, pèlerins sages,
  L'Absinthe aux verts piliers . . .

MOI: Plus ces paysages.
  Qu'est l'ivresse, Amis?

  J'aime autant, mieux, même,
  Pourrir dans l'étang,
  Sous l'affreuse crème,
  Près des bois flottants.

4. LE PAUVRE SONGE

  Peut-être un Soir m'attend
  Où je boirai tranquille
  En quelque vieille Ville,
  Et mourrai plus content:
  Puisque je suis patient!

Wandering Jews of Norway
  Tell me of the snow.
Dear former exiles
  Tell me of the sea.

I: No, no more of these pure drinks,
         These water flowers for glasses.
       Neither legends nor faces
         Slake my thirst;

       Singer, your god-daughter
         Is my thirst so wild
       A mouthless intimate hydra
         Who destroys and afflicts.

3. FRIENDS

       Come, the Wines go to the beaches,
       And the waves by the millions!
       See the wild Bitter
       Rolling from the top of the mountains!
       Let us, wise pilgrims, reach
       The Absinthe with the green pillars . . .

I: No more of these landscapes.
       What is intoxication, Friends?

       I would as soon, or even prefer,
       To rot in the pond,
       Under the horrible scum,
       Near floating pieces of wood.

4. THE POOR MAN DREAMS

       Perhaps an Evening awaits me
       When I will drink peacefully
       In some old Town,
       And die happier:
       Since I am patient!

Si mon mal se résigne,
Si j'ai jamais quelque or,
Choisirai-je le Nord
Ou le Pays des Vignes? . . .
—Ah! songer est indigne

Puisque c'est pure perte!
Et si je redeviens
Le voyageur ancien
Jamais l'auberge verte
Ne peut bien m'être ouverte.

5. CONCLUSION

Les pigeons qui tremblent dans la prairie
Le gibier, qui court et qui voit la nuit,
Les bêtes des eaux, la bête asservie,
Les derniers papillons! . . . ont soif aussi

Mais fondre où fond ce nuage sans guide,
—Oh! favorisé de ce qui est frais!
Expirer en ces violettes humides
Dont les aurores chargent ces forêts?

Bonne pensée du matin

À quatre heures du matin, l'été,
Le sommeil d'amour dure encore.
Sous les bosquets l'aube évapore
    L'odeur du soir fêté.

Mais là-bas dans l'immense chantier
Vers le soleil des Hesperides,
En bras de chemise, les charpentiers
    Déjà s'agitent.

Dans leur désert de mousse, tranquilles,
Ils préparent les lambris précieux
Où la richesse de la ville
    Rira sous de faux cieux.

If my suffering quiets down,
If ever I have some gold,
Will I choose the North
Or the Land of Vineyards? . . .
—Ah! dreaming is shameful

Since it is pure loss!
And if ever I become once again
The old traveler
Never will the green inn
Be open to me.

5. CONCLUSION

The pigeons fluttering in the field
The game, which runs and sees in the dark,
The water animals, the animal enslaved,
The last butterflies! . . . are also thirsty

But can one melt where the guideless cloud melts
—Oh! favored by what is cool!
And expire in these damp violets
Whose dawns fill these forests?

A Good Thought in the Morning

At four in the morning, in summer,
The sleep of love still continues.
Under the arbors dawn evaporates
    The scent of the festive night.

But yonder in the huge lumberyard
Toward the sun of the Hesperides,
In shirtsleeves the carpenters
    Are already moving about.

In their desert of moss, calm,
They prepare the precious panels
Where the city's wealth
    Will laugh under false skies.

Ah! pour ces Ouvriers charmants
Sujets d'un roi de Babylone,
Venus! laisse un peu les Amants,
        Dont l'âme est en couronne.

        O Reine des Bergers,
        Porte aux travailleurs l'eau-de-vie.
        Pour que leurs forces soient en paix
En attendant le bain dans la mer, à midi.

La rivière de Cassis

La Rivière de Cassis roule ignorée
        En des vaux étranges:
La voix de cent corbeaux l'accompagne, vraie
        Et bonne voix d'anges:
Avec les grands mouvements des sapinaies
        Quand plusieurs vents plongent.

Tout roule avec des mystères révoltants
        De campagnes d'anciens temps:
De donjons visités, de parcs importants:
        C'est en ces bords qu'on entend
Les passions mortes des chevaliers errants:
        Mais que salubre est le vent!

Que le piéton regarde à ces claires-voies:
        Il ira plus courageux.
Soldats des forêts que le Seigneur envoie,
        Chers corbeaux délicieux!
Faites fuir d'ici le paysan matois
        Qui trinque d'un moignon vieux.

Ah! for those charming Workmen
Subjects of a Babylonian king,
Venus! leave Lovers for a little while,
         Whose souls are crowned.

         O Queen of Shepherds,
         Take brandy to the workers.
         So that their strength may be at peace
As they wait for the bath in the sea, at noon.

The Cassis River

The Cassis River flows unknown
         In strange valleys:
The voice of a hundred crows accompany it, the true
         Kind voice of angels:
With large movements of fir-groves
         When several winds swoop down.

Everything flows with the repulsive mysteries
         Of ancient landscapes:
Of fortunes visited, of important parks:
         It is within these banks you hear
The dead passions of errant knights:
         But how healthful the wind is!

Let the walker look through these open-work gates:
         He will go on more courageously.
Soldiers of the forest sent by the Lord,
         Dear delightful crows!
Send away from here the crafty peasant
         Who clinks glasses with an old stump of an arm.

Larme [20]

Loin des oiseaux, des troupeaux, des villageoises,
Je buvais, accroupi dans quelque bruyère
Entourée de tendres bois de noisetiers,
Par un brouillard d'après-midi tiède et vert.

Que pouvais-je boire dans cette jeune Oise,
Ormeaux sans voix, gazon sans fleurs, ciel couvert.
Que tirais-je à la gourde de colocase?
Quelque liqueur d'or, fade et qui fait suer

Tel, j'eusse été mauvaise enseigne d'auberge.
Puis l'orage changea le ciel, jusqu'au soir.
Ce furent des pays noirs, des lacs, des perches,
Des colonnades sous la nuit bleue, des gares.

L'eau des bois se perdait sur des sables vierges
Le vent, du ciel, jetait des glaçons aux mares . . .
Or! tel qu'un pêcheur d'or ou de coquillages,
Dire que je n'ai pas eu souci de boire!

Patience [21]

    D'un été.

Aux branches claires des tilleuls
Meurt un maladif hallali.
Mais des chansons spirituelles
Voltigent parmi les groseilles.
Que notre sang rie en nos veines
Voici s'enchevêtrer les vignes.
Le ciel est joli comme un ange
Azur et Onde communient,
Je sors! Si un rayon me blesse
Je succomberai sur la mousse.

Tear

Far from birds and herds and village girls,
I would drink, kneeling in some heather
Surrounded by soft woods of hazel trees,
In an afternoon fog warm and green.

What could I drink from this young Oise,
Voiceless elms, flowerless grass, cloudy sky.
What did I draw from the gourd of the colocynth?
Some golden liquor, insipid, which brings on sweat

Such, I would have been a bad inn sign.
Then the storm changed the sky, until evening.
They were black countries, lakes, poles,
Colonnades under the blue night, railway stations.

The water from the woods disappeared into virgin sand
The wind, from the sky, threw down sheets of ice over the ponds . . .
But! like a fisher for gold or shells,
To say that I gave no thought of drinking!

Patience

Of a summer.

In the bright branches of the lindens
Dies a sickly hunting call.
But lively songs
Fly about in the currant bushes.
So that our blood will laugh in our veins
Here are the vines all entangled.
The sky is pretty as an angel
Azure and Wave commune
I go out! If a ray of light wounds me
I will expire on the moss.

Qu'on patiente et qu'on s'ennuie,
C'est trop simple! . . . Fi de ces peines.
Je veux que l'été dramatique
Me lie à son char de fortune.
Que par toi beaucoup, O Nature,
—Ah moins nul et moins seul! je meure,
Au lieu que les bergers, c'est drôle,
Meurent à peu près par le monde.

Je veux bien que les saisons m'usent.
À Toi, Nature! je me rends,
Et ma faim et toute ma soif;
Et s'il te plaît, nourris, abreuve.
Rien de rien ne m'illusionne:
C'est rire aux parents qu'au soleil;
Mais moi je ne veux rire à rien
Et libre soit cette infortune.[22]

Chanson de la plus haute Tour

Oisive jeunesse
À tout asservie,
Par délicatesse
J'ai perdu ma vie.
Ah! Que le temps vienne
Où les cœurs s'éprennent.

Je me suis dit: laisse,
Et qu'on ne te voie:
Et sans la promesse
De plus hautes joies.
Que rien ne t'arrête
Auguste retraite.

J'ai tant fait patience
Qu'à jamais j'oublie;
Craintes et souffrances
Aux cieux sont parties.
Et la soif malsaine
Obscurcit mes veines.

To be patient and to be bored,
Are too simple! . . . Fie on these cares.
I want dramatic summer
To bind me to its chariot of fortune.
Let me, O Nature, mostly through you
—Ah less worthless and less alone! I die,
In the place where the shepherds, it is strange,
Die approximately throughout the world.

I am willing that the seasons wear me out.
To You, Nature! I give myself over,
And my hunger and all my thirst;
And if you will, feed and water me.
Nothing at all deceives me:
To laugh at the sun is to laugh at one's parents;
But I do not want to laugh at anything
And may this misfortune be free.

Song of the Highest Tower

Idle youth
Enslaved to everything,
Through sensitivity
I wasted my life.
Ah! Let the time come
When hearts fall in love.

I said to myself: stop,
Let no one see you:
And without the promise
Of loftier joys.
Let nothing put you off
Sublime retreat.

I have been patient so long
That I have forgotten everything;
Fears and sufferings
Have left for the skies.
And an unhealthy thirst
Darkens my veins.

Ainsi la Prairie
À l'oubli livrée,
Grandie, et fleurie
D'encens et d'ivraies
Au bourdon farouche
De cent sales mouches.

Ah! Mille veuvages
De la si pauvre âme
Qui n'a que l'image
De la Notre-Dame!
Est-ce que l'on prie
La Vierge Marie?

Oisive jeunesse
À tout asservie,
Par délicatesse
J'ai perdu ma vie.
Ah! Que le temps vienne
Où les cœurs s'éprennent!

L'éternité

Elle est retrouvée.
Quoi? — l'Eternité.
C'est la mer allée
Avec le soleil

Âme sentinelle,
Murmurons l'aveu
De la nuit si nulle
Et du jour en feu.

Des humains suffrages,
Des communs élans
Là tu te dégages
Et voles selon.

Thus the Field
Given over to oblivion,
Grown up, and flowering
With incense and tares
And to the fierce buzzing
Of a hundred dirty flies.

Ah! The thousand bereavements
Of the poor soul
Who has only the image
Of Our Lady!
Do people pray to
The Virgin Mary?

Idle youth
Enslaved to everything,
Through sensitivity
I wasted my life.
Ah! Let the time come
When hearts fall in love!

Eternity

It has been found again.
What has?—Eternity.
It is the sea gone off
With the sun

Sentinel soul,
Let us whisper the vow
Of the night so void
And of the day on fire.

From human approval,
From common impulses
Here you free yourself
And fly off as you will.

Puisque de vous seules,
Braises de satin,
Le Devoir s'exhale
Sans qu'on dise: enfin.

Là pas d'espérance,
Nul orietur.
Science avec patience,
Le supplice est sûr.

Elle est retrouvée.
Quoi?—L'éternité.
C'est la mer allée
Avec le soleil

Âge d'or

Quelqu'une des voix
Toujours angélique
—Il s'agit de moi,—
Vertement s'explique:

Ces mille questions
Qui se ramifient
N'amènent, au fond,
Qu'ivresse et folie;

Reconnais ce tour
Si gai, si facile:
Ce n'est qu'onde, flore,
Et c'est ta famille!

Puis elle chante. O
Si gai, si facile,
Et visible à l'œil nu . . .
—Je chante avec elle,—

Since from you alone,
Embers of satin,
Duty breathes
Without anyone saying: at last.

Here, there is no hope,
No orietur.
Science with patience,
The torture is certain.

It has been found again.
What has?—Eternity.
It is the sea gone off
With the sun

Golden Age

One of the voices
Always angelic
—It is about me,—
Openly expresses itself:

Those thousand questions
Which spread about
Bring, in the end,
Only intoxication and madness;

Recognize this trick
So cheerful, so easy:
It is only wave and flower,
And it is your family!

Then it sings. O
So cheerful, so easy,
And visible to the naked eye . . .
—I sing with it,—

Reconnais ce tour
Si gai, si facile,
Ce n'est qu'onde, flore,
Et c'est ta famille! . . . etc. . . .

Et puis une voix
—Est-elle angélique!—
Il s'agit de moi,
Vertement s'explique;

Et chante à l'instant
En sœur des haleines:
D'un ton Allemand,
Mais ardente et pleine:

Le monde est vicieux;
Si cela t'étonne!
Vis et laisse au feu
L'obscure infortune.

O! joli château!
Que ta vie est claire!
De quel Age es-tu
Nature princière
De Nôtre grand frère! etc. . . . ,[23]

Je chante aussi, moi:
Multiples sœurs! Voix
Pas du tout publiques!
Environnez-moi
De gloire pudique . . . etc. . . . ,

Jeune ménage

La chambre est ouverte au ciel bleu-turquin;
Pas de place: des coffrets et des huches!
Dehors le mur est plein d'aristoloches
Où vibrent les gencives des lutins.

Recognize this trick
So cheerful, so easy,
It is only wave and flower,
And it is your family! . . . etc. . . . .

And then a voice
—How angelic it is!—
It is about me,
Openly expresses itself;

And sings at this moment
A sister of breath:
With a German tone,
But ardent and full:

The world is given to vice;
If that surprises you!
Live and leave to the fire
The dark misfortune.

O! pretty castle!
How bright your life is!
From what Age do you come
Princely nature
Of Our older brother? etc. . . . ,

I too sing:
Many sisters! Voices
Not at all public!
Surround me
With chaste glory . . . etc. . . . ,

Young Couple

The room is open to the turquoise blue sky;
No space: coffers and chests!
Outside the wall is full of birthwort
Where the gums of elves vibrate.

Que ce sont bien intrigues de génies
Cette dépense et ces désordres vains!
C'est la fée africaine qui fournit
La mûre, et les résilles dans les coins.

Plusieurs entrent, marraines mécontentes,
En pans de lumière dans les buffets,
Puis y restent! le ménage s'absente
Peu sérieusement, et rien ne se fait.

Le marié, a le vent qui le floue
Pendant son absence, ici, tout le temps.
Même des fantômes des eaux, errants *
Entrent vaguer aux sphères de l'alcôve.

La nuit, l'amie oh! la lune de miel
Cueillera leur sourire et remplira
De mille bandeaux de cuivre le ciel.
Puis ils auront affaire au malin rat.

—S'il n'arrive pas un feu follet blême,
Comme un coup de fusil, après des vêpres.
— O Spectres saints et blancs de Bethléem,
Charmez plutôt le bleu de leur fenêtre!

* Même des esprits des eaux, malfaisants [24]

"Est-elle almée? [. . .]"

Est-elle almée? . . . aux premières heures bleues
Se détruira-t-elle comme les fleurs feues . . .
Devant la splendide étendue où l'on sente
Souffler la ville énormément florissante!

C'est trop beau! c'est trop beau! mais c'est nécessaire
—Pour la Pêcheuse et la chanson du Corsaire,
Et aussi puisque les derniers masques crurent
Encore aux fêtes de nuit sur la mer pure!

These are really the plottings of genii
This expense and this futile disorder!
It is the African fairy who furnishes
The blackberry, and the hairnets in the corners.

Several, discontented godmothers,
In skirts of light, enter the cupboards,
And stay there! the family is out
For no serious reason, and nothing is accomplished.

The bridegroom, has the wind which cheats him
During his absence, here, all the time.
Even water ghosts, wandering*
Come in to move about in the spheres of the alcove.

At night, my love oh! the honeymoon
Will gather their smiles and fill
The sky with a thousand bands of copper.
Then they will have to face the sly rat.

—If no white will o' the wisp comes,
Like a gunshot, after vespers.
—O holy pale Ghosts of Bethlehem,
See that you charm the blue of their windows!

*Even water sprites, with evil intentions

"Is she an almeh? [. . .]"

Is she an almeh? . . . in the first blue hours
Will she destroy herself like fire-flowers . . .
Before the lavish sweep where you smell
The hugely flowering city's breath!

It is too beautiful! it is too beautiful! but it is necessary
—For the sinning Woman and the Corsair's song,
And also because the last masqueraders believed
Still in the night festivities on the pure sea!

Fêtes de la faim

Ma faim, Anne, Anne,
Fuis sur ton âne.

Si j'ai du *goût,* ce n'est guères
Que pour la terre et les pierres
Dinn! dinn! dinn! dinn! Mangeons l'air,
Le roc, les charbons, le fer

Mes faims, tournez. Paissez, faims,
Le pré des sons!
Attirez le gai venin
Des liserons;

Les cailloux qu'un pauvre brise,
Les vieilles pierres d'églises,
Les galets, fils des déluges,
Pains couchés aux vallées grises!

Mes faims, c'est les bouts d'air noir;
L'azur sonneur;
— C'est l'estomac qui me tire.
C'est le malheur.

Sur terre ont paru les feuilles:
Je vais aux chairs de fruit blettes.
Au sein du sillon je cueille
La doucette et la violette.

Ma faim, Anne, Anne!
Fuis sur ton âne.

Feasts of Hunger

My hunger, Anne, Anne,
Flee on your donkey.

If I have any *taste,* it is for hardly
Anything but earth and stones
Dinn! dinn! dinn! dinn! Let us eat air,
Rock, coal, iron

My hungers, turn about. Graze, hungers,
    On the meadow of bran!
Suck the bright poison
    Of the bindweed;

The rocks a poor man breaks,
The old stones of churches,
The pebbles, sons of floods,
Loaves lying in the gray valleys!

My hungers are bits of black air;
    The blue trumpeter;
—It is my stomach pulling me.
    It is woe.

Over the earth leaves have come out:
I am going to the soft flesh of fruit.
In the heart of the furrow I pick
Lamb's-lettuce and violet.

My hunger, Anne, Anne!
Flee on your donkey.

Les corbeaux

Seigneur, quand froide est la prairie,
Quand, dans les hameaux abattus,
Les longs angelus se sont tus . . .
Sur la nature défleurie
Faites s'abattre des grands cieux
Les chers corbeaux délicieux.

Armée étrange aux cris sévères,
Les vents froids attaquent vos nids!
Vous, le long des fleuves jaunis,
Sur les routes aux vieux calvaires,
Sur les fossés et sur les trous
Dispersez-vous, ralliez-vous!

Par milliers, sur les champs de France,
Où dorment des morts d'avant-hier,
Tournoyez, n'est-ce pas, l'hiver,
Pour que chaque passant repense!
Sois donc le crieur du devoir,
O notre funèbre oiseau noir!

Mais, saints du ciel, en haut du chêne,
Mât perdu dans le soir charmé,
Laissez les fauvettes de mai
Pour ceux qu'au fond du bois enchaîne,
Dans l'herbe d'où l'on ne peut fuir,
La défaite sans avenir.

"L'Enfant qui ramassa les balles [. . .]" [25]

L'Enfant qui ramassa les balles, le Pubère
Où circule le sang de l'exil et d'un Père
Illustre entend germer sa vie avec l'espoir
De sa figure et de sa stature et veut voir
Des rideaux autres que ceux du Trône et des Crèches.
Aussi son buste exquis n'aspire pas aux brèches

The Crows

Lord, when the meadow is cold,
When, in the discouraged hamlets,
The long Angeluses are silenced . . .
Over nature stripped of flowers
Have the dear delightful crows
Swoop down from the great skies.

Strange army with solemn cries,
The cold winds assail your nests!
You—along yellowed rivers,
Over roads with old calvaries,
Over ditches and over holes—
Disperse and rally!

By thousands, over the fields of France,
Where sleep the dead of yesterday,
Turn about in the winter, won't you,
So that each passer-by may remember!
Be then the crier of duty,
O our funereal black bird!

But, saints of the sky, at the top of the oak,
A mast lost in the enchanted evening,
Leave alone the May warblers
For those who, in the depths of the wood,
In the grass from which there is no escape,
Are enslaved by a defeat without a future.

"The Child who picked up the balls [. . .]"

The Child who picked up the balls, the Pubescent
In whom flows the blood of exile and of a famous
Father, hears his life rising up with the hope
Of his face and his figure and wants to see
Curtains different from those of the Throne and Cribs.
And also his handsome head does not aspire to the breaches

De l'Avenir!—Il a laissé l'ancien jouet.—
O son doux rêve ô son bel Enghien*! Son œil est
Approfondi par quelque immense solitude;
"Pauvre jeune homme, il a sans doute l'Habitude!"

*parce que: "Enghien chez soi"!

FRANÇOIS COPPÉE
†

Of the Future!—He has left the old toy.—
O his sweet dream o his fine Enghien*! His eye is
Darkened by some tremendous solitude;
"Poor young man, he has doubtless the Habit!"

*that is to say: "Enghien in your own home"!

FRANÇOIS COPPÉE
†

Poèmes non datés (1872–1873?)

Undated poems (1872–1873?)

"Entends comme brame [. . .]"

Entends comme brame
près des acacias
en avril la rame
viride du pois!

Dans sa vapeur nette,
vers Phœbé! tu vois
s'agiter la tête
de saints d'autrefois . . .

Loin des claires meules
des caps, des beaux toits,
ces chers Anciens veulent
ce philtre sournois . . .

Or ni fériale
ni astrale! n'est
la brume qu'exhale
ce nocturne effet.

Néanmoins ils restent,
— Sicile, Allemagne,
dans ce brouillard triste
et blêmi, justement!

Honte

Tant que la lame n'aura
Pas coupé cette cervelle,
Ce paquet blanc vert et gras
A vapeur jamais nouvelle,

(Ah! Lui, devrait couper son
Nez, sa lèvre, ses oreilles,
Son ventre! et faire abandon
De ses jambes! ô merveille!)

"Listen to how [. . .]"

Listen to how the green
shoot of the pea
bellows near the acacias
in April!

In its clear haze,
toward Phoebe! you see
moving about the heads
of saints of former times . . .

Far from the bright stacks
of the headlands, from the handsome roofs,
these good Ancient men want
this sly philter . . .

Gold neither ferial
nor astral! is
the fog exhaled
by this night effect.

Nevertheless they remain,
—Sicily, Germany,
in this sad and pale
fog, precisely!

Shame

As long as the blade has not
Cut off that brain,
That white green fatty package
With its vapor never fresh,

(Ah! He should cut off his
Nose, his lips, his ears,
His belly! and give up
His legs! o miracle!)

Mais, non, vrai, je crois que tant
Que pour sa tête la lame
Que les cailloux pour son flanc
Que pour ses boyaux la flamme

N'auront pas agi, l'enfant
Gêneur, la si sotte bête,
Ne doit cesser un instant
De ruser et d'être traître

Comme un chat des Monts-Rocheux;
D'empuantir toutes sphères!
Qu'à sa mort pourtant, ô mon Dieu!
S'élève quelque prière!

"Le loup criait sous les feuilles [. . .]"

Le loup criait sous les feuilles
En crachant les belles plumes
De son repas de volailles:
Comme lui je me consume.

Les salades, les fruits
N'attendent que la cueillette;
Mais l'araignée de la haie
Ne mange que des violettes.

Que je dorme! que je bouille
Aux autels de Salomon.
Le bouillon court sur la rouille,
Et se mêle au Cédron.

But, no, truly, I believe that as long
As the blade on his head
And the stones on his side
And the flame on his guts

Have not acted, the troublesome
Child, the so stupid animal,
Must not stop for an instant
Cheating and betraying

Like a Rocky Mountain cat;
Making all spheres stink!
Yet at his death, o Lord,
May some prayer rise up!

"The wolf howled under the leaves [. . .]"

The wolf howled under the leaves
As he spat out the fine feathers
Of his meal of fowl:
Like him I consume myself.

Lettuce and fruit
Wait only to be picked;
But the spider of the hedge
Eats only violets.

Let me sleep! Let me boil
At the altars of Solomon.
Boiling water courses over the rust,
And mixes with the Kidron.

Mémoire [26]

I

L'eau claire; comme le sel des larmes d'enfance,
l'assaut au soleil des blancheurs des corps de femmes;
la soie, en foule et de lys pur, des oriflammes
sous les murs dont quelque pucelle eut la défense;

l'ébat des anges;—non . . . le courant d'or en marche,
meut ses bras, noirs, et lourds, et frais surtout, d'herbe. Elle
sombre, avant [27] le Ciel bleu pour ciel-de-lit, appelle
pour rideaux l'ombre de la colline et de l'arche.

II

Eh! l'humide carreau tend ses bouillons limpides!
L'eau meuble d'or pâle et sans fond les couches prêtes.
Les robes vertes et déteintes des fillettes
font les saules, d'où sautent les oiseaux sans brides.

Plus pure qu'un louis, jaune et chaude paupière
le souci d'eau—ta foi conjugale, o l'Epouse!—
au midi prompt, de son terne miroir, jalouse
au ciel gris de chaleur la Sphère rose et chère.

III

Madame se tient trop debout dans la prairie
prochaine où neigent les fils du travail; l'ombrelle
aux doigts; foulant l'ombelle; trop fière pour elle
des enfants lisant dans la verdure fleurie

leur livre de maroquin rouge! Hélas, Lui, comme
mille anges blancs qui se séparent sur la route,
s'éloigne par delà la montagne! Elle, toute
froide, et noire, court! après le départ de l'homme!

IV

Regret des bras épais et jeunes d'herbe pure!
Or des lunes d'avril au cœur du saint lit! Joie
des chantiers riverains à l'abandon, en proie
aux soirs d'août qui faisaient germer ces pourritures.

Memory

I

Clear water; like the salt of childhood tears,
the assault on the sun by the whiteness of women's bodies;
the silk of banners, in masses and of pure lilies,
under the walls a maid once defended;

the play of angels;—no . . . the golden current on its way,
moves its arms, black, and heavy, and above all cool, with grass. She
sinks, before the blue Sky as a canopy, calls up
for curtains the shadow of the hill and the arch.

II

Ah! the wet surface extends its clear broth!
The water fills the prepared beds with pale bottomless gold.
The green faded dresses of girls
make willows, out of which hop unbridled birds.

Purer than a louis, a yellow and warm eyelid
the marsh marigold—your conjugal faith, o Spouse!—
at prompt noon, from its dim mirror, vies
with the dear rose Sphere in the sky grey with heat.

III

Madame stands too straight in the field
nearby where the filaments from the work snow down; the parasol
in her fingers; stepping on the white flower; too proud for her
children reading in the flowering grass

their book of red morocco! Alas, He, like
a thousand white angels separating on the road,
goes off beyond the mountain! She, all
cold and dark, runs! after the departing man!

IV

Longings for the thick young arms of pure grass!
Gold of April moons in the heart of the holy bed! Joy
of abandoned boatyards, a prey
to August nights which made rotting things germinate.

Qu'elle pleure à présent sous les remparts! l'haleine
des peupliers d'en haut est pour la seule brise.
Puis, c'est la nappe, sans reflets, sans source, grise:
un vieux, dragueur, dans sa barque immobile, peine.

V

Jouet de cet œil d'eau morne, Je n'y puis prendre,
oh! canot immobile! oh! bras trop courts! ni l'une
ni l'autre fleur: ni la jaune qui m'importune,
là; ni la bleue, amie à l'eau couleur de cendre.

Ah! la poudre des saules qu'une aile secoue!
Les roses des roseaux dès longtemps dévorées!
Mon canot, toujours fixe; et sa chaîne tirée
au fond de cet œil d'eau sans bords,—à quelle boue?

Michel et Christine

Zut alors si le soleil quitte ces bords!
Fuis, clair déluge! Voici l'ombre des routes.
Dans les saules, dans la vieille cour d'honneur
L'orage d'abord jette ses larges gouttes.

O cent agneaux, de l'idylle soldats blonds,
Des aqueducs, des bruyères amaigries,
Fuyez! plaine, déserts, prairie, horizons
Sont à la toilette rouge de l'orage!

Chien noir, brun pasteur dont le manteau s'engouffre,
Fuyez l'heure des éclairs supérieurs;
Blond troupeau, quand voici nager ombre et soufre,
Tâchez de descendre à des retraits meilleurs.

Mais moi, Seigneur! voici que mon Esprit vole,
Après les cieux glacés de rouge, sous les
Nuages célestes qui courent et volent
Sur cent Solognes longues comme un railway.

Let her weep now under the ramparts! the breath
of the poplars above is the only breeze.
After, there is the surface, without reflection, without springs, gray:
an old man, dredger, in his motionless boat, labors.

v

Toy of this sad eye of water, I cannot pluck,
o! motionless boat! o! arms too short! neither this
nor the other flower: neither the yellow one which bothers me,
there; nor the friendly blue one in the ash-colored water.

Ah! dust of the willows shaken by a wing!
The roses of the reeds devoured long ago!
My boat still stationary; and its chain caught
in the bottom of this rimless eye of water, — in what mud?

Michel and Christine

The devil with it if the sun leaves these shores!
Vanish, bright flood! Here is the shade of the roads.
In the willows, in the old courtyard
The storm at first sheds its big drops.

O hundred lambs, blond soldiers of the idyl,
From aqueducts and scanty heath,
Flee! plains, deserts, fields, horizons
Are in the red wash of the storm!

Black dog, brown shepherd whose cloak puffs in the wind,
Flee the hour of high lightning;
Blond flock, when the dark and brimstone float about,
Try to go down to better retreats.

But, Lord! my Spirit flies away,
After the icy red skies, under the
Heavenly clouds hastening and flying
Over a hundred Solognes as long as a railway.

Voilà mille loups, mille graines sauvages
Qu'emporte, non sans aimer les liserons,
Cette religieuse après-midi d'orage
Sur l'Europe ancienne où cent hordes iront!

Après, le clair de lune! partout la lande,
Rougissant leurs fronts aux cieux noirs, les guerriers
Chevauchent lentement leurs pâles coursiers!
Les cailloux sonnent sous cette fière bande!

—Et verrai-je le bois jaune et le val clair,
L'Epouse aux yeux bleus, l'homme au front rouge, —ô Gaule,
Et le blanc agneau Pascal, à leurs pieds chers,
—Michel et Christine, —et Christ! —fin de l'Idylle.

"O saisons, ô châteaux [. . .]"

O saisons, ô châteaux
Quelle âme est sans défauts?

O saisons, ô châteaux!

J'ai fait la magique étude
Du Bonheur, que nul n'élude.

O vive lui, chaque fois
Que chante son coq Gaulois.

Mais je n'aurai plus d'envie
Il s'est chargé de ma vie.

Ce Charme! il prit âme et corps
Et dispersa tous efforts.

Que comprendre à ma parole?
Il fait qu'elle fuie et vole!

ô saisons ô châteaux

Behold a thousand wolves, a thousand wild seeds
Which, not without loving the bindweed, are carried off
By this religious afternoon of storms.
Over old Europe where a hundred hordes will pass!

Afterward, moonlight! over the heath,
Reddening their faces against the black skies, the warriors
Slowly ride their pale horses!
Pebbles ring under this proud troop!

—And will I see the yellow wood and the bright valley,
The blue-eyed Bride, the man with the red brow,—o Gaul,
And the white Paschal lamb, at their dear feet,
—Michel and Christine,—and Christ!—end of the Idyl.

"O seasons, o castles [. . .]"

O seasons, o castles,
What soul is without flaws?

O seasons, o castles!

I carried out the magic study
Of Happiness, that no one eludes.

Oh! may he live long, each time
His Gallic cock sings.

But I will have no more desires
It has taken charge of my life.

That Charm! it took my soul and body,
And dispersed every effort.

What can be understood from my words?
It makes them escape and fly off!

o seasons, o castles!

"Plates-bandes d'amarantes [. . .]"

Juillet.   Bruxelles
         Boulevart du Régent,[28]

Plates-bandes d'amarantes jusqu'à
L'agréable palais de Jupiter.
—Je sais que c'est Toi, qui, dans ces lieux,
Mêles ton Bleu presque de Sahara!

Puis, comme rose et sapin du soleil
Et liane ont ici leurs jeux enclos,
Cage de la petite veuve! . . .
                         Quelles
Troupes d'oiseaux! o iaio, iaio! . . .

—Calmes maisons, anciennes passions!
Kiosque de la Folle par affection.
Après les fesses des rosiers, balcon
Ombreux et très-bas de la Juliette.

—La Juliette, ça rappelle l'Henriette,
Charmante station du chemin de fer
Au cœur d'un mont comme au fond d'un verger
Où mille diables bleus dansent dans l'air!

Banc vert où chante au paradis d'orage,
Sur la guitare, la blanche Irlandaise.
Puis de la salle à manger guyanaise
Bavardage des enfants et des cages.

Fenêtre du duc qui fais que je pense
Au poison des escargots et du buis
Qui dort ici-bas au soleil.
                         Et puis
C'est trop beau! trop! Gardons notre silence.

—Boulevart sans mouvement ni commerce
Muet, tout drame et toute comédie,
Réunion des scènes infinie,
Je te connais et t'admire en silence.

"Flowerbands of amaranths [. . .]"

July.   Brussels
                  Boulevart du Régent,

Flowerbands of amaranths up to
The delightful palace of Jupiter.
—I know it is You, who, in this place,
Mingle your almost Sahara Blue!

Then, as rose and fir-tree of the sun
And creeper have their game enclosed here,
The little widow's cage! . . .
                        What
Flocks of birds! o iaio, iaio! . . .

—Calm houses, old passions!
Summerhouse of the Woman driven mad by love.
After the buttocks of the rosebushes, the shadowy
And very low balcony of Juliet.

—Juliet reminds us of Henriette,
A charming railway station
At the heart of a mountain as in the depth of an orchard
Where a thousand blue devils dance in the air!

Green bench where in the stormy paradise,
The white Irish girl sings to the guitar.
Then from the Guyanese dining room
Chatter of children and cages.

The duke's window which makes me think
Of the poison of snails and boxwood
Sleeping down here in the sun.
                      And then
It is too beautiful! too beautiful! Let us keep silent.

—Boulevart with no movement and no business
Mute, every drama and every comedy,
An endless joining of scenes,
I know you and admire you in silence.

"Qu'est-ce pour nous, mon cœur [. . .]"

Qu'est-ce pour nous, mon cœur, que les nappes de sang
Et de braise, et mille meurtres, et les longs cris
De rage, sanglots de tout enfer renversant
Tout ordre; et l'Aquilon encor sur les débris

Et toute vengeance? Rien! . . . —Mais si, toute encor,
Nous la voulons! Industriels, princes, sénats,
Périssez! puissance, justice, histoire, à bas!
Ça nous est dû. Le sang! le sang! la flamme d'or!

Tout à la guerre, à la vengeance, à la terreur,
Mon Esprit! Tournons dans la Morsure: Ah! passez,
Républiques de ce monde! Des empereurs,
Des régiments, des colons, des peuples, assez!

Qui remuerait les tourbillons de feu furieux,
Que nous et ceux que nous nous imaginons frères?
A nous! Romanesques amis: ça va nous plaire.
Jamais nous ne travaillerons, ô flots de feux!

Europe, Asie, Amérique, disparaissez.
Notre marche vengeresse a tout occupé,
Cités et campagnes!—Nous serons écrasés!
Les volcans sauteront! et l'océan frappé . . .

Oh! mes amis!—mon cœur, c'est sûr, ils sont des frères:
Noirs inconnus, si nous allions! allons! allons!
O malheur! je me sens frémir, la vielle terre,
Sur moi de plus en plus à vous! la terre fond,

Ce n'est rien! j'y suis! j'y suis toujours.

"What does it matter for us, my heart [. . .]"

What does it matter for us, my heart, the sheets of blood
And coals, and a thousand murders, and the long cries
Of rage, sobs from every hell upsetting
Every order; and the north wind still over the debris

And all vengeance? Nothing! . . . —But yes, still,
We want it! Industrialists, princes, senates,
Perish! power, justice, history, down with you!
That is our due. Blood! blood! golden flame!

All to war, to vengeance and to terror,
My Spirit! Let us turn about in the Biting Jaws: Ah! vanish,
Republics of this world! Of emperors,
Regiments, colonists, peoples, enough!

Who would stir up the whirlwinds of furious fire,
Except ourselves and those we imagine brothers?
It is for us! Romantic friends: it will give us pleasure.
Never shall we work, o waves of fire!

Europe, Asia, America, disappear.
Our avenging march has occupied every place,
City and country!—We will be overcome!
Volcanoes will explode! and the ocean struck . . .

Oh! my friends!—my heart, it is certain, they are brothers:
Dark strangers, what if we left! come! come!
Woe! woe! I feel myself tremble, the old earth,
On me, more and more yours! the earth melts,

It is nothing! I am here! I am still here.

Proses

Prose

Du temps qu'il était écolier

From His Schoolboy Days

« Le soleil était encore chaud [. . .] »

PROLOGUE

Le soleil était encore chaud; cependant il n'éclairait presque plus la terre; comme un flambeau placé devant les voûtes gigantesques ne les éclaire plus que par une faible lueur, ainsi le soleil, flambeau terrestre, s'éteignait en laissant échapper de son corps de feu une dernière et faible lueur, laissant encore cependant voir les feuilles vertes des arbres, les petites fleurs qui se flétrissaient, et le sommet gigantesque des pins, des peupliers et des chênes séculaires. Le vent rafraîchissant, c'est-à-dire une brise fraîche, agitait les feuilles des arbres avec un bruissement à peu près semblable à celui que faisait le bruit des eaux argentées du ruisseau qui coulait à mes pieds. Les fougères courbaient leur front vert devant le vent. Je m'endormis, non sans m'être abreuvé de l'eau du ruisseau.

II

Je rêvai que . . . . j'étais né à Reims l'an 1503. Reims était alors une petite ville ou, pour mieux dire, un bourg cependant renommé à cause de sa belle cathédrale, témoin du sacre du roi Clovis.

Mes parents étaient peu riches, mais très honnêtes: ils n'avaient pour tout bien qu'une petite maison qui leur avait toujours appartenu et qui était en leur possession vingt ans avant que je ne fus encore né en plus quelque mille francs auxquels il faut encore ajouter les petits louis provenant des économies de ma mère.

Mon père était officier* dans les armées du roi. C'était un homme grand, maigre, chevelure noire, barbe, yeux, peau de même couleur. Quoiqu'il n'eût guère, quand j'étais né, que 48 ou cinquante ans, on lui en aurait certainement bien donné 60 ou 58. Il était d'un caractère vif, bouillant, souvent en colère et ne voulant rien souffrir qui lui déplût.

Ma mère était bien différente: femme douce, calme, s'effrayant de peu de chose, et cependant tenant la maison dans un ordre parfait. Elle était si calme que mon père l'amusait comme une jeune demoiselle. J'étais le plus aimé. Mes frères étaient moins vaillants que moi et cependant plus grands. J'aimais peu l'étude, c'est-à-dire d'apprendre à lire, écrire et compter. Mais si c'était pour arranger une maison, cultiver un jardin, faire des commissions, à la bonne heure, je me plaisais à cela.

"The sun was still hot [. . .]"

PROLOGUE

The sun was still hot; nevertheless it barely illuminated the earth any more; like a torch placed in front of gigantic archways only shines light on them by a faint, the sun, earthly torch, went out by letting a last and faint glimmer escape from its body of fire, and yet still leaving enough light to see green leaves on the trees, little withering flowers, and the gigantic tops of the pine trees, poplars and centuries-old oaks. The refreshing wind, that is to say a cool breeze, shook the trees' leaves with a rustling a little like the one that makes the noise of the silvery stream waters which flowed at my feet. The ferns bent their heads at the wind. I slept, not without drinking some stream water first.

II

I dreamt that . . . . I was born in Reims in the year 1503. Back then Reims was a little city or, more precisely, a village nevertheless known for its beautiful cathedral, witness to the coronation of King Clovis.

My parents were not rich, but very honest: their sole material possessions were a small house that had always belonged to them and which had been theirs for twenty years before I was born and then a few thousand francs to which they had to add the few louis that came from the money my mother put aside.

My father was an officer* in the King's army. He was a large man, thin, with black hair, beard, eyes, and skin of the same color. Even though he couldn't have been, when I was born, more than 48 or fifty years old, he certainly looked more like 60 or 58. He was lively, hotheaded, often angry and having no patience for things he didn't like.

My mother was very different: sweet woman, calm, afraid of the slightest thing, and nevertheless keeping house in perfect order. She was so calm that my father entertained her like a young girl. I was loved more than the others. My brothers were less courageous than I and yet they were taller. I didn't care much for studies, that is to say learning how to read, write and count. But if it was for working around the house, gardening, running errands, early, I enjoyed doing that.

Je me rappelle qu'un jour mon père m'avait promis vingt sous, si je lui faisais bien une division; je commençai; mais je ne pus finir. Ah! combien de fois ne m'a-t-il pas promis des sous, des jouets, des friandises, même une fois cinq francs, si je pouvais lui lire quelque chose. Malgré cela, mon père me mit en classe dès que j'eus 10 ans. Pourquoi, me disais-je, apprendre du grec, du latin? je ne le sais. Enfin, on n'a pas besoin de cela. Que m'importe à moi que je sois reçu . . . à quoi cela sert-il d'être reçu, à rien, n'est-ce pas? Si, pourtant; on dit qu'on n'a une place que lorsqu'on est reçu. Moi, je ne veux pas de place; je serai rentier. Quand même on en voudrait une, pourquoi apprendre le latin? Personne ne parle cette langue. Quelquefois j'en vois sur les journaux; mais, dieu merci, je ne serai pas journaliste. Pourquoi apprendre et de l'histoire et de la géographie? On a, il est vrai, besoin de savoir que Paris est en France, mais on ne demande pas à quel degré de latitude. De l'histoire, apprendre la vie de Chinaldon, de Nabopolassar, de Darius, de Cyrus, et d'Alexandre, et de leurs autres compères remarquables par leurs noms diaboliques, est un supplice?
Que m'importe à moi qu'Alexandre ait été célèbre? Que m'importe . . . Que sait-on si les latins ont existé? C'est peut-être quelque langue forgée; et quand même ils auraient existé, qu'ils me laissent rentier et conservent leur langue pour eux. Quel mal leur ai-je fait pour qu'ils me flanquent au supplice? Passons au grec . . . Cette sale langue n'est parlée par personne, personne au monde! . . .
Ah! saperlipotte de saperlipopette! sapristi! moi je serai rentier; il ne fait pas si bon de s'user les culottes sur les bancs, saperlipopettouille!
Pour être décrotteur, gagner la place de décrotteur, il faut passer un examen; car les places qui vous sont accordées sont d'être ou décrotteur, ou porcher, ou bouvier. Dieu merci, je n'en veux pas, moi, saperlipouille! Avec ça des soufflets vous sont accordés pour récompense; on vous appelle animal, ce qui n'est pas vrai, bout d'homme, etc. . .
ah! saperpouillotte! . . .

La suite prochainement.
Arthur.

(*) colonel des cent-gardes

I recall that one day my father had promised me twenty sous, if I did a division problem for him; I began, but I couldn't finish. Ah! how many times did he promise sous, toys, sweets, even five francs once, if I could read him something. Despite that, my father put me in class as soon as I was 10 years old. Why, I asked myself, learn Greek, Latin? I don't know. Honestly, it's not useful. What do I care if I succeed . . . what is it good for, succeeding at that, for nothing, right? No, it is said that there is work for those who succeed. I don't want work; I will be independently wealthy. Even if one wanted to learn one, why study Latin? No one speaks the language. Sometimes I see a little in the papers; but, thank God, I won't be a journalist. Why study both history and geography? True, it is necessary to know that Paris is in France, but no one asks at what degree of latitude. From history, studying the life of Chinaldon, of Nabopolassar, of Darius, of Cyrus, and of Alexander the Great, and of their other buddies who are memorable for their diabolical names, is this a form of torture?

What do I care if Alexander was famous? What do I care . . . What do we really know about if the Latins really existed? It could be some made-up language; and even if they had existed, they should let me be independently wealthy and keep their language to themselves. Whatever harm did I do to them that they should me subject me to such torture? Let's move on to Greek . . . This filthy language is spoken by no one, no one in the world! . . .

Ah! saperlipotte de saperlipopette! sapristi![29] I will be independently wealthy; wearing out the seat of one's pants on benches is not so great, saperlipopettouille!

To be shoeshine, land the job of shoeshine, you have to take an exam; because the jobs that you get are either shoeshine, or swineherd, or cattleman. Thank God, I don't want to, me, saperlipouille! With a job like that your compensation is slaps across the face; you are called animal, which isn't true, little man, etc. . .

ah! saperpouillotte! . . .

To be continued soon.
Arthur.

(*) colonel with the hundred-guards

Invocation à Vénus [30]

Mère des fils d'Enée, ô délices des Dieux,
Délices des mortels, sous les astres des cieux,
Vénus, tu peuples tout: l'onde où court le navire,
Le sol fécond: par toi tout être qui respire
Germe, se dresse, et voit le soleil lumineux!
Tu parais... À l'aspect de ton front radieux
Disparaissent les vents et les sombres nuages:
L'Océan te sourit; fertile en beaux ouvrages,
La Terre étend les fleurs suaves sous tes pieds;
Le jour brille plus pur sous les cieux azurés!
Dès qu'Avril reparaît, et, qu'enflé de jeunesse,
Prêt à porter à tous une douce tendresse,
Le souffle du zéphyr a forcé sa prison,
Le peuple aérien annonce ta saison:
L'oiseau charmé subit ton pouvoir, ô Déesse;
Le sauvage troupeau bondit dans l'herbe épaisse,
Et fend l'onde à la nage, et tout être vivant,
À ta grâce enchaîné, brûle en te poursuivant!
C'est toi qui, par les mers, les torrents, les montagnes,
Les bois peuplés de nids et les vertes campagnes,
Versant au cœur de tous l'amour cher et puissant,
Les portes d'âge en âge à propager leur sang!
Le monde ne connaît, Vénus, que ton empire!
Rien ne pourrait sans toi se lever vers le jour:
Nul n'inspire sans toi, ni ne ressent d'amour!
À ton divin concours dans mon œuvre j'aspire!...

A. RIMBAUD
Externe au collège de Charleville.

Charles d'Orléans à Louis XI [31]

Sire, le temps a laissé son manteau de pluie; les fouriers d'été sont venus:
donnons l'huys au visage à Mérencolie! Vivent les lays et ballades! mora-
lités et joyeulsetés! Que les clercs de la basoche nous montent les folles
soties: allons ouyr la moralité du Bien-Advisé et Mal-advisé, et la Conver-

224

Invocation to Venus

Mother of Aeneas's sons, o godly delights,
Mortal delights, under the stars in the sky,
Venus, you inhabit all: the wave where the ship sails,
The fecund soil: through you every breathing being
Germinates, rises up, and sees the luminous sun!
You appear . . . At the sight of your radiant face
The winds and dark clouds disappear:
The Ocean smiles at you; fertile in works of good,
The Earth scatters suave flowers under your feet;
The day shines more purely under your azure skies!
As soon as April reappears, and, swollen with youth,
Ready to bring to all a sweet tenderness,
The zephyr's wind forced open its prison,
The aerial people announce your season:
The charmed bird submits to your power, o Goddess;
The wild herd leaps in the thick grass,
And splits the wave while swimming, and every living being,
Enchained to your grace, burns in your pursuit!
It is you who, by the seas, the storms, the mountains,
The nested woods and the green countrysides,
Pouring dear and powerful love into the heart of all,
Carry them from age to age to propagate their race!
The world knows, Venus, but your empire!
Without you nothing could arise to meet the day:
Nothing inspires without you, nor feels love!
To your divine support of my work I aspire! . . .

A. RIMBAUD
Day student at the collège de Charleville.

Charles d'Orléans to Louis XI

Sire, the weather has left its coat of rain; the harbingers of summer have
come: let us shut the door in Melancholia's face! Long live lays and ballads!
moral plays and comedies! Let the Basoche clerks show us the silly farces:
let us hear the morality of the Well-Advised and the Poorly-advised, and

sion du clerc Théophilus, et comme alèrent à Rome Saint Père et Saint Pol, et comment furent martirez! Vivent les dames à rebrassés collets, portant atours et broderyes! N'est-ce pas, Sire, qu'il fait bon dire sous les arbres, quand les cieux sont vêtus de bleu, quand le soleil cler luit, les doux rondeaux, les ballades haut et cler chantées? J'ai ung arbre de la plante d'amours, ou Une fois me dites ouy, ma dame, ou Riche amoureux a toujours l'advantage . . . Mais me voilà bien esbaudi, Sire, et vous allez l'être comme moi: Maistre François Villon, le bon folâstre, le gentil raillart qui rima tout cela, engrillonné, nourri d'une miche et d'eau, pleure et se lamente maintenant au fond du Châtelet! Pendu serez! lui a-t-on dit devant notaire: et le pauvre folet tout transi a fait son épitaphe pour lui et ses compagnons: et les gratieux gallans dont vous aimez tant les rimes, s'attendent danser à Montfaulcon, plus becquetés d'oiseaux que dés à coudre, dans la bruine et le soleil!

Oh! Sire, ce n'est pas pour folle plaisance qu'est là Villon! Pauvres housseurs ont assez de peine! Clergeons attendant leur nomination de l'Université, musards, montreurs de synges, joueurs de rebec qui payent leur escot en chansons, chevaucheurs d'escuryes, sires de deux écus, reîtres cachant leur nez en pots d'étain mieux qu'en casques de guerre[32]; tous ces pauvres enfants secs et noirs comme escouvillons, qui ne voient de pain qu'aux fenêtres, que l'hiver emmitoufle d'onglée, ont choisi maistre François pour mère nourricière! Or nécessité fait gens méprendre, et faim saillir le loup du bois: peut-être l'Escollier, ung jour de famine, a-t-il pris des tripes au baquet des bouchers, pour les fricasser à l'Abreuvoir Popin ou à la taverne du Pestel? Peut-être a-t-il pipé une douzaine de pains au boulanger, ou changé à la Pomme-du-Pin un broc d'eau claire pour un broc de vin de Baigneux? Peut-être, un soir de grande galle au Plat-d'Étain, a-t-il rossé le guet à son arrivée; ou les a-t-on surpris, autour de Montfaulcon, dans un souper conquis par noise, avec une dixaine de ribaudes? Ce sont les méfaits de maistre François! Parce qu'il nous montre ung gras chanoine mignonnant avec sa dame en chambre bien nattée, parce qu'il dit que le chappelain n'a cure de confesser, sinon chambrières et dames, et qu'il conseille aux dévotes, par bonne mocque, de parler contemplation sous les courtines, l'escollier fol, si bien riant, si bien chantant, gent comme esmerillon, tremble sous les griffes des grands juges, ces terribles oiseaux noirs que suivent corbeaux et pies! Lui et ses compagnons, pauvres piteux!, accrocheront un nouveau chapelet de pendus aux bras de la forêt: le vent leur fera chandeaux dans le doux feuillage sonore: et vous, Sire, et tous ceux qui aiment le poète ne pourront rire qu'en pleurs en lisant ses joyeuses bal-

the Conversion of Theophilus the cleric, and how Saint Peter and Saint Paul went to Rome, and how they were martyred! Long live women with bordered collars, with decorations and embroideries! Isn't it true, Sire, when the skies are dressed in blue, when the clear sun shines, that it is good to sing out sweet rondos and loud and clear ballads? I have a tree of the plant of love, or One time tell me Yes, my lady, or Rich in love is always better. . . But here I am exhilarated, Sire, and you shall be as well: Master François Villon, the good rebel, the gentle joker who rhymed all of that, handcuffed, nourished by a bit of bread and water, cries and complains now at the bottom of Châtelet! You shall be hanged! he was told before the notary; and the poor troublemaker all scared to death wrote an epitaph for himself and his companions: and the gracious gallants whose rhymes you love so, wait to dance at Montfaucon, more pecked at by birds than thimbles, in drizzle and in sun!

Oh! Sire, Villon is not some crazy entertainment! Poor dusters have enough hardships! Scholars awaiting their nomination to the University, idlers, monkey-hawkers, rebec players who pay their way in song, stable-jockeys, two-bit kings, mercenary soldiers hiding their noses in pewter pots rather than in helmets of armor; all these poor children, dry and black like firebrands, who only see bread through windows, whom winter wraps in numbing cold, chose master François as their wet-nurse! However, necessity makes people err, and hunger drives the wolf from the woods: perhaps the Student, one day of famine, took tripe from the butcher's tubs, to fricassee them at Popin's Watering Hole or at Pestel's tavern? Perhaps he swiped a dozen breads from the baker, or returned to Pomme-du-Pin a bottle of water for a bottle of Baigneux wine? Could it be that, one night's great gala at the Plat d'Étain, he beat up the guards when he arrived; or were they surprised, near Montfaucon, in a noisy dinner with ten or so whores? These are the evildoings of master François! Since he shows us a fat clergyman playing in bed with his lady in a thickly carpeted room, since he said that the chaplain pays no attention to confession, except from chambermaids and ladies, and that he mockingly advises the followers to speak of contemplation behind curtains, the silly student, so cheerful, so full of song, gentle as a merlin, trembles under the claws of the great judges, those terrible black birds that crows and magpies follow! He and his companions, poor pitiful ones! will attach a new garland of hanged men to the arms of the forest: the wind will bring them soup in the soft sound of leaves: and you, Sire, and all those who love the poet will only be able to laugh through tears in reading his joyous ballads: they will think

lades: ils songeront qu'ils ont laissé mourir le gentil clerc qui chantait si follement, et ne pourront chasser Mérencolie!

Pipeur, larron, maistre François est pourtant le meilleur fils du monde: il rit des grasses souppes jacobines: mais il honore ce qu'a honoré l'église de Dieu, et madame la vierge, et la très sainte trinité! Il honore la Cour de Parlement, mère des bons, et soeur des benoitz anges; aux médisants du royaume de France, il veut presque autant de mal qu'aux taverniers qui brouillent le vin. Et dea! Il sait bien qu'il a trop gallé au temps de sa jeunesse folle! L'hiver, les soirs de famine, auprès de la fontaine Maubuay ou dans quelque piscine ruinée, assis à croppetons devant petit feu de chenevottes, qui flambe par instants pour rougir sa face maigre, il songe qu'il aurait maison et couche molle, s'il eût estudié! . . . Souvent, noir et flou comme chevaucheur d'escovettes, il regarde dans les logis par des mortaises « . .—Ô, ces morceaulx savoureux et frians! ces tartes, ces flans, ces grasses gelines dorées!—Je suis plus affamé que Tantalus!—Du rost! Du rost!—Oh! cela sent plus doux qu'ambre et civettes!—Du vin de Beaulne dans de grandes aiguières d'argent!—Haro! la gorge m'ard! . . . Ô, si j'eusse estudié! . . .—Et mes chausses qui tirent la langue, et ma hucque qui ouvre toutes ses fenêtres, et mon feautre en dents de scie!—Si je rencontrais un piteux Alexander, pour que je puisse, bien recueilli, bien débouté, chanter à mon aise comme Orpheus le doux ménétrier! Si je pouvais vivre en honneur une fois avant que de mourir! . . . » Mais, voilà: souper de rondeaux, d'effets de lune sur les vieux toits, d'effets de lanternes sur le sol, c'est très maigre, très maigre; puis passent, en justes cottes, les mignottes villotières qui font chosettes mignardes pour attirer les passants; puis le regret des tavernes flamboyantes, pleines du cri des buveurs heurtant les pots d'étain et souvent les flamberges, du ricanement des ribaudes, et du chant aspre des rebecs mendiants; le regret des vieilles ruelles noires où saillent follement, pour s'embrasser, des étages de maisons et des poutres énormes; où, dans la nuit épaisse, passent, avec des sons de rapières traînées, des rires et des braieries abominables. . . Et l'oiseau rentre au vieux nid: Tout aux tavernes et aux filles! . . .

Oh! Sire, ne pouvoir mettre plumail au vent par ce temps de joie! La corde est bien triste en mai, quand tout chante, quand tout rit, quand le soleil rayonne sur les murs les plus lépreux! Pendus seront, pour une franche repeue! Villon est aux mains de la Cour de Parlement: le corbel n'écoutera pas le petit oiseau! Sire, ce serait vraiment méfait de pendre ces gentils clercs: ces poètes là, voyez-vous, ne sont pas d'ici bas: laissez les vivre leur vie étrange; laissez les avoir froid et faim, laissez les courir, aimer et chanter: ils sont aussi riches que Jacques Cœur, tous ces fols enfants, car

that they left to die the gentle cleric who sang so merrily, and won't shoo away Melancholia!

Drunk, petty thief, master François is nevertheless the best son of the world: he laughs at fat Jacobin soups: but he honors that which the church of God honored, including the Virgin Mother and the very holy trinity! He honors the Court of Parliament, mother of all that's good, and sister of the blessed angels; to the nay-sayers of the kingdom of France, he wishes almost as much evil as to the tavern-keepers who water down their wine. By God! He knows that he played too much during his days of young folly! In winter, nights of famine, around the Maubué fountain or in some dried up pool, squatting before a small hemp fire, which occasionally heated up and reddened his gaunt face, he thinks that he would have had a house and a soft bed, if he had studied! . . . Often, black and hazy like a rider of little brooms, he looks through mortises into houses "Oh, those savory morsels and delicacies! those tarts, those flans, those fat, golden chickens!—I am hungrier than Tantalus!—Some roast! Some roast!—Oh, that smells sweeter than amber and chives!—Some wine from Beaune in great silver pitchers!—Harrow! my throat burns! . . . Oh, if I had studied! . . . —And my leggings which mock, and my cape which opens all their windows, and my ragged overcoat!—If only I met a pitiful Alexander, so that I, well received despite my unsuitable appearance, could sing at ease like Orpheus the sweet fiddler! If only I could live an honorable moment just once before dying! . . ." But, here: meals of rondos, moonlight cast on the old roofs, light from lanterns on the ground, this is weak, very weak; then pass, well dressed, the pretty flirts who do all the cutesy things to attract the passersby; then the nostalgia for the wild taverns, full of the cries of drinkers hurling tin pots and sometimes swords, of the wenches' laughter, and of the bitter song from beggars' rebecs; the nostalgia for the dark old streets where the floors and enormous ceiling beams jut out crazily, as if to kiss each other; where, in the thick night, laughing and abominable yelling in the air, with the sounds of rapiers dragged along. . . And the bird returns to his old nest: Everything for taverns and women!

Oh! Sire, unable to toss my feather to the wind in this time of joy! The hangman's noose is quite sad in May, when everything sings, when everything laughs, when the sun shines bright on even the most leprous walls! They shall be hanged, for a free meal! Villon is in the hands of the Court of Parliament: the crow will not listen to the little bird! Sire, it would truly be wrong to hang these kind clerics: these poets here, you see, they are not of this world: let them live their strange life; let them be cold and hungry, let them run, love and sing: they are as rich as Jacques Cœur, all these silly

ils ont des rimes pleins l'âme, des rimes qui rient et qui pleurent, qui nous font rire ou pleurer: Laissez les vivre: Dieu bénit tous les miséricords, et le monde bénit les poètes.

A. RIMBAUD

Un cœur sous une soutane:
Intimités d'un séminariste

. . . Ô Thimothina Labinette! Aujourd'hui que j'ai revêtu la robe sacrée, je puis rappeler la passion, maintenant refroidie et dormant sous la soutane, qui l'an passé, fit battre mon cœur de jeune homme sous ma capote de séminariste! . . . .

      1er mai 18 . . . .
. . . Voici le printemps. Le plant de vigne de l'abbé . . . bourgeonne dans son pot de terre: l'arbre de la cour a de petites pousses tendres comme des gouttes vertes sur ses branches; l'autre jour, en sortant de l'étude, j'ai vu à la fenêtre du second quelque chose comme le champignon nasal du sup. . . . Les souliers de J . . . sentent un peu; et j'ai remarqué que les élèves sortent fort souvent pour . . . dans la cour; eux qui vivaient à l'étude comme des taupes, rentassés, enfoncés dans leur ventre, tendant leur face rouge vers le poêle, avec une haleine épaisse et chaude comme celle des vaches! Ils restent fort longtemps à l'air, maintenant, et, quand ils reviennent, ricanent, et referment l'isthme de leur pantalon fort minutieusement,—non, je me trompe, fort lentement,—avec des manières, en semblant se complaire, machinalement, à cette opération qui n'a rien en soi que de très futile . . .

      2 mai. Le sup. . . . est descendu hier de sa chambre, et, en fermant les yeux, les mains cachées, craintif et frileux, il a traîné à quatre pas dans la cour ses pantoufles de chanoine! . . .
      Voici mon cœur qui bat la mesure dans ma poitrine, et ma poitrine qui bat contre mon pupitre crasseux! Oh! je déteste maintenant le temps où les élèves étaient comme de grosses brebis suant dans leurs habits sales, et dormaient dans l'asthmosphère empuantie de l'étude, sous la lumière du gaz, dans la chaleur fade du poêle! . . . J'étends mes bras! je soupire, j'étends mes jambes . . . Je sens des choses dans ma tête, oh! des choses! . . .

children, for they have their souls full of rhymes, rhymes which laugh and cry, which make us laugh or cry: Let them live: God blesses all the merciful: and the world blesses the poets.

A. RIMBAUD

A Heart under a Cassock: Confidences of a Seminarian

. . . O Thimothina Labinette! Today when I have put on the sacred robe, I can recall the passion, now grown cold and dormant under the cassock, which last year, made my heart of a young man beat under my seminarian hood! . . . .

May 1, 18 . . . .
. . . It is spring. The vine slip of Abbé . . . is showing buds in its earthen jar; the tree in the courtyard has small shoots as tender as green drops on its branches. The other day, on leaving the study, I saw at the window of the third floor something like the nasal mushroom of the sup. . . . J's shoes are a bit smelly, and I have noticed that the pupils go out very often in order to . . . in the courtyard. The very ones who lived in the study like thick moles, sunken down into their bellies, extending their red faces toward the stove, with their breath as thick and warm as that of cows! They stay a long time outside now, and when they come back, they jeer and button up the fly of their pants very deliberately—no, that is wrong, very slowly—with mannerisms and seem to take pleasure automatically in that operation which in itself is very futile . . .

May 2 . . . The sup. . . . came down from his room yesterday, and, closing his eyes, his hands hidden, timid and shivering, dragged with great effort in the courtyard his canonical slippers! . . .
Now my heart is beating loudly in my chest, and my chest is beating against my filthy table! Oh! now I loathe the time when pupils were like fat sheep sweating in their dirty clothes and slept in the stinking atmosphere of the study, under gaslight, in the flat warmth from the stove! I stretch out my arms! I sigh and stretch out my legs . . . I feel things in my head, oh! things! . . .

. . . 4 mai . . . . . . Tenez, hier, je n'y tenais plus: j'ai étendu, comme l'ange Gabriel, les ailes de mon cœur. Le souffle de l'esprit sacré a parcouru mon être! J'ai pris ma lyre, et j'ai chanté:

Approchez-vous,
Grande Marie!
Mère chérie!
Du doux Jhésus!
Sanctus Christus!
Ô Vierge enceinte,
Ô mère sainte,
Exaucez-nous!

Ô! si vous saviez les effluves mystérieuses qui secouaient mon âme pendant que j'effeuillais cette rose pœtique! Je pris ma cithare, et comme le Psalmiste, j'élevai ma voix innocente et pure dans les célestes altitudes!!! Ô altitudo altitudinum! . . .

. . . .

. . . 7 mai . . . Hélas! ma pœsie a replié ses ailes, mais, comme Galilée, je dirai, accablé par l'outrage et le supplice: Et pourtant elle se meut! — lisez: elles se meuvent! — J'avais commis l'imprudence de laisser tomber la précédente confidence . . . J . . . l'a ramassée, J . . . , le plus féroce des jansénistes, le plus rigoureux des séides du sup. . . . , et l'a portée à son maître, en secret; mais le monstre, pour me faire sombrer sous l'insulte universelle, avait fait passer ma pœsie dans les mains de tous ses amis!

Hier, le Sup. . . . me mande: j'entre dans son appartement, je suis debout devant lui, fort de mon intérieur: Sur son front chauve frissonnait comme un éclair furtif son dernier cheveux roux; ses yeux émergeaient de sa graisse, mais clames, paisibles; son nez, semblable à une batte, était mû par son branle habituel; il chuchotait un *oremus;* il mouilla l'extrémité de son pouce, tourna quelques feuilles de livre, et sortit un petit papier crasseux, plié . . .

Granananande Maarieie! . . .
Mèèèree Chéééérieie!

Il ravalait ma pœsie! il crachait sur ma rose! il faisait le Brid'oison, le Joseph, le bêtiot, pour salir, pour souiller ce chant virginal; Il bégayait et prolongeait chaque syllabe avec un ricanement de haine concentré: et quand

. . . May 4 . . . . . Now, yesterday, I couldn't stand it! Like Angel Gabriel, I spread the wings of my heart. The breath of the Holy Spirit flooded my being! I took my lyre and sang:

Come close,
Great Mary!
Dear Mother
Of sweet Jesus!
Sanctus Christus!
O Virgin with child
O holy mother,
Hear our prayer!

Oh! if you knew the mysterious effluvia which shook my soul while I plucked the petals of this poetic rose! I took my cithara, and like the Psalmist, raised my innocent pure voice to the heavenly regions! O altitudo altitudinum! . . .

. . . .

. . . May 7 . . . Alas! My poetry has folded its wings, but, like Galileo, I will say, crushed by outrage and suffering: And yet it moves!—read: the wings move!—I had been negligent enough to drop the preceding page of confidences . . . J . . . picked it up, J . . . the most ferocious of Jansenists, the most rigorous of the fanatic supporters of the sup. . . . , and took it secretly to his master; but the monster, to make me undergo insults from everyone, had had my poetry shown to all his friends!

Yesterday, the Sup. . . . sent for me. I went into his apartment. I stood in front of him, strong in my convictions: On his bald brow his last red hair trembled like a furtive gleam; his eyes, quiet and calm, stood out from the fat of his face; his nose, like a beetle, was moved by its usual twitching; he was whispering an *oremus;* he wet the end of his thumb, turned a few book pages, and took out a small greasy folded piece of paper . . .

Greaaaat Maaaary! . . .
Deeeear Mooother!

He debased my poetry! he spat on my nose! he played Brid'oison and Joseph the fool in order to dirty and soil that virginal song; He stuttered and prolonged each syllable with a concentrated sneer of hate: and when he reached the fifth line, . . . *Virgin with chil-ild!* he stopped, distorted the

il fut arrivé au cinquième vers, . . . *Vierge enceineinte!* il s'arrêta, contourna sa nasale, et! il éclata! *Vierge enceinte! Vierge enceinte!* il disait cela avec un ton, en fronçant avec un frisson son abdomen prœminent, avec un ton si affreux, qu'une pudique rougeur couvrit mon front, Je tombai à genoux, les bras vers le plafond, et je m'écriai: Ô mon père! . . .

. . . .

—Votre lýýýre! votre cithâre! jeune homme! votre cithâre! des effluves mystérieuses! qui vous secouaient l'âme! J'aurais voulu voir! Jeune âme, je remarque là dedans, dans cette confession impie, quelque chose de mondain, un abandon dangereux, de l'entraînement, enfin!—

Il se tut, fit frissonner de haut en bas son abdomen: puis, solennel:
—Jeune homme, avez-vous la foi? . . .
—Mon père, pourquoi cette parole? Vos lèvres plaisantent-elles? . . . Oui, je crois à tout ce que dit ma mère . . . la Sainte Eglise!
—Mais . . . Vierge enceinte! . . . C'est la conception, ça, jeune homme; c'est la conception! . . .
—Mon père! je crois à la conception! . . .
—Vous avez raison! jeune homme! C'est une chose . . .
. . . Il se tut . . . —Puis: Le jeune J . . . m'a fait un rapport où il constate chez vous un écartement des jambes, de jour en jour plus notoire, dans votre tenue à l'étude; il affirme vous avoir vu vous étendre de tout votre long sous la table, à la façon d'un jeune homme . . . dégingandé. Ce sont des faits auxquels vous n'avez rien à répondre . . . Approchez-vous, à genoux, tout près de moi; je veux vous interroger avec douceur; répondez: vous écartez beaucoup vos jambes, à l'étude?

Puis il me mettait la main sur l'épaule, autour du cou, et ses yeux devenaient clairs, et il me faisait dire des choses sur cet écartement de jambes . . . Tenez, j'aime mieux vous dire que ce fut dégoûtant, moi qui sais ce que cela veut dire, ces scènes là! . . . Ainsi, on m'avait mouchardé, on avait calomnié mon cœur et ma pudeur,—et je ne pouvais rien dire à cela, les rapports, les lettres Anonymes des élèves les uns contre les autres, au Sup. . . . , étant autorisées, et commandées—, et je venais dans cette chambre, me f . . . sous la main de ce gros! . . . Oh! le séminaire! . . .

. . . .

10 mai—Oh!—mes condisciples sont effroyablement méchants et effroyablement Lascifs. À l'étude, ils savent tous, ces profanes, l'histoire de mes vers, et, aussitôt que je tourne la tête je rencontre la face du poussif D . . . qui me chuchote: Et ta cithare, et ta cithare? et ton journal? Puis,

nasal sound, and burst forth: *Virgin with child! Virgin with child!* he said it with an intonation, in contracting his prominent abdomen with a shudder, with so frightful an intonation that a modest redness covered my brow, I dropped to my knees, and raising my arms to the ceiling, cried out: O Father! . . .

. . . .

—Your lyre! your cithara! young man! your cithara! those mysterious effluvia which shook your soul, I wish I might have seen that! My young soul, I notice in that, in that impious confession, something worldly, a dangerous depravity, a temptation, in a word!—

He stopped, twitched his abdomen from top to bottom, and then solemnly continued:

—Young man, have you faith? . . .

—Father, why do you ask this? Are your lips making fun of me? . . . Yes, I believe everything that my mother . . . Holy Church . . . says!

—But . . . Virgin with child! . . . That is conception, young man; that is conception! . . .

—Father! I believe in the conception!

—You are right! Young man! That is a matter . . .

. . . He stopped speaking . . . Then: —Young J . . . made a report to me in which he says he has noticed you spread your legs more and more noticeably each day, when you are in the study. He claims to have seen you stretch out your legs completely, under the table, in the fashion of a young man . . . moving his rump about. These are facts for which we expect no answer . . . Come close to me, on your knees; I want to question you quietly; tell me: do you spread your legs very much in the study?

Then he put his hand on my shoulder, and around my neck, and his eyes grew bright, and he made me say things about the spreading of my legs . . . Why, I prefer to tell you it was disgusting, because I know what such scenes mean! . . . So, they had spied on me, they had slandered my heart and my modesty—and I had no comeback for that: the reports, the Anonymous letters of the pupils one against the other, and those to the Sup. . . . , authorized, and ordered—, and I came to his room and was . . . under the hand of this fat man! . . . Oh! this seminary! . . .

. . . .

May 10 — Oh!—my classmates are terribly wicked and terribly Lascivious! In the study, all these profane fellows know the story of my verses, and whenever I turn my head, I encounter the face of short-winded D . . . ,

l'idiot L . . . reprend: Et ta lyre? et ta cithare? Puis trois ou quatre chuchotent en chœur: Grande Marie . . . Mère Chérie!

Moi, je suis un grand bênêt:—Jésus, je ne me donne pas de coups de pied!—Mais enfin, je ne moucharde pas, je n'écris pas d'ânonymes, et j'ai pour moi ma sainte pœsie et ma pudeur! . . . .

12 mai . . . Ne devinez-vous pas pourquoi je meurs d'amour?
La fleur me dit: salut: l'oiseau me dit bonjour:
Salut: c'est le printemps! c'est l'ange de tendresse?
Ne devinez-vous pas pourquoi je bous d'ivresse?
Ange de ma grand'mère, ange de mon berceau,
Ne devinez vous pas que je deviens oiseau,
Que ma lyre frissonne et que je bats de l'aile
Comme hirondelle? . . .

J'ai fait ces vers là hier, pendant la récréation; je suis entré dans la chapelle, je me suis enfermé dans un confessionnal, et là, ma jeune pœsie a pu palpiter et s'envoler, dans le rêve et le silence, vers les sphères de l'amour. Puis, comme on vient m'enlever mes moindres papiers dans mes poches, la nuit et le jour, j'ai cousu ces vers en bas de mon dernier vêtement, celui qui touche immédiatement à ma peau, et, pendant l'étude, je tire, sous mes habits, ma pœsie sur mon cœur, et je la presse longuement en rêvant . . . .

15 mai.—Les événements se sont bien pressés, depuis ma dernière confidence, et des événements bien solennels, des événements qui doivent influer sur ma vie future et intérieure d'une façon sans doute bien terrible!

Thimothina Labinette, je t'adore!

Thimothina Labinette, je t'adore! je t'adore! laisse moi chanter sur mon luth, comme le divin Psalmiste sur son Psaltérion, comment je t'ai vue, et comment mon cœur a sauté sur le tien pour un éternel amour!

Jeudi, c'était jour de sortie: nous, nous sortons deux heures; je suis sorti: ma mère, dans sa dernière lettre, m'avait dit: ". . . tu iras, mon fils, occuper superficiellement ta sortie chez monsieur Césarin Labinette, un habitué à ton feu père, auquel il faut que tu sois présenté un jour ou l'autre avant ton ordination; . . ."

. . . Je me présentai à monsieur Labinette, qui m'obligea beaucoup en me reléguant, sans mot dire, dans sa cuisine: sa fille, Thimothine, resta seule avec moi, saisit un linge, essuya un gros bol ventru en l'appuyant con-

who whispers to me: And your cithara, your cithara? and your diary? Then idiotic L. . . . continues: And your lyre? and your cithara? Then three or four whisper in chorus: Great Mary . . . Dear Mother!

And I am a booby: —Jesus, I don't kick myself! —But I don't spy on others, I don't write anonymous letters, and I keep for myself my sacred poetry and my modesty! . . . .

> May 12 . . . Can't you guess why I die from love?
> > The flower says to me: greetings: the bird says hello to me:
> > Greetings, it is spring! it is the angel of tenderness?
> > Can't you guess why I burn with ecstasy?
> > Angel of my grandmother, angel of my cradle,
> > Can't you guess I am becoming a bird,
> > That my lyre trembles and I flap my wing
> > > Like a swallow?

I wrote these verses yesterday, during recess. I went into the chapel and closed myself up in a confessional. There in dreams and silence my young poetry could palpitate and fly off toward the skies of love. Then, since they come day and night and rob me of whatever papers are in my pockets, I sewed these verses into the lower part of my underclothing, which is closest to my skin, and during study hour, I pull, under my clothes, my poetry over my heart, and I press it there for a long time as I dream . . .

May 15.—Events happened one after the other, since my last confidence, and very solemn events they were, events which doubtlessly will influence my future spiritual mutual life in a terrible way!

Thimothina Labinette, I worship you!

Thimothina Labinette, I worship you! I worship you! Let me sing on my lute, as did the divine Psalmist on his Psaltery, how I saw you, and how my heart leapt on to yours for an eternal love!

Thursday was our free day. We go out for two hours. I went out. My mother, in her last letter, had said to me: ". . . my son, go fill up superficially your time off at monsieur Césarin Labinette's, a friend of your late father, to whom you must be introduced some day or other before your ordination; . . ."

. . . I presented myself to Monsieur Labinette, who greatly obliged me by sending me without a word into his kitchen. His daughter, Thimothine, who stayed alone with me, grabbed a towel, dried a large round

tre son cœur, et me dit tout à coup, après un long silence: Eh bien, Monsieur Léonard? . . .

Jusque là, confondu de me voir avec cette jeune créature dans la solitude de cette cuisine, j'avais baissé les yeux et invoqué dans mon cœur le nom sacré de Marie: je relevai le front en rougissant, et, devant la beauté de mon interlocutrice, je ne pus que balbutier un faible: Mademoiselle? . . .

Thimothine! tu étais belle! Si j'étais peintre, je reproduirais sur la toile tes traits sacrés sous ce titre: La Vierge au bol! Mais je ne suis que pœte, et ma langue ne peut te célébrer qu'incomplètement . . .

La cuisinière noire, avec ses trous où flamboyaient les braises comme des yeux rouges, laissait échapper, de ses casseroles à minces filets de fumée, une odeur céleste de soupe aux choux et de haricots; et devant elle, aspirant avec ton doux nez l'odeur de ces légumes, regardant ton gros chat avec tes beaux yeux gris, ô Vierge au bol, tu essuyais ton vase! les bandeaux plats et clairs de tes cheveux se collaient pudiquement sur ton front jaune comme le soleil; de tes yeux courait un sillon bleuatre jusqu'au milieu de ta joue, comme à Santa Teresa! ton nez, plein de l'odeur des haricots, soulevait ses narines délicates; un duvet léger, serpentant sur tes lèvres, ne contribuait pas peu à donner une belle énergie à ton visage; et, à ton menton, brillait un beau signe brun où frissonnaient de beaux poils follets: tes cheveux étaient sagement retenus à ton occiput par des épingles; mais une courte mèche s'en échappait . . . Je cherchai vainement tes seins; tu n'en as pas: tu dédaigne ces ornements mondains: ton cœur est tes seins! . . . : quand tu te retournas pour frapper de ton pied large ton chat doré, je vis tes omoplates saillant et soulevant ta robe, et je fus percé d'amour, devant le tortillement gracieux des deux arcs prononcés de tes reins! . . .

Dès ce moment, je t'adorai: j'adorais, non pas tex cheveux, non pas tes omoplates, non pas ton tortillement inférieurement postérieur: ce que j'aime en une femme, en une vierge, c'est la modestie sainte; ce qui me fait bondir d'amour, c'est la pudeur et la piété; c'est ce que j'adorai en toi, jeune bergère! . . .

Ja tâchais de lui faire voir ma passion; et, du reste, mon cœur, mon cœur me trahissait! Je ne répondais que par des paroles entrecoupées à ses interrogations; plusieurs fois, je lui dis Madame, au lieu de Mademoiselle, dans mon trouble! Peu à peu, aux accents magiques de sa voix, je me sentais succomber; enfin je résolus de m'abandonner, de lâcher tout; et, à je ne sais plus quelle question qu'elle m'adressa, je me renversai en arrière sur ma chaise, je mis une main sur mon cœur, de l'autre, je saisis dans ma poche un chapelet dont je laissai passer la croix blanche, et, un œil vers Thimo-

bowl as she held it against her heart, and said to me abruptly, after a long silence: Well, Monsieur Léonard? . . .

Until then, embarrassed at seeing myself with that young creature in the solitude of that kitchen, I had kept my eyes lowered and invoked in my heart the sacred name of Mary. Blushing, I raised my head, and before the beauty of my interlocutress, I could merely stammer a weak: Mademoiselle? . . .

Thimothine! You were beautiful! If I were a painter, I would reproduce on the canvas your sacred features under the title: The Virgin With the Bowl! But I am merely a poet, and my words can only celebrate you incompletely . . .

The black stove, with its holes where embers blazed like red eyes, let escape from its pots in thin streams of smoke the heavenly smell of cabbage-bean soup. In front of it, smelling the vegetables with your sweet nose and watching your big cat with your beautiful gray eyes, o Virgin with the bowl, you wiped your vessel! the flat light braids of your hair modestly adhered to your brow as yellow as the sun. From your eyes ran a bluish wrinkle to the middle of your cheek, just like Saint Teresa! Your nose, full of the smell of beans, opened its delicate nostrils. A slight down arching over your lips contributed a great deal toward the noble energy on your face. On your chin shone a handsome brown spot where beautiful, playful hairs fluttered. Your hair was cleverly held down over your occiput by pins, but one short lock was loose . . . In vain I looked for your breasts. You don't have any. You scorn such worldly ornaments. Your heart is your breasts! . . . : when you turned about to hit with your large foot your yellow cat, I saw your shoulder blades jutting out and raising your dress, and I was pierced with love, as I faced the gracious twisting of the two pronounced arches of your back! . . .

From that moment I worshipped you. I worshipped, not your hair, not your shoulder blades, not the lower twisting of your posterior. What I love in a woman, in a virgin, is holy modesty. What makes me leap with love is modesty and piety. That is what I worshipped in you, young shepherdess! . . .

I tried to show her my passion, and besides, my heart, my heart betrayed me! I answered her questions only with words half-spoken. Several times in my confusion I said to her Madame rather than Mademoiselle! Gradually I felt I was succumbing to the magic sounds of her voice. And finally I decided to give over and abandon everything; and, at some question or other she asked me, I fell backward on my chair, put one hand on

thine, l'autre au ciel, je répondis douloureusement et tendrement, comme un cerf à une biche:

— Oh! oui! Mademoiselle . . . Thimothina!!!!

Miserere! miserere! — Dans mon œil ouvert délicieusement vers le plafond tombe tout à coup une goutte de saumure, dégouttant d'un jambon planant au dessus de moi, et, lorsque, tout rouge de honte, réveillé dans ma passion, je baissai mon front, je m'aperçus que je n'avais dans ma main gauche, au lieu d'un chapelet, qu'un biberon brun; — ma mère me l'avait confié l'an passé pour le donner au petit de la mère chose! — De l'œil que je tendais au plafond découla la saumure amère: — mais, de l'œil qui te regardait, ô Thimothina, une larme coula, larme d'amour, et larme de douleur! . . . .

. . . .

Quelques temps, une heure après, quand Thimothina m'annonça une collation composée de haricots et d'une omelette au lard, tout ému de ses charmes, je répondis à mi-voix:

— J'ai le cœur si plein, voyez-vous, que cela me ruine l'estomac! — Et je me mis à table; Oh! je le sens encore, son cœur avait répondu au mien dans son appel: pendant la courte collation, elle ne mangea pas:

— Ne trouves-tu pas qu'on sent un goût? répétait elle; son père ne comprenait pas; mais mon cœur le comprit: c'était la Rose de David, la Rose de Jessé, la Rose mystique de l'écriture; c'était l'amour!

Elle se leva brusquement, alla dans un coin de la cuisine, et, me montrant la double fleur de ses reins, elle plongea son bras dans un tas informe de bottes, de chaussures diverses, d'où s'élança son gros chat; et jeta tout cela dans un vieux placard vide; puis elle retourna à sa place, et interrogea l'athmosphère, d'une façon inquiète; tout à coup elle fronça le front et s'écria:

— Cela sent encore! . . .

— Oui, cela sent, répondit son père assez bêtement: (il ne pouvait comprendre, lui, le profane!)

Je m'aperçus bien que tout cela n'était dans ma chair vierge que les mouvements intérieurs de sa passion! je l'adorais, et je savourais avec amour l'omelette dorée, et mes mains battaient la mesure avec la fourchette, et, sous la table, mes pieds frissonnaient d'aise dans mes chaussures! . . .

Mais, ce qui me fut un trait de lumière, ce qui me fut comme un gage d'amour éternel, comme un diamant de tendresse de la part de Thimothina, ce fut l'adorable obligeance qu'elle eut, à mon départ, de m'offrir une paire de chaussettes blanches, avec un sourire et ces paroles:

— Voulez-vous cela pour vos pieds, Monsieur Léonard?

. . . .

my heart, and with the other, I took hold of a rosary in my pocket and let its white crucifix stick out. With one eye toward Thimothine and the other toward heaven, I answered sorrowingly and tenderly, like a deer to a roe:

—Oh! yes! Mademoiselle . . . Thimothina!

Miserere! miserere!—Into my eye ecstatically opened toward the ceiling suddenly falls a drop of brine, trickling down from a ham hovering above me, and when, red with shame, and my passion reawakened, I lowered my head, I saw that I had in my left hand, rather than a rosary, a brown feeding-bottle; my mother had entrusted it to me last year to give it to the infant of mother so and so! From the eye which I turned toward the ceiling ran the bitter brine:—but from the eye looking at you, O Thimothina, a tear rolled, a tear of love, a tear of pain! . . . .

. . . .

About an hour later, when Thimothina announced to me a meal of beans and bacon omelet, I answered in a low voice and very moved by her charms:

—You see, my heart is so full that my stomach is ruined by it!—And I sat down at the table. Oh! I can still feel it. Her heart had answered mine in its call: during the short meal she did not eat.

Don't you smell something? she repeated. Her father did not understand, but my heart understood: it was the Rose of David, the Rose of Jesse, the mystic Rose of scripture, it was love!

She rose abruptly and went into a corner of the kitchen. Showing me the double flower of her buttocks, she dug her arms into a formless pile of boots and different kinds of footgear, out of which leapt her big cat. She threw all that in an old empty closet. Then she came back to her seat and sniffed the air, anxiously. Suddenly she knit her brow and cried out:

—That smell is still here! . . .

—Yes, something is smelling, her father answered rather stupidly: (He was so profane, he could not understand!)

I realized that all that was merely the inner upheaval of passion in my virgin body! I worshipped her, and lovingly savored the golden omelet, and my hands beat out time with the fork, and under the table, my feet trembled deliciously in my shoes! . . .

But what was a flash of light for me, a token of eternal love, a diamond of affection from Thimothina, was her adorable kindness in offering me, when I left, a pair of white socks, with a smile and these words:

—Would you like these for your feet, Monsieur Léonard?

. . . .

16 mai—Thimothina! je t'adore, toi et ton père, toi et ton chat: . . . .

Thimothina
{
Vas devotionis,
Rosa mystica,
Turris davidica, ora pro nobis!
Cœli porta,
Stella maris,
}

17 mai. — Que m'importent à présent les bruits du monde et les bruits de l'étude? Que m'importent ceux que la paresse et la langueur courbent à mes côtés? Ce matin, tous les fronts, appesantis par le sommeil, étaient collés aux tables; un ronflement, pareil au cri du clairon du jugement dernier, un ronflement sourd et lent s'élevait de ce vaste Gethsémani. Moi, stoïque, serein, droit et m'élevant au dessus de tous ces morts comme un palmier au dessus des ruines, méprisant les odeurs et les bruits incongrus, je portai ma tête dans ma main, j'écoutais battre mon cœur plein de Thimothina, et mes yeux se plongeaient dans l'azur du ciel, entrevu par la vitre supérieure de la fenêtre! . . .

—18 mai: Merci à l'Esprit Saint qui m'a inspiré ces vers charmants: ces vers, je vais les enchâsser dans mon cœur; et, quand le ciel me donnera de revoir Thimothina, je les lui donnerai, en échange de ses chaussettes! . . .
Je l'ai intitulée *"La Brise"*:

Dans sa retraite de coton
Dort le zéphyr à douce haleine:
Dans son nid de soie et de laine
Dort le zéphyr au gai menton!

Quand le zéphyr lève son aile
Dans sa retraite de coton,
Quand il court où la fleur l'appelle,
Sa douce haleine sent bien bon!

Ô brise quintessenciée!
Ô quintessence de l'amour!
Quand la rosée est essuyée,
Comme ça sent bon dans le jour!

May 16 Thimothina, I worship you, you and your father, you and your cat: . . . .

Thimothina {
Vas devotionis,
Rosa mystica,
Turris davidica, ora pro nobis!
Cœli porta,
Stella maris,

May 17. — Of what consequence is to me now the tumult of the world and the tumult of the study hall? Of what consequence are those whom laziness and languor bend over close beside me? This morning, every head, heavy with sleep, was glued to the table. Snores, like a blast from the trumpet of the Last Judgment, heavy, slow snores rose up from that huge Gethsemane. But I, stoical, calm, upright, rising above all those dead like a palm tree, listened to the beating of my heart full of Thimothina, and my eyes looked into the blue of the sky, which I could make out through the upper pane of the window! . . .

—May 18: I thank the Holy Spirit who inspired these charming verses. I am going to enshrine these verses in my heart; and, when heaven allows me to see Thimothina again, I will give them to her, in exchange for her socks! . . .

I have called it *The Breeze:*

In its cotton retreat
Sleeps the zephyr with sweet breath:
In its nest of silk and wool
Sleeps the zephyr with the gay chin!

When the zephyr raises its wing
In its cotton retreat,
When it hastens to where the flower calls it,
Its sweet breath smells so good!

O quintessential breeze!
O quintessence of love!
When the dew is dried,
How good it smells during the day!

Jesus! Joseph! Jesus! Marie!
C'est comme une aile de condor
Assoupissant celui qui prie!
Ca nous pénètre et nous endort!

. . . .

La fin est trop intérieure et trop suave: je la conserve dans le tabernacle de mon âme. À la prochaine sortie, je lirai cela à ma divine et odorante Thimothina.

Attendons dans le calme et le recueillement.

. . . .

date incertaine.   Attendons!...

. . . .

16 juin!—Seigneur, que votre volonté se fasse: je n'y mettrai aucun obstacle! Si vous voulez détourner de votre serviteur l'amour de Thimothina, libre à vous, sans doute: mais, Seigneur Jesus, n'avez-vous pas aimé vous même, et la lance de l'amour ne vous a-t-elle pas appris à condescendre aux souffrances des malheureux! Priez pour moi!

Oh! j'attendais depuis longtemps cette sortie de deux heures du 15 juin: j'avais contraint mon âme, en lui disant: Tu seras libre ce jour là. le quinze juin, je m'étais peigné mes quelques cheveux modestes, et, usant d'une odorante pommade rose, je les avais collés sur mon front, comme les bandeaux de Thimothina; je m'étais pommadé les sourcils; j'avais minutieusement brossé mes habits noirs, comblé adroitement certains déficits fâcheux dans ma toilette, et je me présentai à la sonnette espérée de monsieur Césarin Labinette. Il arriva, après un assez long temps, la calotte un peu crânement sur l'oreille, une mèche de cheveux raide et fort pommadée lui cinglant la face comme une balafre, une main dans la poche de sa robe de chambre à fleurs jaunes, l'autre sur le loquet . . . Il me jeta un bonjour sec, fronça le nez en jetant un coup d'œil sur mes souliers à cordons noirs, et s'en alla devant moi, les mains dans ses deux poches, ramenant en devant sa robe de chambre, comme fait l'abbé . . . avec sa soutane, et modelant ainsi à mes regards sa partie inférieure.

Je le suivis.

Il traversa la cuisine, et j'entrai après lui dans son salon. Oh! ce salon! je l'ai fixé dans ma mémoire avec des épingles du souvenir! La tapisserie était à fleurs brunes; sur la cheminée, une énorme pendule en bois noir, à colonnes; deux vases bleus avec des roses; sur les murs, une peinture de la

Jesus! Joseph! Jesus! Mary!
It is like a condor's wing
Making the one who prays doze off!
It penetrates us and puts us to sleep!

.   .   .   .

The ending is too personal and too sweet. I will preserve it in my soul's tabernacle. The next day out, I will read it to my divine, sweet-smelling Thimothina.
Let me wait calmly and meditatively.

.   .   .   .

date unknown.   Let us wait! . . .

.   .   .   .

June 16! Lord, may your will be done. I will put no obstacle in its way! If you will to turn away from your servant Thimothina's love, you are doubt-less free to do this. But, Lord Jesus, don't you love also, and didn't the lance of love teach you how to condescend to the suffering of the wretches! Pray for me!
Oh! a long time I waited for the two o'clock freedom of June 15. I had re-strained my soul by saying to it: you will be free that day: June fifteenth, I combed my modestly sparse hair and, using a pink, strong-smelling po-made, I flattened it against my brow, like Thimothina's braids. I put po-made on my eyebrows, carefully brushed my black habit, skilfully made up for certain deficiencies in my clothes, and hopefully rang monsieur Césarin Labinette's doorbell. He came, after a rather long time, with his skullcap jauntily pulled over one ear, a stiff and heavily pomaded lock of hair cut-ting into his face like a scar, one hand in the pocket of his dressing gown covered with yellow flowers, his other hand on the latch . . . He said hello to me curtly, puckered his nose as he looked quickly at my shoes with their black shoelaces, and went off leading the way, his hands in his two pock-ets, pulling his dressing gown in front of him, as Abbé . . . does with his cassock, thus showing me the outline of his buttocks.
   I followed him.
   He went through the kitchen, and after him I went into the parlor. Oh! that parlor! I have attached it to my mind with the pins of memory! The wallpaper had brown flowers. On the mantel-piece a huge black wooden clock with columns; two blue vases with roses; on the walls, a painting of the battle of Inkerman; and a crayon drawing, by a friend of Césarin, rep-

bataille d'Inkerman; et un dessin au crayon, d'un ami de Césarin, représentant un moulin avec sa meule soufflant un petit ruisseau semblable à un crachat, dessin que charbonnent tous ceux qui commencent à dessiner. La pœsie est bien préférable! . . .

Au milieu du salon, une table à tapis vert, autour de laquelle mon cœur ne vit que Thimothina, quoiqu'il s'y trouvât un ami de monsieur Césarin, ancien executeur des œuvres sacristaines dans la paroisse de . . . , et son épouse, madame de Riflandouille, et que monsieur Césarin lui-même vint s'y accouder de nouveau, aussitôt mon entrée.

Je pris une chaise rembourrée, songeant qu'une partie de moi même allait s'appuyer sur une tapisserie faite sans doute par Thimothina, je saluai tout le monde, et, mon chapeau noir posé sur la table, devant moi, comme un rempart, j'écoutai . . .

Je ne parlais pas; mais mon cœur parlait! Les messieurs continuèrent la partie de cartes commencée: je remarquai qu'ils trichaient à qui mieux mieux, et cela me causa une surprise assez douloureuse.—La partie terminée, ces personnes s'assirent en cercle autour de la cheminée vide; j'étais à un des coins, presque caché par l'énorme ami de Césarin, dont la chaise seule me séparait de Thimothina; je fus content en moi-même du peu d'attention que l'on faisait à ma personne; relégué derrière la chaise du sacristain honoraire, je pouvais laisser voir sur mon visage les mouvements de mon cœur sans être remarqué de personne; je me livrai donc à un doux abandon; et je laissai la conversation s'échauffer et s'engager entre ces trois personnes; car Thimothina ne parlait que rarement; elle jetait sur son séminariste des regards d'amour, et, n'osant le regarder en face, elle dirigeait ses yeux clairs vers mes souliers bien cirés! . . . Moi, derrière le gros sacristain, je me livrais à mon cœur.

Je commençai par me pencher du côté de Thimothina, en levant les yeux au ciel. Elle était retournée. Je me relevai, et, la tête baissée vers ma poitrine, je poussai un soupir; elle ne bougea pas;. Je remis mes boutons, je fis aller mes lèvres, je fis un léger signe de croix; elle ne vit rien. Alors, transporté, furieux d'amour, je me baissai très fort vers elle, en tenant mes mains comme à la communion, et en poussant un Ah! . . . prolongé et douloureux; *Miserere!*. tandis que je gesticulais, que je priais, je tombai de ma chaise avec un bruit sourd, et le gros sacristain se retourna en ricanant, et Thimothina dit à son père:

—Tiens, monsieur Léonard qui coule par terre!

Son père ricana! *Miserere!*

Le sacristain me repiqua, rouge de honte et faible d'amour, sur ma chaise rembourrée, et me fit une place. Mais je baissai les yeux, je voulus

resenting a mill with its wheel shooting forth a little stream similar to spit, the picture which all beginners in drawing blacken with their crayons. Poetry is certainly preferable! . . .

In the middle of the parlor, a table with a green cover, at which my heart saw only Thimothina, although a friend of monsieur Césarin was there also, the former sacristan in the parish of . . . , and his wife madame de Riflandouille, and monsieur Césarin himself sat down again as soon as I entered.

I took an upholstered chair, and thought that one part of my body was going to rest on tapestry doubtless made by Thimothina. I greeted everyone and, placing my black hat on the table, in front of me, like a rampart, I listened . . .

I didn't speak: but my heart spoke! The gentlemen continued the card game they had begun. I noticed that each was rivaling the other in cheating, and this both surprised and pained me.—When the game was over, these people sat in a circle around the empty fireplace. I was in one of the corners, almost hidden by Césarin's large friend whose chair alone separated me from Thimothina. Inwardly I was happy over the lack of attention I was paid. Relegated to a position behind the chair of the honorary sacristan, I could allow the feeling of my heart to show on my face without being seen by anyone. I gently gave myself over to my feelings, and let the conversation become animated and engage those three persons. Thimothina spoke but rarely. She cast loving glances at her seminarian, and, not daring to look directly into my eyes, she directed her clear eyes toward my highly polished shoes! . . . Behind the fat sacristan, I gave over to the feelings of my heart.

I began by leaning toward Thimothina and raising my eyes to heaven. She had turned around. I sat up straight again and, lowering my head toward my chest, I uttered a sigh. She did not budge; I took up my beads again. I made my lips move and made a small sign of the cross. She saw nothing. Then, out of my mind and mad with love, I bent way down toward her, clasping my hands as at communion, and uttering a long painful Ah! *Miserere!*. while I gesticulated, prayed, fell from my chair with a heavy thud, and the fat sacristan turned around jeering, and Thimothina said to her father:

—Why, monsieur Léonard is on the floor!

Her father sneered! *Miserere!*

I was red with shame and weak with love. The sacristan put me back on my upholstered chair, and made a place for it. But I closed my eyes and tried to sleep! These people irked me. They did not guess the love that was

dormir! Cette société m'était importune, elle ne devinait pas l'amour qui souffrait là dans l'ombre: je voulus dormir! mais j'entendis la conversation se tourner sur moi! . . .

Je rouvris faiblement les yeux . . .

Césarin et le sacristain fumaient chacun un cigare maigre, avec toutes les mignardises possibles, ce qui rendait leurs personnes effroyablement ridicules; madame la sacristaine, sur le bord de sa chaise, sa poitrine cave penchée en avant, ayant derrière elle tous les flots de sa robe jaune, qui lui bouffaient jusqu'au cou, et épanouissant autour d'elle son unique volant, effeuillait délicieusement une rose: un sourire affreux entr'ouvrait ses lèvres, et montrait à ses gencives maigres deux dents noires, jaunes, comme la faience d'un vieux poele. — Toi, Thimothina, tu étais belle, avec ta collerette blanche, tes yeux baissés, et tes bandeaux plats!

— C'est un jeune homme d'avenir: son présent inaugure son futur, disait en laissant aller un flot de fumée grise le sacristain . . .

— Oh! monsieur Léonard illustrera la robe, nazilla la sacristaine: les deux yeux parurent . . .

Moi je rougissais, à la façon d'un garçon de bien; je vis que les chaises s'éloignaient de moi, et qu'on chuchotait sur mon compte . . .

Thimothina regardait toujours mes souliers; les deux sales dents me menaçaient . . . le sacristain riait ironiquement: j'avais toujours la tête baissée! . . .

— Lamartine est mort . . . dit tout à coup Thimothina.

Chère Thimothine! C'était pour ton adorateur, pour ton pauvre poète Léonard, que tu jetais dans la conversation ce nom de Lamartine; alors, je relevai le front, je sentis que la pensée seule de la pœsie allait refaire une virginité à tous ces profanes, je sentais mes ailes palpiter, et je dis, rayonnant, l'œil sur Thimothina:

— Il avait de beaux fleurons à sa couronne, l'auteur des *Méditations poetiques!*

— Le cŷgne des vers est défunt! dit la sacristaine.

— Oui, mais il a chanté son chant funèbre, repris-je, enthousiasmé.

— Mais, s'écria la sacristaine, Monsieur Léonard est pœte aussi! Sa mère m'a montré l'an passé des essais de sa muse . . .

Je jouai d'audace: — Oh! Madame, je n'ai apporté ni ma lyre ni ma cithare; mais . . .

— Oh votre cithare! vous l'apporterez un autre jour . . .

— mais, ce néanmoins, si cela ne déplait pas à l'honorable, — et je tirai un morceau de papier de ma poche, — je vais vous lire quelques vers . . . Je les dédie à mademoiselle Thimothina.

suffering in those shadows. I tried to sleep, but I heard the conversation going on around me! . . .

I opened my eyes again slightly.

Césarin and the sacristan each smoked a thin cigar, with every possible delicate mannerism, which made them seem terribly ridiculous; the sacristan's wife, on the edge of her chair, her hollow chest leaning forward, spreading behind her the waves of her yellow dress, which enveloped her to her neck, and her one flounce in full bloom around her, was amorously pulling the petals from a rose. A frightful smile half opened her lips and revealed on her thin gums two black yellow teeth like the stoneware of an old stove. — But you, Thimothina, you were beautiful with your white collar, your lowered eyes, and your flat braids!

— He is a young man with a future: his present inaugurates a future, the sacristan said as he exhaled a wave of gray smoke . . .

— Oh! monsieur Léonard will bring honor to the cloth, said his wife with a nasal twang: her two teeth were visible! . . .

I blushed, in the manner of a well brought up boy. I saw that the chairs were moving away from me and that I was the subject of their whispering . . .

Thimothina still looked at my shoes . . . the two dirty teeth threatened . . . the sacristan laughed ironically . . . I still kept my head down! . . .

— Lamartine is dead . . . said Thimothina suddenly.

Dear Thimothina! It was for your worshipper, for your poor poet Léonard, that you cast into the conversation the name of Lamartine. Then, I raised my head, I felt that the thought of poetry alone would restore virginity to these profane people, I felt my wings quiver, and I said joyously, with my eyes on Thimothina:

— The author of the *Méditations poétiques* had beautiful flowers in his crown!

— The swan of poetry is dead! said the sacristan's wife.

— Yes, but he sang his death song, I replied ardently.

— But, said the sacristan's wife, Monsieur Léonard is a poet also! Last year his mother showed me some attempts of his muse . . .

I made bold to say: — Oh! Madame, I brought neither lyre nor cithara, but . . .

— Oh! you must bring your cithara another day . . .

— but, nevertheless, if it is not displeasing to you, — and I pulled a piece of paper out of my pocket, — I will read you a few verses. . . . I dedicate them to mademoiselle Thimothina.

—Oui! oui! jeune homme! très bien! récitez, récitez, mettez vous au bout de la salle . . .

Je me reculai . . . Thimothine regardait mes souliers . . . La sacristaine faisait la Madone; les deux messieurs se penchaient l'un vers l'autre . . . Je rougis, je toussai, et je dis en chantant tendrement

Dans sa retraite de coton
Dort le zéphyr à douce haleine . . .
Dans son nid de soie et de laine
Dort le zéphyr au gai menton.

Toute l'assistance pouffa de rire: les messieurs se penchaient l'un vers l'autre en faisant de grossiers calembourgs; mais ce qui était surtout effroyable, c'était l'air de la sacristaine, qui, l'œil au ciel faisait la mystique, et souriait avec ses dents affreuses! Thimothina, Thimothina crevait de rire! cela me perça d'une atteinte mortelle, Thimothina se tenait les côtes! . . .

—Un doux zéphyr dans du coton, c'est suave, c'est suave! . . . faisait en reniflant, le père Césarin . . . Je crus m'apercevoir de quelque chose . . . mais cet éclat de rire ne dura qu'une seconde: tous essayèrent de reprendre leur sérieux, qui pétait encore de temps en temps . . .

—Continuez, jeune homme, c'est bien, c'est bien!

Quand le zéphyr lève son aile
Dans sa retraite de coton, . . .
Quand il court où la fleur l'appelle,
Sa douce haleine sent bien bon . . .

Cette fois, un gros rire secoua mon auditoire; Thimothina regarda mes souliers: j'avais chaud, mes pieds brûlaient sous son regard, et nageaient dans la sueur; car je disais: ces chaussettes que je porte depuis un mois, c'est un don de son amour, ces regards qu'elle jette sur mes pieds, c'est un témoignage de son amour: elle m'adore!

Et voici que je ne sais quel petit goût me parut sortir de mes souliers: oh! je compris les rires horribles de l'assemblée! Je compris qu'égarée dans cette société méchante, Thimothina Labinette, Thimothina ne pourrait jamais donner un libre cours à sa passion! Je compris qu'il me fallait dévorer, à moi aussi, cet amour douloureux éclos dans mon cœur une après midi de mai, dans une cuisine des Labinette, devant le tortillement postérieur de la Vierge au bol!

—Quatre heures, l'heure de la rentrée, sonnaient à la pendule du sa-

—Yes! yes! young man! very good! do recite them. Go to the other end of the room . . .

I moved there . . . Thimothina looked at my shoes. The sacristan's wife played the Madonna. The two gentlemen leaned toward one another . . . I blushed, coughed, and said, marking the rhythm tenderly

> In its cotton retreat
> Sleeps the zephyr with sweet breath . . .
> In its nest of silk and wool
> Sleeps the zephyr with the gay chin.

Everyone present guffawed. The men leaned toward one another making coarse puns. But what was especially frightful was the behavior of the sacristan's wife who, her eyes raised to heaven, played the mystic and smiled with her ugly teeth! Thimothina, Thimothina roared laughing. This was a mortal blow to me: Thimothina held her sides! . . . —A sweet zephyr in cotton, why that's very pleasant! . . . Père Césarin said as he sniffed the air . . . I thought I saw something, but the laughter lasted only a second. They all tried to recover their seriousness, although it still broke out from time to time . . .

—Continue, young man, it's very good!

> When the zephyr raises its wing
> In its cotton retreat . . .
> When it hastens to where the flower calls it,
> The sweet breath smells so good . . .

This time heavy laughter shook my listeners. Thimothina looked at my shoes. I was warm, my feet burned as she watched them, and they swam in their sweat; for I said to myself: these socks I have been wearing for a month are a gift of her love, the glances she casts on my feet are a token of her love. She worships me!

Then some slight smell seemed to come from my shoes. Oh! I understood the horrible laughter of those people! I understood that Thimothina Labinette, out of place in that wicked group, Thimothina would never be able to give free reign to her passion! I understood that I too would have to abolish that sorrowful love which had been born in my heart one May afternoon, in the Labinettes' kitchen as I watched the wriggling posterior of the Virgin with the bowl!

—Four o'clock, the time for my return, rang from the parlor clock. Be-

lon; éperdu, brûlant d'amour et fou de douleur, je saisis mon chapeau, je m'enfuis en renversant une chaise, je traversai le corridor en murmurant: J'adore Thimothine, et je m'enfuis au Séminaire sans m'arrêter . . .

Les basques de mon habit noir volaient derrière moi, dans le vent, comme des oiseaux sinistres! . . .

. . . .

. . . .

30 Juin. Désormais, je laisse à la muse divine le soin de bercer ma douleur; martyr d'amour à dix-huit ans, et, dans mon affliction, pensant à un autre martyr du sexe qui fait nos joies et nos bonheurs, n'ayant plus celle que j'aime, je vais aimer la foi! Que le Christ, que Marie me pressent sur leur sein: je les suis: je ne suis pas digne de dénouer les cordons des souliers de Jésus; mais ma douleur! mais mon supplice! Moi aussi, à dix huit ans et sept mois, je porte une croix, une couronne d'épines! mais, dans la main, au lieu d'un roseau, j'ai une cithare! Là sera le dictame à ma plaie! . . . . .

. . . .

—Un an après, 1er Aout—Aujourd'hui, on m'a revêtu de la robe sacrée; je vais servir Dieu; j'aurai une cure et une modeste servante dans un riche village. J'ai la foi; je ferai mon salut, et sans être dispendieux, je vivrai comme un bon serviteur de Dieu avec sa servante. Ma mère la sainte église me réchauffera dans son sein: qu'elle soit bénie! que Dieu soit béni!

. . . . . . Quant à cette passion cruellement chérie que je renferme au fond de mon cœur, je saurai la supporter avec constance: sans la raviver précisément, je pourrai m'en rappeler quelquefois le souvenir: ces choses là sont bien douces!—Moi, du reste, j'étais né pour l'amour et pour la foi!—Peut-etre un jour, revenu dans cette ville, aurai-je le bonheur de confesser ma chère Thimothina? . . . Puis, je conserve d'elle un doux souvenir: depuis un an, je n'ai pas défait les chaussettes qu'elle m'a données . . .

Ces chaussettes-là, mon Dieu! je les garderai à mes pieds jusque dans votre saint Paradis! . . .

wildered, burning with love, crazed with grief, I picked up my hat, upset a chair as I fled, crossed the hall as I murmured: I worship Thimothina, and fled to the Seminary without stopping . . .

The tails of my black habit flapped behind me in the wind like sinister birds! . . .

. . . .

. . . .

June 30. From now on, I leave the divine muse the care of consoling my grief. A love martyr at eighteen and, in my affliction, thinking of another martyr of the sex which creates our joy and happiness, no longer having the one I love, I am going to love religion! May Christ, may Mary press me against their hearts. I follow them. I am not worthy to untie the laces of Jesus' shoes; but O my grief! and O my torture! I too at eighteen years, seven months, bear a cross, a crown of thorns, but in my hand, rather than a reed, I have a cithara! That will be the balm for my wound! . . .

. . . .

— One year later, August 1st—Today they put the sacred robe on me. I am going to serve God. I will have a vicarage and a modest servant in a rich village. I have faith. I will accomplish my salvation, and without being a spendthrift, I will live like a good servant of God with his servant. My mother holy Church will keep me warm in her breast. Bless her! bless God! . . . . . . As for that cruelly loved passion I keep in the bottom of my heart, I will be able to bear it with constancy. Without reviving it in any precise way, at times I will recall its memory: such things are indeed sweet!— Moreover, I was born for love and for faith.— One day perhaps, returning to this town, I will have the happiness of hearing Thimothina's confession? . . . And then, I have a sweet remembrance from her: for a year I have not removed the socks she gave me . . .

O God, I will keep these socks on my feet until I reach your blessed Paradise! . . .

Les déserts de l'amour

AVERTISSEMENT

Ces écritures-ci sont d'un jeune, tout jeune *homme,* dont la vie s'est développée n'importe où; sans mère, sans pays, insoucieux de tout ce qu'on connaît, fuyant toute force morale, comme furent déjà plusieurs pitoyables jeunes hommes. Mais, lui, si ennuyé et si troublé, qu'il ne fit que s'amener à la mort comme à une pudeur terrible et fatale. N'ayant pas aimé de femmes, — quoique plein de sang! — il eut son âme et son cœur, toute sa force, élevés en des erreurs étranges et tristes. Des rêves suivants, — ses amours! — qui lui vinrent dans ses lits ou dans les rues, et de leur suite et de leur fin, de douces considérations religieuses se dégagent peut-être se rapellera-t-on le sommeil continu des Mahométans légendaires, — braves pourtant et circoncis! Mais, cette bizarre souffrance possédant une autorité inquiétante, il faut sincèrement désirer que cette Âme, égarée parmi nous tous, et qui veut la mort, ce semble, rencontre en cet instant-là des consolations sérieuses et soit digne!

C'est certes la même campagne. La même maison rustique de mes parents: la salle même où les dessus de portes sont des bergeries roussies, avec des armes et des lions. Au dîner, il y a un salon, avec des bougies et des vins et des boiseries rustiques. La table à manger est très grande. Les servantes! Elles étaient plusieurs, autant que je m'en suis souvenu. — Il y avait là un de mes jeunes amis anciens, prêtre et vêtu en prêtre, maintenant: c'était pour être plus libre. Je me souviens de sa chambre de pourpre, à vitres de papier jaune: et ses livres, cachés, qui avaient trempé dans l'océan!

Moi j'étais abandonné, dans cette maison de campagne sans fin: lisant dans la cuisine, séchant la boue de mes habits devant les hôtes, aux conversations du salon: ému jusqu'à la mort par le murmure du lait du matin et de la nuit du siècle dernier.

J'étais dans une chambre très sombre: que faisais-je? Une servante vint près de moi: je puis dire que c'était un petit chien: quoiqu'elle fût belle, et d'une noblesse maternelle inexprimable pour moi: pure, connue, toute charmante! Elle me pinça le bras.

Je ne me rappelle même plus bien sa figure: ce n'est pas pour me rappeler son bras, dont je roulai la peau dans mes deux doigts: ni sa bouche, que la mienne saisit comme une petite vague désespérée, minant sans fin quelque chose. Je la renversai dans une corbeille de coussins et de toiles de navire, en un coin noir. Je ne me rappelle plus que son pantalon à dentel-

NOTICE

These writings are of a young, a very young *man,* whose life evolved in no particular place; without a mother, without a country, indifferent to everything that is familiar, avoiding all moral pressure, just like several other pitiful young men. But this fellow was so bored and disturbed that he led himself to death as to some terrible and fatal bashfulness. Not having loved women—although passionate!—his soul and his heart and all his strength were trained in strange, sad errors. From the following dreams—his loves!—which came to him in his bed or in the street, and from their continuation and their ending, pleasing religious considerations may be derived perhaps will one remember the continuous sleep of the legendary Mohammedans—brave nonetheless and circumcised! But this unusual suffering possessing a troublesome authority, one must sincerely hope that this Soul, wandering about among us all, and who, it would seem, wants death, will encounter at that moment serious consolations and be worthy!

This is certainly the same countryside. The same rustic house of my parents: the same room where the frieze panels are russet-colored sheepfolds, with arms and lions. At dinner, there is a parlor with candles and wines and ancient wainscoting. The dining table is very large. The servants! there were several, as far as I could remember.—There was one of my former young friends, a priest and dressed as a priest, now: it was in order to be freer. I remember his dark red room, with windowpanes of yellow paper: and his books, hidden, that had soaked in the ocean!

I was abandoned, in this vast country house: reading in the kitchen, drying the mud of my clothes before my hosts, in the parlor conversations: deadly moved by the murmuring of the morning milk and the night of the last century.

I was in a very dark room: what was I doing? A servant girl came near me: I can say she was a little dog: although she was beautiful, of an inexpressible maternal nobility for me: pure, known, totally charming! She pinched my arm.

I do not even remember any longer her face: that is not in order to recall her arm whose flesh I rolled between my two fingers: nor her mouth, which mine seized like a small desperate wave, endlessly excavating something. I took her in a basket of cushions and ship canvases, in a dark corner. I remember only her white lace panties.—Then, O despair!

las blanches. — Puis, ô désespoir! la cloison devint vaguement l'ombre des arbres, et je me suis abîmé sous la tristesse amoureuse de la nuit.

Cette fois, c'est la Femme que j'ai vue dans la Ville, et à qui j'ai parlé et qui me parle.

J'étais dans une chambre, sans lumière. On vint me dire qu'elle était chez moi: et je la vis dans mon lit, toute à moi, sans lumière! Je fus très ému, et beaucoup parce que c'était la maison de famille: aussi une détresse me prit! j'étais en haillons, moi, et elle, mondaine qui se donnait; il lui fallait s'en aller! Une détresse sans nom: je la pris, et la laissai tomber hors du lit, presque nue; et dans ma faiblesse indicible, je tombai sur elle et me traînai avec elle parmi les tapis sans lumière! La lampe de la famille rougissait l'une après l'autre les chambres voisines. Alors, la femme disparut. Je versai plus de larmes que Dieu n'en a jamais pu demander.

Je sortis dans la ville sans fin. O fatigue! Noyé dans la nuit sourde et dans la fuite du bonheur. C'était comme une nuit d'hiver, avec une neige pour étouffer le monde décidément. Les amis auxquels je criais: où reste-t-elle, répondaient faussement. Je fus devant les vitrages de là où elle va tous les soirs: je courais dans un jardin enseveli. On m'a repoussé. Je pleurais énormément, à tout cela. Enfin je suis descendu dans un lieu plein de poussière, et assis sur des charpentes, j'ai laissé finir toutes les larmes de mon corps avec cette nuit. — Et mon épuisement me revenait pourtant toujours.

J'ai compris qu'elle était à sa vie de tous les jours; et que le tour de bonté serait plus long à se reproduire qu'une étoile. Elle n'est pas revenue, et ne reviendra jamais, l'Adorable qui s'était rendue chez moi, — ce que je n'aurais jamais présumé. — Vrai, cette fois j'ai pleuré plus que tous les enfants du monde.

Proses dites "évangeliques"

"À Samarie, plusieurs ont manifesté leur foi en lui [. . .]"

À Samarie, plusieurs ont manifesté leur foi en lui. Il ne les a pas vus. Samarie la parvenue, l'égoïste, plus rigide observatrice de sa loi protestante que Juda des tables antiques. Là la richesse universelle permettait bien peu de discussion éclairée. Le sophisme, esclave et soldat de la routine, y avait déjà après les avoir flattés, égorgé plusieurs prophètes.
C'était un mot sinistre, celui de la femme à la fontaine: "Vous êtes prophète, vous savez ce que j'ai fait."

the partition vaguely became the shadow from the trees, and I sank into the voluptuous sadness of night.

This time, it is the Woman I saw in the City, and to whom I spoke and who speaks to me.

I was in a room without light. Someone came to tell me she was in my room: and I saw her in my bed, completely mine, without light! I was very moved, and especially so because it was the family house. And therefore I was distressed! I was in rags, and she, a worldly woman, was offering herself. She had to leave! A nameless anguish. I took her, and let her fall out of the bed, almost naked. In my unspeakable weakness, I fell on her and dragged myself with her over the rugs without light! The family lamp reddened one after the other the neighboring rooms. Then the woman disappeared. I shed more tears than God would ever have asked for.

I went into the endless city. O weariness! Drowned in the dark night and in this flight from happiness. It was like a winter night with snow precisely to stifle the world. The friends to whom I cried out: where is she, gave me the wrong answer. I went in front of the windows of the place she goes every evening: I ran to a buried garden. I was repulsed. I wept enormously over all that. Finally I went to a place full of dust, and seated on some framework, I gave vent to all the tears of my body with that night. — And yet my exhaustion still returned.

I understood that she was occupied with her daily life, and that the circuit of kindness would be longer in returning than a star. She did not return, and will never return, that Adorable woman who came to my room — something I would never have supposed. — In truth, this time I wept more than all the children in the world.

Prose Called "Evangelical"

"In Samaria, several displayed their faith in him [. . .]"

In Samaria, several displayed their faith in him. He didn't see them. Samaria the upstart, the egoist, more rigid observer of its protestant law than Judea was of antique tablets. There the universal richness allowed for precious little enlightened discussion. Sophism, slave to and soldier of routine, had after already having flattered them, slit the throats of several prophets. It was a dark word, that of the woman at the fountain: "You are a prophet, you know what I did."

Les femmes et les hommes croyaient aux prophètes. Maintenant on croit à l'homme d'état.

À deux pas de la ville étrangère, incapable de la menacer matériellement, s'il était pris comme prophète, puisqu'il s'était montré là si bizarre, qu'aurait-il fait?

Jésus n'a rien pu dire à Samarie.

"L'air léger et charmant de la Galilée [. . .]"

L'air léger et charmant de la Galilée: les habitants le reçurent avec une joie curieuse: ils l'avaient vu, secoué par la sainte colère, fouetter les changeurs et les marchands de gibier du temple. Miracle de la jeunesse pâle et furieuse, croyaient-ils.

Il sentit sa main aux mains chargées de bagues et à la bouche d'un officier. L'officier était à genoux dans la poudre: et sa tête était assez plaisante, quoique à demi chauve.

Les voitures filaient dans les étroites rues [de la ville]; un mouvement, assez fort pour ce bourg; tout semblait devoir être trop content ce soir-là.

Jésus retira sa main: il eut un mouvement d'orgueil enfantin et féminin. "Vous autres, si vous ne voyez [point] des miracles, vous ne croyez point."

Jésus n'avait point encor fait de miracles. Il avait, dans une noce, dans une salle à manger verte et rose, parlé un peu hautement à la Sainte Vierge. Et personne n'avait parlé du vin de Cana à Capharnaum, ni sur le marché, ni sur les quais. Les bourgeois peut-être.

Jésus dit: "Allez, votre fils se porte bien." L'officier s'en alla, comme on porte quelque pharmacie légère, et Jésus continua par les rues moins fréquentées. Des liserons [orange], des bourraches montraient leur lueur magique entre les pavés. Enfin il vit au loin la prairie poussiéreuse, et les boutons d'or et les marguerites demandant grâce au jour.

"Bethsaïda, la piscine [. . .]"

Bethsaïda, la piscine des cinq galeries, était un point d'ennui. Il semblait que ce fût un sinistre lavoir, toujours accablé de la pluie et noir; et les mendiants s'agitant sur les marches intérieures blêmies par ces lueurs d'orages précurseurs des éclairs d'enfer, en plaisantant sur leurs yeux bleus aveugles, sur les linges blancs ou bleus dont s'entouraient leurs moignons. O buanderie militaire, ô bain populaire. L'eau était toujours noire, et nul infirme n'y tombait même en songe.

The women and the men believed in prophets. Now we believe in men of state.

Two steps from the foreign city, unable to threaten it materially, if he had been taken for a prophet, since he had appeared so strange to them there, what would he have done?

Jesus could not to say a word in Samaria.

"The light and charming air of Galilee [. . .]"

The light and charming air of Galilee: the inhabitants received it with a curious joy: they had seen it, shaken by the holy anger, whipping the temple's moneychangers and fowl merchants. Miracle of pale and furious youth, they thought.

He felt his hand in the ring-laden hands and in the mouth of an officer. The officer was on his knees in the dust: and his heat was pleasant enough, although half balding.

The carriages flew through the narrow streets [of the city]; a bustling, rather intense for that town; everything seemed that it should be too right that evening.

Jesus pulled his hand away: it was a movement of childish and feminine pride. "The rest of you, if you do not see miracles [at all], you do not believe at all."

Jesus had not yet performed any miracles. He had, at a wedding, in a green and pink dining room, raised his voice a little to the Holy Virgin. And no one had spoken about the wine of Cana at Capharnaum, neither at the market, nor on the quays. The bourgeois perhaps.

Jesus said: "Go, your son is fine." The officer went away, as if he had taken some mild medicine, and Jesus continued on less traveled roads. Some [orange] bindweeds and some borages revealed their magical glow from between the paving stones. Finally off in the distance he saw the dusty prairie, and the buttercups and daisies asking for the mercy of daylight.

"Bethsaida, the pool [. . .]"

Bethsaida, the pool with five galleries, was a point of boredom. It resembled a sinister washhouse, always harassed with rain, and black; and the beggars stirring about on the lower steps whitened by those glimmers of storms, forerunners of hellish lightning, as they joked about their blind blue eyes, about the white or blue clothes wrapped around their stumps.

C'est là que Jésus fit la première action grave; avec les infâmes infirmes. Il y avait un jour, de février, mars ou avril, où le soleil de 2 h. ap. midi, laissait s'étaler une grande faux de lumière sur l'eau ensevelie, et comme, là-bas, loin derrière les infirmes, j'aurais pu voir tout ce que ce rayon seul éveillait de bourgeons et de cristaux et de vers, dans le reflet, pareil à un ange blanc couché sur le côté, tous les reflets infiniment pâles remuaient.

Alors tous les péchés, fils légers et tenaces du démon, qui pour les cœurs un peu sensibles, rendaient ces hommes plus effrayants que les monstres, voulaient se jeter à cette eau. Les infirmes descendaient, ne raillant plus; mais avec envie.

Les premiers entrés sortaient guéris, disait-on. Non. Les péchés les rejetaient sur les marches, et les forçaient de chercher d'autres postes: car leur Démon ne peut rester qu'aux lieux où l'aumône est sûre.

Jésus entra aussitôt après l'heure de midi. Personne ne lavait ni ne descendait de bêtes. La lumière dans la piscine était jaune comme les dernières feuilles des vignes. Le divin maître se tenait contre une colonne: il regardait les fils du Péché; le démon tirait sa langue en leur langue; et riait au monde.

Le Paralytique se leva, qui était resté couché sur le flanc, [franchit la galerie,] et ce fut d'un pas singulièrement assuré qu'ils le virent franchir la galerie et disparaître dans la ville, les Damnés.

O laundry for the military, O baths for the populace. The water was always black, and no cripple ever fell in, even in his dreams.

That is where Jesus performed his first serious act; with the filthy cripples. There was one day, in February, March, or April, when the two-o'clock sun allowed a large scythe of light to spread out over the buried water; and as, in the distance, far behind the cripples, I could have seen everything that this ray alone awakened in the form of buds, crystals, and worms, in the reflection, similar to a white angel lying on his side, all the infinitely pale reflections stirred.

Then all the sins, slight, tenacious sons of the demon, who for some-what sensitive hearts made these men more terrifying than monsters, tried to hurl themselves into that water. The cripples went down, no longer derisive; but with desire.

It was said that the first who went in came out cured. The sins cast them back on to the steps, and forced them to look for other places: because their Demon can stay only in places where he is sure of getting alms.

Jesus went in immediately after the hour of noon. No one was washing the animals or leading them to the water. The light in the pool was yellow like the last leaves of the vineyard. The divine master was standing against a column: he was watching the sons of Sin. The demon was sticking out his tongue in their tongues; and ridiculing everyone.

The Paralytic, who had remained lying on his side, stood up, [crossed the gallery,] and the Damned saw him cross the gallery with an unusually firm step and disappear into the city.

Une saison en enfer (1873)

A Season in Hell (1873)

Jadis, si je me souviens bien, ma vie était un festin où s'ouvraient tous les cœurs, où tous les vins coulaient.

Un soir, j'ai assis la Beauté sur mes genoux.—Et je l'ai trouvée amère.—Et je l'ai injuriée.

Je me suis armé contre la justice.

Je me suis enfui. O sorcières, ô misère, ô haine, c'est à vous que mon trésor a été confié!

Je parvins à faire s'évanouir dans mon esprit toute l'espérance humaine. Sur toute joie pour l'étrangler j'ai fait le bond sourd de la bête féroce.

J'ai appelé les bourreaux pour, en périssant, mordre la crosse de leurs fusils. J'ai appelé les fléaux, pour m'étouffer avec le sable, le sang. Le malheur a été mon dieu. Je me suis allongé dans la boue. Je me suis séché à l'air du crime. Et j'ai joué de bons tours à la folie.

Et le printemps m'a apporté l'affreux rire de l'idiot.

Or, tout dernièrement m'étant trouvé sur le point de faire le dernier *couac!* j'ai songé à rechercher la clef du festin ancien, où je reprendrais peut-être appétit.

La charité est cette clef.—Cette inspiration prouve que j'ai rêvé!

"Tu resteras hyène, etc. . . . ," se récrie le démon qui me couronna de si aimables pavots. "Gagne la mort avec tous tes appétits, et ton égoïsme et tous les péchés capitaux."

Ah! j'en ai trop pris:—Mais, cher Satan, je vous en conjure, une prunelle moins irritée! et en attendant les quelques petites lâchetés en retard, vous qui aimez dans l'écrivain l'absence des facultés descriptives ou instructives, je vous détache ces quelques hideux feuillets de mon carnet de damné.

Mauvais sang

J'ai de mes ancêtres gaulois l'œil bleu blanc, la cervelle étroite, et la maladresse dans la lutte. Je trouve mon habillement aussi barbare que le leur. Mais je ne beurre pas ma chevelure.

Les Gaulois étaient les écorcheurs de bêtes, les brûleurs d'herbes les plus ineptes de leur temps.

D'eux, j'ai: l'idolâtrie et l'amour du sacrilège;—oh! tous les vices, colère, luxure,—magnifique, la luxure;—surtout mensonge et paresse.

J'ai horreur de tous les métiers. Maîtres et ouvriers, tous paysans, ignobles. La main à plume vaut la main à charrue.—Quel siècle à mains! —Je n'aurai jamais ma main. Après, la domesticité même trop loin. L'honnêteté

Long ago, if my memory serves me, my life was a banquet where every-one's heart was generous, and where all wines flowed.

One evening I pulled Beauty down on my knees.—I found her embit-tered and I cursed her.

I took arms against justice.

I ran away. O witches, poverty, hate—I have confided my treasure to you!

I was able to expel from my mind all human hope. On every form of joy, in order to strangle it, I pounced stealthily like a wild animal.

I called to my executioners to let me bite the ends of their guns, as I died. I called to all plagues to stifle me with sand and blood. Disaster was my god. I stretched out in mud. I dried myself in criminal air. I played clever tricks on insanity.

Spring brought to me an idiot's terrifying laughter.

But recently, on the verge of giving my last *croak,* I thought of look-ing for the key to the ancient banquet where I might possibly recover my appetite.

Charity is the key. This lofty thought proves I dreamt it!

"You will remain a hyena . . . etc.," yells the demon who crowned me with such delightful poppies. "Reach your death with all your lusts, with your selfishness and all the capital sins."

Ah! I've taken too much on. Dear Satan, I beg you, show a less glaring eye! While waiting for the few small acts of cowardice still to come, for you who like in a writer an absence of descriptive or discursive faculties, I tear out these few miserable pages from my notebook of the damned.

Bad Blood

From my Gallic ancestors I have blue-white eyes, a narrow skull, and clum-siness in wrestling. My clothes are as barbaric as theirs. But I don't butter my hair.

The Gauls were flayers of animals and the most inept scorchers of grass in their time.

From them I inherit: idolatry and love of sacrilege,—oh! all vices: anger, lust—lust that is grandiose—and especially deceit and sloth.

I loathe all trades. All of them, foremen and workmen, are base peas-ants. A writer's hand is no better than a ploughman's. What a century of

de la mendicité me navre. Les criminels dégoûtent comme des châtrés: moi, je suis intact, et ça m'est égal.

Mais! qui a fait ma langue perfide tellement, qu'elle ait guidé et sauvegardé jusqu'ici ma paresse? Sans me servir pour vivre même de mon corps, et plus oisif que le crapaud, j'ai vécu partout. Pas une famille d'Europe que je ne connaisse.—J'entends des familles comme la mienne, qui tiennent tout de la déclaration des Droits de l'Homme.—J'ai connu chaque fils de famille!

————

Si j'avais des antécedents à un point quelconque de l'histoire de France! Mais non, rien.

Il m'est bien évident que j'ai toujours été race inférieure. Je ne puis comprendre la révolte. Ma race ne se souleva jamais que pour piller: tels les loups à la bête qu'ils n'ont pas tuée.

Je me rappelle l'histoire de la France fille aînée de l'Eglise. J'aurais fait, manant, le voyage de terre sainte; j'ai dans la tête des routes dans les plaines souabes, des vues de Byzance, des remparts de Solyme; le culte de Marie, l'attendrissement sur le crucifié s'éveillent en moi parmi mille féeries profanes.—Je suis assis, lépreux, sur les pots cassés et les orties, au pied d'un mur rongé par le soleil.—Plus tard, reître, j'aurais bivaqué sous les nuits d'Allemagne.

Ah! encore: je danse le sabbat dans une rouge clairière, avec des vieilles et des enfants.

Je ne me souviens pas plus loin que cette terre-ci et le christianisme. Je n'en finirais. pas de me revoir dans ce passé. Mais toujours seul; sans famille; même, quelle langue parlais-je? Je ne me vois jamais dans les conseils du Christ; ni dans les conseils des Seigneurs,—représentants du Christ.

Qu'étais-je au siècle dernier: je ne me retrouve qu'aujourd'hui. Plus de vagabonds, plus de guerres vagues. La race inférieure a tout couvert—le peuple, comme on dit, la raison; la nation et la science.

Oh! la science! On a tout repris. Pour le corps et pour l'âme,—le viatique,—on a la médecine et la philosophie,—les remèdes de bonnes femmes et les chansons populaires arrangées. Et les divertissements des princes et les jeux qu'ils interdisaient! Géographie, cosmographie, mécanique, chimie! . . .

La science, la nouvelle noblesse! Le progrès. Le monde marche! Pourquoi ne tournerait-il pas?

C'est la vision des nombres. Nous allons à l'*Esprit*. C'est très-certain, c'est oracle, ce que je dis. Je comprends, et ne sachant m'expliquer sans paroles païennes, je voudrais me taire.

hands! I will never possess my hand. After, domesticity even too far off. I am sickened by the uprightness of begging. Because I am intact and don't care, criminals disgust me as if they were castrates.

But who made my tongue so perfidious that it has guided and preserved my sloth up until now? Without making use of my body in any way, and lazier than a toad, I have lived everywhere. I know every family in Europe. I mean families like my own owing everything to the Declaration of the Rights of Man. I have known the eldest son of every family!

If I only had ancestors at some point in the history of France!
No! no antecedent.

It is very clear to me that I have always belonged to an inferior race. I am unable to understand revolt. My race never rose up except to loot: like wolves over the animal they did not kill.

I recall the history of France, eldest daughter of the Church. As a serf I would have made the journey to the Holy Land. In my mind I have roads through the Swabian plains, images of Byzantium and the ramparts of Jerusalem: the cult of Mary, pity for the Crucified One well up in me among a thousand profane visions.—I, a leper, am seated on shards and nettles, at the foot of a sun-devoured wall.—Later, as a mercenary, I would have bivouacked under German nights.

Ah! again! I am dancing the witches' sabbath in a red clearing with old women and children.

I don't remember farther back than this land and Christianity. I shall never have enough of seeing myself in that past. But always alone. Without a family. Yes, what was the language I spoke? I never see myself at the councils of Christ, or at the councils of Lords—representatives of Christ.

What was I in the last century? I recognize myself only today. No more vagabonds, no more vague wars. The inferior race has covered everything: the people, as they say; reason, nation, and science.

Oh! science! Everything has been reconsidered. For the body and the soul—the viaticum—there is medicine and philosophy—old wives' remedies and rearranged popular songs. The diversions of princes and the games they forbade! Geography, cosmography, mechanics, chemistry! . . .

Science, the new nobility! Progress. The world marches on! Why shouldn't it turn back?

It is the vision of numbers. We are moving toward the *Spirit*. I tell you it is very certain, oracular. I understand, and not knowing how to explain this without using pagan words, I prefer to be silent.

Le sang païen revient! L'Esprit est proche, pourquoi Christ ne m'aide-t-il pas, en donnant à mon âme noblesse et liberté. Hélas! l'Evangile a passé! l'Evangile! l'Evangile.

J'attends Dieu avec gourmandise. Je suis de race inférieure de toute éternité.

Me voici sur la plage armoricaine. Que les villes s'allument dans le soir. Ma journée est faite; je quitte l'Europe. L'air marin brûlera mes poumons; les climats perdus me tanneront. Nager, broyer l'herbe, chasser, fumer surtout; boire des liqueurs fortes comme du métal bouillant,—comme faisaient ces chers ancêtres autour des feux.

Je reviendrai, avec des members de fer, la peau sombre, l'œil furieux: sur mon masque, on me jugera d'une race forte. J'aurai de l'or: je serai oisif et brutal. Les femmes soignent ces féroces infirmes retour des pays chauds. Je serai mêlé aux affaires politiques. Sauvé.

Maintenant je suis maudit, j'ai horreur de la patrie. Le meilleur, c'est un sommeil bien ivre, sur la grève.

On ne part pas.—Reprenons les chemins d'ici, chargé de mon vice, le vice qui a poussé ses racines de souffrance à mon côté, dès l'âge de raison— qui monte au ciel, me bat, me renverse, me traîne.

La dernière innocence et la dernière timidité. C'est dit. Ne pas porter au monde mes dégoûts et mes trahisons.

Allons! La marche, le fardeau, le désert, l'ennui et la colère.

A qui me louer? Quelle bête faut-il adorer? Quelle sainte image attaque-t-on? Quels cœurs briserai-je? Quel mensonge dois-je tenir? —Dans quel sang marcher?

Plutôt, se garder de la justice.—La vie dure, l'abrutissement simple,— soulever, le poing desséché, le couvercle du cercueil, s'asseoir, s'étouffer. Ainsi point de vieillesse, ni de dangers: la terreur n'est pas française.

—Ah! je suis tellement délaissé que j'offre à n'importe quelle divine image des élans vers la perfection.

O mon abnégation, ô ma charité merveilleuse! ici-bas, pourtant!

De profundis Domine, suis-je bête!

Encore tout enfant, j'admirais le forçat intraitable sur qui se referme toujours le bagne; je visitais les auberges et les garnis qu'il aurait sacrés par son séjour; je voyais *avec son idée* le ciel bleu et le travail fleuri de la campagne; je flairais sa fatalité dans les villes. Il avait plus de force qu'un saint,

The pagan blood comes back. The Spirit is near. Why doesn't Christ help me by giving my soul nobility and freedom? Alas! the Gospel has gone by! The Gospel! The Gospel.

Gluttonously I am waiting for God. I am of an inferior race from all eternity.

Here I am on the shore of Brittany. Let the cities light up in the evening. My day is done. I am leaving Europe. The sea air will burn my lungs. Lost climates will tan me. I will swim, trample the grass, hunt, and smoke especially. I will drink alcohol as strong as boiling metal—just as my dear ancestors did around their fires.

I will come back with limbs of iron and dark skin and a furious look. By my mask they will think I am from a strong race. I will have gold. I will be lazy and brutal. Women take care of these ferocious invalids, back from the torrid countries. I will go into politics. Saved.

Now I am an outcast. I loathe my country. The best thing for me is a drunken sleep on the beach.

You cannot get away.—Let me follow the roads here again, burdened with my vice, the vice that sank its roots of suffering at my side as early as the age of reason—and that rises to the sky, batters me, knocks me down, drags me after it.

The last innocence and the last shyness. It has been said. I will not take into the world my betrayals and what disgusts me.

Let's move on! The march, the burden, the desert, boredom, anger.

To whom can I sell myself? What beast must I worship? What sacred image are we attacking? Whose heart shall I break? What lie should I tell?—In whose blood shall I walk?

Rather, let me keep away from justice.—The hard life, simple brutishness—let me lift up with a withered fist the coffin's lid, and sit down and be stifled. Thus, no old age, no perils. Terror is not French.

—Ah! I am so alone that I offer to any divine image my desires for perfection.

Oh my abnegation, oh my marvelous charity! here on earth, however! *De profundis Domine,* a fool I am!

While still a child, I admired the obdurate convict on whom the prison gates always close. I visited the inns and furnished rooms he hallowed by his stay. *With his mind* I saw the blue sky and the work of the flowering

plus de bon sens qu'un voyageur—et lui, lui seul! pour témoin de sa gloire et de sa raison.

Sur les routes, par des nuits d'hiver, sans gîte, sans habits, sans pain, une voix étreignait mon cœur gelé: "Faiblesse ou force: te voilà, c'est la force. Tu ne sais ni où tu vas ni pourquoi tu vas, entre partout, réponds à tout. On ne te tuera pas plus que si tu étais cadavre." Au matin j'avais le regard si perdu et la contenance si morte, que ceux que j'ai rencontrés *ne m'ont peut-être pas vu.*

Dans les villes la boue m'apparaissait soudainement rouge et noire, comme une glace quand la lampe circule dans la chambre voisine, comme un trésor dans la forêt! Bonne chance, criais-je, et je voyais une mer de flammes et de fumée au ciel; et, à gauche, à droite, toutes les richesses flambant comme un milliard de tonnerres.

Mais l'orgie et la camaraderie des femmes m'étaient interdites. Pas même un compagnon. Je me voyais devant une foule exaspérée, en face du peloton d'exécution, pleurant du malheur qu'ils n'aient pu comprendre, et pardonnant!—Comme Jeanne d'Arc!—"Prêtres, professeurs, maîtres, vous vous trompez en me livrant à la justice. Je n'ai jamais été de ce peuple-ci; je n'ai jamais été chrétien; je suis de la race qui chantait dans le supplice; je ne comprends pas les lois; je n'ai pas le sens moral, je suis une brute: vous vous trompez . . ."

Oui, j'ai les yeux fermés à votre lumière. Je suis une bête, un nègre. Mais je puis être sauvé. Vous êtes de faux nègres, vous maniaques, féroces, avares. Marchand, tu es nègre; magistrat, tu es nègre; général, tu es nègre; empereur, vieille démangeaison, tu es nègre: tu as bu d'une liqueur non taxée, de la fabrique de Satan.—Ce peuple est inspiré par la fièvre et le cancer. Infirmes et vieillards sont tellement respectables qu'ils demandent à être bouillis.—Le plus malin est de quitter ce continent, où la folie rôde pour pourvoir d'otages ces misérables. J'entre au vrai royaume des enfants de Cham.

Connais-je encore la nature? me connais-je?—*Plus de mots.* J'ensevelis les morts dans mon ventre. Cris, tambour, danse, danse, danse, danse! Je ne vois même pas l'heure où, les blancs débarquant, je tomberai au néant.

Faim, soif, cris, danse, danse, danse, danse!

Les blancs débarquent. Le canon! Il faut se soumettre au baptême, s'habiller, travailler.

J'ai reçu au cœur le coup de la grâce. Ah! je ne l'avais pas prévu!

fields. I sniffed his doom in cities. He had more strength than a saint, more good sense than a traveler—and he, he alone, the witness to his glory and rightness.

On the roads, on winter nights, homeless, without clothes, without bread, a voice clenched my frozen heart: "Weakness or strength: you are there, it is strength. You do not know where you are going, or why you are going. Go in anywhere. Answer everything. They will not kill you any more than if you were a dead body." In the morning I had so vacant a look and so dead an expression, that those I met *perhaps did not see me*.

In cities the mud seemed to me suddenly red and black, like a mirror when the lamp moves about in the next room, like a treasure in the forest! Good luck, I cried, and I saw a sea of flames and smoke in the sky; and on the left and on the right, every kind of richness flaming like a billion thunderbolts.

But debauchery and the companionship of women were denied me. Not even a friend. I saw myself in front of an infuriated mob, facing the firing-squad, weeping over the unhappiness which they would not have been able to understand, and forgiving!—Like Joan of Arc!—"Priests, teachers, masters, you are wrong to turn me over to justice. I have never belonged to this race. I have never been Christian. I am of the breed that sang under torture. I do not understand your laws. I have no moral sense. I am a brute. You are making a mistake."

Yes, my eyes are closed to your light. I am a beast, a savage. But I can be saved. You are false savages, you maniacs, wild and miserly. Merchant, you are a savage. Magistrate, you are a savage. General, you are a savage. Emperor, old mange, you are a savage. You have drunk untaxed liquor from Satan's still.—This people is inspired by fever and cancer. Invalids and old men are so respectable that they *ask* to be boiled.—The shrewdest thing would be to leave this continent, where madness prowls about to provide hostages for these wretches. I am entering upon the true kingdom of the children of Ham.

Do I know nature yet? Do I know myself? —*No more words*. I will bury the dead in my belly. Yells, drum, dance, dance, dance, dance! I can't even see the time when the whites will land and I will fall into the void.

Hunger, thirst, yells, dance, dance, dance, dance!

The white men are landing. The cannon! We will have to be baptized and put on clothes and work.

I have been shot in the heart by grace. Ah! I had not foreseen it!

Je n'ai point fait le mal. Les jours vont m'être légers, le repentir me sera épargné. Je n'aurai pas eu les tourments de l'âme presque morte au bien, où remonte la lumière sévère comme les cierges funéraires. Le sort du fils de famille, cercueil prématuré couvert de limpides larmes. Sans doute la débauche est bête, le vice est bête; il faut jeter la pourriture à l'écart. Mais l'horloge ne sera pas arrivée à ne plus sonner que l'heure de la pure douleur! Vais-je être enlevé comme un enfant, pour jouer au paradis dans l'oubli de tout le malheur!

Vite! est-il d'autres vies? — Le sommeil dans la richesse est impossible. La richesse a toujours été bien public. L'amour divine seul octroie les clefs de la science. Je vois que la nature n'est qu'un spectacle de bonté. Adieu chimères, idéals, erreurs.

Le chant raisonnable des anges s'élève du navire sauveur: c'est l'amour divin. — Deux amours! je puis mourir de l'amour terrestre, mourir de dévouement. J'ai laissé des âmes dont la peine s'accroîtra de mon départ! Vous me choisissez parmi les naufragés; ceux qui restent sont-ils pas mes amis?

Sauvez-les!

La raison m'est née. Le monde est bon. Je bénirai la vie. J'aimerai mes frères. Ce ne sont plus des promesses d'enfance. Ni l'espoir d'échapper à la vieillesse et à la mort. Dieu fait ma force, et je loue Dieu.

————————

L'ennui n'est plus mon amour. Les rages, les débauches, la folie, dont je sais tous les élans et les désastres, — tout mon fardeau est déposé. Apprécions sans vertige l'étendue de mon innocence.

Je ne serais plus capable de demander le réconfort d'une bastonnade. Je ne me crois pas embarqué pour une noce avec Jésus-Christ pour beau-père.

Je ne suis pas prisonnier de ma raison. J'ai dit: Dieu. Je veux la liberté dans le salut: comment la poursuivre? Les goûts frivoles m'ont quitté. Plus besoin de dévouement ni d'amour divin. Je ne regrette pas le siècle des cœurs sensibles. Chacun a sa raison, mépris et charité: je retiens ma place au sommet de cette angélique échelle de bon sens.

Quant au bonheur établi, domestique ou non . . . non, je ne peux pas. Je suis trop dissipé, trop faible. La vie fleurit par le travail, vieille vérité: moi, ma vie n'est pas assez pesante, elle s'envole et flotte loin au-dessus de l'action, ce cher point du monde.

Comme je deviens vieille fille, à manquer du courage d'aimer la mort!

Si Dieu m'accordait le calme céleste, aérien, la prière, — comme les anciens saints. — Les saints! des forts! les anachorètes, des artistes comme il n'en faut plus!

I have not committed evil. My days will weigh light and I shall be spared repentance. I shall not have gone through the torments of the soul, almost dead to good, from which rises a grave flame like funeral tapers. The fate of the family's son, a premature coffin covered with limpid tears. Yes, debauchery is stupid and vice is stupid. What is rotten must be thrown aside. But the clock will not have been able to strike anything save the hour of pure pain. Am I going to be carried off like a child to play in Paradise and forget all misfortune?

Quick! Are there other lives?—To sleep in the midst of wealth is impossible. Wealth has always been public property. Only divine love gives over the keys of science. I see that nature is but a spectacle of goodness. Farewell chimeras, ideals, errors.

The reasonable song of the angels rises up from the rescue ship: it is divine love.—Two loves! I may die of earthly love or die of devotion. I have left behind me souls whose suffering will increase at my going. You choose me from among the shipwrecked. Aren't those who remain my friends?

Save them!

Reason was born in me. The world is good. I will bless life. I will love my brothers. These are not the promises of a child. Nor the hope of escaping old age and death. God is my strength, and I give Him praise.

Boredom is no longer my love. Rage, debauchery, madness—I know all their aspirations and disasters—all my burden is laid aside. Without being dazed, let us evaluate the extent of my innocence.

I would no longer be able to ask for the comfort of a beating. I do not believe I have embarked on a wedding with Jesus Christ as father-in-law.

I am not a prisoner of my reason. I said: God. I want freedom in salvation. How can I pursue it? I have no more taste for frivolity. No more need of devotion or divine love. I do not regret the age of tender hearts. Each is right, scorn and charity. I reserve my place at the top of the angelic ladder of common sense.

As for established happiness, domestic or otherwise . . . no, I cannot. I am too worn out, too weak. Life flowers through work, an old truth. My life does not weigh enough. It soars up and floats far above action, that dear central point of the world.

What an old maid I am becoming, in lacking the courage to love death!

If God would grant me heavenly, aerial calm and prayer—like ancient saints.—Saints are the strong ones! Anchorites are artists not wanted any more!

Farce continuelle! Mon innocence me ferait pleurer. La vie est la farce à mener par tous.

———————

Assez! Voici la punition. — *En marche!*

Ah! les poumons brûlent, les tempes grondent! la nuit roule dans mes yeux, par ce soleil! le cœur . . . les membres . . .

Où va-t-on? au combat? Je suis faible! les autres avancent. Les outils, les armes . . . le temps! . . .

Feu! feu sur moi! Là! ou je me rends. — Lâches! — Je me tue! Je me jette aux pieds des chevaux!

Ah! . . .

— Je m'y habituerai.

Ce serait la vie française, le sentier de l'honneur!

Nuit de l'enfer

J'ai avalé une fameuse gorgée de poison. — Trois fois béni soit le conseil qui m'est arrivé! — Les entrailles me brûlent. La violence du venin tord mes membres, me rend difforme, me terrasse. Je meurs de soif, j'étouffe, je ne puis crier. C'est l'enfer, l'éternelle peine! Voyez comme le feu se relève! Je brûle comme il faut. Va, démon!

J'avais entrevu la conversion au bien et au bonheur, le salut. Puis-je décrire la vision, l'air de l'enfer ne souffre pas les hymnes! C'était des millions de créatures charmantes, un suave concert spirituel, la force et la paix, les nobles ambitions, que sais-je?

Les nobles ambitions!

Et c'est encore la vie! — Si la damnation est éternelle! Un homme qui veut se mutiler est bien damné, n'est-ce pas? Je me crois en enfer, donc j'y suis. C'est l'exécution du catéchisme. Je suis esclave de mon baptême. Parents, vous avez fait mon malheur et vous avez fait le vôtre. Pauvre innocent! — L'enfer ne peut attaquer les païens. — C'est la vie encore! Plus tard, les délices de la damnation seront plus profondes. Un crime, vite, que je tombe au néant, de par la loi humaine.

Tais-toi, mais tais-toi! . . . C'est la honte, le reproche, ici: Satan qui dit que le feu est ignoble, que ma colère est affreusement sotte. — Assez! . . . Des erreurs qu'on me souffle, magies, parfums faux, musiques puériles. — Et dire que je tiens la vérité, que je vois la justice: j'ai un jugement sain et arrêté, je suis prêt pour la perfection . . . Orgueil. — La peau de ma tête se

An endless farce? My innocence would make me weep. Life is the farce we all play.

Enough! Here is the punishment.—*Forward, march!*

Ah! my lungs are burning, my temples pound! I see black in this sunlight! My heart . . . My limbs . . .

Where are we going? Into battle? I am weak! Others are advancing. Tools, weapons . . . time! . . .

Fire! Fire at me! Stop! or I'll surrender.—Cowards!—I'll kill myself! I'll throw myself in front of the horses!

Ah! . . .

—I will get used to it.

That would be the French way of life, the path of honor!

Night in Hell

I swallowed a monstrous mouthful of poison.—Thrice blessed be the idea that came to me! My entrails are burning. The poison's violence twists my limbs, deforms me and hurls me to the ground. I am dying of thirst and am choking. I can't cry out. It is hell and eternal punishment. See how the fire rises up again! I am burning as I should. Come on, demon!

I had caught a glimpse of my conversion to the good and to happiness, salvation. Can I describe the vision? The air of hell does not permit hymns. They were millions of charming creatures, a sweet spiritual concert, strength and peace, noble ambitions, how can I know what?

Noble ambitions!

And this is still life!—And damnation is eternal! A man who tries to mutilate himself is surely damned, isn't he? I think I am in hell, and therefore I am. It is the result of the catechism. I am a slave to my baptism. Parents, you have caused my misfortune and your own. Poor innocent!—Hell has no power over pagans.—This is still life! Later, the delights of damnation will be all the greater. A crime, quick, so I can drop into the void, in accordance with the law of man.

Be quiet! Will you be quiet! . . . Here, there is shame and reprobation. Satan says the fire is contemptible and my anger totally ridiculous.— Enough! . . . They are whispering errors to me, magic, strange perfumes, childish melodies.—And to think that I have truth, that I see justice. My judgment is sound and certain. I am ready for perfection . . . Pride.—My

dessèche. Pitié! Seigneur, j'ai peur. J'ai soif, si soif! Ah! l'enfance, l'herbe, la pluie, le lac sur les pierres, *le clair de lune quand le clocher sonnait douze* . . . le diable est au clocher, à cette heure. Marie! Sainte–Vierge! . . . —Horreur de ma bêtise.

Là-bas, ne sont-ce pas des âmes honnêtes, qui me veulent du bien . . . Venez . . . J'ai un oreiller sur la bouche, elles ne m'entendent pas, ce sont des fantômes. Puis, jamais personne ne pense à autrui. Qu'on n'approche pas. Je sens le roussi, c'est certain.

Les hallucinations sont innombrables. C'est bien ce que j'ai toujours eu: plus de foi en l'histoire, l'oubli des principes. Je m'en tairai: poëtes et visionnaires seraient jaloux. Je suis mille fois le plus riche, soyons avare comme la mer.

Ah ça! l'horloge de la vie s'est arrêtée tout à l'heure. Je ne suis plus au monde.—La théologie est sérieuse, l'enfer est certainement *en bas*—et le ciel en haut.—Extase, cauchemar, sommeil dans un nid de flammes.

Que de malices dans l'attention dans la campagne . . . Satan, Ferdinand, court avec les graines sauvages . . . Jésus marche sur les ronces purpurines, sans les courber . . . Jésus marchait sur les eaux irritées. La lanterne nous le montra debout, blanc et des tresses brunes, au flanc d'une vague d'émeraude . . .

Je vais dévoiler tous les mystères: mystères religieux ou naturels, mort, naissance, avenir, passé, cosmogonie, néant. Je suis maître en fantasmagories.

Écoutez! . . .

J'ai tous les talents!—Il n'y a personne ici et il y a quelqu'un: je ne voudrais pas répandre mon trésor.—Veut-on des chants nègres, des danses de houris? Veut-on que je disparaisse, que je plonge à la recherche de l'*anneau?* Veut-on? Je ferai de l'or, des remèdes.

Fiez-vous donc à moi, la foi soulage, guide, guérit. Tous, venez,— même les petits enfants,—que je vous console, qu'on répande pour vous son cœur,—le cœur merveilleux!—Pauvres hommes, travailleurs! Je ne demande pas de prières; avec votre confiance seulement, je serai heureux.

—Et pensons à moi. Ceci me fait peu regretter le monde. J'ai de la chance de ne pas souffrir plus. Ma vie ne fut que folies douces, c'est regrettable.

Bah! faisons toutes les grimaces imaginables.

Décidément, nous sommes hors du monde. Plus aucun son. Mon tact a disparu. Ah! mon château, ma Saxe, mon bois de saules. Les soirs, les matins, les nuits, les jours . . . Suis-je las!

scalp is drying up. Pity! Lord, I am afraid. I am thirsty, so thirsty! Ah! Childhood, grass, rain, lake water on the pebbles, *moonlight when the bell tower rang twelve* . . . The devil is in the tower at this moment. Mary! Holy Virgin! . . . —The horror of my stupidity.

Back there, are they not good souls who wish me well . . . Come . . . A pillow is over my mouth. They cannot hear me, they are ghosts. Besides, no one ever thinks of anyone else. Let no one come near. I am certain that I smell scorched.

There are countless hallucinations. In truth it is what I have always had: no faith in history and the forgetting of principles. I will not speak of this: poets and visionaries would be jealous. I am the richest a thousand times over. Let me be as avaricious as the ocean.

Why! the clock of life stopped just now. I am no longer in the world.— Theology is serious, hell is certainly *down below*—and heaven up above.— Ecstasy, nightmare, sleep in a nest of flames.

Oh! the malice in attentiveness in the country . . . Satan, Old Nick, runs about with the wild grain . . . Jesus is walking over the scarlet brambles, without bending them down . . . Once Jesus walked on the troubled waters. The lantern showed him to us, standing and pale, with long dark hair, beside an emerald wave . . .

I intend to unveil all mysteries: religious mysteries or those of nature, death, birth, the future, the past, cosmogony, the void. I am a master of hallucinations.

Listen! . . .

I possess every talent!—There is no one here and there is someone. I would not like to expend my treasure.—Do you want primitive songs or houri dances? Do you want me to disappear and dive after the *ring*? Do you? I will make gold and remedies.

Then trust in me. Faith relieves and guides and cures. Come all, even the little children—and I will comfort you, and pour out my heart for you—my marvelous heart!—Poor men, workers! I am not asking for prayers. With your trust alone, I will be happy.

—Just think of me. This hardly makes me miss the world. I am lucky enough not to suffer any more. My life was only sweet madness, and that is too bad.

Bah! Let us make all possible faces.

Decidedly we are out of the world. No more sound. My touch has gone. Ah! my castle, my Saxony, my willow grove. The evenings, mornings nights, days. How tired I am!

Je devrais avoir mon enfer pour la colère, mon enfer pour l'orgueil, — et l'enfer de la caresse; un concert d'enfers.

Je meurs de lassitude. C'est le tombeau, je m'en vais aux vers, horreur de l'horreur! Satan, farceur, tu veux me dissoudre, avec tes charmes. Je réclame. Je réclame! un coup de fourche, une goutte de feu.

Ah! remonter à la vie! Jeter les yeux sur nos difformités. Et ce poison, ce baiser mille fois maudit! Ma faiblesse, la cruauté du monde! Mon Dieu, pitié, cachez-moi, je me tiens trop mal! — Je suis caché et je ne le suis pas.

C'est le feu qui se relève avec son damné.

Délires

I

Vierge folle

L'époux infernal

Écoutons la confession d'un compagnon d'enfer:

"O divin Époux, mon Seigneur, ne refusez pas la confession de la plus triste de vos servantes. Je suis perdue. Je suis soûle. Je suis impure. Quelle vie!

"Pardon, divin Seigneur, pardon! Ah! pardon! Que de larmes! Et que de larmes encore plus tard, j'espère!

"Plus tard, je connaîtrai de divin Époux! Je suis née soumise à Lui. — L'autre peut me battre maintenant!

"A présent, je suis au fond du monde! O mes amies! . . . non, pas mes amies . . . Jamais délires ni tortures semblables . . . Est-ce bête!

"Ah! je souffre, je crie. Je souffre vraiment. Tout pourtant m'est permis, chargée du mépris des plus méprisables cœurs.

"Enfin, faisons cette confidence, quitte à la répéter vingt autres fois, — aussi morne, aussi insignifiante!

"Je suis esclave de l'Époux infernal, celui qui a perdu les vierges folles. C'est bien ce démon-là. Ce n'est pas un spectre, ce n'est pas un fantôme. Mais moi qui ai perdu la sagesse, qui suis damnée et morte au monde, — on ne me tuera pas! — Comment vous le décrire! Je ne sais même plus parler. Je suis en deuil, je pleure, j'ai peur. Un peu de fraîcheur, Seigneur, si vous voulez, si vous voulez bien!

"Je suis veuve . . . — J'étais veuve . . . — mais oui, j'ai été bien sérieuse jadis, et je ne suis pas née pour devenir squelette! . . . — Lui était presque

I should have my hell for anger, for pride—and the hell of caresses; a concert of hells.

I am dying of weariness. It is the tomb. I am going to the worms, horror of horrors! Satan, joker, you are trying to dissolve me with your charms. I object. I object! Give me a poke with your pitchfork! A drop of fire.

Ah! if I could rise again into life! and cast my eyes on our deformities. And that poison, that kiss damned a hundred times! My weakness, the world's cruelty. Pity, God, hide me, I misbehave!—I am hidden and I am not hidden.

The fire rises up again with its damned.

Delirium

I

The Foolish Virgin

The Infernal Bridegroom

Let us listen to the confession of a hell-mate:

"O heavenly Bridegroom, my Lord, do not refuse the confession of the saddest of your servant girls. I am lost and drunk and impure. What a life!

"Forgive me, heavenly Lord, forgive me! Ah! forgive me! So many tears! And so many more tears later, I hope!

"Later, I will know the heavenly Bridegroom! I was born His servant. —The other can beat me now!

"At this moment I am at the bottom of the world, O my friends! . . . no, not my friends . . . Never delirium and torture like this . . . How idiotic!

"Ah! I am suffering and cry out. I really suffer. Yet everything is allowed me, burdened with the scorn of the most contemptible hearts.

"And now let me speak this confidence, even if I repeat it twenty times over—as lugubrious and insignificant as it is now!

"I am the slave of the infernal Bridegroom, who attacked the foolish virgins. He is that demon. He is no ghost, no phantom. But I who have lost all reason, who am damned and dead to the world—will not be killed! How can I describe him to you! I can no longer speak. I am in mourning, weeping and terrified. Lord, cool my brow, if you will, if only you will!

"I am a widow . . . I once was a widow . . . Yes, I was once very serious, and I was not born to become a skeleton! . . . —He was almost a child . . .

un enfant . . . Ses délicatesses mystérieuses m'avaient séduite. J'ai oublié tout mon devoir humain pour le suivre. Quelle vie! La vraie vie est absente. Nous ne sommes pas au monde. Je vais où il va, il le faut. Et souvent il s'emporte contre moi, *moi, la pauvre âme*. Le Démon!—C'est un Démon, vous savez, *ce n'est pas un homme*.

"Il dit: 'Je n'aime pas les femmes. L'amour est à réinventer, on le sait. Elles ne peuvent plus que vouloir une position assurée. La position gagnée, cœur et beauté sont mis de côté: il ne reste que froid dédain, l'aliment du mariage, aujourd'hui. Ou bien je vois des femmes, avec les signes du bonheur, dont, moi, j'aurai pu faire de bonnes camarades, dévorées tout d'abord par des brutes sensibles comme des brutes sensibles comme des bûchers . . .'

"Je l'écoute faisant de l'infamie une gloire, de la cruauté un charme. 'Je suis de race lointaine: mes pères étaient Scandinaves: ils se perçaient les côtes, buvaient leur sang.—Je me ferai des entailles partout le corps, je me tatouerai, je veux devenir hideux comme un Mongol: tu verras, je hurlerai dans les rues: Je veux devenir bien fou de rage. Ne me montre jamais de bijoux, je ramperais et me tordrais sur le tapis. Ma richesse, je la voudrais tachée de sang partout. Jamais je ne travaillerai . . .' Plusieurs nuits, son démon me saisissant, nous nous roulions, je luttais avec lui!—Les nuits, souvent, ivre, il se poste dans des rues ou dans des maisons, pour m'épouvanter mortellement.—'On me coupera vraiment le cou: ce sera dégoûtant.' Oh! ces jours où il veut marcher avec l'air de crime!

"Parfois il parle, en une façon de patois attendri, de la mort qui fait repentir, des malheureux qui existent certainement, des travaux pénibles, des départs qui déchirent les cœurs. Dans les bouges où nous nous enivrions, il pleurait en considérant ceux qui nous entouraient, bétail de la misère. Il relevait les ivrognes dans les rues noires. Il avait pitié d'une mère méchante pour les petits enfants.—Il s'en allait avec des gentillesses de petite fille au catéchisme.—Il feignait d'être éclairé sur tout, commerce, art, médecine.—Je le suivais, il le faut!

"Je voyais tout le décor dont, en esprit, il s'entourait; vêtements, draps, meubles: je lui prêtais des armes, une autre figure. Je voyais tout ce qui le touchait, comme il aurait voulu le créer pour lui. Quand il me semblait avoir l'esprit inerte, je le suivais, moi, dans des actions étranges et compliquées, loin, bonnes ou mauvaises: j'étais sûre de ne jamais entrer dans son monde. A côté de son cher corps endormi, que d'heures des nuits j'ai veillé, cherchant pourquoi il voulait tant s'évader de la réalité. Jamais homme n'eut pareil vœu. Je reconnaissais,—sans craindre pour lui,— qu'il pouvait être un sérieux danger dans la société.—Il a peut-être des

His mysteriously delicate feelings had seduced me. I forgot all my human duty to follow him. What a life! Real life is absent. We are not in the world. I go where he goes. I have to. And often he flies into a rage at *me, poor me.* The Demon! He is a demon, you know. *He is not a man.*

"He said: 'I do not like women: Love is to be reinvented, that is clear. All they can want now is a secure position. When security is reached, their hearts and their beauty are set aside. Only cold scorn is left, the food of marriage today, Or I see women, with signs of happiness, whom I could have made close comrades, devoured first by brutes as sensitive as a log of wood . . . !'

"I listen to him making infamy into glory, cruelty into charm. 'I am from a distant race: my ancestors were Scandinavians; they used to pierce their sides and drink their own blood.—I will make gashes on my entire body and tattoo it. I want to be as hideous as a Mongol. You will see, I will howl in the streets. I want to become mad with rage. Never show me jewels, for I would grovel and writhe on the floor. I would like my wealth spattered with blood all over. I shall never work . . .' On several nights, his demon seizing me, we rolled on the ground and I fought with him!—Often at night, drunk, he lay in wait in the streets or in houses, to frighten me to death.—'They will really cut my throat; it will be revolting!' Oh! those days when he tries to walk about with a criminal air!

"Sometimes he talks, in a kind of tender patois, about death bringing repentance, about the wretches who must exist, about painful work, and heartbreaking farewells. In the dives where we used to get drunk, he would weep as he watched the herd of poverty-stricken people about us. He used to lift up drunkards in the dark streets. He felt the pity of a bad mother for small children.—He used to go off with the charm of a little girl going to catechism class.—He pretended to be informed about everything, business, art, medicine.—I used to follow him. I had to!

"I saw the entire setting with which he surrounded himself in his mind; clothes, sheets, furniture: I lent him weapons, and another face. I saw everything that affected him as he would like to have created it for himself. When his mind seemed inactive to me, I followed him in strange, complicated actions, very far, good or bad. I was sure that I would never enter his world. How many night hours have I stayed awake beside his dear sleeping body, wondering why he wanted so much to escape from reality. Never did a man have such a wish. I recognized—without fearing for him—that he could be a serious danger for society.—Does he have perhaps secrets for *changing life*? No, he is only looking for them, I told myself. In a word, his charity is bewitched, and I am its prisoner. No other soul

secrets pour *changer la vie*? Non, il ne fait qu'en chercher, me répliquais-je. Enfin sa charité est ensorcelée, et j'en suis la prisonnière. Aucune autre âme n'aurait assez de force,—force de désespoir!—pour la supporter,—pour être protégée et aimée par lui. D'ailleurs, je ne me le figurais pas avec une autre âme: on voit son Ange, jamais l'Ange d'un autre,—je crois. J'étais dans son âme comme dans un palais qu'on a vidé pour ne pas voir une personne si peu noble que vous: voilà tout. Hélas! je dépendais bien de lui. Mais que voulait-il avec mon existence terne et lâche? Il ne me rendait pas meilleure, s'il ne me faisait pas mourir! Tristement dépitée, je lui dis quelquefois: 'Je te comprends.' Il haussait les épaules.

"Ainsi, mon chagrin se renouvelant sans cesse, et me trouvant plus égarée à mes yeux,—comme à tous les yeux qui auraient voulu me fixer, si je n'eusse été condamnée pour jamais à l'oubli de tous!—j'avais de plus en plus faim de sa bonté. Avec ses baisers et ses étreintes amies, c'était bien un ciel, un sombre ciel, où j'entrais, et où j'aurais voulu être laissée, pauvre, sourde, muette, aveugle. Déjà j'en prenais l'habitude. Je nous voyais comme deux bons enfants, libres de se promener dans le Paradis de tristesse. Nous nous accordions. Bien émus, nous travaillions ensemble. Mais, après une pénétrante caresse, il disait: 'Comme ça te paraîtra drôle, quand je n'y serai plus, ce par quoi tu as passé. Quand tu n'auras plus mes bras sous ton cou, ni mon cœur pour t'y reposer, ni cette bouche sur tes yeux. Parce qu'il faudra que je m'en aille, très loin, un jour. Puis il faut que j'en aide d'autres: c'est mon devoir. Quoique ce ne soit guère ragoûtant . . . , chère âme . . .' Tout de suite je me pressentais, lui parti, en proie au vertige, précipitée dans l'ombre la plus affreuse: la mort. Je lui faisais promettre qu'il ne me lâcherait pas. Il l'a faite vingt fois, cette promesse d'amant, C'était aussi frivole que moi lui disant: 'Je te comprends.'

"Ah! je n'ai jamais été jalouse de lui. Il ne me quittera pas, je crois. Que devenir? Il n'a pas une connaissance; il ne travaillera jamais. Il veut vivre somnambule. Seules, sa bonté et sa charité lui donneraient-elles droit dans le monde réel? Par instants, j'oublie la pitié où je suis tombée: lui me rendra forte, nous voyagerons, nous chasserons dans les déserts, nous dormirons sur les pavés des villes inconnues, sans soins, sans peines. Ou je me réveillerai, et les lois et les mœurs auront changé,—grâce à son pouvoir magique,—le monde, en restant le même, me laissera à mes désirs, joies, nonchalances. Oh! la vie d'aventures qui existe dans les livres des enfants, pour me récompenser, j'ai tant souffert, me la donneras-tu? Il ne peut pas. J'ignore son idéal. Il m'a dit avoir des regrets, des espoirs: cela ne doit pas me regarder. Parle-t-il à Dieu? Peut-être devrais-je m'adresser à Dieu. Je suis au plus profond de l'abîme, et je ne sais plus prier.

would have enough strength—strength of despair—to endure it, to be protected and loved by him. Besides, I could not imagine him with another soul. I believe we see our own Angel, and never anyone else's Angel. I was in his soul as in a palace that had been emptied in order not to see so mean a person as myself, that is all. Alas! I counted on him. But what did he want with my dull and craven existence? He made me no better, if he did not drive me to distraction. Sometimes when I was sad and angry, I said to him: 'I understand you.' He would shrug his shoulders.

"So, my sadness being always renewed, and being in my own eyes more lost than ever—as in the eyes of all those who would have liked to watch me if I had not been condemned forever to be forgotten by everyone! More and more I hungered for his charity. With his kisses and friendly embrace, it was a heaven, a dark heaven where I entered, and I would like to have been left, poor, deaf, dumb and blind. Already it had become my habit. I saw us as two good children free to walk about in the Paradise of sorrow. We got on together. We worked together in a state of joy. But after a penetrating caress, he would say: 'It will seem strange to you, when I am not here any more—after all you have gone through. When you will no longer have my arms under your neck, and my heart to lay your head on, and my lips on your eyes. Because one day I will have to go off, very far off. You see, it is my duty to help others. Although it is not very attractive . . . , dear heart . . .' Immediately with him gone, I saw myself overcome with dizziness and hurled down into the most horrible darkness of death. I made him promise that he would not abandon me. Twenty times he gave me that lover's promise. It was as pointless as when I said to him: 'I understand you.'

"Oh! I was never jealous of him. He will not leave me, I think. What could he do? He knows nothing and will never work. He wants the life of a sleepwalker. Will his kindness and charitableness give him the right to live in the real world? At moments I forget the terrible state I have fallen into. He will make me strong. We will travel and hunt in deserts. We will sleep on the pavements of unknown cities, uncared for and without worries. Or else I will wake up, and laws and customs will have changed— thanks to his magical power; or the world, remaining the same, will leave me to my desires and joys and carefree ways. Oh! will you give me, who have suffered so much, as a reward the life of adventure that is in children's books? He cannot. I do not know what his ideal is. He told me he has regrets and hopes. But that is no concern of mine. Does he speak to God? Perhaps I should appeal to God. I am in the lowest depths and I have forgotten how to pray.

"S'il m'expliquait ses tristesses, les comprendrais-je plus que ses railleries? Il m'attaque, il passe mes heures à me faire honte de tout ce qui m'a pu toucher au monde, et s'indigne si je pleure.

"—Tu vois cet élégant jeune homme, entrant dans la belle et calme maison: il s'appelle Duval, Dufour, Armand, Maurice, que sais-je? Une femme s'est dévouée à aimer ce méchant idiot: elle est morte, c'est certes une sainte au ciel, à présent. Tu me feras mourir comme il a fait mourir cette femme. C'est notre sort, à nous, cœurs charitables . . ." Hélas! il avait des jours où tous les hommes agissant lui paraissaient les jouets de délires grotesques: il riait affreusement, longtemps.—Puis, il reprenait ses manières de jeune mère, de sœur aimée. S'il était moins sauvage, nous serions sauvés! Mais sa douceur aussi est mortelle. Je lui suis soumise.—Ah! je suis folle!

"Un jour peut-être il disparaîtra merveilleusement; mais il faut que je sache, s'il doit remonter à un ciel, que je voie un peu l'assomption de mon petit ami!"

Drôle de ménage!

Délires

II

Alchimie du verbe

A moi. L'histoire d'une de mes folies.

Depuis longtemps je me vantais de posséder tous les paysages possibles, et trouvais dérisoires les célébrités de la peinture et de la poésie moderne.

J'aimais les peintures idiotes, dessus de portes, décors, toiles de saltimbanques, enseignes, enluminures populaires; la littérature démodée, latin d'église, livres érotiques sans orthographe, romans de nos aïeules, contes de fées, petits livres de l'enfance, opéras vieux, refrains niais, rhythmes naïfs.

Je rêvais croisades, voyages de découvertes dont on n'a pas de relations, républiques sans histoires, guerres de religion étouffées, révolutions de mœurs, déplacements de races et de continents: je croyais à tous les enchantements.

J'inventai la couleur des voyelles!—A noir, E blanc, I rouge, O bleu, U vert.—Je réglai la forme et le mouvement de chaque consonne, et, avec des rhythmes instinctifs, je me flattai d'inventer un verbe poétique accessible, un jour ou l'autre, à tous les sens. Je réservais la traduction.

"If he explained his sadness to me, would I understand it any better than his mockery? He attacks me and spends hours making me feel shame for everything that ever touched me, and he is shocked if I cry.

"—Do you see that elegantly dressed young man going into the handsome refined house? His name is Duval, Dufour, Armand, Maurice, or something else. A woman offered her love to that low idiot. She is dead and is certainly now a saint in heaven. You will kill me as he killed that woman. It is our fate, the fate of all loving hearts . . ." Alas! There were days when all active men seemed to him playthings of grotesque madness. He used to laugh long and frightfully.—Then he would recover his manners of a young mother, of an older sister. If he were less wild, we would be saved! But his tenderness too is mortal. I am a slave to him.—Oh! I am mad!

"One day perhaps he will disappear as by a miracle. But if he is to go to some heaven again, I must know it in order to catch sight of my little friend's ascension!"

A strange couple!

Delirium

II

Alchemy of the Word

It is my turn. The story of one of my follies.

For a long time I had boasted of having every possible landscape, and found laughable the celebrated names of painting and modern poetry.

I liked stupid paintings, door panels, stage sets, back-drops for acrobats, signs, popular engravings, old-fashioned literature, church Latin, erotic books with bad spelling, novels of our grandmothers, fairy tales, little books from childhood, old operas, ridiculous refrains, naïve rhythms.

I dreamed of crusades, of unrecorded voyages of discovery, of republics with no history, of hushed-up religious wars, revolutions in customs, displacements of races and continents: I believed in every kind of witchcraft.

I invented the color of the vowels!—*A* black, *E* white, *I* red, *O* blue, *U* green.—I regulated the form and movement of each consonant, and, with instinctive rhythms, I prided myself on inventing a poetic language accessible, some day, to all the senses. I reserved translation rights.

Ce fut d'abord une étude. J'écrivais des silences, des nuits, je notais l'inexprimable. Je fixais des vertiges.

Loin des oiseaux, des troupeaux, des villagoises,
Que buvais-je, à genoux dans cette bruyère
Entourée de tendres bois de noisetiers,
Dans un brouillard d'après-midi tiède et vert?

Que pouvais-je boire dans cette jeune Oise,
—Ormeaux sans voix, gazon sans fleurs, ciel couvert!—
Boire à ces gourdes jaunes, loin de ma case
Chérie? Quelque liqueur d'or qui fait suer.

Je faisais une louche enseigne d'auberge.
—Un orage vint chasser le ciel. Au soir
L'eau des bois se perdait sur les sables vierges,
Le vent de Dieu jetait des glaçons aux mares;

Pleurant, je voyais de l'or—et ne pus boire.——

———————

A quatre heures du matin, l'été,
Le sommeil d'amour dure encore.
Sous les bocages s'évapore
        L'odeur du soir fêté.

Là-bas, dans leur vaste chantier
Au soleil des Hespérides,
Déjà s'agitent—en bras de chemise—
        Les Charpentiers.

Dans leurs Déserts de mousse, tranquilles,
Ils préparent les lambris précieux
        Où la ville
        Peindra de faux cieux.

O, pour ces Ouvriers charmants
Sujets d'un roi de Babylone,
Vénus! quitte un instant les Amants
Dont l'âme est en couronne.

It was at first a study. I wrote out silences and the nights. I recorded the inexpressible. I described frenzies.

> Far from birds, herds and village girls,
> What did I drink, on my knees in the heather
> Surrounded by a soft woods of hazel trees,
> In a warm green afternoon mist?
>
> What could I drink from this young Oise,
> —Voiceless elms, flowerless grass, cloudy sky!—
> Drinking from those yellow gourds, far from my beloved
> Cabin? Some golden liquor that brings on sweat.
>
> I was a disreputable sign for an inn.
> —A storm chased the sky away. At night
> The water of the evening woods sank into the virgin sand,
> And God's wind cast icicles into the ponds;
>
> Weeping, I saw gold—and could not drink.——

> At four in the morning, in summer,
> Love's sleep still lasts.
> Under the trees the scent
>   Of the festive night evaporates.
>
> Yonder, in their vast lumberyard
> Under the sun of the Hesperides,
> Carpenters—in shirtsleeves—
>   Are already moving about.
>
> In their Deserts of moss, quiet,
> They prepare precious panels
>   Where the city
>   Will paint false skies.
>
> O, for those charming Workmen
> Subjects of a Babylonian king,
> Venus! leave for a moment the Lovers
> Whose souls are crowned.

O Reine des Bergers,
Porte aux travailleurs l'eau-de-vie,
Que leurs forces soient en paix
En attendant le bain dans la mer à midi.

La vieillerie poétique avait une bonne part dans mon alchimie du verbe.

Je m'habituai à l'hallucination simple: je voyais très-franchement une mosquée à la place d'une usine, une école de tambours faite par des anges, des calèches sur les routes du ciel, un salon au fond d'un lac; les monstres, les mystères; un titre de vaudeville dressait des épouvantes devant moi.

Puis j'expliquai mes sophismes magiques avec l'hallucination des mots!

Je finis par trouver sacré le désordre de mon esprit. J'étais oisif, en proie à une lourde fièvre: j'enviais la félicité des bêtes,—les chenilles, qui représentent l'innocence des limbes, les taupes, le sommeil de la virginité!

Mon caractère s'aigrissait. Je disais adieu au monde dans d'espèces de romances:

Chanson de la plus haute Tour

Qu'il vienne, qu'il vienne,
Le temps dont on s'éprenne.

J'ai tant fait patience
Qu'à jamais j'oublie.
Craintes et souffrances
Aux cieux sont parties.
Et la soif malsaine
Obscurcit mes veines.

Qu'il vienne, qu'il vienne,
Le temps dont on s'éprenne.

Telle la prairie
A l'oubli livrée,
Grandie, et fleurie
D'encens et d'ivraies,
Au bourdon farouche
Des sales mouches.

Qu'il vienne, qu'il vienne,
Le temps dont on s'éprenne.

O Queen of Shepherds,
Take brandy to the workers,
So their strength may be at peace
As they wait for their noon bath in the sea.

Poetic old-fashionedness figured largely in my alchemy of the word.

I grew accustomed to pure hallucination: I saw quite frankly a mosque in place of a factory, a school of drummers made up of angels, carriages on roads in the sky, a parlor at the bottom of the lake; monsters, mysteries. The title of a vaudeville conjured up horrors before me.

Then I explained my magic sophisms with the hallucination of words!

At the end I looked on the disorder of my mind as sacred. I was idle, a prey to a heavy fever. I envied the happiness of animals—caterpillars representing the innocence of limbo, moles, the sleep of virginity!

My disposition grew embittered. I said farewell to the world in the form of light poems:

Song of the Highest Tower

May it come, may it come,
The time we will fall in love with.

I have been patient so long
That I have forgotten everything.
Fears and suffering
Have left for the skies.
And an unhealthy thirst
Darkens my veins.

May it come, may it come,
The time we will fall in love with.

Like the field
Given over to oblivion,
Grown up, and flowering
With incense and tares,
And to the fierce buzzing
Of dirty flies.

May it come, may it come,
The time we will fall in love with.

J'aimai le désert, les vergers brûlés, les boutiques fanées, les boissons tié-
dies. Je me traînais dans les ruelles puantes et, les yeux fermés, je m'offrais
au soleil, dieu de feu.

"Général, s'il reste un vieux canon sur tes remparts en ruines, bombarde-
nous avec des blocs de terre sèche. Aux glaces des magasins splendides!
dans les salons! Fais manger sa poussière à la ville. Oxyde les gargouilles.
Emplis les boudoirs de poudre de rubis brûlante . . ."

Oh! le moucheron enivré à la pissotière de l'auberge, amoureux de la
bourrache, et que dissout un rayon!

Faim

Si j'ai du goût, ce n'est guère
Que pour la terre et les pierres.
Je déjeune toujours d'air,
De roc, de charbons, de fer.

Mes faims, tournez. Paissez, faims,
    Le pré des sons.
Attirez le gai venin
    Des liserons.

Mangez les cailloux qu'on brise,
Les vieilles pierres d'églises;
Les galets des vieux déluges,
Pains semés dans les vallées grises.

———————

Le loup criait sous les feuilles
En crachant les belles plumes
De son repas de volailles:
Comme lui je me consume.

Les salades, les fruits
N'attendent que la cueillette;
Mais l'araignée de la haie
Ne mange que des violettes.

Que je dorme! que je bouille
Aux autels de Salomon.
Le bouillon court sur la rouille,
Et se mêle au Cédron.

I loved the desert, burnt orchards, musty shops, tepid drinks. I dragged myself through stinking alleys, and with my eyes closed, gave myself over to the sun, the god of fire.

"General, if an old cannon remains on your ruined ramparts, bombard us with lumps of dried earth. In the mirrors of luxurious stores! in parlors! Make the city eat its own dust. Oxidize the gargoyles. Fill bedrooms with the burning powder of rubies . . ."

Oh! the drunken gnat in the inn's urinal, in love with diuretic borage and dissolved by a sunbeam!

Hunger

If I have any taste, it is for hardly
Anything but earth and stones.
I always feed on air,
Rock, coal, and iron.

My hungers, turn about. Graze, hungers,
    On the meadow of bran.
Suck the bright poison
    Of the bindweed.

Eat the rocks that are broken,
The old stones of churches;
The pebbles of old floods,
Bread scattered in gray valleys.

———————

The wolf cried under the leaves
As he spat out the fine feathers
Of his meal of fowl:
Like him I consume myself.

Lettuce and fruit
Wait only to be picked;
But the spider of the hedge
Eats only violets.

Let me sleep! Let me boil
At the altars of Solomon.
Boiling water courses over the rust,
And mixes with the Kidron.

Enfin, ô bonheur, ô raison, j'écartais du ciel l'azur, qui est du noir, et je vécus, étincelle d'or de la lumière *nature*. De joie, je prenais une expression bouffonne et égarée au possible:

> Elle est retrouvée!
> Quoi? l'éternité.
> C'est la mer mêlée
>   Au soleil.

> Mon âme éternelle,
> Observe ton vœu
> Malgré la nuit seule
> Et le jour en feu.

> Donc tu te dégages
> Des humains suffrages,
> Des communs élans!
> Tu voles selon . . .

> —Jamais l'espérance,
>   Pas d'*orietur*.
> Science et patience,
> Le supplice est sûr.

> Plus de lendemain,
> Braises de satin,
>   Votre ardeur
>   Est le devoir.

> Elle est retrouvée!
> — Quoi? — l'Éternité.
> C'est la mer mêlée
>   Au soleil.

————————

Je devins un opéra fabuleux: je vis que tous les êtres ont une fatalité de bonheur: l'action n'est pas la vie, mais une façon de gâcher quelque force, un énervement. La morale est la faiblesse de la cervelle.

A chaque être, plusieurs *autres* vies me semblaient dues. Ce monsieur ne sait ce qu'il fait: il est un ange. Cette famille est une nichée de chiens. De-

At last, o happiness, o reason, I removed from the sky the blue that is black, and I lived like a spark of gold of *pure* light. From joy I took an expression as buffoonish and strange as possible:

It has been found again!
What has? eternity.
It is the sea mixed
        With the sun.

My eternal soul,
Observe your vow
In spite of the night
And the day on fire.

So, you free yourself
From human approval,
From common impulses!
You fly off as . . .

Never any hopes,
        No *orietur*.
Science and patience,
The suffering is sure.

No more tomorrow,
Embers of satin,
        Your ardor
        Is duty.

It has been found again!
—What has? —Eternity.
It is the sea mixed
        With the sun.

———————

I became a fabulous opera. I saw that all beings have a fatality for happiness. Action is not life, but a way of spoiling some force, an enervation. Morality is a weakness of the brain.

To each being it seemed to me that several *other* lives were due. This gentleman does not know what he is doing. He is an angel. This family is

vant plusieurs hommes, je causai tout haut avec un moment d'une de leurs autres vies. —Ainsi, j'ai aimé un porc.

Aucun des sophismes de la folie, —la folie qu'on enferme, —n'a été oublié par moi: je pourrais les redire tous, je tiens le système.

Ma santé fut menacée. La terreur venait. Je tombais dans des sommeils de plusieurs jours, et, levé, je continuais les rêves les plus tristes. J'étais mûr pour le trépas, et par une route de dangers ma faiblesse me menait aux confins du monde et de la Cimmérie, patrie de l'ombre et des tourbillons.

Je dus voyager, distraire les enchantements assemblés sur mon cerveau. Sur la mer, que j'aimais comme si elle eût dû me laver d'une souillure, je voyais se lever la croix consolatrice. J'avais été damné par l'arc-en-ciel. Le Bonheur était ma fatalité, mon remords, mon ver: ma vie serait toujours trop immense pour être dévouée à la force et à la beauté.

Le Bonheur! Sa dent, douce à la mort, m'avertissait au chant du coq, — *ad matutinum,* au *Christus venit,* —dans les plus sombres villes:

> O saisons, ô châteaux!
> Quelle âme est sans défauts?

J'ai fait la magique étude
Du bonheur, qu'aucun n'élude.

Salut à lui, chaque fois
Que chante le coq gaulois.

Ah! je n'aurai plus d'envie:
Il s'est chargé de ma vie.

Ce charme a pris âme et corps
Et dispersé les efforts.

> O saisons, ô châteaux!

L'heure de sa fuite, hélas!
Sera l'heure du trépas.

> O saisons, ô châteaux!

———

Cela s'est passé. Je sais aujourd'hui saluer la beauté.

a litter of dogs. In front of several men, I talked out loud with one moment of one of their other lives.—In that way, I loved a pig.

Not one sophistry of madness—madness that is locked up—was forgotten by me. I could say them all again. I know the system.

My health was threatened. Terror came. I used to fall into a sleep of several days, and, when up, I continued the saddest dreams. I was ripe for death, and along a road of dangers my weakness led me to the edge of the world and Cimmeria, a land of darkness and whirlwinds.

I had to travel, to divert the enchantments assembled over my head. Over the sea, which I loved as if it were washing me of a stain, I saw the consoling cross rise. I had been damned by the rainbow. Happiness was my fatality, my remorse, my worm: my life would always be too immense to be devoted to strength and beauty.

Happiness! Its tooth, sweet to death, warned me at the crowing of the cock,—*ad matutinum,* at the *Christus venit,*—in the darkest cities:

> O seasons, o castles!
> What soul is without flaws?

> I carried out the magic study
> Of happiness, which no man evades.

> A salute to it each time
> The Gallic cock sings.

> Ah! I will have no more desires:
> It has taken charge of my life.

> This charm has taken body and soul
> And dispersed all efforts.

> O seasons, o castles!

> The hour of its flight, alas,
> Will be the hour of my death.

> O seasons, o castles!

———

That is over. Today I can greet beauty.

L'impossible

Ah! cette vie de mon enfance, la grande route par tous les temps, sobre surnaturellement, plus désintéressé que le meilleur des mendiants, fier de n'avoir ni pays, ni amis, quelle sottise c'était. —Et je m'en aperçois seulement!

—J'ai eu raison de mépriser ces bonshommes qui ne perdraient pas l'occasion d'une caresse, parasites de la propreté et de la santé de nos femmes, aujourd'hui qu'elles sont si peu d'accord avec nous.

J'ai eu raison dans tous mes dédains: puisque je m'évade!

Je m'évade!

Je m'explique.

Hier encore, je soupirais: "Ciel! sommes-nous assez de damnés ici-bas! Moi, j'ai tant de temps déjà dans leur troupe! Je les connais tous. Nous nous reconnaissons toujours; nous nous dégoûtons. La charité nous est inconnue. Mais nous sommes polis; nos relations avec le monde sont très—convenables." Est-ce étonnant? Le monde! les marchands, les naïfs! —Nous ne sommes pas déshonorés. —Mais les élus, comment nous recevraient-ils? Or il y a des gens hargneux et joyeux, de faux élus, puisqu'il nous faut de l'audace ou de l'humilité pour les aborder. Ce sont les seuls élus. Ce ne sont pas des bénisseurs!

M'étant retrouvé deux sous de raison —ça passe vite! —je vois que mes malaises viennent de ne m'être pas figuré assez tôt que nous sommes à l'Occident. Les marais occidentaux! Non que je croie la lumière altérée, la forme exténuée, le mouvement égaré . . . Bon! voici que mon esprit veut absolument se charger de tous les développements cruels qu'a subis l'esprit depuis la fin de l'Orient . . . Il en veut, mon esprit!

. . . Mes deux sous de raison sont finis! —L'esprit est autorité, il veut que je sois en Occident. Il faudrait le faire taire pour conclure comme je voulais.

J'envoyais au diable les palmes des martyrs, les rayons de l'art, l'orgueil des inventeurs, l'ardeur des pillards; je retournais à l'Orient et à la sagesse première et éternelle. —Il paraît que c'est un rêve de paresse grossière!

Pourtant, je ne songeais guère au plaisir d'échapper aux souffrances modernes. Je n'avais pas en vue la sagesse bâtarde du Coran. —Mais n'y a-t-il pas un supplice réel en ce que, depuis cette déclaration de la science, le christianisme, l'homme *se joue,* se prouve les évidences, se gonfle du plaisir de répéter ces preuves, et ne vit que comme cela! Torture subtile, niaise; source de mes divagations spirituelles. La nature pourrait s'ennuyer, peut-être! M. Prudhomme est né avec le Christ.

The Impossible

Ah! that life of my childhood, the highway in all weather, supernaturally sober, more disinterested than the best of beggars, proud to have neither a country nor friends, what madness this was.—And only now do I realize it!

—I was right to despise those fellows who never lost the chance of a caress, parasites of the cleanliness and health of our women today when they are so little in agreement with us.

I was right in all my scorn, since I am escaping!

I am escaping!

Let me explain.

Just yesterday I was sighing: "Heavens! Aren't there enough of us who are damned here below? Already I have been so long in their troop! I know them all. We always recognize one another. Each of us disgusts the other. Charity is unknown to us. But we are polite. Our relationship with the world is very correct." Is this surprising? The world! merchants, simple souls!—We are not dishonored.—But how would the elect receive us? Now, there are surly and joyous men, the false elect, since we need boldness or humility to approach them. They are the only elect. They are not blessers!

Since I have recovered two cents worth of reason—it disappears fast!—I see that my discomfort comes from not being understood early enough that we are in the West. The western swamps! Not that I believe light is adulterated, or form exhausted, or movement gone astray . . . My spirit is insistent upon taking over all the cruel developments which the spirit has undergone since the end of the East . . . My spirit does indeed insist!

. . . My two cents worth of reason is over!—The spirit is authority. It wants me to be in the West. I would have to silence it to conclude as I wished.

May the devil take martyrs' palms, rays of art, pride of inventors, enthusiasm of plunderers! I returned to the East and to the first eternal wisdom.—It seems like a dream of vulgar sloth!

Yet I never thought of the pleasure of escaping from today's suffering. I did not have in mind the bastard wisdom of the Koran.—But is there not real torture in the fact that, since the declaration of science, and Christianity, man *deludes himself,* proving obvious truth, puffing up with the pleasure of repeating his proofs, and living only in this way? A subtle, ridiculous torture; source of my spiritual meanderings. Nature might be bored, perhaps! M. Prudhomme was born with Christ.

N'est-ce pas parce que nous cultivons la brume! Nous mangeons la fièvre avec nos légumes aqueux. Et l'ivrognerie! et le tabac! et l'ignorance! et les dévouements!—Tout cela est-il assez loin de la pensée de la sagesse de l'Orient, la patrie primitive? Pourquoi un monde moderne, si de pareils poisons s'inventent!

Les gens d'Église diront: C'est compris. Mais vous voulez parler de l'Éden. Rien pour vous dans l'histoire des peuples orientaux.—C'est vrai; c'est à l'Éden que je songeais! Qu'est-ce que c'est pour mon rêve, cette pureté des races antiques!

Les philosophes: Le monde n'a pas d'âge. L'humanité se déplace, simplement. Vous êtes en Occident, mais libre d'habiter dans votre Orient, quelque ancien qu'il vous le faille,—et d'y habiter bien. Ne soyez pas un vaincu. Philosophes, vous êtes de votre Occident.

Mon esprit, prends garde. Pas de partis de salut violents. Exerce-toi!— Ah! la science ne va pas assez vite pour nous!

—Mais je m'aperçois que mon esprit dort.

S'il était bien éveillé toujours à partir de ce moment, nous serions bientôt à la vérité, qui peut-être nous entoure avec ses anges pleurant! . . . —S'il avait été éveillé jusqu'à ce moment-ci, c'est que je n'aurais pas cédé aux instincts délétères, à une époque immémoriale! . . .—S'il avait toujours été bien éveillé, je voguerais en pleine sagesse! . . .

O pureté! pureté!

C'est cette minute d'éveil qui m'a donné la vision de la pureté!—Par l'esprit on va à Dieu!

Déchirante infortune!

L'éclair

Le travail humain! c'est l'explosion qui éclaire mon abîme de temps en temps.

"Rien n'est vanité; à la science, et en avant!" crie l'Ecclésiaste moderne, c'est-à-dire *Tout le monde*. Et pourtant les cadavres des méchants et des fainéants tombent sur le cœur des autres . . . Ah! vite, vite un peu; là-bas, par delà la nuit, ces récompenses futures, éternelles . . . les échappons-nous? . . .

— Qu'y puis-je? Je connais le travail; et la science est trop lente. Que la prière galope et que la lumière gronde . . . je le vois bien. C'est trop simple, et il fait trop chaud; on se passera de moi. J'ai mon devoir, j'en serai fier à la façon de plusieurs, en le mettant de côté.

Isn't it because we cultivate fog? We eat fever with our watery vegetables. And drunkenness! and tobacco! and ignorance! and devotedness!—Isn't all that quite far from thought of Oriental wisdom, and the original native land? Why a modern world, if such poisons are invented?

Churchmen will say: It is agreed. But you mean Eden. Nothing for you in the history of Oriental peoples.—It is true; I was thinking of Eden! What is its relation with my dream, this purity of ancient races!

Philosophers: The world is ageless. Humanity simply moves about. You are in the West, but free to live in your East, as ancient as you need—and to live well there. Do not be one of the conquered. Philosophers, you are of your West.

My spirit, take care. No violent decisions about salvation. Start working! —Ah! science does not move fast enough for us!

—But I see my spirit is sleeping.

If it were always wide awake from this moment on, we would soon reach truth, who perhaps surrounds us with her weeping angels! . . . If it had been awake until this moment, I would not have given in to my deleterious instincts at an immemorial time! . . . —If it had always been awake, I would be sailing in full wisdom! . . .

O purity! purity!

This moment of awakening gave me the vision of purity!—Through the spirit man goes to God!

What heartbreaking misfortune!

Lightning

Work of man! this is the explosion which lights up my abyss from time to time.

"Nothing is vanity; science and onward!" cries the modern Ecclesiastes, namely *Everyone*. And yet the bodies of the wicked and the slothful fall on the hearts of others. Ah! come quickly! out there, beyond the night . . . shall we miss those future eternal rewards?

—What can I do? I understand what work is, and science moves too slowly. I see clearly that prayer gallops and light thunders. This is too simple. And it is too hot. People will get along without me. I have my duty. I will be proud of it in the fashion of several others, by putting it aside.

Ma vie est usée. Allons! feignons, fainéantons, ô pitié! Et nous existerons en nous amusant, en rêvant amours monstres et univers fantastiques, en nous plaignant et en querellant les apparences du monde, saltimbanque, mendiant, artiste, bandit,—prêtre! Sur mon lit d'hôptial, l'odeur de l'ences m'est revenue si puissante; gardien des aromates sacrés, confesseur, martyr . . .

Je reconnais là ma sale éducation d'enfance. Puis quoi! . . . Aller mes vingt ans, si les autres vont vingt ans . . .

Non! non! à présent je me révolte contre la mort! Le travail paraît trop léger à mon orgueil: ma trahison au monde serait un supplice trop court. Au dernier moment, j'attaquerais à droite, à gauche . . .

Alors,—oh!—chère pauvre âme, l'éternité serait-elle pas perdue pour nous!

Matin

N'eus-je pas *une fois* une jeunesse aimable, héroïque, fabuleuse, à écrier sur des feuilles d'or,—trop de chance! Par quel crime, par quelle erreur, ai-je mérité ma faiblesse actuelle? Vous qui prétendez que des bêtes poussent des sanglots de chagrin, que des malades désespèrent, que des morts rêvent mal, tâchez de raconter ma chute et mon sommeil. Moi, je ne puis pas plus m'expliquer que le mendiant avec ses continuels *Pater* et *Ave Maria*. *Je ne sais plus parler!*

Pourtant, aujourd'hui, je crois avoir fini la relation de mon enfer. C'était bien l'enfer; l'ancien, celui dont le fils de l'homme ouvrit les portes.

Du même désert, à la même nuit, toujours mes yeux las se réveillent à l'étoile d'argent, toujours, sans que s'émeuvent les Rois de la vie, les trois mages, le cœur, l'âme, l'esprit. Quand irons-nous, par delà les grèves et les monts, saluer la naissance du travail nouveau, la sagesse nouvelle, la fuite des tyrans et des démons, la fin de la superstition, adorer—les premiers!— Noël sur la terre!

Le chant des cieux, la marche des peuples! Esclaves, ne maudissons pas la vie.

My life is worn out. Come! let's pretend, let's be idle, O pity! We will exist by amusing ourselves, by dreaming of monstrous loves and fantastic universes, by complaining and quarreling with the appearances of the world—clown, beggar, artist, bandit—priest! On my hospital bed the odor of incense came back to me so strong: keeper of the sacred aromatics, confessor, martyr . . .

Therein I recognize my filthy education of childhood. But what of it? . . . Let my twenty years go, if others go their twenty years . . .

No! no! Now I revolt against death! Work seems too slight to my pride: my betrayal to the world would be too brief a torture. At the last moment, I would attack right and left . . .

Then—oh!—poor dear soul, would not eternity be lost to us!

Morning

Once did not I have a delightful youth, heroic and fabulous, to be written on sheets of gold,—too much luck! Through what crime, through what error did I deserve my present weakness? You who say that animals sob from grief, that the sick despair, that the dead have bad dreams, try to relate my fall and my sleep. I can no more explain myself than the beggar with his endless *Paters* and *Ave Marias*. *I have forgotten how to speak!*

Yet today I think I have finished the story of my hell. It was really hell; the old hell, the one whose gates were opened by the son of man.

From the same wilderness, in the same night, my tired eyes always awaken to the silver star, although the Kings of life, the three magi, the heart, the soul, and spirit, are not moved. Where shall we go beyond the shores and the mountains, to salute the birth of the new work, and the new wisdom, the flight of tyrants and demons, the end of superstition, and be the first to worship Christmas on earth?

The song of heavens, the marching of nations! Slaves, let us not curse life.

Adieu

L'automne déjà!—Mais pourquoi regretter un éternel soleil, si nous sommes engagés à la découverte de la clarté divine,—loin des gens qui meurent sur les saisons.

L'automne. Notre barque élevée dans les brumes immobiles tourne vers le port de la misère, la cité énorme au ciel taché de feu et de boue. Ah! les haillons pourris, le pain trempé de pluie, l'ivresse, les mille amours qui m'ont crucifié! Elle ne finira donc point cette goule reine de millions d'âmes et de corps morts *et qui seront jugés!* Je me revois la peau rongée par la boue et la peste, des vers plein les cheveux et les aisselles et encore de plus gros vers dans le cœur, étendu parmi les inconnus sans âge, sans sentiment ... J'aurais pu y mourir ... L'affreuse évocation! J'exècre la misère.

Et je redoute l'hiver parce que c'est la saison du comfort!

—Quelquefois je vois au ciel des plages sans fin couvertes de blanches nations en joie. Un grand vaisseau d'or, au-dessus de moi, agite ses pavillons multicolores sous les brises du matin. J'ai créé toutes les fêtes, tous les triomphes, tous les drames. J'ai essayé d'inventer de nouvelles fleurs, de nouveaux astres, de nouvelles chairs, de nouvelles langues. J'ai cru acquérir des pouvoirs surnaturels. Eh bien! je dois enterrer mon imagination et mes souvenirs! Une belle gloire d'artiste et de conteur emportée!

Moi! moi qui me suis dit mage ou ange, dispensé de toute morale, je suis rendu au sol, avec un devoir à chercher, et la réalité rugueuse à étreindre! Paysan!

Suis-je trompé? la charité serait-elle sœur de la mort, pour moi?

Enfin, je demanderai pardon pour m'être nourri de mensonge. Et allons. Mais pas une main amie! et où puiser le secours?

———————

Oui, l'heure nouvelle est au moins très-sévère.

Car je puis dire que la victoire m'est acquise: les grincements de dents, les sifflements de feu, les soupirs empestés se modèrent. Tous les souvenirs immondes s'effacent. Mes derniers regrets détalent,—des jalousies pour les mendiants, les brigands, les amis de la mort, les arriérés de toutes sortes.—Damnés, si je me vengeais!

Il faut être absolument moderne.

Point de cantiques: tenir le pas gagné. Dure nuit! le sang séché fume sur ma face, et je n'ai rien derrière moi, que cet horrible arbrisseau! ... Le combat spirituel est aussi brutal que la bataille d'hommes; mais la vision de la justice est le plaisir de Dieu seul.

Farewell

Autumn already!—But why regret an eternal sun, if we are committed to the discovery of divine light,—far from those who die with the seasons.

Autumn. Our boat, in the motionless mist, turns toward the harbor of wretchedness, the huge city under a sky stained with fire and mud. Ah! the rotten rags, the rain-soaked bread, the drunkenness, the thousand loves that crucified me! She will never be done, then, that ghoul queen of a million souls and dead bodies, *and which will be judged!* I see myself again, with my skin eaten by mud and plague, worms in my hair and armpits and still bigger worms in my heart, lying among strangers without age, without feeling . . . I could have died there . . . It is an unbearable memory! I despise poverty.

And I dread winter because it is the season of comfort!

—Sometimes I see in the sky endless beaches covered with white joyous nations. A huge golden vessel, above me, waves its multicolored flags in the morning wind. I have created all celebrations, all triumphs, all dramas. I have tried to invent new flowers, new stars, new flesh, new tongues. I believed I had acquired supernatural powers. Well! I have to bury my imagination and my memories! A fine reputation of an artist and storyteller lost sight of!

I who called myself magus or angel, exempt from all morality, I am thrown back to the earth, with a duty to find, and rough reality to embrace! Peasant!

Was I wrong? Could charity be the sister of death for me?

At least I will ask forgiveness for having fed on lies. Let us go now.

But not a friendly hand! Where can I find help?

Yes, at least the new hour is very harsh.

For I can say that victory is mine: the gnashing of teeth, the hissing of fire, the reeking sighs abate. All filthy memories fade out. My last regrets scamper off: envy of beggars, brigands, friends of death, backward creatures of all sorts.—You who are damned, what if I avenged myself!

We must be absolutely modern.

No hymns. I must hold what has been gained. Hard night! The dried blood smokes on my face, and I have nothing behind me except that horrible tree! . . . A spiritual battle is as brutal as a battle of men; but the vision of justice is the pleasure of God alone.

However this is the vigil. Let us welcome all the influxes of vigor and

Cependant c'est la veille. Recevons tous les influx de vigueur et de tendresse réelle. Et à l'aurore, armés d'une ardente patience, nous entrerons aux splendides villes.

Que parlais-je de main amie! Un bel avantage, c'est que je puis rire des vieilles amours mensongères, et frapper de honte ces couples menteurs, — j'ai vu l'enfer des femmes là-bas; — et il me sera loisible de *posséder la vérité dans une âme et un corps.*

avril–août, 1873

real tenderness. And, at dawn, armed with ardent patience, we will enter magnificent cities.

What was I saying about a friendly hand? One fine advantage is that I can laugh at old lying loves and strike with shame those lying couples—I saw the hell of women down there—and I shall be free *to possess truth in one body and soul.*

April–August, 1873

Illuminations (1872–1874?)

Illuminations (1872–1874?)

Après le déluge

Aussitôt que l'idée du Déluge se fût rassise,

Un lièvre s'arrêta dans les sainfoins et les clochettes mouvantes et dit sa prière à l'arc-en-ciel à travers la toile de l'araignée.

Oh les pierres précieuses qui se cachaient, — les fleurs qui regardaient déjà.

Dans la grande rue sale les étals se dressèrent, et l'on tira les barques vers la mer étagée là-haut comme sur les gravures.

Le sang coula, chez Barbe-Bleue, — aux abattoirs, — dans les cirques, où le sceau de Dieu blêmit les fenêtres. Le sang et le lait coulèrent.

Les castors bâtirent. Les "mazagrans" fumèrent dans les estaminets.

Dans la grande maison de vitres encore ruisselante les enfants en deuil regardèrent les merveilleuses images.

Une porte claqua, et sur la place du hameau, l'enfant tourna ses bras, compris des girouettes et des coqs des clochers de partout, sous l'éclatante giboulée.

Madame . . . établit un piano dans les Alpes. La messe et les premières communions se célébrèrent aux cent mille autels de la cathédrale.

Les caravanes partirent. Et le Splendide Hôtel fut bâti dans le chaos de glaces et de nuit du pôle.

Depuis lors, la Lune entendit les chacals piaulant par les déserts de thym, — et les églogues en sabots grognant dans le verger. Puis, dans la futaie violette, bourgeonnante, Eucharis me dit que c'était le printemps.

Sourds, étang, — Ecume, roule sur le pont et pardessus les bois; — draps noirs et orgues, — éclairs et tonnerre, — montez et roulez; — Eaux et tristesses, montez et relevez les Déluges.

Car depuis qu'ils se sont dissipés, — oh les pierres précieuses s'enfouissant, et les fleurs ouvertes! — c'est un ennui! et la Reine, la Sorcière qui allume sa braise dans le pot de terre, ne voudra jamais nous raconter ce qu'elle sait, et que nous ignorons.

Enfance

I

Cette idole, yeux noirs et crin jaune, sans parents ni cour, plus noble que la fable, mexicaine et flamande; son domaine, azur et verdure inso-

After the Flood

As soon as the idea of the Flood had subsided,

A hare stopped in the clover and the swinging flower bells and said its prayer through the spider's web to the rainbow.

The precious stones were hiding, and already the flowers were beginning to look up.

The butchers' blocks rose in the dirty main street, and boats were hauled down to the sea, piled high as in pictures.

Blood flowed in Bluebeard's house, in the slaughterhouses, in the circuses, where the seal of God whitened the windows. Blood and milk flowed.

Beavers set about building. Coffee urns let out smoke in the bars.

In the large house with windows still wet children in mourning looked at exciting pictures.

A door slammed. On the village square the child swung his arms around, and was understood by the weather vanes and the steeple cocks everywhere, under the pelting rain.

Madame X installed a piano in the Alps. Mass and first communions were celebrated at the hundred thousand altars of the cathedral.

The caravans departed. And the Hôtel Splendide was built in the chaos of ice and polar night.

Since then, the Moon has heard jackals yelping in thyme deserts,—and eclogues in wooden shoes growling in the orchard. Finally, in the violet budding grove, Eucharis told me spring was here.

Gush forth, waters of the pond,—Foam, pour over the bridge and over the woods;—black shrouds and organs,—lightning and thunder,—rise up and spread everywhere. Waters and sorrows, rise up and bring back the Floods.

For ever since they have gone,—oh! the precious stones buried and the opened flowers!—we have been bored! The Queen, the Witch lighting her coal in the earthen pot, will never tell us what she knows and what we shall never know.

Childhood

I

This idol, black-eyed and yellow-haired, no parents and no palace, but more princely than the Mexican and Flemish fairy story. His land of bla-

lents, court sur des plages nommées, par des vagues sans vaisseaux, de noms férocement grecs, slaves, celtiques.

À la lisière de la forêt—les fleurs de rêve tintent, éclatent, éclairent,—la fille à lèvre d'orange, les genoux croisés dans le clair déluge qui sourd des prés, nudité qu'ombrent, traversent et habillent les arcs-en-ciel, la flore, la mer.

Dames qui tournoient sur les terrasses voisines de la mer; enfantes et géantes, superbes noires dans la mousse vert-de-gris, bijoux debout sur le sol gras des bosquets et des jardinets dégelés—jeunes mères et grandes sœurs aux regards pleins de pèlerinages, sultanes, princesses de démarches et de costume tyranniques, petites étrangères et personnes doucement malheureuses.

Quel ennui, l'heure du "cher corps" et "cher cœur."

II

C'est elle, la petite morte, derrière les rosiers.—La jeune maman trépassée descend le perron—La calèche du cousin crie sur le sable—Le petit frère—(il est aux Indes!) là, devant le couchant, sur le pré d'œillets:—les vieux qu'on a enterrés tout droits dans le rempart aux giroflées.

L'essaim des feuilles d'or entoure la maison du général. Ils sont dans le midi.—On suit la route rouge pour arriver à l'auberge vide. Le château est à vendre; les persiennes sont détachées.—Le curé aura remporté la clef de l'église.—Autour du parc, les loges des gardes sont inhabitées . . . Les palissades sont si hautes qu'on ne voit que les cimes bruissantes. D'ailleurs il n'y a rien à voir là-dedans.

Les prés remontent aux hameaux sans coqs, sans enclumes. L'écluse est levée. O les calvaires et les moulins du désert, les îles et les meules.

Des fleurs magiques bourdonnaient. Les talus *le* berçaient. Des bêtes d'une élégance fabuleuse circulaient. Les nuées s'amassaient sur la haute mer faite d'une éternité de chaudes larmes.

III

Au bois il y a un oiseau, son chant vous arrête et vous fait rougir.

Il y a une horloge qui ne sonne pas.

Il y a une fondrière avec un nid de bêtes blanches.

Il y a une cathédrale qui descend et un lac qui monte.

Il y a une petite voiture abandonnée dans le taillis, ou qui descend le sentier en courant, enrubannée.

tant blue and green, covers beaches named, by shipless waves, with names that are ferociously Greek, Slav, Celtic.

At the forest's edge — the dream flowers tinkle, burst, illuminate — the girl with the orange lips, her knees crossed in the limpid flood rising up from the fields, a naked body shadowed, penetrated, and clothed by rainbows, flowers, the ocean.

Ladies strolling on the terraces near the sea; giants and children, magnificent blacks in the green-gray moss, jewels erect on the rich ground of groves and thawed gardens — young mothers and tall sisters whose eyes reflect their pilgrimages, sultanas, princesses of tyrannical walk and costume, foreign girls and some others sweetly unhappy.

The boredom of saying "dear body," "dear heart."

II

That's she, the little girl behind the rose bushes, and she's dead. — The young mother, also dead, is coming down the steps — The cousin's carriage crunches the sand — The small brother (he's in India!) over there in the field of pinks, in front of the sunset: — the old men they've buried upright in the wall covered with gillyflowers.

A swarm of gold leaves smothers the general's house. They're in the south. — You take the red road to reach the empty inn. The château's up for sale and the shutters are coming loose. — The priest must have taken away the key of the church. Around the park, the keepers' cottages are uninhabited . . . The fences are so high that you can only see the tree tops moving in the wind. Anyway there's nothing to see there.

The fields roll up to the villages without roosters and without anvils. The sluice is open. Oh! the crosses and the windmills of the desert, the islands and the haystacks!

Magic flowers were buzzing. The slopes rocked *him* like a cradle. Animals of fabulous beauty walked about. Clouds were massed together over the high seas, made of the warm tears of all time.

III

In the woods there's a bird whose singing stops you and makes you blush.

There's a clock which doesn't strike.

There's a clay-pit with a nest of white animals.

There's a cathedral coming down and a lake going up.

There's a little carriage abandoned in the woods or rolling down the path, with ribbons all over it.

Il y a une troupe de petits comédiens en costumes, aperçus sur la route à travers la lisière du bois.

Il y a enfin, quand l'on a faim et soif, quelqu'un qui vous chasse.

IV

Je suis le saint, en prière sur la terrasse,—comme les bêtes pacifiques paissent jusqu'à la mer de Palestine.

Je suis le savant au fauteuil sombre. Les branches et la pluie se jettent à la croisée de la bibliothèque.

Je suis le piéton de la grand'route par les bois nains; la rumeur des écluses couvre mes pas. Je vois longtemps la mélancolique lessive d'or du couchant.

Je serais bien l'enfant abandonné sur la jetée partie à la haute mer, le petit valet, suivant l'allée dont le front touche le ciel.

Les sentiers sont âpres. Les monticules se couvrent de genêts. L'air est immobile. Que les oiseaux et les sources sont loin! Ce ne peut être que la fin du monde, en avançant.

V

Qu'on me loue enfin ce tombeau, blanchi à la chaux avec les lignes du ciment en relief—très loin sous terre.

Je m'accoude à la table, la lampe éclaire très vivement ces journaux que je suis idiot de relire, ces livres sans intérêt.

A une distance énorme au-dessus de mon salon souterrain, les maisons s'implantent, les brumes s'assemblent. La boue est rouge ou noire. Ville monstrueuse, nuit sans fin!

Moins haut, sont des égouts. Aux côtés, rien que l'épaisseur du globe. Peut-être les gouffres d'azur, des puits de feu. C'est peut-être sur ces plans que se rencontrent lunes et comètes, mers et fables.

Aux heures d'amertume je m'imagine des boules de saphir, de métal. Je suis maître du silence. Pourquoi une apparence de soupirail blêmirait-elle au coin de la voûte?

Conte

Un Prince était vexé de ne s'être employé jamais qu'à la perfection des générosités vulgaires. Il prévoyait d'étonnantes révolutions de l'amour, et

There's a troupe of child actors, in costume, whom you can see on the road through the edge of the wood.

And then there's someone who chases you off when you're hungry and thirsty.

IV

I am the saint in prayer on the terrace like the peaceful animals that graze as far as the sea of Palestine.

I am the scholar in his dark armchair. Branches and rain beat against the library window.

I am the wanderer along the main road running through the dwarfish woods. The noise of the sluices drowns my footsteps. For a long time I can see the sad golden wash of the sunset.

I might be the child abandoned on the wharf setting out for the high seas, or the farmhand, following the path whose top reaches the sky.

The pathways are rough. The slopes are covered with broom. The air is still. How far away are the birds and the springs of water! This must be the end of the world, lying ahead.

V

Now hire for me the tomb, whitewashed with the lines of cement in bold relief—far underground.

I lean my elbows on the table, and the lamp lights brightly the newspapers I am fool enough to reread, and the absurd books.

At a tremendous distance above my subterranean room, houses grow like plants, and fogs gather. The mud is red or black. Monstrous city, endless night!

Not so high up are the sewers. At my side, nothing but the thickness of the globe. Perhaps there are pits of azure and wells of fire. On those levels perhaps moons and comets, seas and fables meet.

In moments of depression I imagine sapphire and metal balls. I am master of silence. Why should the appearance of a cellar window turn pale at the corner of the ceiling?

Story

A Prince was tired of merely spending his time perfecting conventionally generous impulses. He could foretell amazing revolutions of love, and

soupçonnait ses femmes de pouvoir mieux que cette complaisance agrémentée de ciel et de luxe. Il voulait voir la vérité, l'heure du désir et de la satisfaction essentiels. Que ce fût ou non une aberration de piété, il voulut. Il possédait au moins un assez large pouvoir humain.

Toutes les femmes qui l'avaient connu furent assassinées. Quel saccage du jardin de la beauté! Sous le sabre, elles le bénirent. Il n'en commanda point de nouvelles.—Les femmes réapparurent.

Il tua tous ceux qui le suivaient, après la chasse ou les libations.—Tous le suivaient.

Il s'amusa à égorger les bêtes de luxe. Il fit flamber les palais. Il se ruait sur les gens et les taillait en pièces.—La foule, les toits d'or, les belles bêtes existaient encore.

Peut-on s'extasier dans la destruction, se rajeunir par la cruauté! Le peuple ne murmura pas. Personne n'offrit le concours de ses vues.

Un soir il galopait fièrement. Un Génie apparut, d'une beauté ineffable, inavouable même. De sa physionomie et de son maintien ressortait la promesse d'un amour multiple et complexe! d'un bonheur indicible, insupportable même! Le Prince et le Génie s'anéantirent probablement dans la santé essentielle. Comment n'auraient-ils pas pu en mourir? Ensemble donc ils moururent.

Mais ce Prince décéda, dans son palais, à un âge ordinaire. Le prince était le Génie. Le Génie était le Prince.

La musique savante manque à notre désir.

Parade

Des drôles très solides. Plusieurs ont exploité vos mondes. Sans besoins, et peu pressés de mettre en œuvre leurs brillantes facultés et leur expérience de vos consciences. Quels hommes mûrs! Des yeux hébétés à la façon de la nuit d'été, rouges et noirs, tricolores, d'acier piqué d'étoiles d'or; des facies déformés, plombés, blêmis, incendiés; des enrouements folâtres! La démarche cruelle des oripeaux!—Il y a quelques jeunes,—comment regarderaient-ils Chérubin?—pourvus de voix effrayantes et de quelques ressources dangereuses. On les envoie prendre du dos en ville, affublés d'un *luxe* dégoûtant.

O le plus violent Paradis de la grimace enragée! Pas de comparaison avec vos Fakirs et les autres bouffonneries scéniques. Dans des costumes improvisés avec le goût du mauvais rêve ils jouent des complaintes, des tragédies

suspected his wives of being able to give him more than their complacency, enhanced with ideals and wealth. He wanted to see truth and the time of full desire and satisfaction. He wanted this, even if it was a misuse of piety. At least he possessed a large reserve of human power.

All the wives who had known him were murdered. What slaughter of the garden of beauty! They blessed him when the sword came down. He did not order any new wives.—The wives reappeared.

He killed the men who followed him, after hunting or drinking with them.—They all followed him.

He took delight in cutting the throats of the pet animals. He set fire to the palaces. He fell on the servants and hacked them to pieces.—The crowd, the gold roofs, the splendid animals were still there.

Can man reach ecstasy in destruction and be rejuvenated by cruelty? His people made no complaint and no one offered him any advice.

One evening when he was proudly riding his horse, a Genie appeared, of unspeakable, unmentionable beauty. His face and his bearing gave promise of a rich complex love! of an indescribable, unbearable happiness. The Prince and the Genie killed one another probably in the prime of life. How could they have failed to die of it? Together, therefore, they died.

But this Prince passed away, in his palace, at a normal age. The prince was the Genie. The Genie was the Prince.

Our desires are deprived of cunning music.

Circus

Husky fellows. Some of them have exploited your worlds. Without cares and in no hurry to use their brilliant faculties and their knowledge of your consciences. What virile men! Eyes deadened, like a summer's night, red and black, tricolored, of steel spotted with golden stars; faces deformed, ashen, pale, ruddy; wild hoarseness! The cruel demeanor of decorations!—There are some young fellows—what would they think of Cherubino?—with dangerous voices and terrifying resources. They are sent to the city for trade, decked out in disgusting *finery.*

Oh! the most violent Paradise of the enraged smile! No comparison with your Fakirs and other stage antics. In improvised costumes and in the style of a bad dream they recite sad poems and perform tragedies of brigands and spiritual demigods such as history or religion never had. Popular and maternal scenes are mixed with bestial poses and love by Chinese,

de malandrins et de demi-dieux spirituels comme l'histoire ou les religions ne l'ont jamais été. Chinois, Hottentots, bohémiens, niais, hyènes, Molochs, vieilles démences, démons sinistres, ils mêlent les tours populaires, maternels, avec les poses et les tendresses bestiales. Ils interpréteraient des pièces nouvelles et des chansons "bonnes filles." Maîtres jongleurs, ils transforment le lieu et les personnes et usent de la comédie magnétique. Les yeux flambent, le sang chante, les os s'élargissent, les larmes et des filets rouges ruissellent. Leur raillerie ou leur terreur dure une minute, ou des mois entiers.

J'ai seul la clef de cette parade sauvage.

Antique

Gracieux fils de Pan! Autour de ton front couronné de fleurettes et de baies tes yeux, des boules précieuses, remuent. Tachées de lies brunes, tes joues se creusent. Tes crocs luisent. Ta poitrine ressemble à une cithare, des tintements circulent dans tes bras blonds. Ton cœur bat dans ce ventre où dort le double sexe. Promène-toi, la nuit, en mouvant doucement cette cuisse, cette seconde cuisse et cette jambe de gauche.

Being Beauteous

Devant une neige un Être de Beauté de haute taille. Des sifflements de mort et des cercles de musique sourde font monter, s'élargir et trembler comme un spectre ce corps adoré; des blessures écarlates et noires éclatent dans les chairs superbes. Les couleurs propres de la vie se foncent, dansent, et se dégagent autour de la Vision, sur le chantier. Et les frissons s'élèvent et grondent et la saveur forcenée de ces effets se chargeant avec les sifflements mortels et les rauques musiques que le monde, loin derrière nous, lance sur notre mère de beauté, — elle recule, elle se dresse. Oh! nos os sont revêtus d'un nouveau corps amoureux.

×   ×   ×

O la face cendrée, l'écusson de crin, les bras de cristal! le canon sur lequel je dois m'abattre à travers la mêlée des arbres et de l'air léger!

Hottentots, gypsies, fools, hyenas, Molochs, old fits of madness and wily demons. They would interpret new plays and sentimental songs. As master jugglers they transform the place and the characters and use magnetic comedy. Their eyes catch fire, their blood sings, their bones grow big, tears and red rivulets stream. Their farce or their terror lasts a minute or for months on end.

I alone have the key of this wild circus.

Ancient

Graceful son of Pan! Under your brow crowned with flowers and berries, your eyes, precious balls, move. Spotted with dark streaks, your cheeks look hollow. Your fangs glisten. Your chest is like a lyre and tinklings move up and down your white arms. Your heart beats in that abdomen where your double sex sleeps. Walk at night and move gently this thigh, then this other thigh and this left leg.

Being Beauteous

Standing tall before snow, a Being of Beauty. Death whistles and rings of muffled music cause this worshipped body to rise up, expand; and tremble like a ghost. Scarlet and black wounds break out on the proud flesh. The very colors of life deepen, dance, and stand out from the Vision, in the yard. Tremblings rise and threaten and the persistent taste of these effects combining with the whistle of men and the discordant music which the world, far behind us, throws to our mother of beauty. She draws back and stands up. Our bones are reclothed with a new and amorous body.

×　　×　　×

Oh! the ashen face, the horsehair emblem, the crystal arms! The cannon on which I must fall, in the medley of trees and light air!

Vies

I

O les énormes avenues du pays saint, les terrasses du temple! Qu'a-t-on fait du brahmane qui m'expliqua les Proverbes? D'alors, de là-bas, je vois encore même les vieilles! Je me souviens des heures d'argent et de soleil vers les fleuves, la main de la campagne sur mon épaule, et de nos caresses debout dans les plaines poivrées.—Un envol de pigeons écarlates tonne autour de ma pensée—Exilé ici j'ai eu une scène où jouer les chefs-d'œuvre dramatiques de toutes les littératures. Je vous indiquerais les richesses inouïes. J'observe l'histoire des trésors que vous trouvâtes. Je vois la suite! Ma sagesse est aussi dédaignée que le chaos. Qu'est mon néant, auprès de la stupeur qui vous attend?

II

Je suis un inventeur bien autrement méritant que tous ceux qui m'ont précédé; un musicien même, qui ai trouvé quelque chose comme la clef de l'amour. À présent, gentilhomme d'une campagne aigre au ciel sobre j'essaye de m'émouvoir au souvenir de l'enfance mendiante, de l'apprentissage ou de l'arrivée en sabots, des polémiques, des cinq ou six veuvages, et quelques noces où ma forte tête m'empêcha de monter au diapason des camarades. Je ne regrette pas ma vieille part de gaîeté divine: l'air sobre de cette aigre campagne alimente fort activement mon atroce scepticisme. Mais comme ce scepticisme ne peut désormais être mis en œuvre, et que d'ailleurs je suis dévoué à un trouble nouveau,—j'attends de devenir un très méchant fou.

III

Dans un grenier où je fus enfermé à douze ans j'ai connu le monde, j'ai illustré la comédie humaine. Dans un cellier j'ai appris l'histoire. À quelque fête de nuit dans une cité du Nord j'ai rencontré toutes les femmes des anciens peintres. Dans un vieux passage à Paris on m'a enseigné les sciences classiques. Dans une magnifique demeure cernée par l'Orient entier j'ai accompli mon immense œuvre et passé mon illustre retraite. J'ai brassé mon sang. Mon devoir m'est remis. Il ne faut même plus songer à cela. Je suis réellement d'outre-tombe, et pas de commissions.

Lives

I

Oh! the huge avenues of the holy land, the terraces of the temple! What has happened to the brahmin who taught me the Proverbs? From then and from there I can still see even the old women! I remember silvery hours and sun near rivers, the hand of the country on my shoulder, and our caresses as we stood in the fiery fields.—A flight of red pigeons thunders around my thoughts—In exile here I had a stage on which to perform the dramatic masterpieces of all literatures. I might tell you about unheard-of wealth. I follow the story of the treasures you found. I see the next chapter! My wisdom is as neglected as chaos is. What is my void, compared with the stupefaction awaiting you?

II

I am a far more deserving inventor than all those who went before me; a musician, in fact, who found something resembling the key of love. At present, a noble from a meager countryside with a dark sky I try to feel emotion over the memory of a mendicant childhood, over my apprenticeship when I arrived wearing wooden shoes, polemics, five or six widowings, and a few wild escapades when my strong head kept me from rising to the same pitch as my comrades. I don't miss what I once possessed of divine happiness: the calm of this despondent countryside gives a new vigor to my terrible scepticism. But since this scepticism can no longer be put into effect, and since I am now given over to a new worry—I expect to become a very wicked fool.

III

In an attic where at the age of twelve I was locked up, I knew the world and illustrated the human comedy. In a wine cellar I learned history. At some night celebration, in a northern city, I met all the wives of former painters. In an old back street in Paris I was taught the classical sciences. In a magnificent palace, surrounded by all the Orient, I finished my long work and spent my celebrated retirement. I have invigorated my blood. I am released from my duty. I must not even think of that any longer. I am really from beyond the tomb, and without work.

Départ [34]

Assez vu. La vision s'est rencontrée à tous les airs.
Assez eu. Rumeurs des villes, le soir, et au soleil, et toujours.
Assez connu. Les arrêts de la vie. — O Rumeurs et Visions!
Départ dans l'affection et le bruit neufs?

Royauté

Un beau matin, chez un peuple fort doux, un homme et une femme superbes criaient sur la place publique: "Mes amis, je veux qu'elle soit reine!" "Je veux être reine!" Elle riait et tremblait. Il parlait aux amis de révélation, d'épreuve terminée. Ils se pâmaient l'un contre l'autre.

En effet, ils furent rois toute une matinée où les tentures carminées se relevèrent sur les maisons, et toute l'après-midi, où ils s'avancèrent du côté des jardins de palmes.

À une raison

Un coup de ton doigt sur le tambour décharge tous les sons et commence la nouvelle harmonie.

Un pas de toi, c'est la levée des nouveaux hommes et leur en-marche.

Ta tête se détourne: le nouvel amour! Ta tête se retourne, — le nouvel amour!

"Change nos lots, crible les fléaux, à commencer par le temps," te chantent ces enfants. "Elève n'importe où la substance de nos fortunes et de nos vœux" on t'en prie.

Arrivée de toujours, qui t'en iras partout.

Matinée d'ivresse

O *mon* Bien! o *mon* Beau! Fanfare atroce où je ne trébuche point! chevalet féerique! Hourra pour l'œuvre inouïe et pour le corps merveilleux, pour la première fois! Cela commença sous les rires des enfants, cela finira par eux. Ce poison va rester dans toutes nos veines même quand, la fanfare tour-

Departure

Seen enough. The vision met itself in every kind of air.

Had enough. Noises of cities in the evening, in the sunlight, and forever.

Known enough. The haltings of life.—Oh! Noises and Visions!

Departure into new affection and sound?

Royalty

One fine morning, in a land of very gentle people, a handsome man and woman cried out in the public square. "My friends, I want her to be queen!" "I want to be queen!" She laughed and trembled. He spoke to his friends of a revelation, of a trial ended. They swooned over each other.

They actually were monarchs for an entire morning when crimson draperies were hung from the houses, and for the entire afternoon when they walked toward the palm gardens.

To Reason

A tap with your finger on the drum releases all sounds and begins the new harmony.

One step of yours, and the new men rise up and march.

Your head turns aside: new love! Your head turns back: new love!

The children sing to you: "Change our fate, overcome the plague, and begin with time." They beg you, "Raise where you wish the substance of our fortune and our prayers."

You will go everywhere, since you have come from all time.

Morning of Drunkenness

Oh *my* Good! oh *my* Beautiful! Terrible fanfare of music where I never lose step! magical rack! Hurrah for the miraculous work and for the marvelous body, for the first time! It all began with the laughter of children, and will end there. This poison will still be in our veins even when the fanfare dies

nant, nous serons rendu à l'ancienne inharmonie. Ô maintenant nous si digne de ces tortures! rassemblons fervemment cette promesse surhumaine faite à notre corps et à notre âme créés: cette promesse, cette démence! L'élégance, la science, la violence! On nous a promis d'enterrer dans l'ombre l'arbre du bien et du mal, de déporter les honnêtetés tyranniques, afin que nous amenions notre très pur amour. Cela commença par quelques dégoûts et cela finit, — ne pouvant nous saisir sur-le-champ de cette éternité, — cela finit par une débandade de parfums.

Rire des enfants, discrétion des esclaves, austérité des vierges, horreur des figures et des objets d'ici, sacrés soyez-vous par le souvenir de cette veille. Cela commençait par toute la rustrerie, voici que cela finit par des anges de flamme et de glace.

Petite veille d'ivresse, sainte! quand ce ne serait que pour le masque dont tu nous as gratifié. Nous t'affirmons, méthode! Nous n'oublions pas que tu as glorifié hier chacun de nos âges. Nous avons foi au poison. Nous savons donner notre vie tout entière tous les jours.

Voici le temps des *Assassins*.

Phrases

Quand le monde sera réduit en un seul bois noir pour nos quatre yeux étonnés, — en une plage pour deux enfants fidèles, — en une maison musicale pour notre claire sympathie, — je vous trouverai.

Qu'il n'y ait ici-bas qu'un vieillard seul, calme et beau, entouré d'un "luxe inouï," — et je suis à vos genoux.

Que j'aie réalisé tous vos souvenirs, — que je sois celle qui sait vous garrotter, — je vous étoufferai.

———————

Quand nous sommes très forts, — qui recule? très gais, — qui tombe de ridicule? Quand nous sommes très méchants, — que ferait-on de nous.

Parez-vous, dansez, riez, — Je ne pourrai jamais envoyer l'Amour par la fenêtre.

———————

— Ma camarade, mendiante, enfant monstre! comme ça t'est égal, ces malheureuses et ces manœuvres, et mes embarras. Attache-toi à nous avec ta voix impossible, ta voix! unique flatteur de ce vil désespoir.

away and we return to the earlier discord. And now that we are so worthy of this torture, let us fervently gather in the superhuman promise made to our created body and soul. This promise, this madness! Elegance, science, violence! They promised us they would bury in the darkness the tree of good and evil, and deport tyrannical codes of honesty so that we may bring forward our very pure love. It all began with feelings of disgust and it ended—since we could not seize its eternity on the spot—it ended with a riot of perfumes.

Laughter of children, discretion of slaves, coldness of virgins, horror of figures and objects from here, be consecrated by the memory of that night. It began in slyness and it came to an end with angels of fire and ice.

Brief night of intoxication, holy night! even if it was only for the mask you bequeathed to us. We assert you, method! We are not forgetting that yesterday you glorified each of our ages. We believe in that poison. We can give all of our existence each day.

Behold the age of *Murderers*.

Phrases

When the world is reduced to a single dark wood for our two pairs of dazzled eyes—to a beach for two faithful children—to a musical house for our clear understanding—then I shall find you.

When there is only one old man on earth, lonely, peaceful, handsome, living in unsurpassed luxury, then I am at your feet.

When I have realized all your memories,—when I am the girl who can tie your hands,—then I will stifle you.

———————

When we are very strong, who draws back? or very happy, who collapses from ridicule? When we are very bad, what can they do to us.

Dress up, dance, laugh. I will never be able to throw Love out of the window.

———————

—Comrade of mine, beggar girl, monstrous child! How little you care about the wretched women, and the machinations and my embarrassment. Join us with your impossible voice, oh your voice! the one flatterer of this base despair.

Une matinée couverte, en Juillet. Un goût de cendres vole dans l'air;—une odeur de bois suant dans l'âtre,—les fleurs rouies,—le saccage des promenades—la bruine des canaux par les champs—pourquoi pas déjà les joujoux et l'encens?

×　　×　　×

J'ai tendu des cordes de clocher à clocher; des guirlandes de fenêtre à fenêtre; des chaînes d'or d'étoile à étoile, et je danse.

×　　×　　×

Le haut étang fume continuellement. Quelle sorcière va se dresser sur le couchant blanc? Quelles violettes frondaisons vont descendre?

×　　×　　×

Pendant que les fonds publics s'écoulent en fêtes de fraternité, il sonne une cloche de feu rose dans les nuages.

×　　×　　×

Avivant un agréable goût d'encre de Chine, une poudre noire pleut doucement sur ma veillée.—Je baisse les feux du lustre, je me jette sur le lit, et, tourné du côté de l'ombre je vous vois, mes filles! mes reines!

×　　×　　×

Ouvriers

O cette chaude matinée de février. Le Sud inopportun vint relever nos souvenirs d'indigents absurdes, notre jeune misère.

Henrika avait une jupe de coton à carreau blanc et brun, qui a dû être portée au siècle dernier, un bonnet à rubans, et un foulard de soie. C'était bien plus triste qu'un deuil. Nous faisons un tour dans la banlieue. Le temps était couvert et ce vent du Sud excitait toutes les vilaines odeurs des jardins ravagés et des prés desséchés.

Cela ne devait pas fatiguer ma femme au même point que moi. Dans une flache laissée par l'inondation du mois précédent à un sentier assez haut elle me fit remarquer de très petits poissons.

La ville, avec sa fumée et ses bruits de métiers, nous suivait très loin dans les chemins. O l'autre monde, l'habitation bénie par le ciel et les ombrages! Le sud me rappelait les misérables incidents de mon enfance, mes désespoirs d'été, l'horrible quantité de force et de science que le sort a toujours éloignée de moi. Non! nous ne passerons pas l'été dans cet avare pays où nous ne serons jamais que des orphelins fiancés. Je veux que ce bras durci ne traîne plus *une chère image*.

A dark morning in July. The taste of ashes in the air, the smell of wood sweating in the hearth, steeped flowers, the devastation of paths, drizzle over the canals in the fields, why not already playthings and incense?

× × ×

I stretched out ropes from spire to spire; garlands from window to window; golden chains from star to star, and I dance.

× × ×

The high pond is constantly steaming. What witch will rise up against the white sunset? What purple flowers are going to descend?

× × ×

While public funds disappear in brotherly celebrations, a bell of pink fire rings in the clouds.

× × ×

Arousing a pleasant taste of Chinese ink, a black powder gently rains on my night.—I lower the jets of the chandelier, throw myself on the bed, and, turning toward the dark, I see you, O my daughters and queens!

× × ×

Workers

O that warm February morning. The unseasonable South came to stimulate our memories of ridiculous poverty, all our youthful want.

Henrika had on a skirt of brown and white checkered cotton which must have been worn a hundred years ago, a bonnet with ribbons, and a silk scarf. It was sadder than mourning. We took a walk in the suburbs. The sky was gray and that wind from the South brought out all the bad smells from the ruined gardens and the dried-up meadows.

This did not tire my wife as much as myself. In a pool left by the flood of the month before, on quite a high path, she showed me some very small fish.

The city, with its smoke and noise from the looms, followed us as far as we walked. Oh! that other world, that dwelling blessed by heaven and the cool shade! The south wind reminded me of the wretched events of my childhood, of my torments in summertime, of the horrible amount of strength and knowledge which fate has always taken away from me. No! we will not spend the summer in this miserly place where we will never be anything but betrothed orphans. I do not want these strong arms to drag any longer *a beloved image.*

Les ponts

Des ciels gris de cristal. Un bizarre dessin de points, ceux-ci droits, ceux-là bombés, d'autres descendant ou obliquant en angles sur les premiers, et ces figures se renouvelant dans les autres circuits éclairés du canal, mais tous tellement longs et légers que les rives, chargées de dômes s'abaissent et s'amoindrissent. Quelques-uns de ces ponts sont encore chargés de masures. D'autres soutiennent des mâts, des signaux, de frêles parapets. Des accords mineurs se croisent, et filent, des cordes montent des berges. On distingue une veste rouge, peut-être d'autres costumes et des instruments de musique. Sont-ce des airs populaires, des bouts de concerts seigneuriaux, des restants d'hymnes publics? L'eau est grise et bleue, large comme un bras de mer.—Un rayon blanc, tombant du haut du ciel, anéantit cette comédie.

Ville

Je suis un éphémère et point trop mécontent citoyen d'une métropole crue moderne parce que tout goût connu a été éludé dans les ameublements et l'extérieur des maisons aussi bien que dans le plan de la ville. Ici vous ne signaleriez les traces d'aucun monument de superstition. La morale et la langue sont réduites à leur plus simple expression, enfin! Ces millions de gens qui n'ont pas besoin de se connaître amènent si pareillement l'éducation, le métier et la vieillesse, que ce cours de vie doit être plusieurs fois moins long que ce qu'une statistique folle trouve pour les peuples du continent. Aussi comme, de ma fenêtre, je vois des spectres nouveaux roulant à travers l'épaisse et éternelle fumée de charbon,—notre ombre des bois, notre nuit d'été!—des Erinnyes nouvelles, devant mon cottage qui est ma patrie et tout mon cœur puisque tout ici ressemble à ceci,—la Mort sans pleurs, notre active fille et servante, un Amour désespéré, et un joli Crime piaulant dans la boue de la rue.

Ornières

À droite l'aube d'été éveille les feuilles et les vapeurs et les bruits de ce coin du parc, et les talus de gauche tiennent dans leur ombre violette les mille rapides ornières de la route humide. Défilé de féeries. En effet:

Bridges

Gray crystal skies. A strange pattern of bridges, some straight, some arched, others going down or veering off at angles to the first, and these shapes repeating themselves in other lighted circuits of the canal, but all of them so long and light that the banks heavy with domes are lowered and shrunken. Some of these bridges are still covered with hovels. Others support masts, signals, thin parapets. Minor chords cross one another and diminish, ropes come up from the shores. You can see a red jacket and perhaps other costumes and musical instruments. Are they popular tunes, bits of castle concerts, remnants of public hymns? The water is gray and blue, as wide as an arm of the sea. —A white ray, falling from the top of the sky, blots out this comedy.

City

I am an ephemeral and not-too-discontented citizen of a metropolis obviously modern because every known taste has been avoided in the furnishings and in the outsides of the houses as well as in the layout of the city. Here you would not discover the least sign of any monument of superstition. In short, morals and speech are reduced to their simplest expression. These millions of people who have no need of knowing one another conduct their education, their trade, and their old age with such similarity that the duration of their lives must be several times shorter than, according to some insane statistics, is the case with the people on the continent. From my window, I see new ghosts rolling through thick, everlasting coal smoke, —our shadow in the woods, our summer night!—new Furies in front of my cottage which is my country and my heart since everything here resembles it—Death without tears, our active daughter and servant, a desperate Love, and a pretty Crime crying in the mud of the street.

Ruts

On the right the summer dawn stirs up leaves and mists and noises from that corner of the park, and the mounds on the left-hand side hold in their purple shade the countless swift ruts of the wet road. Fairy procession. Yes,

des chars chargés d'animaux de bois doré, de mâts et de toiles bariolées, au grand galop de vingt chevaux de cirque tachetés, et les enfants et les hommes sur leurs bêtes les plus étonnantes;—vingt véhicules, bossés, pavoisés et fleuris comme des carrosses anciens ou de contes, pleins d'enfants attifés pour une pastorale suburbaine;—Même des cercueils sous leur dais de nuit dressant les panaches d'ébène, filant au trot des grandes juments bleues et noires.

Villes [35]

Ce sont des villes! C'est un peuple pour qui se sont montrés ces Alleghanys et ces Libans de rêve! Des chalets de cristal et de bois qui se meuvent sur des rails et des poulies invisibles. Les vieux cratères ceints de colosses et de palmiers de cuivre rugissent mélodieusement dans les feux. Des fêtes amoureuses sonnent sur les canaux pendus derrière les chalets. La chasse des carillons crie dans les gorges. Des corporations de chanteurs géants accourent dans des vêtements et des oriflammes éclatants comme la lumière des cimes. Sur les plateformes au milieu des gouffres les Rolands sonnent leur bravoure. Sur les passerelles de l'abîme et les toits des auberges l'ardeur du ciel pavoise les mâts. L'écroulement des apothéoses rejoint les champs des hauteurs où les centauresses séraphiques évoluent parmi les avalanches. Au-dessus du niveau des plus hautes crêtes une mer troublée par la naissance éternelle de Vénus, chargée de flottes orphéoniques et de la rumeur des perles et des conques précieuses,—la mer s'assombrit parfois avec des éclats mortels. Sur les versants des moissons de fleurs grandes comme nos armes et nos coupes, mugissent. Des cortèges de Mabs en robes rousses, opalines, montent des ravines. Là-haut, les pieds dans la cascade et les ronces, les cerfs tettent Diane. Les Bacchantes des banlieues sanglotent et la lune brûle et hurle. Vénus entre dans les cavernes des forgerons et des ermites. Des groupes de beffrois chantent les idées des peuples. Des châteaux bâtis en os sort la musique inconnue. Toutes les légendes évoluent et les élans se ruent dans les bourgs. Le paradis des orages s'effondre. Les sauvages dansent sans cesse la fête de la nuit. Et une heure je suis descendu dans le mouvement d'un boulevard de Bagdad où des compagnies ont chanté la joie du travail nouveau, sous une brise épaisse, circulant sans pouvoir éluder les fabuleux fantômes des monts où l'on a dû se retrouver.

Quels bons bras, quelle belle heure me rendront cette région d'où viennent mes sommeils et mes moindres mouvements?

wagons loaded with animals of gilded wood, poles, and gaily-striped cloth, to the gallop of twenty spotted circus horses, and children and men on their most amazing beasts; — twenty vehicles embossed, with flags and flowers like ancient or story-book carriages, full of children all dressed for an outing in the suburbs; — Coffins, too, under their dark canopy with their pitch-black plumes, rolling along to the trot of large blue and black mares.

Cities

They are cities! They are a people for whom these Alleghanies and dream Lebanons have risen up. Swiss chalets of crystal and wood move along invisible rails and pulleys. Old craters girdled by colossi and copper palm trees roar tunefully in the midst of fires. The sounds of love feasts ring out over the canals suspended behind the chalets. The pack of chimes clamors in the gorges. Guilds of gigantic singers come together in clothes and banners as shining as the light on mountain tops. On platforms, within precipices, Rolands blare forth their valor. On foot bridges spanning the abyss and on the roofs of inns, the burning sky decks out masts. The collapse of apotheoses joins the fields with the highlands where seraphic centauresses move about in avalanches. Above the level of the highest crests a sea, disturbed by the eternal birth of Venus, heavy with Orphic navies and the roar of pearls and precious shells, — the sea sometimes grows dark with mortal splendor. On the slopes harvests of flowers as big as our weapons and our tankards bellow. Long lines of Mabs in red and opal dresses come up from the valleys. There, with their feet in the waterfall and the briars, deer suckle at the breasts of Diana. The Bacchantes of the suburbs sob and the moon burns and shouts. Venus goes into the caverns of blacksmiths and hermits. Groups of belfries intone the ideas of the people. Unfamiliar music comes from castles built of bones. All legends gyrate and the impulses of the living hurl themselves about in the villages. The paradise of storms comes to its end. The savages dance ceaselessly in the celebration of night. And for one hour I went down into the animated Baghdad boulevard where groups sang of the joy of new work, in a sluggish breeze, moving about without eluding the fabulous phantoms of mountains where people had to find themselves again.

What good arms, what precious hour will give me back that place from whence come my sleep and my slightest movements?

Vagabonds

Pitoyable frère! Que d'atroces veillées je lui dus! "Je ne me saisissais pas fervemment de cette entreprise. Je m'étais joué de son infirmité. Par ma faute nous retournerions en exil, en esclavage." Il me supposait un guignon et une innocence très bizarres, et il ajoutait des raisons inquiétantes.

Je répondais en ricanant à ce satanique docteur, et finissais par gagner la fenêtre. Je créais, par delà la campagne traversée par des bandes de musique rare, les fantômes du futur luxe nocturne.

Après cette distraction vaguement hygiénique je m'étendais sur une paillasse. Et, presque chaque nuit, aussitôt endormi, le pauvre frère se levait, la bouche pourrie, les yeux arrachés, — tel qu'il se rêvait! — et me tirait dans la salle en hurlant son songe de chagrin idiot.

J'avais en effet, en toute sincérité d'esprit, pris l'engagement de le rendre à son état primitif de fils du soleil, — et nous errions, nourris du vin des cavernes et du biscuit de la route, moi pressé de trouver le lieu et la formule.

Villes

L'acropole officielle outre les conceptions de la barbarie moderne les plus colossales. Impossible d'exprimer le jour mat produit par le ciel immuablement gris, l'éclat impérial des bâtisses, et la neige éternelle du sol. On a reproduit dans un goût d'énormité singulier toutes les merveilles classiques de l'architecture. J'assiste à des expositions de peinture dans des locaux vingt fois plus vastes qu'Hampton-Court. Quelle peinture! Un Nabuchodonosor norvégien a fait construire les escaliers des ministères; les subalternes que j'ai pu voir sont déjà plus fiers que des Brahmas, et j'ai tremblé à l'aspect des gardiens de colosses et officiers de constructions. Par le groupement des bâtiments en squares, cours et terrasses fermées, on évince les cochers. Les parcs représentent la nature primitive travaillée par un art superbe. Le haut quartier a des parties inexplicables: un bras de mer, sans bateaux, roule sa nappe de grésil bleu entre des quais chargés de candélabres géants. Un pont court conduit à une poterne immédiatement sous le dôme de la Sainte-Chapelle. Ce dôme est une armature d'acier artistique de quinze mille pieds de diamètre environ.

Sur quelques points des passerelles de cuivre, des plates-formes, des escaliers qui contournent les halles et les piliers, j'ai cru pouvoir juger la pro-

Vagabonds

Poor brother! What terrible nights I owed him! "I had no deep feeling for the affair. I played on his weakness. Through my fault, we would return to exile and slavery." He believed I had a very bizarre kind of bad luck and innocence, and he added upsetting reasons.

With a jeer I answered my satanic doctor, and left by the window. Along the countryside, streaked with bands of rare music, I created phantoms of a future night parade.

After that vaguely hygienic distraction I lay down on straw. And almost every night, as soon as I was asleep, my poor brother would get up, his mouth dry and his eyes protruding—just as he dreamed himself to be!— and would drag me into the room yelling his dream of a sad fool.

In deepest sincerity, I had pledged to convert him back into his primitive state of a sun-child,—and we wandered, sustained by wine from caverns and traveler's crust, with me impatient to find the place and the formula.

Cities

The official acropolis surpasses the most colossal conceptions of modern barbarism. Impossible to express the flat daylight produced by this unchanging gray sky, the imperial glitter of the buildings, and the eternal snow on the ground. In a singular taste for the gigantic they reproduced all the classical architectural marvels, and I visit exhibitions of paintings in rooms twenty times larger than Hampton Court. What paintings! A Norwegian Nebuchadnezzar built the stairways of the government buildings; the underlings I saw are already prouder than Brahmins, and I trembled at the sight of the guards of the colossi and the building officials. By arranging the buildings into squares, closed courtyards, and terraces, they cheat the cab-drivers. The parks represent a primitive nature artfully and proudly laid out. The upper part of the city has inexplicable parts: a river from the sea, without boats, unfolds its blue slate water between wharves supporting tremendous candelabra. A short bridge leads to a postern right under the dome of the Sainte-Chapelle. This dome is an artistic framework of steel, about fifteen thousand feet in diameter.

From a few points of the copper foot-bridges, and platforms and stairways surrounding the markets and pillars, I thought I could estimate the

fondeur de la ville: c'est le prodige dont je n'ai pas pu me rendre compte: quels sont les niveaux des autres quartiers sur ou sous l'acropole? Pour l'étranger de notre temps la reconnaissance est impossible. Le quartier commerçant est un circus d'un seul style, avec galeries à arcades. On ne voit pas de boutiques. Mais la neige de la chaussée est écrasée; quelque nababs aussi rares que les promeneurs d'un matin de dimanche à Londres, se dirigent vers une diligence de diamants. Quelques divans de velours rouge: on sert des boissons polaires dont le prix varie de huit cents à huit mille roupies. À l'idée de chercher des théâtres sur ce circus, je me réponds que les boutiques doivent contenir des drames assez-sombres (?) Je pense qu'il y a une police; mais la loi doit être tellement étrange, que je renonce à me faire une idée des aventuriers d'ici.

Le faubourg aussi élégant qu'une belle rue de Paris est favorisé d'un air de lumière. L'élément démocratique compte quelques cents âmes. Là encore les maisons ne se suivent pas; le faubourg se perd bizarrement dans la campagne, le "Comté" qui remplit l'occident éternel des forêts et des plantations prodigieuses où les gentilshommes sauvages chassent leurs chroniques sous la lumière qu'on a créée.

Veillées

I

C'est le repos éclairé, ni fièvre ni langueur, sur le lit ou sur le pré.
C'est l'ami ni ardent ni faible. L'ami.
C'est l'aimée ni tourmentante ni tourmentée. L'aimée.
L'air et le monde point cherchés. La vie.
—Etait-ce donc ceci?
—Et le rêve fraîchit.

II

L'éclairage revient à l'arbre de bâtisse. Des deux extrémités de la salle, décors quelconques, des élévations harmoniques se joignent. La muraille en face du veilleur est une succession psychologique de coupes de frises, de bandes athmosphériques et d'accidences géologiques. —Rêve intense et rapide de groupes sentimentaux avec des êtres de tous les caractères parmi toutes les apparences.

depth of the city: this is the miracle I was not able to judge: what are the levels of the other parts above or below the acropolis? For the foreigner of our day, reconnoitering is impossible. The business quarter is a circus constructed in a uniform style, with arcade galleries. You cannot see any shops. But the snow on the highway is flattened; a few nabobs as rare as Sunday morning walkers in London, are moving toward a diamond coach. A few divans of red velvet. They serve North Pole drinks at a price between eight hundred and eight thousand rupees. While on the point of looking for theatres in this circus, I tell myself that the shops must contain fairly tragic dramas (?) I think there are policemen. But the law must be so unusual that I give up imagining what adventurers are like here.

The suburb as elegant as a beautiful street in Paris enjoys an air of light. The democratic constituency numbers a few hundred souls. Here too the houses do not follow one another. The suburb melts strangely into the country, the "County" filling the eternal west with forests and gigantic plantations, where savage nobles hunt their news columns in the light which they invented.

Vigils

I

It is enlightened rest, neither fever nor languor, on the bed or on the grass.

It is the friend, who is neither strong nor weak. The friend.

It is the beloved, not tormenting nor tormented. The beloved.

The air and the world not sought after. Life.

—Was it this then?

—And the dream brought coolness.

II

The lighting comes back to the beam. From the two far sides of the room, commonplace settings, harmonic elevations merge. The wall opposite the guard is a psychological series of sections of friezes, atmospheric bands, and geological occurrences. —An intense, swift dream of sentimental groups with men of all characters in the midst of all appearances.

Les lampes et les tapis de la veillée font le bruit des vagues, la nuit, le long de la coque et autour du steerage.

La mer de la veillée, telle que les seins d'Amélie.

Les tapisseries, jusqu'à mi-hauteur, des taillis de dentelle, teinte d'émeraude, où se jettent les tourterelles de la veillée.

. . . .

La plaque du foyer noir, de réels soleils des grèves: ah! puits des magies; seule vue d'aurore, cette fois.

Mystique

Sur la pente du talus les anges tournent leurs robes de laine dans les herbages d'acier et d'émeraude.

Des prés de flammes bondissent jusqu'au sommet du mamelon. À gauche le terreau de l'arête est piétiné par tous les homicides et toutes les batailles, et tous les bruits désastreux filent leur courbe. Derrière l'arête de droite la ligne des orients, des progrès.

Et tandis que la bande en haut du tableau est formée de la rumeur tournante et bondissante des conques des mers et des nuits humaines,

La douceur fleurie des étoiles et du ciel et du reste descend en face du talus, comme un panier,—contre notre face, et fait l'abîme fleurant et bleu là-dessous.

Aube

J'ai embrassé l'aube d'été.

Rien ne bougeait encore au front des palais. L'eau était morte. Les camps d'ombres ne quittaient pas la route du bois. J'ai marché, réveillant les haleines vives et tièdes, et les pierreries regardèrent, et les ailes se levèrent sans bruit.

La première entreprise fut, dans le sentier déjà empli de frais et blêmes éclats, une fleur qui me dit son nom.

Je ris au wasserfall blond qui s'échevela à travers les sapins: à la cime argentée je reconnus la déesse.

Alors je levai un à un les voiles. Dans l'allée, en agitant les bras. Par la

The lamps and the rugs of the vigil make the sound of waves at night along the keel and around the steerage deck.

The sea of the vigil, like the breasts of Amelia.

The tapestries, half-way up, the lace undergrowth, emerald-colored, where the doves of the vigil fly.

. . . .

The plaque of the black earth, real suns of the shores: ah! well of magic; this time, a solitary vision of dawn.

Mystic

On the slope of the hill the angels whirl their woollen robes in the steel and emerald grasses.

Meadows of flame leap up to the top of the rise. On the left, the earth of the crest has been trampled on by all the murderers and battles, and all the sounds of disaster flash in their orbit. Behind the crest on the right, the line of the East and progress.

And while the band at the top of the picture is formed by the whirling and leaping noise of conch shells and nights of men,

The flowering beauty of the stars and of the sky and of all else comes down opposite the hill, like a basket,—close to our face, and makes the hollow below sweet smelling and blue.

Dawn

I have held the summer dawn in my arms.

Nothing moved as yet on the fronts of the palaces. The water was dead. Swarms of shadows refused to leave the road to the wood. I walked along, awakening the warm, alive air. Stones looked up, and wings rose up silently.

The first occurrence, in the path already filled with cool white shimmerings, was a flower which told me its name.

I laughed at the blond waterfall which tumbled down through the pine trees. At its silver top I recognized the goddess.

Then I took off her veils one by one. In the path, where I waved my

plaine, où je l'ai dénoncée au coq. À la grand'ville elle fuyait parmi les clochers et les dômes, et courant comme un mendiant sur les quais de marbre, je la chassais.

En haut de la route, près d'un bois de lauriers, je l'ai entourée avec ses voiles amassées, et j'ai senti un peu son immense corps. L'aube et l'enfant tombèrent au bas du bois.

Au réveil il était midi.

Fleurs

D'un gradin d'or,—parmi les cordons de soie, les gazes grises, les velours verts et les disques de cristal qui noircissent comme du bronze au soleil,—je vois la digitale s'ouvrir sur un tapis de filigranes d'argent, d'yeux et de chevelures.

Des pièces d'or jaune semées sur l'agate, des piliers d'acajou supportant un dôme d'émeraudes, des bouquets de satin blanc et de fines verges de rubis entourent la rose d'eau.

Tels qu'un dieu aux énormes yeux bleus et aux formes de neige, la mer et le ciel attirent aux terrasses de marbre la foule des jeunes et fortes roses.

Nocturne vulgaire

Un souffle ouvre des brèches operadiques dans les cloisons,—brouille le pivotement des toits rongés,—disperse les limites des foyers,—eclipse les croisées.—Le long de la vigne, m'étant appuyé du pied à une gargouille,—je suis descendu dans ce carrosse dont l'époque est assez indiquée par les glaces convexes, les panneaux bombés et les sophas contournés—Corbillard de mon sommeil, isolé, maison de berger de ma niaiserie, le véhicule vire sur le gazon de la grande route effacée: et dans un défaut en haut de la glace de droite tournoient les blêmes figures lunaires, feuilles, seins;

—Un vert et un bleu très foncés envahissent l'image. Dételage aux environs d'une tache de gravier.

—Ici, va-t-on siffler pour l'orage, et les Sodomes,—et les Solymes,—et les bêtes féroces et les armées,

—(Postillon et bêtes de songe reprendront-ils sous les plus suffocantes futaies, pour m'enfoncer jusqu'aux yeux dans la source de soie).

arms. In the field, where I gave away her name to the cock. In the city she fled between steeples and domes; and running like a thief along the marble wharves, I chased her.

Where the road mounts, near a laurel wood, I wrapped her in all her veils and felt something of the immensity of her body. Dawn and the child collapsed at the edge of the wood.

On waking, it was midday.

Flowers

From a gold terrace,—amidst silken cords, gray veils, green velvets and crystal discs which darken like bronze in the sun,—I see the foxglove opening on a tapestry of silver threads, eyes, and hair.

Pieces of yellow gold sown on the agate, mahogany pillars supporting an emerald dome, bouquets of white satin and delicate stalks of rubies surround the water-rose.

Like a god with large blue eyes and a snow body, the sea and the sky entice to the marble stairs the swarm of young, strong roses.

Daily Nocturne

A gust of wind makes operatic cracks in the partitions,—confuses the pivoting of worm-eaten roofs—blows away the walls of hearth,—blots out the windows.—Along the vine, leaning with one foot on a gargoyle,—I came into this coach whose age is indicated by its convex mirrors, its swelling panels, and its round sofas—Hearse of my sleep, all alone, shepherd's hut of my tomfoolery, the carriage turns on the grass of the fading highway: and in a blemish at the top of the right-hand glass white lunar figures, leaves, and breasts revolve;

—A very deep green and blue invade the picture. We can unharness near a patch of gravel.

—Here, we can whistle for the storm, and Sodoms,—and Solymas,—and wild beasts and armies,

—(Will the post chaise and dream animals take over in the most stifling groves to push me down to the level of my eyes in the silk water?)

—Et nous envoyer, fouettés à travers les eaux clapotantes et les boissons répandues, rouler sur l'aboi des dogues . . .

—Un souffle disperse les limites du foyer.

Marine

Les chars d'argent et de cuivre—
Les proues d'acier et d'argent—
Battent l'écume,—
Soulèvent les souches des ronces—
Les courants de la lande,
Et les ornières immenses du reflux
Filent circulairement vers l'est,
Vers les piliers de la forêt,—
Vers les fûts de la jetée,
Dont l'angle est heurté par des tourbillons de lumière.

Fête d'hiver

La cascade sonne derrière les huttes d'opéra-comique. Des girandoles prolongent, dans les vergers et les allées voisins du Méandre,—les verts et les rouges du couchant. Nymphes d'Horace coiffés au Premier Empire,—Rondes Sibériennes, Chinoises de Boucher.

Angoisse

Se peut-il qu'Elle me fasse pardonner les ambitions continuellement écrasées,—qu'une fin aisée répare les âges d'indigence,—qu'un jour de succès nous endorme sur la honte de notre inhabileté fatale,

(O palmes! diamant!—Amour! force!—plus haut que toutes joies et gloires!—de toutes façons, partout,—démon, dieu,—Jeunesse de cet être-ci; moi!)

Que des accidents de féerie scientifique et des mouvements de fraternité sociale soient chéris comme restitution progressive de la franchise première? . . .

—And send us, whipped by the thumping waters and the spilled drinks, to roll over the barking of the bulldogs . . .

—A gust of wind blows away the walls of the hearth.

Seapiece

Chariots of silver and copper—
Bows of steel and silver—
Beat the foam—
Raise up the stumps of bramble—
The currents of the moor
And the huge ruts of the ebb tide
Flow circularly toward the East,
Toward the pillars of the forest,—
Toward the poles of the pier,
Whose angle is struck by whirls of light.

Winter Party

The waterfall resounds behind the *opéra-comique* cabins. Candelabra continue, in the neighboring orchards and paths of the Labyrinth,—the greens and reds of the sunset. Nymphs of Horace with First Empire head-dress,—Siberian dances, Chinese women by Boucher.

Agony

Can She have me pardoned for my ambition so everlastingly repressed? Can wealth at the end of my life make up for my years of poverty? Can one day's success make me forget the shame of my fatal awkwardness,

(Oh! palms and diamonds! Love and power! higher than joy and fame!—at any rate, everywhere, a demon and a god, myself the Youth of this being!)

Can accidents of scientific fantasy and organizations of social brother-hood be cherished as the progressive restoration of original innocency? . . .

Mais la Vampire qui nous rend gentils commande que nous nous amusions avec ce qu'elle nous laisse, ou qu'autrement nous soyons plus drôles.

Rouler aux blessures, par l'air lassant et la mer; aux supplices, par le silence des eaux et de l'air meurtriers; aux tortures qui rient, dans leur silence atrocement houleux.

Métropolitain

Du détroit d'indigo aux mers d'Ossian, sur le sable rose et orange qu'a lavé le ciel vineux viennent de monter et de se croiser des boulevards de cristal habités incontinent par de jeunes familles pauvres qui s'alimentent chez les fruitiers. Rien de riche.—La ville!

Du désert de bitume fuient droit en déroute avec les nappes de brumes échelonnées en bandes affreuses au ciel qui se recourbe, se recule et descend, formé de la plus sinistre fumée noire que puisse faire l'Océan en deuil, les casques, les roues, les barques, les croupes.—La bataille!

Lève la tête: ce pont de bois, arqué; les derniers potagers de Samarie; ces masques enluminés sous la lanterne fouettée par la nuit froide; l'ondine niaise à la robe bruyante, au bas de la rivière; les crânes lumineux dans les plans [36] de pois—et les autres fantasmagories—la campagne.

Des routes bordées de grilles et de murs, contenant à peine leurs bosquets, et les atroces fleurs qu'on appellerait cœurs et sœurs, Damas damnant de longueur,—possessions de féeriques aristocraties ultra-Rhénanes, Japonaises, Guaranies, propres encore à recevoir la musique des anciens— et il y a des auberges qui pour toujours n'ouvrent déjà plus—il y a des princesses, et si tu n'es pas trop accablé, l'étude des astres—le ciel.

Le matin où avec Elle, vous vous débattîtes parmi les éclats de neige, les lèvres vertes, les glaces, les drapeaux noirs et les rayons bleus, et les parfums pourpres du soleil des pôles,—ta force.

Barbare

Bien après les jours et les saisons, et les êtres et les pays,

Le pavillon en viande saignante sur la soie des mers et des fleurs arctiques; (elles n'existent pas.)

But the Vampire who makes us behave stipulates that we play with what she leaves us, or otherwise that we start being funnier.

Let me roll in my wounds, through the heavy air and the sea; in my pains, through the silence of water and the harmful air; in the tortures which jeer at me, through their fiendish and billowy silence.

Metropolitan

From the indigo straits to Ossian's seas, over the rose-orange sand washed by a wine-colored sky, crystal boulevards have risen up and crossed, immediately settled by poor young families who get their food at the fruit dealers. Nothing rich.—Just the city!

From the asphalt desert flee in a straight line helmets, wheels, barges, rumps—in confusion with the sheets of fog spaced in horrible bands in the sky which bends back, withdraws and comes down, formed by the most treacherous black smoke which the Ocean in mourning can make.—Just the battle!

Look up: this wood bridge, arched; these last vegetable gardens of Samaria; these illuminated masks under the lantern whipped by the cold night; the silly water nymph in her noisy dress, in the lower part of the river; these luminous skulls in the pea rows—and other bewitchments—just the country.

These roads lined with fences and walls, their gardens bursting over them and the terrible flowers called hearts and sisters, damask damning slowly—possessions of fairy-like aristocracies beyond the Rhenish, Japanese, Guaranian, still capable of receiving the music of the ancients—and there are inns which will never open again now—there are princesses, and if you are not too overwrought, the study of the stars—just the sky.

In the morning when with Her, you fought in those shimmerings of snow, the green lips, the ice, the black flags and blue rays, and the red perfumes of the polar sun,—just your strength.

Barbarian

Long after the days and the seasons, and the people and the countries,

The flag of red meat over the silk of the seas and the Arctic flowers (but they do not exist.)

Remis des vieilles fanfares d'héroïsme—qui nous attaquent encore le cœur et la tête—loin des anciens assassins—

Oh! Le pavillon en viande saignante sur la soie des mers et des fleurs arctiques; (elles n'existent pas)

Douceurs!

Les brasiers pleuvant aux rafales de givre,—Douceurs!—les feux à la pluie du vent de diamants jetée par le cœur terrestre éternellement carbonisé pour nous.—O monde!—

(Loin des vieilles retraites et des vieilles flammes, qu'on entend, qu'on sent,)

Les brasiers et les écumes. La musique, virement des gouffres et choc des glaçons aux astres.

O Douceurs, o monde, o musique! Et là, les formes, les sueurs, les chevelures et les yeux, flottant. Et les larmes blanches, bouillantes,—o douceurs!—et la voix féminine arrivée au fond des volcans et des grottes arctiques.

Le pavillon . . .

Promontoire

L'aube d'or et la soirée frissonnante trouvent notre brick en large en face de cette Villa et de ses dépendances, qui forment un promontoire aussi étendu que l'Epire et le Péloponnèse, ou que la grande île du Japon, ou que l'Arabie! Des fanums qu'éclaire la rentrée des théories, d'immenses vues de la défense des côtes modernes; des dunes illustrées de chaudes fleurs et de bacchanales; de grands canaux de Carthage et des Embankments d'une Venise louche, de molles éruptions d'Etnas et des crevasses de fleurs et d'eaux des glaciers, des lavoirs entourés de peupliers d'Allemagne; des talus de parcs singuliers penchant des têtes d'Arbres du Japon; et les façades circulaires des "Royal" ou des "Grand" de Scarbro' ou de Brooklyn; et leurs railways flanquent, creusent, surplombent les dispositions de cet Hôtel, choisies dans l'histoire des plus élégantes et des plus colossales constructions de l'Italie, de l'Amérique et de l'Asie, dont les fenêtres et les terrasses à présent pleines d'éclairages, de boissons et de brises riches, sont ouvertes à l'esprit des voyageurs et des nobles—qui permettent, aux heures du jour, à toutes les tarentelles des côtes,—et même aux ritournelles des vallées illustres de l'art, de décorer merveilleusement les façades du Palais-Promontoire.

Recovering from the old fanfares of heroism—which still attack our heart and our head—far from the former assassins—

Oh! The flag of red meat over the silk of the seas and the Arctic flowers (but they do not exist)

Happiness!

The blazing fires streaming in the frosty gusts,—Happiness! The fires in the rain of the wind of diamonds hurled down by the world's heart endlessly burned for us.—O world!—

(Far from the old places and the old fire we hear and smell.)

Fires and foam. Music, turning of the abysses and collisions of icicles with the stars.

O happiness, o world, o music! Here, forms, sweating, hair and eyes, floating. And white tears, boiling—o happiness!—and the voice of a woman coming from the depths of the volcanoes and arctic grottoes.

The flag . . .

Promontory

The golden dawn and the tremendous evening find our brig out at sea, opposite this Villa and its dependencies, which form a promontory as extensive as Epirus and the Peloponnesus, or as the large island of Japan, or Arabia! Temples lighted up by the return of theories, tremendous views of modern coastal defenses; dunes illuminated by warm flowers and bacchanalia; great canals of Carthage and Embankments of a degenerate Venice, mild erupting Etnas and crevasses of flowers and glacier waters, outside laundries surrounded by German poplars; mounds in odd parks where the top of a Japanese tree bends down; and circular façades of "Royals" or "Grands" of Scarborough or Brooklyn; and their railways flank, hollow out, and dominate the outlay of this Hotel, which has been picked from the history of the most ornate and the biggest buildings of Italy, America, and Asia, whose windows and terraces now full of lighting appliances, drinks, and redolent breezes, are opened to the spirit of the travelers and nobles—who allow by day all the tarantellas of the coast,— and even the ritournellas of the illustrious valleys of art, to decorate in a miraculous way the façades of the Promontory Palace.

Scènes

L'ancienne Comédie poursuit ses accords et divise ses Idylles:
Des boulevards de tréteaux.

Un long pier en bois d'un bout à l'autre d'un champ rocailleux où la foule barbare évolue sous les arbres dépouillés.

Dans des corridors de gaze noire suivant le pas des promeneurs aux lanternes et aux feuilles.

Des oiseaux des mystères s'abattent sur un ponton de maçonnerie mû par l'archipel couvert des embarcations des spectateurs.

Des scènes lyriques accompagnées de flûte et de tambour s'inclinent dans des réduits ménagés sous les plafonds, autour des salons de clubs modernes ou des salles de l'Orient ancien.

La féerie manœuvre au sommet d'un amphithéâtre couronné par les taillis, — Ou s'agite et module pour les Béotiens, dans l'ombre des futaies mouvantes sur l'arête des cultures.

L'opéra-comique se divise sur une scène à l'arête d'intersection de dix cloisons dressées de la galerie aux feux.

Soir historique

En quelque soir, par exemple, que se trouve le touriste naïf, retiré de nos horreurs économiques, la main d'un maître anime le clavecin des prés; on joue aux cartes au fond de l'étang, miroir évocateur des reines et des mignonnes, on a les saintes, les voiles, et les fils d'harmonie, et les chromatismes légendaires, sur le couchant.

Il frissonne au passage des chasses et des hordes. La comédie goutte sur les tréteaux de gazon. Et l'embarras des pauvres et des faibles sur ces plans stupides!

A sa vision esclave, — l'Allemagne s'échafaude vers des lunes; les déserts tartares s'éclairent — les révoltes anciennes grouillent dans le centre du Céleste empire, par les escaliers et les fauteuils de rocs — un petit monde blême et plat, Afrique et Occidents, va s'édifier. Puis un ballet de mers et de nuits connues, une chimie sans valeur, et des mélodies impossibles.

La même magie bourgeoise à tous les points où la malle nous déposera! Le plus élémentaire physicien sent qu'il n'est plus possible de se soumettre à cet atmosphère personnel, brume de remords physiques, dont la constatation est déjà une affliction.

Scenes

Ancient Comedy continues its harmonies and divides up in Idylls:
Streets of stages.

A long wooden pier stretching from one end of a rocky field to the other, where the wild crowd wanders under the bare trees.

In corridors of black gauze following the steps of passers-by under the lanterns and leaves.

Birds from mystery plays come down on to the stonework of the pontoon bridge which is moved up and down by the protected line of spectators' boats.

Lyric scenes accompanied by flute and drum bow gracefully in corners under the ceilings, round modern club rooms or ancient Oriental halls.

The fairy-play takes place at the top of an amphitheatre crowned with foliage — Or is performed in a modulated key for Boetians, in the darkness of moving trees or the crest of fields.

The *opéra-comique* is divided on a stage at the line of intersection of ten partitions placed between the gallery and the footlights.

Historic Evening

For example, on some evening when the innocent tourist has retired from our economic turmoil, the hands of the master bring to life the harpsichord of the fields. They play cards at the bottom of the lake, a mirror reflecting queens and favorites. They have saints, veils, weavings of harmony and chromatic legends in the sunset.

He shudders at the passing of hunts and hordes. Comedy trickles on to the lawn platforms. And the embarrassment of the poor and the feeble on these stupid floor plans!

Before his slavish vision, — Germany builds itself up toward the moons; Tartar deserts are lighted up — ancient revolutions rumble in the center of the Celestial empire, over the rock stairways and armchairs — a small, white, flat world, Africa and the Wests, is going to be erected. Then a ballet of well-known seas and nights, a valueless chemistry, and impossible melodies.

The same middle-class magic wherever the mail train puts us down! The most elementary physicist feels it is no longer possible to undergo this personal atmosphere, a fog of physical remorse, whose very existence is already a trial.

Non!—Le moment de l'étuve, des mers enlevées, des embrasements souterrains, de la planète emportée, et des exterminations conséquentes, certitudes si peu malignement indiquées dans la bible et par les Nornes et qu'il sera donné à l'être sérieux de surveiller.—Cependant ce ne sera point un effet de légende!

Mouvement

Le mouvement de lacet sur la berge des chutes du fleuve,
Le gouffre à l'étambot,
La célérité de la rampe,
L'énorme passade du courant
Mènent par les lumières inouïes
Et la nouveauté chimique
Le voyageurs entourés des trombes du val
Et du strom.

Ce sont les conquérants du monde
Cherchant la fortune chimique personnelle;
Le sport et le confort voyagent avec eux;
Ils emmènent l'éducation
Des races, des classes et des bêtes, sur ce Vaisseau.
Repos et vertige
A la lumière diluvienne,
Aux terribles soirs d'étude.

Car de la causerie parmi les appareils,—le sang; les fleurs, le feu, les
    bijoux—
Des comptes agités à ce bord fuyard,
—On voit, roulant comme une digue au delà de la route hydraulique
    motrice,
Monstrueux, s'éclairant sans fin,—leur stock d'études;
Eux chassés dans l'extase harmonique
Et l'héroïsme de la découverte.

Aux accidents atmosphériques les plus surprenants
Un couple de jeunesse s'isole sur l'arche,
—Est-ce ancienne sauvagerie qu'on pardonne?—
Et chante et se poste.

No!—The moment of the cauldron, of seas swept away, of underground conflagrations, of the planet carried off, of resulting exterminations, certainties indicated with so little maliciousness in the bible and by the Norns which it will be the duty of a serious man to watch.—Yet it will not give the impression of a legend!

Motion

The swaying motion on the bank of the river falls,
The chasm at the sternpost,
The swiftness of the hand-rail,
The huge passing of the current
Conduct by unimaginable lights
And chemical newness
Voyagers surrounded by the waterspouts of the valley
And the current.

They are the conquerors of the world
Seeking a personal chemical fortune;
Sports and comfort travel with them;
They take the education
Of races, classes, and animals, on this Boat.
Repose and dizziness
To the torrential light,
To the terrible nights of study.

For from the talk among the apparatus,—blood, flowers, fire,
    jewels—
From the agitated accounts on this fleeing deck,
—You can see, rolling like a dyke beyond the hydraulic motor
    road,
Monstrous, illuminated endlessly,—their stock of studies;
Themselves driven into harmonic ecstasy
And the heroism of discovery.

In the most startling atmospheric happenings
A youthful couple withdraws into the archway,
—Is it an ancient coyness that can be forgiven?—
And sings and stands guard.

Bottom

La réalité étant trop épineuse pour mon grand caractère, — je me trouvai néanmoins chez ma dame, en gros oiseau gris bleu s'essorant vers les moulures du plafond et traînant l'aile dans les ombres de la soirée.

Je fus, au pied du baldaquin supportant ses bijoux adorés et ses chefs-d'œuvre physiques, un gros ours aux gencives violettes et au poil chenu de chagrin, les yeux aux cristaux et aux argents des consoles.

Tout se fit ombre et aquarium ardent. Au matin, — aube de juin batailleuse, — je courus aux champs, âne, claironnant et brandissant mon grief, jusqu'à ce que les Sabines de la banlieue vinrent se jeter à mon poitrail.

H

Toutes les monstruosités violent les gestes atroces d'Hortense. Sa solitude est la mécanique érotique, sa lassitude, la dynamique amoureuse. Sous la surveillance d'une enfance elle a été, à des époques nombreuses, l'ardente hygiène des races. Sa porte est ouverte à la misère. Là, la moralité des êtres actuels se décorpore en sa passion ou en son action. — O terrible frisson des amours novices sur le sol sanglant et par l'hydrogène clarteux! trouvez Hortense.

Dévotion

À ma sœur Louise Vanaen de Voringhem: — Sa cornette bleue tournée à la mer du Nord. — Pour les naufragés.

À ma sœur Léonie Aubois d'Ashby. Baou — l'herbe d'été bourdonnante et puante. — Pour la fièvre des mères et des enfants.

À Lulu, — démon — qui a conservé un goût pour les oratoires du temps des Amies et de son éducation incomplète. Pour les hommes! — À madame
. . .

À l'adolescent que je fus. À ce saint vieillard, ermitage ou mission.

À l'esprit des pauvres. Et à un très haut clergé.

Aussi bien à tout culte en telle place de culte mémoriale et parmi tels événements qu'il faille se rendre, suivant les aspirations du moment ou bien notre propre vice sérieux.

Ce soir à Circeto des hautes glaces, grasse comme le poisson, et enluminée comme les dix mois de la nuit rouge, — (son cœur ambre et spunk),

Bottom

Reality being too prickly for my lofty character, — I became at my lady's a big blue-gray bird flying up near the moldings of the ceiling and dragging my wings after me in the shadows of the evening.

At the foot of the baldaquino supporting her precious jewels and her physical masterpieces, I was a fat bear with purple gums and thick sorry-looking fur, my eyes of crystal and silver from the consoles.

Evening grew dark like a burning aquarium. In the morning, — a battling June dawn, — I ran to the fields, an ass, trumpeting and brandishing my grievance, until the Sabines came from the suburbs to hurl themselves on my chest.

H

All forms of monstrosity violate the atrocious gestures of Hortense. Her solitude is erotic mechanics, her weariness is the dynamics of love. Under the guardianship of childhood she has been, at many periods of time, the passionate hygiene of races. Her door is opened to poverty. There, the morals of real beings disembody in her passion or her action. — O terrible thrill of new loves on the blood covered ground and in the white hydrogen! find Hortense.

Devotions

To Sister Louise Vanaen de Voringhem: — Her blue coif turned toward the North Sea. — Pray for the shipwrecked.

To Sister Léonie Aubois d'Ashby. Baou — the buzzing, smelly summer grass. — Pray for the fever of mothers and children.

To Lulu, — a devil — who has kept a taste for oratories of the time of friends and her incomplete education. Pray for men! To Madame . . .

To the adolescent I once was. To that holy elder, hermitage or mission.

To the spirit of the poor. And to a very high-ranking clergy.

As well as to every devotion in every place of age-old worship and to such events where one has to go, to observe the aspirations of the moment or our own ingrained vice.

This evening to Circeto of the cold heights, fat as a fish, and illuminated like the ten months of the red night, — (her heart amber and spirited), — for

—pour ma seule prière muette comme ces régions de nuit et précédant des bravoures plus violentes que ce chaos polaire.

À tout prix et avec tous les airs, même dans des voyages métaphysiques. —Mais plus *alors*.

Démocratie

"Le drapeau va au paysage immonde, et notre patois étouffe le tambour.

"Aux centres nous alimenterons la plus cynique prostitution. Nous massacrerons les révoltes logiques.

"Aux pays poivrés et détrempés! —au service des plus monstrueuses exploitations industrielles ou militaires.

"Au revoir ici, n'importe où. Conscrits du bon vouloir, nous aurons la philosophie féroce; ignorants pour la science, roués pour le confort; la crevaison pour le monde qui va. C'est la vraie marche. En avant, route!"

Fairy

Pour Hélène se conjurèrent les sèves ornementales dans les ombres vierges et les clartés impassibles dans le silence astral. L'ardeur de l'été fut confiée à des oiseaux muets et l'indolence requise à une barque de deuils sans prix par des anses d'amours morts et de parfums affaissés.

—Après le moment de l'air des bûcheronnes à la rumeur du torrent sous la ruine des bois, de la sonnerie des bestiaux à l'écho des vals, et des cris des steppes—

Pour l'enfance d'Hélène frissonnèrent les fourrures et les ombres, —et le sein des pauvres, et les légendes du ciel.

Et ses yeux et sa danse supérieurs encore aux éclats précieux, aux influences froides, au plaisir du décor et de l'heure uniques.

Guerre

Enfant, certains ciels ont affiné mon optique: tous les caractères nuancèrent ma physionomie. Les Phénomènes s'émurent. —à présent l'inflexion

my one prayer silent as those night regions and preceding bravery more vi-
olent than this polar chaos.

At all costs and in every manner, even in metaphysical journeys.—But
no more *thens*.

Democracy

"The flag's off to that filthy place, and our speech drowns the sound of
the drum.

"In the centers we'll feed the most cynical whoring. We'll smash all log-
ical revolts.

"To the peppery dried-up countries!—in the service of the most gigan-
tic industrial or military exploitation.

"Goodbye to this place, no matter where we're off to. We conscripts of
good will are going to display a savage philosophy; ignorant in science,
rakes where our comfort is concerned; and let the world blow up! This is
the real march. Forward, men!"

Fairy World

For Helen the decorative sap conspired in the virginal darkness and the
impassive light in the astral silence. The heat of summer was entrusted to
silent birds and the appropriate languor to a priceless mourning barge
moving through waters of dead loves and collapsed perfumes.

—After the time when the wives of the woodcutters sang to the sound
of the cascade in the ruins of the forest, after the bells of the animals
sounded to the echo of the valleys and the cries of the steppes—

For Helen's childhood the furs and the shadows trembled,—and the
breast of the poor, and the legends of heaven.

And her eyes and her dancing still superior to the shafts of precious
light, to waves of cold, to the pleasure of the unique setting and the unique
moment.

War

Child, certain skies have sharpened my eyesight: their characters cast shad-
ows on my face. The Phenomena grew excited.—and now the everlasting

éternelle des moments et l'infini des mathématiques me chassent par ce monde où je subis tous les succès civils, respecté de l'enfance étrange et des affections énormes.—Je songe à une Guerre, de droit ou de force, de logique bien imprévue.

C'est aussi simple qu'une phrase musicale.

Génie

Il est l'affection et le présent puisqu'il a fait la maison ouverte à l'hiver écumeux et à la rumeur de l'été—lui qui a purifié les boissons et les aliments—lui qu'est le charme des lieux fuyant et le délice surhumain des stations.— Il est l'affection et l'avenir, la force et l'amour que nous, debout dans les rages et les ennuis, nous voyons passer dans le ciel de tempête et les drapeaux d'extase.

Il est l'amour, mesure parfaite et réinventée, raison merveilleuse et imprévue, et l'éternité: machine aimée des qualités fatales. Nous avons tous eu l'épouvante de sa concession et de la nôtre: o jouissance de notre santé, élan de nos facultés, affection égoïste et passion pour lui,—lui qui nous aime pour sa vie infinie . . .

Et nous nous le rappelons et il voyage . . . Et si l'Adoration s'en va, sonne, sa Promesse, sonne: "Arrière ces superstitions, ces anciens corps, ces ménages et ces ages. C'est cette époque-ci qui a sombré!"

Il ne s'en ira pas, il ne redescendra pas d'un ciel, il n'accomplira pas la rédemption des colères de femmes et de gaîetés des hommes et de tout ce péché: car c'est fait, lui étant, et étant aimé.

O ses souffles, ses têtes, ses courses; la terrible célérité de la perfection des formes et de l'action.

O fécondité de l'esprit et immensité de l'univers!

Son corps! Le dégagement rêvé, le brisement de la grâce croisée de violence nouvelle!

Sa vue, sa vue! tous les agenouillages anciens et les peines *relevés* à sa suite.

Son jour! l'abolition de toutes souffrances sonores et mouvantes dans la musique plus intense.

Son pas! les migrations plus énormes que les anciennes invasions.

O Lui et nous! l'orgueil plus bienveillant que les charités perdues.

O monde!—et le chant clair des malheurs nouveaux!

Il nous a connu tous et nous a tous aimé, sachons, cette nuit d'hiver, de

inflection of moments and the infinity of mathematics hunt me throughout this world where I experience civic popularity, respected by strange children and overpowering affections.—I dream of a War, of justice or power, of unsuspected logic.

It is as simple as a musical phrase.

Genie

He is affection and the present moment because he has thrown open the house to the snow foam of winter and to the noises of summer—he who purified drinking water and food—who is the enchantment fleeing places and the superhuman delight of resting places.—He is affection and future, the strength and love which we, erect in rage and boredom, see pass by in the sky of storms and the flags of ecstasy.

He is love, perfect and reinvented measure, miraculous, unforeseen reason, and eternity: machine loved for its qualities of fate. We have all known the terror of his concession and ours: delight in our health, power of our faculties, selfish affection and passion for him,—he who loves us because his life is infinity . . .

And we recall him and he sets forth . . . And if Adoration moves, rings, his Promise, rings: "Down with these superstitions, these other bodies, these couples and ages. This is the time which has gone under!"

He will not go away, he will not come down again from some heaven, he will not redeem the anger of women, the laughter of men, or all that sin: for it is done now, since he is and since he is loved.

His breathing, his heads, his racings; the terrifying swiftness of form and action when they are perfect.

Fertility of the mind and vastness of the world!

His body! the dreamed-of liberation, the collapse of grace joined with new violence!

All that he sees! all the ancient kneelings and the penalties *canceled* as he passes by.

His day! the abolition of all noisy and restless suffering within more intense music.

His step! migrations more tremendous than early invasions.

O He and I! pride more benevolent than lost charity.

O world!—and the limpid song of new woe!

He knew us all and loved us, may we, this winter night, from cape to

cap en cap, du pôle tumultueux au château, de la foule à la plage, de regards en regards, forces et sentiments las, le héler et le voir, et le renvoyer, et sous les marées et au haut des déserts de neige, suivre ses vues, —*ses souffles*—son corps,—son jour.

Jeunesse

I.

DIMANCHE

Les calculs de côté, l'inévitable descente du ciel et la visite des souvenirs et la séance des rhythmes occupent la demeure, la tête et le monde de l'esprit.

—Un cheval détale sur le turf suburbain, et le long des cultures et des boisements, percé par la peste carbonique. Une misérable femme de drame, quelque part dans le monde, soupire après des abandons improbables. Les desperadoes languissent après l'orage, l'ivresse et les blessures. De petits enfants étouffent des malédictions le long des rivières.—

Reprenons l'étude au bruit de l'œuvre dévorante qui se rassemble et remonte dans les masses.

II.

SONNET

Homme de constitution ordinaire, la chair n'était-elle pas un fruit pendu dans le verger,—o journées enfantes!—le corps un trésor à prodiguer;—o aimer, le péril ou la force de Psyché? La terre avait des versants fertiles en princes et en artistes, et la descendance et la race nous poussaient aux crimes et aux deuils: le monde votre fortune et votre péril. Mais à présent, ce labeur comblé, toi, tes calculs,—toi, tes impatiences—ne sont plus que votre danse et votre voix, non fixées et point forcées, quoique d'un double événement d'invention et de succès—une raison,—en l'humanité fraternelle et discrète par l'univers sans images;—la force et le droit réfléchissent la danse et la voix à présent seulement appréciées.

III.

VINGT ANS

Les voix instructives exilées . . . L'ingénuité physique amèrement rassise . . .—Adagio—Ah! l'égoïsme infini de l'adolescence, l'optimisme stu-

cape, from the noisy pole to the castle, from the crowd to the beach, from vision to vision, our strength and our feelings tired, hail him and see him and send him away, and under tides and on the summit of snow deserts follow his eyes,—*his breathing*—his body,—his day.

Youth

I.

SUNDAY

When homework is done, the inevitable descent from heaven and the visitation of memories, and the session of rhythms invade the dwelling, the head and the world of the spirit.

—A horse scampers off along the suburban turf, and the gardens and the wood lots, besieged by the carbonic plague. Somewhere in the world, a wretched melodramatic woman is sighing for unlikely desertions. Desperadoes are languishing for storms, drunkenness, wounds. Little children are stifling curses along the rivers.—

I must study some more to the sound of the consuming work which forms in all the people and rises up in them.

II.

SONNET

Man of usual constitution, wasn't the flesh a fruit hanging in the orchard? —o childhood days!—wasn't the body a treasure to spend?—o to love, the peril or the strength of Psyche? The earth had slopes fertile in princes and artists, and your descendants and your race drove you to crime and mourning: the world your fortune and your peril. But now that this work is done, you and your calculations,—you and your impatience—are only your dance and your voice, not fixed and not forced, although they are the reason for a double event made up of invention and success, in brotherly and discreet humanity throughout the universe without pictures;—force and right reflect the dance and the voice which are only now appreciated.

III.

TWENTY YEARS OLD

The exiled voices teach . . . Physical candor bitterly put in its place . . . —Adagio—Oh! infinite egoism of adolescence, and studious optimism:

dieux: que le monde était plein de fleurs cet été! Les airs et les formes mourant . . . —Un chœur, pour calmer l'impuissance et l'absence! Un chœur de verres, de mélodies nocturnes . . . En effet les nerfs vont vite chasser.

IV.

Tu en es encore à la tentation d'Antoine. L'ébat du zèle écourté, les tics d'orgueil puéril, l'affaissement et l'effroi.

Mais tu te mettras à ce travail: toutes les possibilités harmoniques et architecturales s'émouvront autour de ton siège. Des êtres parfaits, imprévus, s'offriront à tes expériences. Dans tes environs affluera rêveusement la curiosité d'anciennes foules et de luxes oisifs. Ta mémoire et tes sens ne seront que la nourriture de ton impulsion créatrice. Quant au monde, quand tu sortiras, que sera-t-il devenu? En tout cas, rien des apparences actuelles.

Solde

À vendre ce que les Juifs n'ont pas vendu, ce que noblesse ni crime n'ont goûté, ce qu'ignore l'amour maudit et la probité infernale des masses: ce que le temps ni la science n'ont pas à reconnaître:

Les Voix reconstituées; l'éveil fraternel de toutes les énergies chorales et orchestrales et leurs applications instantanées; l'occasion, unique, de dégager nos sens!

À vendre les Corps sans prix, hors de toute race, de tout monde, de tout sexe, de toute descendance! Les richesses jaillissant à chaque démarche! Solde de diamants sans contrôle!

À vendre l'anarchie pour les masses; la satisfaction irrépressible pour les amateurs supérieurs; la mort atroce pour les fidèles et les amants!

À vendre les habitations et les migrations, sports, féeries et comforts parfaits, et le bruit, le mouvement et l'avenir qu'ils font!

À vendre les applications de calcul et les sauts d'harmonie inouïs. Les trouvailles et les termes non soupçonnés, possession immédiate,

Élan insensé et infini aux splendeurs invisibles aux délices insensibles, —et ses secrets affolants pour chaque vice—et sa gaîté effrayante pour la foule—

—À vendre les Corps, les voix, l'immense opulence inquestionable, ce qu'on ne vendra jamais. Les vendeurs ne sont pas à bout de solde! Les voyageurs n'ont pas à rendre leur commission de si tôt!

how full of flowers was the world that summer! Melodies and forms dying . . . —A choir, to pacify impotence and absence! A choir of glasses, of night tunes . . . Yes, and one's nerves go out quickly to hunt.

IV.

You are still at the stage of the temptation of St. Anthony. The struggle with diminished zeal, grimacings of a child's insolence, collapse and fright.

But you will begin this work. All the possibilities of harmony and architecture will rise up around your seat. Perfect and unpredictable beings will offer themselves for your experiments. Around you the curiosity of ancient crowds and idle luxuries will move in dreamily. Your memory and your senses will only serve to feed your creative urge. What will happen to the world when you leave it? Nothing, in any case, will remain of what is now visible.

Sale

For sale what the Jews have not sold, what nobility and crime have not enjoyed, what the fatal love and the infernal honesty of the masses do not know: what time and science need not recognize:

Revised Voices; the brotherly awakening of all choral and orchestral power and their immediate application; the unique opportunity of freeing our senses!

For sale priceless Bodies, not belonging to any known race, world, sex, progeny! Wealth rising up at each step! Sale of diamonds with no control!

For sale anarchy for the masses; irrepressible satisfaction for superior amateurs; terrible death for the faithful and lovers!

For sale dwellings and migrations, sports, fantasies and perfect comfort, with the noise, movement, and future they create!

For sale results of mathematics and unheard-of scales of harmony. Discoveries and unsuspected terminologies, immediate possession,

Wild and infinite leap to splendor invisible to immaterial delights,— and ravishing secrets for each vice—and terrifying gaiety for the masses—

—For sale Bodies, voices, the tremendous, unquestionable wealth, what will never be sold. The salesmen have not reached the end of the sale! Travelers do not have to render accounts immediately!

Correspondance

Selected Letters

Correspondance

Selected Letters

Charleville (Ardennes), le 24 mai 1870

Cher Maître,

Nous sommes aux mois d'amour; j'ai dix-sept ans.[37] L'âge des espérances et des chimères, comme on dit, — et voici que je me suis mis, enfant touché par le doigt de la Muse, — pardon si c'est banal, — à dire mes bonnes croyances, mes espérances, mes sensations, toutes ces choses des poètes, — moi j'appelle cela du printemps.

Que si je vous envoie quelques-uns de ces vers, — et cela en passant par Alph. Lemerre, le bon éditeur, — c'est que j'aime tous les poètes, tous les bons Parnassiens, — puisque le poète est un Parnassien, — épris de la beauté idéale; c'est que j'aime en vous, bien naïvement, un descendant de Ronsard, un frère de nos maîtres de 1830, un vrai romantique, un vrai poète. Voilà pourquoi. — C'est bête, n'est-ce pas, mais enfin? . . .

Dans deux ans, dans un an peut-être, je serai à Paris. — Anch'io, messieurs du journal, je serai Parnassien! — Je ne sais ce que j'ai là . . . qui veut monter . . . — Je jure, cher maître, d'adorer toujours les deux déesses, Muse et Liberté.

Ne faites pas trop la moue en lisant ces vers: . . . Vous me rendriez fou de joie et d'espérance, si vous vouliez, cher Maître, *faire faire* à la pièce *Credo in unam* une petite place entre les Parnassiens, . . . Je viendrais à la dernière série du *Parnasse:* cela ferait le Credo des poètes! . . . —Ambition! ô Folle!

Arthur Rimbaud[38]

Charleville, 25 août 1870

Monsieur,

Vous êtes heureux, vous, de ne plus habiter Charleville! — Ma ville natale est supérieurement idiote entre les petites villes de province. Sur cela, voyez-vous, je n'ai plus d'illusions. Parce qu'elle est à côté de Mézières, — une ville qu'on ne trouve pas, — parce qu'elle voit pérégriner dans ses rues deux ou trois cents de pioupious, cette benoîte population gesticule, prud'hommesquement spadassine, bien autrement que les assiégés de Metz et de Strasbourg! C'est effrayant, les épiciers retraités qui revêtent l'uniforme! C'est épatant, comme ça a du chien, les notaires, les vitriers, les percepteurs, les menuisiers, et tous les ventres, qui, chassepot au cœur,

To Théodore de Banville

Charleville (Ardennes), 24 May 1870

Dear Maître,

We are in the months of love; I am seventeen. The age of hope and dreams, they say—and now I have begun, a child touched by the finger of the Muse—excuse me if this is banal—to express my good beliefs, my hopes, my sensations, all those things dear to poets—and this I call the spring.

If I send you some of these verses—and this thanks to Alph. Lemerre, the good publisher—it is because I love all poets, all good Parnassians—since the poet is a Parnassian—in love with ideal beauty. It is because I esteem in you, quite simply, a descendant of Ronsard, a brother of our masters of 1830, a real romantic, a real poet. That is why. This is foolishness, isn't it? but still?

In two years, in one year perhaps, I will be in Paris.—*Anch'io,* gentlemen of the press, I will be a Parnassian! I do not know what is inside me . . . that wants to come out. . . . I swear, *cher Maître,* I will always worship the two goddesses, the Muse and Liberty.

Do not frown too much as you read these verses: . . . You would make me delirious with joy and hope, if you were willing, *cher Maître,* to make room for the poem *Credo in unam* among the Parnassians, . . . I would like to be in the last issue of *Parnasse;* it would become the Creed of the poets! . . . O mad Ambition!

Arthur Rimbaud

To Georges Izambard

Charleville, 25 August 1870

Monsieur,

You are lucky not to be living now in Charleville!—My native town is the supremely stupid provincial town. You see, on this subject I have no more illusions. Because it is beside Mézières—a town you can't find—because it sees wandering about in its streets two or three hundred soldiers, this benighted population gesticulates like a bullying M. Prudhomme, in a very different manner than the besieged of Metz and Strasbourg! Retired grocers clothed in their uniforms are a terrible spectacle! It is astonishing, to see how lively they are, notaries, glaziers, tax-collectors, carpenters, and all the fat-bellied dignitaries with rifles over their hearts, patrolling at the

font du patrouillotisme aux portes de Mézières; ma patrie se lève! . . . Moi, j'aime mieux la voir assise: ne remuez pas les bottes! c'est mon principe.

Je suis dépaysé, malade, furieux, bête, renversé; j'espérais des bains de soleil, des promenades infinies, du repos, des voyages, des aventures, des bohémienneries enfin; j'espérais surtout des journaux, des livres . . . Rien! Rien! Le courrier n'envoie plus rien aux libraires; Paris se moque de nous joliment: pas un seul livre nouveau! c'est la mort! Me voilà réduit, en fait de journaux, à l'honorable *Courrier des Ardennes,* propriétaire, gérant, directeur, rédacteur en chef et rédacteur unique, A. Pouillard! Ce journal résume les aspirations, les vœux et les opinions de la population, ainsi jugez! c'est du propre! . . . —On est exilé dans sa patrie!!!!

Heureusement, j'ai votre chambre:—Vous vous rappelez la permission que vous m'avez donnée.—J'ai emporté la moitié de vos livres! J'ai pris *Le Diable à Paris.* Dites-moi un peu s'il y a jamais eu quelque chose de plus idiot que les dessins de Grandville?—J'ai *Costal l'Indien,* j'ai *La Robe de Nessus,* deux romans intéressants. Puis, que vous dire? . . . J'ai lu tous vos livres, tous; il y a trois jours, je suis descendu aux *Epreuves,* puis aux *Glaneuses,*— oui, j'ai relu ce volume!—puis ce fut tout! . . . Plus rien; votre bibliothèque, ma dernière planche de salut, était épuisée! . . . —Le *Don Quichotte* m'apparut; hier, j'ai passé, deux heures durant, la revue des bois de Doré: maintenant, je n'ai plus rien!

Je vous envoie des vers; lisez cela un matin, au soleil, comme je les ai faits: vous n'êtes plus professeur, maintenant, j'espère! . . . —

. . . .

—Vous aviez l'air de vouloir connaître Louisa Siefert, quand je vous ai prêté ses derniers vers; je viens de me procurer des parties de son premier volume de poésies, les *Rayons perdus,* 4ᵉ édition; j'ai là une pièce très émue et fort belle, *Marguerite:*

> . . . .
> Moi j'étais à l'écart, tenant sur mes genoux
> Ma petite cousine aux grands yeux bleus si doux:
> C'est une ravissante enfant que Marguerite
> Avec ses cheveux blonds; sa blouche si petite
> Et son teint transparent . . . .
> . . . .
> Marguerite est trop jeune. Oh! si c'était ma fille,
> Si j'avais une enfant, tête blonde et gentille,
> Fragile créature en qui je revivrais,
> Rose et candide avec de grands yeux indiscrets!

gates of Mézières: my country is rising up! . . . I prefer to see it seated: don't bestir yourself! that is my principle.

I am at a loss, ill, mad, stupid, astounded; I had hoped for sunbaths, long walks, rest, travel, adventure, bohemian larks, in a word; especially I had hoped for newspapers and books. . . . But there is nothing! The mail delivers nothing to bookstores; Paris is coyly making fun of us: not a single new book! everything is dead! In the way of newspapers, I am reduced to the honorable *Courrier des Ardennes,* owner, manager, director, head editor, and sole editor, A. Pouillard! This paper summarizes the aspirations, desires, and opinions of the population. You can judge for yourself what it is like! . . . —We are exiled in our own country!

Fortunately I have your room: you remember the permission you gave me. I have borrowed half of your books! I took *Le Diable à Paris.* Tell me if there is anything more idiotic than the drawings of Grandville?—I have *Costal l'Indien* and *La Robe de Nessus,* two interesting novels. What else is there to say? I have read all your books, all of them. Three days ago I sank as low as *Les Epreuves* and *Les Glaneuses.* Yes, I reread that volume! That was all there was! . . . Nothing left—I had exhausted your library, my last spiritual resource. . . . —I found *Don Quichotte.* Yesterday for two hours I went over Doré's woodcuts. Now I have nothing!

I am sending you some poems. Read them some morning in the sunlight where I composed them. You are not a teacher now, I hope! . . . —

. . . .

—You seemed to want to know more of Louisa Siefert, when I lent you her most recent poems; I just acquired parts of her first volume of poems, *Rayons perdus,* 4th edition; here is a very moving and beautiful piece, *Marguerite:*

. . . .
I was off to one side, holding on my lap
My little cousin with big blue eyes so sweet:
Marguerite is a ravishing girl
With her blonde hair; her mouth so small
And her fair skin . . . .

. . . .
Marguerite is too young. Oh! If she were my daughter,
If I had a child with a head so blonde and gentle,
Delicate creature in whom I would be reborn
Pink and candid with big indiscreet eyes!

Des larmes sourdent presque au bord de ma paupière
Quand je pense à l'enfant qui me rendrait si fière,
Et que je n'aurai pas, que je n'aurai jamais;
Cal l'avenir, cruel en celui que j'aimais,
De cette enfant aussi veut que je désespère . . .

. . . .

Jamais on ne dira de moi: c'est une mère!
Et jamais un enfant ne me dira: maman!
C'en est fini pour moi du céleste roman
Que toute jeune fille à mon âge imagine . . .

. . . .

—Ma vie, à dix-huit ans, compte tout un passé.

—C'est aussi beau que les plaintes d'Antigone ἀνύμφη,[39] dans Sophocle.
J'ai les *Fêtes galantes* de Paul Verlaine, un joli in-12 écu. C'est fort bizarre,
très drôle; mais vraiment, c'est adorable. Parfois de fortes licences: ainsi,

Et la tigresse épou | vantable d'Hyrcanie

est un vers de ce volume. Achetez, je vous le conseille, *La Bonne Chanson*,
un petit volume de vers du même poète: ça vient de paraître chez Lemerre;
je ne l'ai pas lu: rien n'arrive ici; mais plusieurs journaux en disent beau-
coup de bien.
—Au revoir, envoyez-moi une lettre de 25 pages—poste restante—et
bien vite!

A. Rimbaud

P.S.—A bientôt, des révélations sur la vie que je vais mener après . . .
vacances . . .

À Georges Izambard

Paris, le 5 septembre 1870

Cher Monsieur,

Ce que vous me conseilliez de ne pas faire, je l'ai fait: je suis allé à Paris,
quittant la maison maternelle! J'ai fait ce tour le 29 août.
Arrêté en descendant de wagon pour n'avoir pas un sou et devoir treize

Tears rise almost fill my eyelids
When I think of the child who would make me so proud,
Whom I will not have, whom I will never have;
Because fate, cruel in all that I loved,
Of this child also wishes that I despair. . .

. . . .
Never will one say of me: she is a born mother!
And never will a child say to me: Mommy!
It's over for me, the dreamy story
That every young girl my age imagines. . .

. . . .
—My life, at eighteen, includes a full past.

—This is as beautiful as Antigone's laments *anumphē,* in Sophocles.—I
have Paul Verlaine's *Fêtes galantes,* in a pocket-size edition. It's extremely
strange, very funny; but really, it's adorable. Sometimes with serious li-
cense; for example,

And the terrible ti | gress of Hyrcania [40]

is a line from this volume.—I advise you to buy *La Bonne Chanson,* a small
volume of poems from the same poet: Lemerre has just brought it out; I
haven't read it; nothing gets this far; but it has been well reviewed in sev-
eral newspapers.
—Goodbye. Send me a letter of 25 pages—in care of the post office—and
quickly!

A. Rimbaud

P.S. Soon I will give you revelations about the life I am going to lead af-
ter . . . vacation. . . .

To Georges Izambard

Paris, 5 September 1870

Cher Monsieur,

What you advised me not to do, I did. I went to Paris and left my
mother's home. I took this trip August 29.

Arrested as I got off the train, for not having a centime and owing the

francs de chemin de fer, je fus conduit à la préfecture, et, aujourd'hui, j'attends mon jugement à Mazas! oh!—*J'espère en vous* comme en ma mère; vous m'avez toujours été comme un frère: je vous demande instamment cette aide que vous m'offrîtes. J'ai écrit à ma mère, au procureur impérial, au commissaire de police de Charleville; si vous ne recevez de moi aucune nouvelle mercredi, avant le train qui conduit de Douai à Paris, *prenez ce train, venez ici me réclamer par lettre, ou en vous présentant au procureur,* en priant, en *répondant de moi,* en *payant ma dette! Faites tout ce que vous pourrez,* et, quand vous recevrez cette lettre, écrivez, vous aussi, *je vous l'ordonne,* oui, *écrivez à ma pauvre mère* (Quai de la Madeleine, 5, Charlev.) *pour la consoler! Ecrivez-moi* aussi; faites tout! Je vous aime comme un frère, je vous aimerai comme un père.

Je vous serre la main   Votre pauvre

Arthur Rimbaud à Mazas

Et si vous parvenez à me libérer, vous m'emmènerez à Douai avec [vous].

À Georges Izambard

Charleville, le 2 novembre 1870

Monsieur,

—À vous seul ceci. —

Je suis rentré à Charleville un jour après vous avoir quitté. Ma mère m'a reçu, et je suis là . . . tout à fait oisif. Ma mère ne me mettrait en pension qu'en janvier 71.

Et bien! j'ai tenu ma promesse.

Je meurs, je me décompose dans la platitude, dans la mauvaiseté, dans la grisaille. Que voulez-vous, je m'entête affreusement à adorer la liberté libre, et . . . un tas de choses que "ça fait pitié", n'est-ce pas?—Je devais repartir aujourd'hui même; je le pouvais: j'étais vêtu de neuf, j'aurais vendu ma montre, et vive la liberté!—Donc je suis resté! je suis resté!—et je voudrai repartir encore bien des fois—Allons, chapeau, capote, les deux poings dans les poches et sortons!—Mais je resterai, je resterai. Je n'ai pas promis cela. Mais je le ferai pour mériter votre affection: vous me l'avez dit. Je la mériterai.

La reconnaissance que je vous ai, je ne saurais pas vous l'exprimer aujourd'hui plus que l'autre jour. Je vous la prouverai. Il s'agirait de faire

railroad thirteen francs, I was taken to the prefecture, and today am awaiting the verdict in Mazas! — Oh! *My hope is in you* as in my mother. You have always been a brother to me and now I am asking for the help you offered me. I have written to my mother, to the imperial procurator, to the head of the police in Charleville. If you hear nothing from me on Wednesday, before the train that leaves Douai for Paris, *take that train, come here to claim me by letter, or go to the procurator* to intercede, *to vouch for me* and *pay my debt! Do all you can,* and, when you receive this letter, write, you too, *I order you,* yes, *write to my poor mother* (Quai de la Madeleine, 5, Charlev.) *to console her! Write also to me.* Do all this! I love you as a brother, I will love you as a father.

I shake your hand   Your poor

Arthur Rimbaud at Mazas

And if you succeed in freeing me, you will take me with you to Douai.

To Georges Izambard

Charleville, 2 November 1870

Monsieur,

— This is for you alone. —

I returned to Charleville the day after leaving you. My mother took me in, and here I am . . . without any occupation. My mother will not put me back in school before January '71.

So, I kept my promise.

I am dying, I am decomposing in dulness, in paltry wickedness, in grayness. What can I say? — in a terrible way I insist on worshipping free freedom, and so many things that *I am to be pitied,* isn't it true? I was to set out again today. I could have done so. I had new clothes on, I would have sold my watch, and long live freedom! — But I stayed back! I stayed back! — I will want to leave many more times — Let's go, hat, coat, my two fists in my pockets and we're off! But I will stay, I will stay. I did not promise to. But I will do so to deserve your affection. You told me this. I will deserve it.

The gratitude I feel for you, I could not express today any more than any other day. I will prove it to you. If it were a question of doing some-

quelque chose pour vous, que je mourrais pour le faire, — je vous en donne ma parole. — J'ai encore un tas de choses à dire . . .

Ce "sans-cœur" de

A. Rimbaud

À Georges Izambard

Charleville, 13 mai 1871

Cher Monsieur!

Vous revoilà professeur. On se doit à la Société, m'avez-vous dit; vous faites partie des corps enseignants: vous roulez dans la bonne ornière. — Moi aussi, je suis le principe: je me fais cyniquement *entretenir;* je déterre d'anciens imbéciles de collège: tout ce que je puis inventer de bête, de sale, de mauvais, en action et en paroles, je le leur livre: on me paie en bocks et en filles. *Stat mater dolorosa, dum pendet filius.* — Je me dois à la Société, c'est juste, — et j'ai raison. — Vous aussi, vous avez raison, pour aujourd'hui. Au fond, vous ne voyez en votre principe que poésie subjective: votre obstination à regagner le râtelier universitaire — pardon! — le prouve. Mais vous finirez toujours comme un satisfait qui n'a rien fait, n'ayant rien voulu faire. Sans compter que votre poésie subjective sera toujours horriblement fadasse. Un jour, j'espère, — bien d'autres espèrent la même chose, — je verrai dans votre principe la poésie objective, je la verrai plus sincèrement que vous ne le feriez! — Je serai un travailleur: c'est l'idée qui me retient, quand les colères folles me poussent vers la bataille de Paris, — où tant de travailleurs meurent pourtant encore tandis que je vous écris! Travailler maintenant, jamais, jamais; je suis en grève.

Maintenant, je m'encrapule le plus possible. Pourquoi? Je veux être poète, et je travaille à me rendre *Voyant:* vous ne comprenez pas du tout, et je ne saurais presque vous expliquer. Il s'agit d'arriver à l'inconnu par le dérèglement de *tous les sens.* Les souffrances sont énormes, mais il faut être fort, être né poète, et je me suis reconnu poète. Ce n'est pas du tout ma faute. C'est faux de dire: Je pense: On devrait dire: On me pense. — Pardon du jeu de mots. —

Je est un autre. Tant pis pour le bois qui se trouve violon, et Nargue aux inconscients, qui ergotent sur ce qu'ils ignorent tout à fait!

Vous n'êtes pas *Enseignant* pour moi. Je vous donne ceci: est-ce de la satire, comme vous diriez? Est-ce de la poésie? C'est de la fantaisie, toujours. — Mais, je vous en supplie, ne soulignez ni du crayon, ni trop de la pensée:

thing for you, I would die in order to do it. I give you my word.—I still have many things to say. . . .

This "heartless"

A. Rimbaud

To Georges Izambard

Charleville, 13 May 1871

Cher Monsieur!

You are a teacher again. You have told me we owe a duty to Society. You belong to the teaching body: you move along in the right track. I also follow the principle: cynically I am having myself *kept*. I dig up old imbeciles from school: I serve them with whatever I can invent that is stupid, filthy, mean in acts and words. They pay me in beer and liquor. *Stat mater dolorosa, dum pendet filius.*—My duty is to Society, that is true—and I am right.—You too are right, for now. In reality, all you see in your principle is subjective poetry: your obstinacy in reaching the university trough—excuse me—proves this. But you will always end up a self-satisfied man who has done nothing because he wanted to do nothing. Not to mention that your subjective poetry will always be horribly insipid. One day, I hope— many others hope the same thing—I will see objective poetry according to your principle, I will see it more sincerely than you would! I will be a worker: this idea holds me back, when mad anger drives me toward the battle of Paris—where so many workers are dying as I write to you! Work now?—never, never, I am on strike.

Now, I am degrading myself as much as possible. Why? I want to be a poet, and I am working to make myself a *Seer:* you will not understand this, and I don't know how to explain it to you. It is a question of reaching the unknown by the derangement of *all the senses.* The sufferings are enormous, but one has to be strong, one has to be born a poet, and I know I am a poet. This is not at all my fault. It is wrong to say: I think: One ought to say: people think me.—Pardon the pun [penser, "to think"; panser, "to groom"].—

I is someone else. It is too bad for the wood which finds itself a violin and Scorn for the heedless who argue over what they are totally ignorant of!

You are not a *Teacher* for me. I give you this: is it satire, as you would say? Is it poetry? It is fantasy, always.—But I beg you, do not underline it with your pencil or too much with your thought:

Le cœur supplicié [41]

Mon triste cœur bave à la poupe. . . .
Mon cœur est plein de caporal!
Ils y lancent des jets de soupe,
Mon triste cœur bave à la poupe . . .
Sous les quolibets de la troupe
Qui lance un rire général
Mon triste cœur bave à la poupe,
Mon cœur est plein de caporal!

Ithyphalliques et pioupiesques
Leurs insultes l'ont dépravé;
À la vesprée, ils font des fresques
Ithyphalliques et pioupiesques;
Ô flots abracadabrantesques,
Prenez mon cœur, qu'il soit sauvé!
Ithyphalliques et pioupiesques
Leurs insultes l'ont dépravé!

Quand ils auront tari leurs chiques,
Comment agir, ô cœur volé?
Ce seront des refrains bachiques
Quand ils auront tari leurs chiques!
J'aurai des sursauts stomachiques
Si mon cœur triste est ravalé!
Quand ils auront tari leurs chiques
Comment agir, ô cœur volé?

Ça ne veut pas rien dire. [42] — *Répondez-moi:* chez Mr Deverrière, pour A. R..

Bonjour de cœur,   Art. Rimbaud

À Paul Demeny

Charleville, 15 mai 1871

J'ai résolu de vous donner une heure de littérature nouvelle. Je commence de suite par un psaume d'actualité:

The Tortured Heart

My sad heart slobbers at the poop. . . .
My heart is full of tobacco-spit!
They spew streams of soup at it,
My sad heart slobbers at the poop . . .
Under the jeerings of the soldiers
Who break out laughing
My sad heart slobbers at the poop,
My heart is full of tobacco-spit!

Ithyphallic and soldierish
Their insults have depraved it;
At vespers, they make frescoes
Ithyphallic and soldierish;
O abracadabratic waves,
Take my heart, let it be saved!
Ithyphallic and soldierish
Their insults have depraved it!

When they have used up their quid,
How will I act, O stolen heart?
There will be Bacchic refrains
When they have used up their quid!
I will have stomach retchings
If my sad heart is degraded!
When they have used up their quid
How will I act, O stolen heart?

This does not mean nothing. —*Answer me:* care of M' Deverrière, for A. R..

Warm greetings,   Art. Rimbaud

To Paul Demeny

Charleville, 15 May 1871

I have decided to give you an hour of new literature. I begin at once with a song of today:

Chant de guerre parisien

Le printemps est évident, car . . .

· · · · · · · · · · · · · ·

A. RIMBAUD

—Voici de la prose sur l'avenir de la poésie—

Toute poésie antique aboutit à la poésie grecque, Vie harmonieuse. —De la Grèce au mouvement romantique, —moyen-âge, —il y a des lettrés, des versificateurs. D'Ennius à Théroldus, de Théroldus à Casimir Delavigne, tout est prose rimée, un jeu, avachissement et gloire d'innombrables générations idiotes: Racine est le pur, le fort, le grand. —On eût soufflé sur ses rimes, brouillé ses hémistiches, que le Divin Sot serait aujourd'hui aussi ignoré que le premier venu auteur d'*Origines*. —Après Racine, le jeu moisit. Il a duré deux mille ans!

Ni plaisanterie, ni paradoxe. La raison m'inspire plus de certitudes sur le sujet que n'aurait jamais eu de colères un Jeune-France. Du reste, libre aux *nouveaux!* d'exécrer les ancêtres: on est chez soi et l'on a le temps.

On n'a jamais bien jugé le romantisme; qui l'aurait jugé? Les critiques!! Les romantiques, qui prouvent si bien que la chanson est si peu souvent l'œuvre, c'est-à-dire la pensée chantée *et comprise* du chanteur?

Car Je est un autre. Si le cuivre s'éveille clairon, il n'y a rien de sa faute. Cela m'est évident: j'assiste à l'éclosion de ma pensée: je la regarde, je l'écoute: je lance un coup d'archet: la symphonie fait son remuement dans les profondeurs, ou vient d'un bond sur la scène.

Si les vieux imbéciles n'avaient pas trouvé du Moi que la signification fausse, nous n'aurions pas à balayer ces millions de squelettes qui, depuis un temps infinie! ont accumulé les produits de leur intelligence borgnesse, en s'en clamant les auteurs!

En Grèce, ai-je dit, vers et lyres *rhythment l'Action*. Après, musique et rimes sont jeux, délassements. L'étude de ce passé charme les curieux: plusieurs s'éjouissent à renouveler ces antiquités: —c'est pour eux. L'intelligence universelle a toujours jeté ses idées, naturellement; les hommes ramassaient une partie de ces fruits du cerveau: on agissait par, on en écrivait des livres: telle allait la marche, l'homme ne se travaillant pas, n'étant pas encore éveillé, ou pas encore dans la plénitude du grand songe. Des fonctionnaires, des écrivains: auteur, créateur, poète, cet homme n'a jamais existé!

La première étude de l'homme qui veut être poète est sa propre connaissance, entière; il cherche son âme, il l'inspecte, il la tente, l'apprend.

Parisian War Song

Spring is evident, for . . .

. . . .

A. RIMBAUD

—Here is some prose on the future of poetry—
All ancient poetry ended in Greek poetry, harmonious life.—From Greece
to the romantic movement—Middle Ages—there are writers and versi-
fiers. From Ennius to Theroldus, from Theroldus to Casimir Delavigne, it
is all rhymed prose, a game, degradation and glory of countless idiotic
generations: Racine is pure, strong and great.—If his rhymes had been
blown out and his hemistichs mixed up, the Divine Fool would today be
as unknown as any old author of *Origins.*—After Racine, the game gets
moldy. It has lasted two thousand years!

Neither joke, nor paradox. Reason fills me with more certainty on the
subject than a member of Jeune-France[43] would have ever been with rage.
Moreover, *newcomers!* are free to condemn the ancestors. We are at home
and we have the time.

Romanticism has never been carefully judged; who would have judged
it? The critics!! The romantics, who prove so obviously that a song is
so seldom a work, that is to say, a thought sung *and understood* by the
singer?

For I is someone else. If brass wakes up a trumpet, it is not its fault. This
is obvious to me: I am present at this birth of my thought: I watch it and
listen to it: I draw a stroke of the bow: the symphony makes its stir in the
depths, or comes on to the stage in a leap.

If old imbeciles had not discovered only the false meaning of the Ego,
we would not have to sweep away those millions of skeletons which, for
time immemorial! have accumulated the results of their one-eyed intellects
by claiming to be the authors!

In Greece, as I have said, verses and lyres *give rhythm to Action.* After
that, music and rhymes are games and pastimes. The study of this past
delights the curious: several rejoice in reviving those antiquities—it is for
them. Universal intelligence has always thrown out its ideas, naturally;
men picked up a part of these fruits of the mind: people acted through
them and wrote books about them. Things continued thus: man not
working on himself, not yet being awake, or not yet in the fullness of the
great dream. Civil servants, writers: author, creator, poet, that man never
existed!

Dès qu'il la sait, il doit la cultiver; Cela semble simple: en tout cerveau s'accomplit un développement naturel; tant *d'égoïstes* se proclament auteurs; il en est bien d'autres qui *s'*attribuent leur progrès intellectuel!—Mais il s'agit de faire l'âme monstrueuse: à l'instar des comprachicos, quoi! Imaginez un homme s'implantant et se cultivant des verrues sur le visage.

Je dis qu'il faut être *voyant,* se faire *voyant.*

Le Poète se fait *voyant* par un long, immense et raisonné *dérèglement* de *tous les sens.* Toutes les formes d'amour, de souffrance, de folie; il cherche lui-même, il épuise en lui tous les poisons, pour n'en garder que les quintessences. Ineffable torture où il a besoin de toute la foi, de toute la force surhumaine, où il devient entre tous le grand malade, le grand criminel, le grand maudit,—et le suprême Savant!—Car il arrive à l'*inconnu!* Puisqu'il a cultivé son âme, déjà riche, plus qu'aucun! Il arrive à l'inconnu, et quand, affolé, il finirait par perdre l'intelligence de ses visions, il les a vues! Qu'il crève dans son bondissement par les choses inouïes et innommables: viendront d'autres horribles travailleurs; ils commenceront par les horizons où l'autre s'est affaissé!

—La suite à six minutes—

Ici j'intercale un second psaume *hors du texte:* veuillez tendre une oreille complaisante,—et tout le monde sera charmé.—J'ai l'archet en main, je commence:

Mes petites amoureuses

Un hydrolat lacrymal lave . . .

. . . .

A. R.

Voilà. Et remarquez bien que, si je ne craignais de vous faire débourser plus de 60 c. de port,—moi pauvre effaré qui, depuis sept mois, n'ai pas tenu un sul rond de bronze!—je vous livrerais encore mes *Amants de Paris,* cent hexamètres, Monsieur, et ma *Mort de Paris,* deux cents hexamètres!——Je reprends:

Donc le poète est vraiment voleur de feu.

Il est chargé de l'humanité, des *animaux* même; il devra faire sentir, palper, écouter ses inventions; si ce qu'il rapporte *de là-bas* a forme, il donne forme; si c'est informe, il donne de l'informe. Trouver une langue;

The first study of the man who wants to be a poet is the knowledge of himself, complete. He looks for his soul, inspects it, tests it, learns it. As soon as he knows it, he must cultivate it; It seems simple: in every mind a natural development takes place; so many *egoists* call themselves authors, there are many others who attribute their intellectual progress *to themselves!*—But the soul must be made monstrous: in the fashion of the comprachicos,[44] if you will! Imagine a man implanting and cultivating warts on his face.

I say one must be a *seer,* make oneself a *seer.*

The Poet makes himself a *seer* by a long, gigantic and rational *derangement* of *all the senses.* All forms of love, suffering, and madness. He searches himself. He exhausts all poisons in himself and keeps only their quintessences. Unspeakable torture where he needs all his faith, all his superhuman strength, where he becomes among all men the great patient, the great criminal, the one accursed—and the supreme Scholar!—Because he reaches the *unknown!* Since he cultivated his soul, rich already, more than any man! He reaches the unknown, and when, bewildered, he ends by losing the intelligence of his visions, he has seen them. Let him die as he leaps through unheard of and unnamable things: other horrible workers will come; they will begin from the horizons where the other one collapsed!

—To be continued in six minutes—

Here I interpolate a second psalm *to accompany the text:* please lend a friendly ear—and everyone will be delighted.—The bow is in my hand and I begin:

My Little Lovers

A lacrymal tincture washes . . .

. . . .

A. R.

That's that. And note carefully that if I were not afraid of making you spend more than sixty centimes on postage—I poor terrified one who for seven months have not had a single copper!—I would also give you my *Lovers of Paris,* one hundred hexameters, sir, and my *Death of Paris,* two hundred hexameters!———I continue:
Therefore the poet is truly the thief of fire.

—Du reste, toute parole étant idée, le temps d'un langage universel viendra! Il faut être académicien,—plus mort qu'un fossile,—pour parfaire un dictionnaire, de quelque langue que ce soit. Des faibles se mettraient à *penser* sur la première lettre de l'alphabet, qui pourraient vite ruer dans la folie!——

Cette langue sera de l'âme pour l'âme, résumant tout, parfums, sons, couleurs, de la pensée accrochant la pensée et tirant. Le poète définirait la quantité d'inconnu s'éveillant en son temps dans l'âme universelle: il donnerait plus—que la formule de sa pensée, que la notation *de sa marche au Progrès!* Enormité devenant norme, absorbée par tous, il serait vraiment *un multiplicateur de progrès!*

Cet avenir sera matérialiste, vous le voyez;—Toujours pleins du *Nombre* et de l'*Harmonie,* ces poèmes seront faits pour rester.—Au fond, ce serait encore un peu la Poésie grecque. L'art éternel aurait ses fonctions; comme les poètes sont citoyens. La Poésie ne rhythmera plus l'action; elle *sera en avant.*

Ces poètes seront! Quand sera brisé l'infini servage de la femme, quand elle vivra pour elle et par elle, l'homme,—jusqu'ici abominable,—lui ayant donné son renvoi, elle sera poète, elle aussi! La femme trouvera de l'inconnu! Ses mondes d'idées différeront-ils des nôtres?—Elle trouvera des choses étranges, insondables, repoussantes, délicieuses; nous les prendrons, nous les comprendrons.

En attendant, demandons aux *poètes* du *nouveau,*—idées et formes. Tous les habiles croiraient bientôt avoir satisfait à cette demande:—Ce n'est pas cela!

Les premiers romantiques ont été *voyants* sans trop bien s'en rendre compte: la cultuer de leurs âmes s'est commencée aux accidents: locomotives abandonnées, mais brûlantes, que prennent quelque temps les rails.—Lamartine est quelquefois voyant, mais étranglé par la forme vieille.—Hugo, *trop cabochard,* a bien du *vu* dans les derniers volumes: *Les misérables* sont un vrai *poème.* J'ai *Les châtiments* sous main; *Stella* donne à peu près la mesure de la *vue* de Hugo. Trop de Belmontet et de Lamennais, de Jéhovahs et de colonnes, vieilles énormités crevées.

Musset est quatorze fois exécrable pour nous, générations douloureuses et prises de visions,—que sa paresse d'ange a insultées! Ô! les contes et les proverbes fadasses! Ô les *Nuits!* ô *Rolla,* ô *Namouna,* ô la *Coupe!* Tout est français, c'est-à-dire haïssable au suprême degré; français, pas parisien! Encore une œuvre de cet odieux génie qui a inspiré Rabelais, Voltaire, Jean La Fontaine; commenté par M. Taine! Printanier, l'esprit de Musset! Charmant, son amour! En voilà, de la peinture à l'émail, de la poésie

He is responsible for humanity, even for the *animals;* he will have to have his inventions smelt, felt, and heard; if what he brings back *from down there* has form, he gives form; if it is formless, he gives formlessness. A language must be found.

—Moreover, every word being an idea, the time of a universal language will come! One has to be an academician, —deader than a fossil, —to complete a dictionary in any language whatsoever. Weak people would begin *to think* about the first letter of the alphabet, and they would soon rush into madness!——

This language will be of the soul for the soul, containing everything, smells, sounds, colors, thought holding on to thought and pulling. The poet would define the amount of the unknown awakening in his time in the universal soul: he would give more—than the formulation of his thought, than the expression *of his march toward Progress!* Enormity becoming normal, absorbed by all, he would really be a *multiplier of progress!*

This future will be materialistic, as you see;—Always filled with *Number* and *Harmony,* these poems will be made to endure.—Fundamentally, it would be Greek poetry again in a way. Eternal art would have its functions; since poets are citizens. Poetry will not lend its rhythm to action, it *will be in advance.*

These poets will exist. When the endless servitude of woman is broken, when she lives for and by herself, man—heretofore abominable—having given her her release, she too will be a poet! Woman will find some of the unknown! Will her world of ideas differ from ours?—She will find strange, unfathomable, repulsive, delicious things; we will take them, we will understand them.

Meanwhile, let us ask the *poets* for the *new*—ideas and forms. All the clever ones will soon believe they have satisfied this demand—It is not so!

The first Romantics were *seers* without wholly realizing it: the cultivation of their souls began accidentally: abandoned locomotives, their fires still on, which the rails carry for some time.—Lamartine is at times a seer, but strangled by the old form.—Hugo, *too ham,* has *vision* in his last volumes: *Les misérables* is a real *poem.* I have *Les châtiments* with me; *Stella* gives approximately the extent of Hugo's *vision.* Too many Belmontets and Lamennais, Jehovahs and columns, old broken enormities.

Musset is fourteen times loathsome to us, suffering generations obsessed by visions—insulted by his angelic sloth! O! the insipid tales and proverbs! O the *Nuits!* O *Rolla,* O *Namouna,* O the *Coupe!* It is all French, namely detestable to the highest degree; French, not Parisian! One more work of that odious genius who inspired Rabelais, Voltaire, Jean La Fon-

solide! On savourera longtemps la poésie *française,* mais en France. Tout garçon épicier est en mesure de débobiner une apostrophe Rollaque; tout séminariste en porte les cinq cents rimes dans le secret d'un carnet. À quinze ans, ces élans de passion mettent les jeunes en rut; à seize ans, ils se contentent déjà de les réciter avec *cœur;* à dix-huit ans, à dix-sept même, tout collégien qui a le moyen, fait le *Rolla,* écrit un *Rolla!* Quelques-uns en meurent peut-être encore. Musset n'a rien su faire: il y avait des visions derrière la gaze des rideaux: il a fermé les yeux. Français, panadif, traîné de l'estaminet au pupitre de collège, le beau mort est mort, et, désormais, ne nous donnons même plus la peine de le réveiller par nos abominations!

Les seconds romantiques sont très *voyants:* Th. Gautier, Lec de Lisle, Th. de Banville. Mais inspecter l'invisible et entendre l'inouï étant autre chose que reprendre l'esprit des choses mortes, Baudelaire est le premier voyant, roi des poètes, *un vrai Dieu.* Encore a-t-il vécu dans un milieu trop artiste; et la forme si vantée en lui est mesquine: les inventions d'inconnu réclament des formes nouvelles.

Rompue aux formes vieilles, parmi les innocents, A. Renaud,—a fait son *Rolla;*—L. Grandet,—a fait son *Rolla;*—les gaulois et les Musset, G. Lafenestre, Coran, Cl. Popelin, Soulary, L. Salles; les écoliers, Marc, Aicard, Theuriet; les morts et les imbéciles, Autran, Barbier, L. Pichat, Lemoyne, les Deschamps, les Desessarts; les journalistes,—L. Cladel, Robert Luzarches, X. de Ricard; les fantaisistes, C. Mendès; les bohèmes; les femmes; les talents, Léon Dierx et Sully-Prudhomme, Coppée;—la nouvelle école, dite parnassienne, a deux voyants, Albert Mérat et Paul Verlaine, un vrai poète.—Voilà.—Ainsi je travaille à me rendre *Voyant.*—Et finissons par un chant pieux.

Accroupissements

Bien tard, quand il se sent l'estomac écœuré,

. . . .

Vous seriez exécrable de ne pas répondre: vite, car dans huit jours je serai à Paris, peut-être.

Au revoir.   A. Rimbaud

taine; with M. Taine's commentary! Springlike, Musset's wit! Charming, his love! There you have enamel painting and solid poetry! *French* poetry will be enjoyed for a long time, but in France. Every grocer's boy is able to reel off a Rollaesque speech; every seminarian carries the five hundred rhymes hidden in his notebook. At fifteen, these bursts of passion make boys horny; at sixteen, they are satisfied to recite them with *feeling;* at eighteen, even at seventeen, every schoolboy who has the ability, makes a *Rolla,* writes a *Rolla!* Some still die from this perhaps. Musset could do nothing: there were visions behind the gauze of the curtains: he closed his eyes. French, lifeless dragged from tavern to schoolroom desk, the fine cadaver is dead, and, henceforth let's not even bother to wake him up with our abominations!

The second Romantics are very much seers: Th. Gautier, Lec. de Lisle, Th. de Banville. But since inspecting the invisible and hearing the unheard of is different from recovering the spirit of dead things, Baudelaire is the first seer, king of poets, *a real god!* And yet he lived in too artistic a world; and the form so highly praised in him is trivial: inventions of the unknown call for new forms.

Broken-in to old forms, among the innocent, A. Renaud—has written his *Rolla;* L. Grandet has written his *Rolla;* the Gauls and the Mussets, G. Lafenestre, Coran, Cl. Popelin, Soulary, L. Salles; the pupils Marc, Aicard, Theuriet; the dead and the imbeciles, Autran, Barbier, L. Pichat, Lemoyne, the Deschamps, the Desessarts; the journalists,—L. Cladel, Robert Luzarches, X. de Ricard; the fantasists, C. Mendès; les bohemians; the women; the talents, Léon Dierx and Sully-Prudhomme, Coppée; the new school, called Parnassian, has two seers: Albert Mérat and Paul Verlaine, a real poet.—There you are.—So, I work to make myself into a *Seer.*—And let's dose with a pious hymn.

Squattings

Very late, when he feels his stomach sicken,

. . . .

You would be loathsome not to answer: quickly, because in a week, I will be in Paris, perhaps.

Goodbye,   A. Rimbaud

À Paul Demeny

Charleville, 10 juin 1871

À M P. Demeny

Les poètes de sept ans

. . . .

Les pauvres à l'église

. . . .

Voici,—ne vous fâchez pas,—un motif à dessins drôles: c'est une an-
tithèse aux douces vignettes pérennelles où batifolet les cupidons, où s'es-
sorent les cœurs panachés de flammes, fleurs vertes, oiseaux mouillés, pro-
montoires de Leucade, etc. . . —ces triolets, eux aussi, au reste, iront

Où les vignettes pérennelles,
Où les doux vers.

Voici:—ne vous fâchez pas!—

Le cœur du pitre

Mon triste Cœur bave à la poupe,
Mon cœur est plein de caporal;
Ils y lancent des jets de soupe
Mon triste Cœur bave à la poupe.
Sous les quolibets de la troupe
Qui pousse un rire général,
Mon triste cœur bave à la poupe
Mon cœur est plein de caporal!

Ithyphalliques et pioupiesques
Leurs insultes l'ont dépravé:
À la vesprée, ils font des fresques
Ithyphalliques et pioupiesques:
Ô flots abracadabrantesques
Prenez mon cœur, qu'il soit sauvé:
Ithyphalliques et pioupiesques
Leurs insultes l'ont dépravé!

To Paul Demeny

Charleville, 10 June 1871

To M P. Demeny

Seven-year-old Poets

. . . .

The Poor in Church

. . . .

Here,—don't be upset,—a series of funny sketches: it's antidote to the sweet perennial vignettes where cupids frolic, where flame-decorated hearts soar, green flowers, moistened birds, Leucadian promontories, etc. . . — moreover these triolets, they too, will go

> *Where the perennial vignettes,*
> *Where the sweet verses.*

Here:—don't be upset!—

The Fool's Heart

My sad Heart slobbers at the poop,
My heart is full of tobacco-spit;
They spew streams of soup at it
My sad Heart slobbers at the poop.
Under the jeering of the soldiers
Who break out laughing,
My sad heart slobbers at the poop
My heart is full of tobacco-spit!

Ithyphallic and soldierish
Their insults have depraved it:
At vespers they make frescoes
Ithyphallic and soldierish:
O, abracadabratic waves
Take my heart, let it be saved:
Ithyphallic and soldierish
Their insults have depraved it!

Quand ils auront tari leurs chiques,
Comment agir, ô cœur volé?
Ce seront des refrains bachiques
Quand ils auront tari leurs chiques:
J'aurai des sursauts stomachiques
Si mon cœur triste est ravalé:
Quand ils auront tari leurs chiques,
Comment agir, ô cœur volé?

Voilà ce que je fais.—J'ai trois prières à vous adresser: brûlez, *je le veux,* et je crois que vous respecterez ma volonté comme celle d'un mort, brûlez *tous les vers que je fus assez sot* pour vous donner lors *de mon séjour à Douai* : ayez la bonté de m'envoyer, s'il vous est possible et s'il vous plaît, un exemplaire de vos *Glaneuses,* que je voudrais relire et qu'il m'est impossible d'acheter, ma mère ne m'ayant gratifié d'aucun rond de bronze depuis six mois,—pitié!—: enfin, veuillez bien me répondre, quoi que ce soit, pour cet envoi et pour le précédent.

Je vous souhaite un bon jour, ce qui est bien bon. Ecrivez à : M. Deverrière, 95, sous les Allées, pour

A. Rimbaud.

À Théodore de Banville

Charleville, Ardennes, 15 août 1871

A Monsieur Théodore de Banville
Ce qu'on dit au Poète à propos de fleurs

Monsieur et Cher Maître,

Vous rappelez-vous avoir reçu de province, en juin 1870, cent ou cent cinquante hexamètres mythologiques intitulés *Credo in unam?* Vous fûtes assez bon pour répondre!

C'est le même imbécile qui vous envoie les vers ci-dessus, signés Alcide Bava.—Pardon.

J'ai dix-huit ans.—J'aimerai toujours les vers de Banville.

L'an passé je n'avais que dix-sept ans!

Ai-je progressé?

Alcide Bava
A. R.

When they have used up their quid,
How will I act, O stolen heart?
There will be Bacchic refrains
When they have used up their quid:
I will have stomach retchings
If my sad heart is degraded:
When they have used up their quid,
How will I act, O stolen heart?

Here's what I'm doing. —I pray to you three things: burn, *I want you to,* and I trust that you will respect my wish like that of a dying man, burn *all the verses that I was stupid enough* to give you during *my visit to Douai:* be good enough to send me, if you can and if you, a copy of your *Glaneuses,* which I would like to reread and which it is impossible for me to buy, my mother not having given me a single bronze coin for six months,—take pity!—: Finally, please respond to me, anything at all, to this letter and to the previous one.

I wish you a good day, which is quite good. Write to: Mr. Deverrière, 95, sous les Allées, for

A. Rimbaud.

To Théodore de Banville

Charleville, Ardennes, 15 August 1871

To Monsieur Théodore de Banville
What is said to the Poet about flowers

Sir and Cher Maître,

Do you remember receiving from the province, in June 1870, a hundred or a hundred and fifty mythological hexameters entitled *Credo in unam?* You were kind enough to answer!

The same imbecile is sending you the above verses, signed Alcide Bava— I beg your pardon.

I am eighteen. —I will always love the verses of Banville.
Last year I was only seventeen!
Have I made any progress?

Alcide Bava
A. R.

À Paul Demeny

Charleville (Ardennes) 28 août 1871

Monsieur,

Vous me faites recommencer ma prière: soit. Voici la complainte complète. Je cherche des paroles calmes: mais ma science de l'art n'est pas bien profonde. Enfin, voici:

Situation du prévenu: j'ai quitté depuis plus d'un an la vie ordinaire, pour ce que vous savez. Enfermé sans cesse dans cette inqualifiable contrée ardennaise, ne fréquentant pas un homme, recueilli dans un travail infâme, inepte, obstiné, mystérieux, ne répondant que par le silence aux questions, aux apostrophes grossières et méchantes, me montrant digne dans ma position extra-légale, j'ai fini par provoquer d'atroces résolutions d'une mère aussi inflexible que soixante-treize administrations à casquettes de plomb.

Elle a voulu m'imposer le travail,—perpétuel, à Charleville (Ardennes)! Une place pour tel jour, disait-elle, ou la porte.

Je refusais cette vie; sans donner mes raisons: c'eût été pitoyable. Jusqu'aujourd'hui, j'ai pu tourner ces échéances. Elle, en est venue à ceci: souhaiter sans cesse mon départ inconsidéré, ma fuite! Indigent, inexpérimenté, je finirais par entrer aux établissements de correction. Et, dès ce moment, silence sur moi!

Voilà le mouchoir de dégoût qu'on m'a enfoncé dans la bouche. C'est bien simple.

Je ne demande rien, je demande un renseignement. Je veux travailler libre: mais à Paris, que j'aime. Tenez: je suis un piéton, rien de plus; j'arrive dans la ville immense sans aucune ressource matérielle: mais vous m'avez dit: Celui qui désire être ouvrier à quinze sous par jour s'adresse là, fait cela, vit comme cela. Je m'adresse là, je fais cela, je vis comme cela. Je vous ai prié d'indiquer des occupations peu absorbantes, parce que la pensée réclame de larges tranches de temps. Absolvant le poète, ces balançoires matérielles se font aimer. Je suis à Paris: il me faut une *économie* positive! Vous ne trouvez pas cela sincère? Moi, ça me semble si étrange, qu'il me faille vous protester de mon sérieux!

J'avais eu l'idée ci-dessus: la seule qui me parût raisonnable: je vous la rends sous d'autres termes. J'ai bonne volonté, je fais ce que je puis, je parle aussi compréhensiblement qu'un malheureux!

Pourquoi tancer l'enfant qui, non doué de principes zoologiques, désirerait un oiseau à cinq ailes? On le ferait croire aux oiseaux à six queues, ou à trois becs! On lui prêterait un Buffon des familles: ça le déleurre.

Donc, ignorant de quoi vous pourriez m'écrire, je coupe les explica-

Charleville (Ardennes) 28 August 1871

Sir,

You make me begin my prayer over again: so be it. Here is the entire complaint. I am looking for calm words: but my knowledge of the art is not very profound. But here it is:

Situation of the accused: for more than a year I gave up ordinary living, for what you know. Closed up without respite in this unmentionable Ardennes country, seeing not a single man, engaged in an infamous, inept, obstinate, mysterious work, answering questions and coarse evil apostrophies by silence, appearing worthy in my extralegal position, I provoked at the end frightful resolutions of a mother as inflexible as seventy-three administrations with steel helmets.

She tried to force me to perpetual work, in Charleville (Ardennes)! Take the job on such a day, she said, or get out.

I refused that life; without giving my reasons: it would have been pitiful. Up until now I have been able to avoid these terms. She, has come to this: to hope constantly for my impulsive departure, my flight! Poor and inexperienced, I would end up in a house of correction. And from then on, nothing would be known about me!

This is the disgusting handkerchief that has been stuffed into my mouth. It is all quite simple.

I am not asking for anything, but I am asking for some information. I want to be free when I work but in Paris, which I love. You see: I am a pedestrian, nothing more than that; I come to the huge city without any material resources: but you said to me: the man who wants to be a worker at fifteen sous a day comes here, does that, lives in this way. I come here, do that, live in this way. I begged you to tell me of work not too absorbing because thought demands large blocks of time. Absolving the poet, this sort of material nonsense is agreeable. I am in Paris: I need a positive economy! Don't you find this sincere? It seems so strange to me that I have to argue with you about my seriousness!

I had had the above idea: the only one that seemed reasonable to me: I give it to you in other terms. I have good determination, I do what I can, I speak as comprehensibly as any wretch!

Why scold a child who, not endowed with zoological principles, might want a five-winged bird? You would make him belive in birds with six tails or three beaks! You would lend him a family Buffon: that would de-lure him.

tions, et continue à me fier à vos expériences, à votre obligeance que j'ai bien bénie, en recevant votre lettre, et je vous engage un peu à partir de mes idées,—s'il vous plaît . . .

Recevriez-vous sans trop d'ennui des échantillons de mon travail?

A. Rimbaud

À P. Verlaine

[Charleville, septembre 1871] [45]

[. . .] J'ai le projet de faire un grand poème, et je ne puis travailler à Charleville. Je suis empêché de venir à Paris, étant sans ressources. Ma mère est veuve et extrêmement dévote. Elle ne me donne que dix centimes tous les dimanches pour payer ma chaise à l'église. [. . .]

De P. Verlaine à A. Rimbaud

[Paris, septembre 1871] [46]

[. . .] Venez, chère grande âme, on vous appelle, on vous attend. [. . .]

À Ernest Delahaye

Parmerde, Juinphe 72

Mon ami,

Oui, surprenante est l'existence dans le cosmorama Arduan. La province, où on se nourrit de farineux et de boue, où l'on boit du vin du cru et de la bière du pays, ce n'est pas ce que je regrette. Aussi tu as raison de la dénoncer sans cesse. Mais ce lieu-ci: distillation, composition, tout étroitesses; et l'été accablant: la chaleur n'est pas très constante, mais de voir que le beau temps est dans les intérêts de chacun, et que chacun est un porc, je hais l'été, qui me tue quand il se manifeste un peu. J'ai une soif à craindre la gangrène: les rivières ardennaises et belges, les cavernes, voilà ce que je regrette.

Il y a bien ici un lieu de boisson que je préfère. Vive l'académie d'Absomphe, malgré la mauvaise volonté des garçons. C'est le plus délicat et le plus tremblant des habits, que l'ivresse par la vertu de cette sauge de glaciers, l'absomphe. Mais pour, après, se coucher dans la merde!

So, not knowing what you might write to me about, I cut short all explanations, and continue to trust your experiments, your kindness which I have blessed, in receiving your letter, and I engage you somewhat with these ideas . . . if you will . . .

Would you accept without too much dismay some samples of my work?

A. Rimbaud

To P. Verlaine

[Charleville, September 1871]

[. . .] I have undertaken the project of a great poem, and I cannot work in Charleville. Having no money, I am unable to come to Paris. My mother is widowed and extremely devout. She gives me only ten centimes each Sunday to pay for my seat at church. [. . .]

From P. Verlaine to A. Rimbaud

[Paris, September 1871]

[. . .] Come, great dear soul, we call you, we are waiting for you. [. . .]

To Ernest Delahaye

Parshit, Junish 72

My friend,

Yes, surprising is existence in the Ardennes cosmorama. The province where you eat flour and mud, where you drink local wine and local beer, is not what I miss. You are right to keep on denouncing it. But this place: distillation, composition, all narrowness; and the oppressive summer: the heat is not continuous, but in seeing that good weather is in the interest of all, and that each one is a pig, I hate the summer which kills me when it shows itself even a bit. I am so thirsty that I fear gangrene: what I miss are the Belgian and Ardennes rivers and caves.

There is a drinking place I prefer here. Long live the Academy of Absinth, in spite of the ill-temper of the waiters. It is the most delicate, the most tremulous of garments—this drunkenness induced by virtue of that sage of the glaciers, *absomphe* (absinth) In order to recline in shit afterward!

Toujours même geinte, quoi! Ce qu'il y a de certain, c'est merde à Perrin. Et au comptoir de l'Univers, qu'il soit en face du square ou non. Je ne maudis pas l'Univers, pourtant.—Je souhaite très fort que l'Ardenne soit occupée et pressurée de plus en plus immodérément. Mais tout cela est encore ordinaire.

Le sérieux, c'est qu'il faut que tu te tourmentes beaucoup. Peut-être que tu aurais raison de beaucoup marcher et lire. Raison en tout cas de ne pas te confiner dans les bureaux et maisons de famille. Les abrutissements doivent s'exécuter loin de ces lieux-là. Je suis loin. de vendre du baume, mais je crois que les habitudes n'offrent pas des consolations, aux pitoyables jours.

Maintenant, c'est la nuit que je travaince. De minuit à 5 du matin. Le mois passé, me chambre, rue M^r-le-Prince, donnait sur un jardin du lycée Saint-Louis. Il y avait des arbres énormes sous ma fenêtre étroite. À 3 heures du matin, la bougie pâlit: tous les oiseaux crient à la fois dans les arbres: c'est fini. Plus de travail. Il me fallait regarder les arbres, le ciel, saisis par cette heure indicible, première du matin. Je voyais les dortoirs du lycée, absolument sourds. Et déjà le bruit saccadé, sonore, délicieux des tombereaux sur les boulevards.—Je fumais ma pipe-marteau, en crachant sur les tuiles, car c'était une mansarde, ma chambre. À 5 heures, je descendais à l'achat de quelque pain; c'est l'heure. Les ouvriers sont en marche partout. C'est l'heure de se soûler chez les marchands de vin, pour moi. Je rentrais manger, et me couchais à 7 heures du matin, quand le soleil faisait sortir les cloportes de dessous les tuiles. Le premier matin en été et les soirs de décembre, voilà ce qui m'a ravi toujours ici.

Mais, en ce moment, j'ai une chambre jolie, sur une cour sans fond mais de 3 mètres carrés.—La rue Victor Cousin fait coin sur la place de la Sorbonne par le café du Bas-Rhin, et donne sur la rue Soufflot, à l'autre extrém.——Là, je bois de l'eau toute la nuit, je ne vois pas le matin, je ne dors pas, j'étouffe. Et voilà.

Il sera certes fait droit à ta réclamation! N'oublie pas de chier sur *La Renaissance,* journal littéraire et artistique, si tu le rencontres. J'ai évité jusqu'ici les pestes d'émigrés Caropolmerdis.[47] Et merde aux saisons et colrage.[48]

Courage.

A. R.

Always the same whining! What is certain is shit on Perrin. And on the bar of the Café de l'Univers, whether it faces the square or not. Yet I don't curse the Univers. I strongly hope that the Ardenne will be occupied and pressed more and more rigorously. But all this is still banal.

What is bad is you will have to be greatly tormented. Perhaps you would be right to walk a great deal and read. A reason in any case not to be confined in offices and homes. Stupefactions have to be carried out far from such places. I am far from selling balm, but I think that habits do not offer consolations on wretched days.

Now, it is nighttime I am crossing through. From midnight to five in the morning. Last month, my room, on rue Monsieur-le-Prince, looked out on a garden of the lycée Saint-Louis. There were huge trees under my narrow window. At three in the morning, the candle went pale: all the birds cry at once in the trees: it is over. No more work. I had to look at the trees and the sky, seized by that unspeakable hour, the first in the morning. I saw the lycée dormitories, absolutely muted. And already the jerky, sonorous, delightful noise of the carts on the boulevards. I smoked my hammer-pipe, spitting on the tiles, for my room was a garret. At five o'clock, I went down stairs to buy bread; it was the time. Workmen were walking everywhere. For me, it was the time to get drunk at wine merchants'. I returned to my room to eat, and went to bed at seven in the morning when the sun makes the woodlice come out from under the tiles. What has always delighted me here is the early morning in summer and the December evenings.

But at this moment, I have an attractive room, on an endless courtyard three meters square.—The street Victor-Cousin forms a corner on the square of the Sorbonne with the café du Bas-Rhin, and opens on to the rue Soufflot at the other end.—There, I drink water all night, I can't see in the morning, I don't sleep, I stifle. There's my story.

Your claims will certainly be honored! Don't forget to shit on *La Renaissance,* a literary newspaper of the arts, if you come across it. Up until now I have avoided the plagues of Charleshitty emigrants. And shit on the seasons and coulrage.

Courage.

A. R.

À Ernest Delahaye

Laïtou (Roche) (canton d'Attigny) mai 73

Cher ami, tu vois mon existence actuelle dans l'aquarelle ci-dessous.
O Nature! ô ma mère!

Quelle chierie! et quels monstres d'innocence, ces paysans. Il faut, le
soir, faire deux lieux, et plus, pour boire un peu. La *Mother* m'a mis là dans
un triste trou.

Je ne sais comment en sortir: j'en sortirai pourtant. Je regrette cet atroce
Charlestown, l'Univers, la Bibliothè., etc. . . . . Je travaille pourtant assez
régulièrement, je fais de petites histoires en prose, titre général: Livre
païen, ou Livre nègre. C'est bête et innocent. O innocence! innocence; in-
nocence, innoc . . . fléau!

Verlaine doit t'avoir donné la malheureuse commission de parlementer
avec le sieur Devin, imprimeux du Nôress. Je crois que ce Devin pourrait
faire le livre de Verlaine à assez bon compte et presque proprement. (S'il
n'emploie pas les caractères emmerdés du Nôress. il serait capable d'en
coller un cliché, une annonce!)

Je n'ai rien de plus à te dire, la contemplostate de la Nature m'absorcu-
lant tout entier. Je suis à toi, o Nature, o ma mère!

Je te serre les mains, dans l'espoir d'un revoir que j'active autant que
je puis.

R.

Je rouvre ma lettre. Verlaine doit t'avoir proposé un rendez-vol au Di-
manche 18, à Boulion. Moi je ne puis y aller. Si tu y vas, il te chargera proba-
blement de quelques fraguemants en prose de moi ou de lui, à me retourner.

La mère Rimb. retournera à Charlestown dans le courant de Juin, c'est
sûr, et je tâcherai de rester dans cette jolie ville quelque temps.

Le soleil est accablant et il gèle le matin. J'ai été avant-hier voir les Pruss-
mars à Vouziers, une sous-préfecte de 10000 âmes, à sept kilom. d'ici. Ca
m'a ragaillardi.

Je suis abominablement gêné. Pas un livre, pas un cabaret à portée de
moi, pas un incident dans la rue. Quelle horreur que cette campagne fran-
çaise. Mon sort dépend de ce livre, pour lequel une demi-douzaine d'his-
toires atroces sont encore à inventer. Comment inventer des atrocités ici?
Je ne t'envoie pas d'histoires, quoique j'en aie déjà trois, *ça coûte tant!* En-
fin, voilà!

Bon revoir, tu verras ça.

Rimb.

Laïtou (Roche) (canton of Attigny) May 73

Dear friend, You can see my present life in this enclosed drawing.
O Nature! O mother of mine!

What a tough shit! and what monsters of innocence these peasants are!
At night, to have a drink, you have to walk two leagues or more. The
Mother has put me in this sad hole of a place.

I don't know how to get out of it, but I will. I miss that vile Charles-
town, l'Univers (café), the library, etc. . . . Yet I work quite steadily, I am
writing little stories in prose, general title: Pagan Book, or Negro Book.
It is crazy and innocent. O innocence! innocence; innocence, innoc—
plague!

Verlaine must have given you the wretched commission of arguing
with Lord Devin, printer of the *Nord-Est*. I think this Devin could do Ver-
laine's book reasonably and quite satisfactorily. (If he doesn't use the shitty
typing characters of the Nord-Est. He would be capable of sticking an il-
lustration on it or an ad!)

I have nothing more to tell you, the contemplation of nature com-
pletely filling my ass. I am yours, O Nature, O mother!

I shake your hands, in the hope of a reunion I am activating as much as
possible.

R.

I open my letter which I closed. Verlaine must have proposed to you a
rendezvous Sunday the 18th in Boulion. I can't go. If you go, he will prob-
ably give you a few fragments of my prose or his to return to me.

Mother Rimb. will return to Charlestown sometime in June, this is cer-
tain, and I will try to stay in that pretty town a little while.

The sun is strong and it is freezing in the morning. The day before yes-
terday I went to see the Prussians in Vouziers, a subprefecture of 10,000
souls, seven kilometers from here. This cheered me up.

I am absolutely thwarted. Not a book, not a bar within reach, not
an incident in the street. How horrible this French countryside is! My
fate depends on this book, for which I still have to invent a half-dozen
atrocious stories. How can I invent atrocities here? I am not sending
you any stories, although I already have three. *It costs too much!* That's all
for now!

Goodbye to you. You'll see it later.

Rimb.

Laïtou (Roches) (canton d'Attigny) Mai 73

Cher ami, tu vois mon existence actuelle

dans l'aquarelle ci-dessous.

O Nature! o ma mère!

Quelle chierie! et quels monstres d'innocence
ces paysans. Il faut, le soir, faire deux
lieues, et plus, pour
boire un peu. La
Mother m'a mis dans
un triste trou.

Laitou,
Mon village

Je ne sais comment en
sortir : j'en sortirai, pourtant. Je regrette
cet atroce Charlestown, l'Univers, la
Bibliothèque, etc... Je travaille pourtant assez
régulièrement; je fais de petites histoires, en prose,
titre général : Livre païen, ou Livre nègre.
C'est bête et innocent. O innocence! innocence,
innocence, innoc..., fléau!

Verlaine doit t'avoir donné la malheureuse
commission de parlementer avec le sieur Devin,
imprimeur du Nôress. — Je crois que ce Devin
pourrait faire le livre de Verlaine à assez
bon compte et presque proprement. (S'il n'emploie
pas les caractères emmerdés du Nôress. il serait
capable d'en coller un cliché, une annonce!)

Je n'ai rien de plus à te dire, la contemplation
de la Nature m'absorculant tout entier. Je suis
à Toi, o Nature, o ma mère!

Je te serre les mains, dans l'espoir d'un
revoir que j'active autant que je puis. R.

Prochainement je t'enverrai des timbres pour m'acheter et m'envoyer le *Faust de Goethe,* Biblioth. populaire. Ça doit coûter un sou ce transport. Dis-moi s'il n'y a pas des traduct. de Shakespeare dans les nouveaux livres de cette biblioth.

Si même tu peux m'en envoyer le catalogue le plus nouveau, envoie.

R.

À Verlaine

Londres, vendredi après-midi (4–5 juillet 1873)

Reviens, reviens, cher ami, seul ami, reviens. Je te jure que je serai bon. Si j'étais maussade avec toi, c'est une plaisanterie où je me suis entêté, je m'en repens plus qu'on ne peut dire. Reviens, ce sera bien oublié. Quel malheur que tu aies cru à cette plaisanterie. Voilà deux jours que je ne cesse de pleurer. Reviens. Sois courageux, cher ami. Rien n'est perdu. Tu n'as qu'a refaire le voyage. Nous revivrons ici bien courageusement, patiemment. Ah! je t'en supplie. C'est ton bien, d'ailleurs. Reviens, tu retrouveras toutes tes affaires. J'espère que tu sais bien à présent qu'il n'y avait rien de vrai dans notre discussion. L'affreux moment! Mais toi, quand je te faisais signe de quitter le bateau, pourquoi ne venais-tu pas? Nous avons vécu deux ans ensemble pour arriver à cette heure-là! Que vas-tu faire? Si tu ne veux pas revenir ici, veux-tu que j'aille te trouver où tu es?

Oui, c'est moi qui ai eu tort.

Oh tu ne m'oublieras pas, dis?

Non, tu ne peux pas m'oublier.

Moi, je t'ai toujours là.

Dis, réponds à ton ami, est-ce que nous ne devons plus vivre ensemble?

Sois courageux. Réponds-moi vite.

Je ne puis rester ici plus longtemps.

N'écoute que ton bon cœur.

Vite, dis si je dois te rejoindre.

A toi toute la vie.

Rimbaud

Vite, réponds, je ne puis rester ici plus tard que lundi soir. Je n'ai pas encore un penny, je ne puis mettre ça à la poste. J'ai confié à *Vermersch* tes livres et tes manuscrits.

Si je ne dois plus te revoir, je m'engagerai dans la marine ou l'armée.

Soon I will send you stamps to buy for me and send Goethe's *Faust,* in the Bibliothèque populaire *edition. It will cost one sou for mailing.*

Tell me if there aren't any Shakespeare translations in the new books of that edition.

And if you could send me the newest catalogue, do so.

R.

To Verlaine

London, Friday afternoon (4–5 July 1873)

Come back, come back, dear friend, my one friend, come back. I swear I will behave. If I was surly with you, it was a joke. I couldn't stop. I am more repentant than I can say. Come back, everything will be forgotten. How terrible that you took that joke seriously. For two days now I haven't stopped crying. Come back. Be brave, dear friend. Nothing is lost. You have only to make the journey again. We will live here again courageously and patiently. Oh! I beg you. It is for your good, moreover. Come back, you will find all your things here. I hope you realize now there was nothing real in our discussions. That terrible moment. But why didn't you come, when I signaled you to get off the boat? We lived together two years, to come to this moment. What are you going to do? If you don't want to come back here, do you want me to come to you?

Yes, I was in the wrong.

Oh you won't forget me, will you?

No, you can't forget me.

I still have you here.

Listen, answer your friend, aren't we to live together any more?

Be brave. Answer me quickly.

I cannot stay here much longer.

Listen only to your good heart.

Quick, tell me if I should come to you.

Yours, all my life.

Rimbaud

Answer quickly, I cannot stay here any later than Monday evening. I haven't another penny, I can't put this in the mail. I have given your books and manuscripts to Vermersch to take care of.

If I am not to see you again, I will enlist in the navy or the army.

O reviens, à toutes les heures je repleure. Dis-moi de te retrouver, j'irai, dis-le-moi, télégraphie-moi—Il faut que je parte lundi soir, où vas-tu, que veux-tu faire?

À *Verlaine*

(Londres, 4–5 juillet 1873)

Cher ami,

J'ai ta lettre datée *"En mer."* Tu as tort, cette fois, et très tort. D'abord rien de positif dans ta lettre: ta femme ne viendra pas ou viendra dans trois mois, trois ans, que sais-je? Quant à claquer, je te connais. Tu vas donc, en attendant ta femme et ta mort, te démener, errer, ennuyer des gens. Quoi, toi, tu n'as pas encore reconnu que les colères étaient aussi fausses d'un côté que de l'autre! Mais c'est toi qui aurais les derniers torts, puisque, même après que je t'ai rappelé, tu as persisté dans tes faux sentiments. Crois-tu que ta vie sera plus agréable avec d'autres que moi: *Réfléchis-y!*—Ah! certes non!—

Avec moi seul tu peux être libre, et puisque je te jure d'être très gentil à l'avenir, que je déplore toute ma part de torts, que j'ai enfin l'esprit net, que je t'aime bien, si tu ne veux pas revenir, ou que je te rejoigne, tu fais un crime, et *tu t'en repentiras de* LONGUES ANNÉES par *la perte de toute liberté, et des ennuis plus atroces* peut-être que tous ceux que tu as éprouvés. Après ça, resonge à ce que tu étais avant de me connaître.

Quant à moi, je ne rentre pas chez ma mère. Je vais à Paris, je tâcherai d'être parti lundi soir. Tu m'auras forcé à vendre tous tes habits, je ne puis faire autrement. Ils ne sont pas encore vendus: ce n'est que lundi matin qu'on me les emporterait. Si tu veux m'adresser des lettres à Paris, envoie à L. Forain, 289, rue St.-Jacques, pour A. Rimbaud. Il saura mon adresse.

Certes, si ta femme revient, je ne te compromettrai pas en t'écrivant,—je n'écrirai jamais.

Le seul vrai mot, c'est: reviens, je veux être avec toi, je t'aime. Si tu écoutes cela, tu montreras du courage et un esprit sincère.

Autrement, je te plains.

Mais je t'aime, je t'embrasse et nous nous reverrons.

Rimbaud

8 Great Colle, etc. . . . jusqu'à lundi soir, ou mardi à midi, si tu m'appelles.

Oh! come back. I am crying all the time. Tell me to come to you, and I will come, tell me, send me a wire—I have to leave Monday evening, where are you going, what do you want to do?

To Verlaine

(London, 4–5 July 1873)

Dear friend,

I have your letter dated "At sea." You are wrong this time. First there is nothing positive in your letter: your wife is not coming or she will come in three months, or three years, or sometime. As for dying, I know you. So, while waiting for your wife and your death, you are going to struggle, wander about, and bore people. What! Haven't you yet realized that our anger was false on both sides! But it is you who will be wrong in the end, because, even after I called you back, you persisted in your false sentiments. Do you think life will be happier with others than it was with me? *Think about this!*—oh! certainly not!—

With me alone you can be free, and since I swear to you I will behave in the future, I am sorry for my part in the wrong, that my mind is clear at last, that I am fond of you, if you don't want to come back or don't want me to join you, you are committing a crime, and *you will repent of this for* LONG YEARS TO COME by *losing all freedom, and by more atrocious suffering* perhaps than any you have felt. After this, think of what you were before knowing me.

As for myself, I am not going back to my mother's. I am going to Paris, I will try to be gone by Monday. You will have forced me to sell all your clothes. I can do nothing else. They are not yet sold: they won't be taken from me until Monday morning. If you want to write to me in Paris, write to L. Forain, 289, rue Saint-Jacques (for A. Rimbaud). He will know my address.

Believe me, if your wife comes back, I will not compromise you by writing to you. I will never write.

The one true word is: come back. I want to be with you, I love you. If you heed this, you will show courage and sincerity.

Otherwise, I pity you.

But I love you, I embrace you and we will see one another again.

Rimbaud

8 Great Colle, etc. . . . until Monday evening, or Tuesday at noon, if you call me.

Aux siens

Alexandrie, décembre 1878

Chers amis,

Je suis arrivé ici après une traversée d'une dizaine de jours, et, depuis une quinzaine que je me retourne ici, voici seulement que les choses commencent à mieux tourner! Je vais avoir un emploi prochainement; et je travaille déjà assez pour vivre, petitement il est vrai. Ou bien je serai occupé dans une grande exploitation agricole à quelque dix lieues d'ici (j'y suis déjà allé, mais il n'y aurait rien avant quelques semaines); — ou bien j'entrerai prochainement dans les douanes anglo-égyptiennes, avec bon traitement; — ou bien, je crois plutôt que je partirai prochainement pour Chypre, l'île anglaise, comme interprète d'un corps de travailleurs. En tous cas, on m'a promis quelque chose; et c'est avec un ingénieur français — homme obligeant et de talent — que j'ai affaire. Seulement voici ce qu'on demande de moi: un mot de toi, maman, avec légalisation de la mairie et portant ceci:

"Je soussignée, épouse Rimbaud, propriétaire à Roche, déclare que mon fils Arthur Rimbaud sort de travailler sur ma propriété, qu'il a quitté Roche de sa propre volonté, le 20 octobre 1878, et qu'il s'est conduit honorablement ici et ailleurs, et qu'il n'est pas actuellement sous le coup de la loi militaire.

Signé: Ep. R. . . ."

Et le cachet de la mairie qui est le plus nécessaire.

Sans cette pièce on ne me donnera pas un placement fixe, quoique je croie qu'on continuerait à m'occuper incidemment. Mais gardez-vous de dire que je ne suis resté que quelque temps à Roche, parce qu'on m'en demanderait plus long, et ça n'en finirait pas; ensuite ça fera croire aux gens de la compagnie agricole que je suis capable de diriger des travaux.

Je vous prie en grâce de m'envoyer ce mot le plus tôt possible: la chose est bien simple et aura de bons résultats, au moins celui de me donner un bon placement pour tout l'hiver.

Je vous enverrai prochainement des détails et des descriptions d'Alexandrie et de la vie égyptienne. Aujourd'hui, pas le temps. Je vous dis au revoir. Bonjour à F[rédéric], s'il est là. Ici il fait chaud comme l'été à Roche.

Des nouvelles.

A. Rimbaud
Poste française, Alexandrie,
Égypte.

To his family

Dear friends,

I got here after a crossing of about ten days, and it is only now that I have been here two weeks that things are beginning to look better! I will soon have a job, and I am already working enough in order to live, though in a small way. Either I will be engaged in a large agricultural enterprise about ten leagues from here (I have already been there, but there will be nothing for a few weeks); or I will soon join the Anglo-Egyptian Customs, with a good salary;—or else, I think rather that I will soon leave for Cyprus, the English island, as an interpreter for a labor corps. In any case, I have been promised something; and it is with a French engineer—an obliging, talented man—that I am dealing. However, this is what they are asking me for: a word from you, mother, notarized by the city hall, and saying this:

"I the undersigned, wife of Rimbaud, property-owner in Roche, declare that my son Arthur Rimbaud has recently worked on my property; that he left Roche of his own free will on October 20th 1878, and that he behaved honorably here and elsewhere, and that he is not at the present moment liable to military law.

Signed: Wife of R . . ."
Plus the city hall stamp, which is the most necessary thing.

Without this form I will not be given a regular job, although I believe they would continue to employ me at times. But be careful not to say that I stayed only a little while in Roche, because they would ask me more about it, and there would be no end to it; then, it will make the people in the agricultural company believe I am able to take charge of the work.

I beg you please send me this note as soon as possible: the matter is very simple and will have good results, at least it will give me a good job for the entire winter.

I will soon send you details and descriptions of Alexandria and of Egyptian life. No time today. I'll say goodbye. Hello to Frédéric, if he is there. It is as warm here as it is in summer in Roche.

Give me the news.

A. Rimbaud
French Post Office, Alexandria,
Egypt.

Aux siens

E. Jean et Thial fils
Entrepreneurs

Larnaca (Chypre),
le 15 février 1879.

Chers amis,

Je ne vous ai pas écrit plus tôt, ne sachant de quel côté on me ferait tourner. Cependant vous avez dû recevoir une lettre d'Alexandrie où je vous parlais d'un engagement prochain pour Chypre. Demain 16 février il y aura juste deux mois que je suis employé ici. Les patrons sont à Larnaca, le port principal de Chypre. Moi je suis surveillant d'une carrière au désert, au bord de la mer: on fait un canal aussi. Il y a aussi à faire l'embarquement des pierres sur les cinq bateaux et le vapeur de la Compagnie. Il y a aussi un four à chaux, briqueterie, etc. . . . Le premier village est à une heure de marche. Il n'y a ici qu'un chaos de rocs, la rivière et la mer. Il n'y a qu'une maison. Pas de terre, pas de jardins, pas un arbre. En été, il y a quatre-vingts degrés de chaleur. A présent, on en a souvent cinquante. C'est l'hiver. Il pleut quelquefois. On se nourrit de gibier, de poules, etc. . . . Tous les Européens ont été malades, excepté moi. Nous avons été ici vingt Européens au plus au camp. Les premiers sont arrivés le 9 décembre. Il y en a trois ou quatre de morts. Les ouvriers chypriotes viennent des villages environnants; on en a employé jusqu'à soixante par jour. Moi je les dirige: je pointe les journées, dispose du matériel, je fais les rapports à la Compagnie, tiens le compte de la nourriture et de tous les frais; et je fais la paie; hier, j'ai fait une petite paie de cinq cents francs aux ouvriers grecs.

Je suis payé au mois, cent cinquante francs, je crois: je n'ai encore rien reçu qu'une vingtaine de francs. Mais je vais bientôt être payé entièrement et je crois même congédié, comme je crois qu'une nouvelle compagnie va venir s'installer en notre place et prendre tout à la tâche. C'est dans cette incertitude que je retardais d'écrire. En tous cas, ma nourriture ne me coûtant que 2,25 par jour, et ne devant pas grand'chose au patron, il me restera toujours de quoi attendre d'autre travail, et il y en aura toujours pour moi ici dans Chypre. On va faire des chemins de fer, des forts, des casernes, des hôpitaux, des ports, des canaux, etc. . . . Le 1ᵉʳ mars on va donner des concessions de terrains, sans autres frais que l'enregistrement des actes.

Que se passe-t-il chez vous? Préféreriez-vous que je rentre? Comment vont les petites affaires? Ecrivez-moi au plus tôt.

Arthur Rimbaud.
poste restante, à Larnaca
(Chypre)

Je vous écris ceci au désert et ne sais quand faire partir.

E. Jean et Thial fils	Larnaca (Cyprus)
Entrepreneurs	15 February 1879

Dear friends,

I didn't write to you earlier, not knowing where I would be sent. But you must have received a letter from Alexandria where I told you of a new job for Cyprus. Tomorrow February 16 I will have been employed here exactly two months. The head men are in Larnaca, the principal harbor of Cyprus. I am the supervisor of a quarry in the desert, at the edge of the sea. They are also making a canal. Also rocks have to be put on the five boats and the steamer of the Company. There is also a limekiln, a brick-yard, etc. . . . The first village is one hour walking distance. Here there is only a chaos of rocks, the river, and the sea. There is only one house. No soil, no gardens, not a tree. In summer, the temperature goes up to eighty degrees. Now, it is often fifty. It is winter. It rains sometimes. We eat game, chicken, etc. All the Europeans have been sick, except myself. At the most, there have been twenty Europeans among us in the camp. The first came on the 9th of December. Three or four have died. The Cypriot workers come from surrounding villages. Up to sixty have been employed by the day. I am in charge of them. I schedule the day's work, give out the material, I make reports to the Company, keep an account of the food and all expenses, and give out the pay. Yesterday I distributed pay of 500 francs to the Greek workmen.

I am paid by the month, 150 francs, I believe. So far I have received only twenty francs or so. I will soon be paid completely and then probably dismissed, since I think a new company is coming to settle down here and take over the entire direction. It was because of this uncertainty that I put off writing. In any case, my food costing me only 2,25 francs a day, and owing almost nothing to the boss, I will have enough if I have to wait for other work, and there will always be work for me here in Cyprus. They are going to build railroads, forts, barracks, hospitals, harbors, canals, etc. . . . On the first of March, land concessions will be given out, without cost except the registering of the deeds.

What is happening at home? Would you prefer I come back? How is everything getting along? Write to me as soon as possible.

Arthur Rimbaud.
P.O., Larnaca
(Cyprus)

I am writing this in the desert and I don't know when it will leave.

Mont-Troodos (Chypre), dimanche 23 mai 1880

Excusez-moi de n'avoir pas écrit plus tôt. Vous avez peut-être eu besoin de savoir où j'étais; mais jusqu'ici j'ai réellement été dans l'impossibilité de vous faire parvenir de mes nouvelles.

Je n'ai rien trouvé à faire en Egypte et je suis parti pour Chypre il y a presque un mois. En arrivant, j'ai trouvé mes anciens patrons en faillite. Au bout d'une semaine, j'ai cependant trouvé l'emploi que j'occupe à présent. Je suis surveillant au palais que l'on bâtit pour le gouverneur général, au sommet du Troodos, la plus haute montagne de Chypre (2.100 mètres).

Jusqu'ici j'étais seul avec l'ingénieur, dans une des baraques en bois qui forment le camp. Hier sont arrivés une cinquantaine d'ouvriers et l'ouvrage va marcher. Je suis seul surveillant, jusqu'ici je n'ai que deux cents francs par mois. Voici quinze jours que je suis payé, mais je fais beaucoup de frais: il faut toujours voyager à cheval; les transports sont excessivement difficiles, les villages très loin, la nourriture très chère. De plus, tandis qu'on a très chaud dans les plaines, à cette hauteur-ci il fait, et fera encore pendant un mois, un froid désagréable; il pleut, grêle, vente à vous renverser. Il a fallu que je m'achète matelas, couvertures, paletot, bottes, etc., etc.

Il y a au sommet de la montagne un camp où les troupes anglaises arriveront dans quelques semaines, dès qu'il fera trop chaud dans la plaine et moins froid sur la montagne. Alors le service des provisions sera assuré.

Je suis donc, à présent, au service de l'administration anglaise: je compte être augmenté prochainement et rester employé jusqu'à la fin de ce travail, qui se finira probablement vers septembre. Ainsi, je pourrai gagner un bon certificat, pour être employé dans d'autres travaux qui vont probablement suivre, et mettre de côté quelques cents francs.

Je me porte mal; j'ai des battements de cœur qui m'ennuient fort. Mais il vaut mieux que je n'y pense pas. D'ailleurs qu'y faire? Cependant l'air est très sain ici. Il n'y a sur la montagne que des sapins et des fougères.

Je fais cette lettre aujourd'hui dimanche; mais il faut que je la mette à la poste à dix lieues d'ici, dans un port nommé Limassol, et je ne sais quand je trouverai l'occasion d'y aller ou d'y envoyer. Probablement pas avant huitaine.

A présent, il faut que je vous demande un service. J'ai absolument besoin, pour mon travail, de deux livres intitulés, l'un:

Album des Scieries forestières et agricoles, en anglais, prix 3 francs, contenant 128 dessins.

Mount Troodos (Cyprus) Sunday 23 May 1880.

Excuse me for not having written earlier. You perhaps needed to know where I was. But up until now it has really been impossible for me to send you news of myself.

There was no job for me in Egypt, and I left for Cyprus almost a month ago. On arriving, I found my former employers bankrupt. At the end of a week, however, I found my present employment. I am a supervisor in the palace that is being built for the governor-general, at the top of the Troodos, the highest mountain of Cyprus (2,100 meters.)

Until now I have been alone with the engineer, in one of the wooden shanties which make up the camp. Yesterday about fifty workmen came and the work will progress. I am the only supervisor. Until now I have had only two hundred francs a month. I was paid two weeks ago, but I have many expenses. I always have to travel on horseback, means of conveyance are extremely difficult, villages far apart, food very expensive. Moreover, while it is very warm on the plains, at this altitude it is, and will be for a month, disagreeably cold. The rain, hail, and wind are strong enough to knock you over. I have had to buy a mattress, blanket, a jacket, boots, etc., etc.

At the top of the mountain there is a camp where the English troops will arrive in a few weeks, as soon as it is too warm on the plain and less cold on the mountain. Then the service of supplies will be assured.

So, I am now in the service of the English administration. I hope my salary will be raised very soon, and I hope to remain employed until the completion of this work, which will probably end about September. If this happens, I will earn a good recommendation to be employed in other enterprises which will probably follow, and put aside a few hundred francs.

My health is not good. I suffer from palpitations which worry me. But it is better for me not to think about this. Anyway, what could I do? The air is excellent here. There are only fir-trees and ferns on the mountain.

I am writing this letter today Sunday. But I must post it ten leagues from here, at a harbor called Limassol, and I don't know when I will find the opportunity of going there or of sending this letter there. Probably not before a week.

And now I have to ask you to do me a service. For my work I have great need of two books entitled, first:

Album of Forest and Farm Sawmills, in English, price 3 francs, containing 128 drawings.

(Pour cela, écrire vous-mêmes à M. Arbey, constructeur-mécanicien, cours de Vincennes, Paris.)

Ensuite:

Le Livre de poche du Charpentier, collection de 140 épures, par Merly, prix 6 francs.

(A demander chez Lacroix, éditeur, rue des Saints-Pères, Paris.)

Il faut que vous me demandiez et m'envoyiez ces deux ouvrages au plus tôt, à l'adresse ci-dessous:

> Monsieur Arthur Rimbaud
> Poste restante.
>
> Limassol (Chypre)

Il faudra que vous payiez ces ouvrages, je vous en prie. *La poste ici ne prend pas d'argent, je ne puis donc vous en envoyer.* Il faudrait que j'achète un petit objet quelconque, que la poste accepterait, et je cacherais l'argent dedans. Mais c'est défendu et je ne tiens pas à le faire. Prochainement cependant, si j'ai autre chose à vous faire envoyer, je tâcherai de vous faire parvenir de l'argent de cette manière.

Vous savez combien de temps il faut, aller et retour, pour Chypre; et là où je me trouve, je ne compte pas, avec toute la diligence, avoir ces livres avant *six semaines.*

Jusqu'ici je n'ai encore parlé que de moi. Pardonnez-moi. C'est que je pensais que vous devez vous trouver en bonne santé, et au mieux pour le reste. Vous avez bien sûr plus chaud que moi. Et donnez-moi bien des nouvelles du petit train. Et le père Michel? et Cotaîche?

Je vais tâcher de vous faire prochainement un petit envoi du fameux vin de la Commanderie.

Je me recommande à votre souvenir.

A vous.

> Arthur Rimbaud
> Poste restante, Limassol (Chypre).

A propos, j'oubliais l'affaire du livret. Je vais prévenir le consul de France ici, et il arrivera de la chose ce qu'il en arrivera.

(For this, you should write to M. Arbey, builder-mechanic, cours de Vincennes, Paris.)

Second:

The Pocket Book of the Carpenter, collection of 140 drawings, by Merly, price 6 francs.

(Ask for this at Lacroix', publisher, rue des Saints-Pères, Paris.)

Please order these two books as soon as possible and send them to me, at this address:

Monsieur Arthur Rimbaud

P.O.

Limassol (Cyprus)

You will have to pay for these books. *The post office does not accept money, and so I can't send you any.* I would have to buy some small object which the post office would accept, and hide the money inside. But this is forbidden and I don't want to do it. Soon, however, if I have something else to have you send, I will try to send you the money in this way.

You know how much time is necessary, to go and to come, for Cyprus; and here where I am, with all speed, I don't expect to have these books before *six weeks.*

Thus far I have spoken only about myself. Excuse me. I thought that you must be in good health, and everything else was fine. It is certainly warmer there than here. Give me news of everything at home. How is père Michel? and Cotaîche?

I am going to try to send you soon some of the famous wine of the Commanderie (attached to religious order).

Don't forget me.

Yours.

Arthur Rimbaud

P.O., Limassol (Cyprus).

By the way, I forgot the business about the booklet. I will tell the French consul here, and he will see what happens.

Aux siens

Aden, 25 août 1880

Chers amis,

Il me semble que j'avais posté dernièrement une lettre pour vous, contant comme j'avais malheureusement dû quitter Chypre et comment j'étais arrivé ici après avoir roulé la mer Rouge.

Ici, je suis dans un bureau de marchand de café. L'agent de la Compagnie est un général en retraite. On fait passablement d'affaires, et on va faire beaucoup plus. Moi, je ne gagne pas beaucoup, ça ne fait pas plus de six francs par jour; mais si je reste ici, et il faut bien que j'y reste, car c'est trop éloigné de partout pour qu'on ne reste pas plusieurs mois avant de seulement gagner quelques centaines de francs pour s'en aller en cas de besoin, si je reste, je crois que l'on me donnera un poste de confiance, peut-être une agence dans une autre ville, et ainsi je pourrais gagner quelque chose un peu plus vite.

Aden est un roc affreux, sans un seul brin d'herbe ni une goutte d'eau bonne: on boit l'eau de mer distillée. La chaleur y est excessive, surtout en juin et septembre qui sont les deux canicules. La température constante, nuit et jour, d'un bureau très frais et très ventilé est de 35 degrés. Tout est très cher et ainsi de suite. Mais, il n'y a pas: je suis comme prisonnier ici, et, assurément, il me faudra y rester au moins trois mois avant d'être un peu sur mes jambes ou d'avoir un meilleur emploi.

Et à la maison? La moisson est finie?

Contez-moi vos nouvelles.

Arthur Rimbaud

Aux siens

Aden, 22 septembre 1880

Chers amis,

Je reçois votre lettre du 9 sep[tembr]e, et, comme un courrier part demain pour la France, je réponds.

Je suis aussi bien qu'on peut l'être ici. La maison fait plusieurs centaines de mille francs d'affaires par mois. Je suis le seul employé et tout passe par mes mains, je suis très au courant du commerce du café à présent. J'ai absolument la confiance du patron. Seulement, je suis mal payé: je n'ai que cinq francs par jour, nourri, logé, blanchi, etc., etc., avec cheval et voiture, ce qui représente bien une douzaine de francs par jour. Mais comme je suis

To his family

Aden, 25 August 1880

Dear friends,

It seems to me that I recently mailed a letter for you, telling how unfortunately I had to leave Cyprus and how I reached here after rolling over the Red Sea.

Here I am in the office of a coffee merchant. The agent of the Company is a retired general. The business is fairly prosperous, and it will improve. I don't earn very much, not more than six francs a day. But if I stay here, and I will have to stay here, for it is too far off from everywhere for me not to stay several months before earning even a few hundred francs that would allow me to leave if I had to. If I stay, I think they will give me a position of trust, perhaps an agency in another city, and thus I could earn something more quickly.

Aden is a frightful rock, without a single blade of grass or a drop of good water, They drink distilled sea water. The heat is excessive here, especially in June and September which are the two canicular months. The constant temperature, night and day, of a very cool and well-ventilated office is 35 degrees [C.]. Everything is expensive and so forth. But I have to stay: I am like a prisoner here, and certainly I will have to stay at least three months before getting back on my legs or getting a better job.

How are things at home? Is the harvest in?

Give me the news.

Arthur Rimbaud

To his family

Aden, 22 September 1880

Dear friends,

I have received your letter of September 9, and since the mail for France is leaving tomorrow, I am writing now.

I am as comfortable as one can be here. The business brings in several hundred thousand francs a month. I am the only employee and everything goes through me, by now I am very well versed in the coffee trade. I have the complete trust of the director. But I am badly paid. I get only five francs a day, with board, room, and laundry, etc., etc., a horse and carriage, which obviously represents about twelve francs a day. But since I am the

le seul employé un peu intelligent d'Aden, à la fin de mon deuxième mois ici, c'est-à-dire le 16 octobre, si l'on ne me donne pas deux cents francs par mois, en dehors de tous frais, je m'en irai. J'aime mieux partir que de me faire exploiter. J'ai d'ailleurs déjà environ 200 francs en poche. J'irais probablement à Zanzibar, où il y a à faire. Ici aussi, d'ailleurs, il y a beaucoup à faire. Plusieurs sociétés commerciales vont s'établir sur la côte d'Abyssinie. La maison a aussi des caravanes dans l'Afrique; et il est encore possible que je parte par là, où je me ferais des bénéfices et où je m'ennuierais moins qu'à Aden, qui est, tout le monde le reconnaît, le lieu le plus ennuyeux du monde, après toutefois celui que vous habitez.

J'ai 40 degrés de chaleur ici, à la maison: on sue des litres d'eau par jourici. Je voudrais seulement qu'il y ait 60 degrés, comme quand je restais à Massaouah!

Je vois que vous avez eu un bel été. Tant mieux. C'est la revanche du fameux hiver.

Les livres ne me sont pas parvenus, parce que (j'en suis sûr) q[uel]qu'un se les sera appropriés à ma place, aussitôt que j'ai eu quitté le Troodos. J'en ai toujours besoin, ainsi que d'autres livres, mais je ne vous demande rien, parce que je n'ose pas envoyer d'argent avant d'être sûr que je n'aurai pas besoin de cet argent, par exemple si je partais à la fin du mois.

Je vous souhaite mille chances et un été de 50 ans sans cesser.

Répondez-moi toujours à la même adresse; si je m'en vais, je ferai suivre.

Rimbaud

—Bien faire mon adresse, parce qu'il y a ici un Rimbaud agent des Messageries maritimes. On m'a fait payer 10 centimes de sup[plément] d'affranch[issement].

Je crois qu'il ne faut pas encourager Frédéric à venir s'établir à Roche, s'il y a tant soit peu d'occupation ailleurs. Il s'ennuierait vite, et on ne peut compter qu'il y resterait. Quant à l'idée de se marier, quand on n'a pas le sou ni la perspective ni le pouvoir d'en gagner, n'est-ce pas une idée misérable? Pour ma part, celui qui me condamnerait au mariage dans des circonst[ances] pareilles ferait mieux de m'assassiner tout de suite. Mais chacun son idée, ce qu'il pense ne me regarde pas, ne me touche en rien, et je lui souhaite tout le bonheur possible sur terre et particulièrement dans le canton d'Attigny (Ardennes).

A vous

only somewhat intelligent employee in Aden, at the end of my second month here, that is, the 16th of October, if they don't give me two hundred francs a month, in addition to all expenses, I will leave. I prefer to leave rather than be exploited. Moreover I have about 200 francs in cash. I would probably go to Zanzibar where there are possibilities. But, here too, there are many possibilities. Several business houses will be established along the Abyssinian coast. This company also has caravans in Africa, and it is still possible that I will go there, where I would earn a good salary and where I would be less bored than in Aden, which is, as everyone knows, the most boring place in the world, second only to the place where you live.

It is 40 degrees here, inside: we sweat liters of water every day here. I only wish it were 60 degrees, as it was when I was at Massaouah!

I see that you had a fine summer. That is good. It is a revenge over the hard winter.

The books did not reach me because (I am sure of this) someone helped himself to them in my name, as soon as I left Troodos. I still need them, and other books too, but I am not asking you for anything, because I don't dare send money before being sure that I won't need this money if I leave at the end of the month, for example.

I wish you good luck and a summer that will last forever.

Always write to me at the same address. If I leave, I will have mail forwarded.

Rimbaud

—Write the address clearly, because there is a Rimbaud here, agent of the Messageries maritimes [sea transport]. They made me pay an additional ten centimes for delivery.

I don't believe you should encourage Frédéric to settle down in Roche, as long as he has some kind of employment elsewhere. He would be quickly bored, and you couldn't rely on his staying there. As for the marriage idea, when you haven't a sou or the prospect or the capacity of earning anything, it is a miserable idea. In my case, the one who would force me to get married under such circumstances would do better to kill me outright. But let each of us make up his own mind! What he thinks does not concern me, does not affect me in the least, and I wish him all possible happiness on this earth, and particularly in the canton of Attigny (Ardennes).

Yours

Aux siens

Harar, le 15 février 1881

Chers amis,

J'ai reçu votre lettre du 8 décembre, et je crois même vous avoir écrit une fois depuis. J'en ai, d'ailleurs, perdu la mémoire en campagne.

Je vous rappelle que je vous ai fait envoyer 300 francs: 1°. d'Aden; 2°. de Harar a la date du 10 décembre environ; 3°. de Harar à la date du 10 janvier environ. Je compte qu'en ce moment vous avez déjà reçu ces trois envois de cent francs et mis en route ce que je vous ai demandé. Je vous remercie dès à présent de l'envoi que vous m'annoncez, mais que je ne recevrai pas avant deux mois d'ici, peut-être.

Envoyez-moi *Les constructions métalliques,* par Monge, prix: 10 francs.

Je ne compte pas rester longtemps ici; je saurai bientôt quand je partirai. Je n'ai pas trouvé ce que je présumais; et je vis d'une façon fort ennuyeuse et sans profits. Dès que j'aurai 1.500 ou 2.000 francs, je partirai, et j'en serai bien aise. Je compte trouver mieux un peu plus loin. Ecrivez-moi des nouvelles des travaux de Panama: aussitôt ouverts, j'irai. Je serai même heureux de partir d'ici, dès à présent. J'ai pincé une maladie, peu dangereuse par elle-même; mais ce climat-ci est traître pour toute espèce de maladie. On ne guérit jamais d'une blessure. Une coupure d'un millimètre à un doigt suppure pendant des mois et prend la gangrène très facilement. D'un autre côté, l'administration égyptienne n'a que des médecins et des médicaments insuffisants. Le climat est très humide en été: c'est malsain; je m'y déplais au possible, c'est beaucoup trop froid pour moi.

En fait de livres, ne m'envoyez plus de ces manuels *Roret.*

Voici quatre mois que j'ai commandé des effets à Lyon, et je n'aurai encore rien avant deux mois.

Il ne faut pas croire que ce pays-ci soit entièrement sauvage. Nous avons l'armée, artillerie et cavalerie, égyptienne, et leur administration. Le tout est identique à ce qui existe en Europe; seulement, c'est un tas de chiens et de bandits. Les indigènes sont des Gallas, tous agriculteurs et pasteurs: gens tranquilles, quand on ne les attaque pas. Le pays est excellent, quoique relativement froid et humide; mais l'agriculture n'y est pas avancée. Le commerce ne comporte principalement que les peaux des bestiaux, qu'on trait pendant leur vie et qu'on écorche ensuite; puis du café, de l'ivoire, de l'or; des parfums, encens, musc, etc. Le mal est que l'on est à 60 lieues de la mer et que les transports coûtent trop.

Je suis heureux de voir que votre petit manège va aussi bien que pos-

To his family

Harar, 15 February 1881

Dear friends,

I received your letter of December 8th, and I think I even wrote you once since then. But I have forgotten about it since I have been in the country.

I remind you that I had 300 francs sent to you: 1st. from Aden; 2nd. from Harar, about December 10th; 3rd. from Harar, about January 10th. I trust that by now you have already received three lots of a hundred francs, and sent on what I asked you for. I thank you now for what you tell me you have sent, but I won't receive it until two months from now perhaps.

Send me *Construction in Metal* by Monde, priced at 10 francs.

I don't intend to stay here very long. Soon I will know when I am leaving. I did not find what I thought I would find; and I am living in a very boring and unprofitable way. As soon as I have 1,500 or 2,000 francs, I will leave, and I will be glad to. I hope to find something better farther on. Give me news of the Panama project: as soon as it is opened, I will go there. I will even be glad to leave here, now. I caught an illness, not very dangerous in itself; but this climate is treacherous for any kind of illness. A wound never heals! A cut on the finger a millimeter long suppurates for months and very easily catches gangrene. In addition to this, the Egyptian administration has an insufficient number of doctors and medicine. The climate is very humid in summer: it is unhealthy; I find it unpleasant and much too cold for me.

About books: don't send me any more *Roret* manuals.

Four months ago I ordered some things from Lyon and I'll receive nothing for two months.

You musn't believe that this country is completely uncivilized. We have the Egyptian army, artillery and cavalry, and their administration. All this is identical with what exists in Europe; the difference is they are a pack of dogs and bandits. The natives are Gallas, all farmers and shepherds: peaceful people when they are not attacked. The country is excellent, although relatively cold and damp; but agriculture is not advanced. Trade is carried on principally in hides of animals, which are milked when alive, and then flayed; then there is coffee, ivory, and gold; perfumes, incense, musk, etc. The trouble is that we are sixty leagues from the sea and transportation is too expensive.

I am happy to know that your little scheme is prospering as well as pos-

sible. Je ne vous souhaite pas une réédition de l'hiver 1879–80, dont je me souviens assez pour éviter à jamais l'occasion d'en subir un semblable.

Si vous trouviez un exemplaire dépareillé du Bottin, Paris et Étranger, (quand ce serait un ancien), pour *quelques francs,* envoyez-le-moi, en caisse: j'en ai spécialement besoin.

Fourrez-moi aussi une demi-livre de graines de betterave saccharifère dans un coin de l'envoi.

Demandez—si vous avez de l'argent de reste—chez Lacroix le *Dictionary of Engineering military and civil,* prix 15 francs. Ceci n'est pas fort pressé.

Soyez sûrs que j'aurai soin de mes livres.

Notre matériel de photographie et de préparation d'histoire naturelle n'est pas encore arrivé, et je crois que je serai parti avant qu'il n'arrive.

J'ai une foule de choses à demander; mais il faut que vous m'envoyiez le Bottin d'abord.

A propos, comment n'avez-vous pas retrouvé le dictionnaire arabe? Il doit être à la maison cependant.

Dites à F[rédéric] de chercher dans les papiers arabes un cahier intitulé: *Plaisanteries, jeux de mots,* etc., en arabe; et il doit y avoir aussi une collection de *dialogues,* de *chansons* ou je ne sais quoi, utile à ceux qui apprennent la langue. S'il y a un ouvrage en arabe, envoyez; mais tout ceci comme emballage seulement, car ça ne vaut pas le port.

Je vais vous faire envoyer une vingtaine de kilos café moka à mon compte, si ça ne coûte pas trop de douane.

Je vous dis: à bientôt! dans l'espoir d'un temps meilleur et d'un travail moins bête; car, si vous présupposez que je vis en prince, moi je suis sûr que je vis d'une façon fort bête et fort embêtante.

Ceci part avec une caravane, et ne vous parviendra pas avant fin mars. C'est un des agréments de la situation. C'est même le pire.

A vous,

Rimbaud

Aux siens

Aden, le 18 janvier 1882

Chers amis,

Je reçois votre lettre du 27 décembre 1881, contenant une lettre de Delahaye. Vous me dites m'avoir écrit deux fois au sujet du reçu de cette somme

sible. I don't wish you another edition of the winter of 1879–80, which I remember well enough to avoid forever the possibility of undergoing another one like it.

If you find an odd copy of the *Bottin, Paris et Étranger* [telephone directory] (even if it is an old one), for *a few francs,* send it to me in a packing case. I particularly need one.

Also stick half a pound of sugar-beet seed in a corner of the box.

If you have any money left over, ask Lacroix for the *Dictionary of Engineering military and civil,* priced at 15 francs. This is not very urgent.

You can be sure that I will take care of my books.

Our photographic and naturalist materials have not yet come, and I think I will have gone before they come.

I have a lot of things to ask you for, but first you must send me the *Bottin.*

By the way, how was it you didn't find the Arabic dictionary? It must be in the house somewhere.

Tell Frédéric to look in the Arabic papers for a notebook entitled: *Plaisanteries, jeux de mots* [*Jokes, Puns*] in Arabic; and there must be also a collection of *dialogues,* or *songs* or something or other, useful to those who are learning the language. If there is a book in Arabic, send it; but all this only as packing, because it is not worth the postage.

I am going to have twenty kilos or so of Moka coffee sent to you at my expense, if it doesn't cost too much duty.

Let me say now: I will see you soon! in the hope of better weather and a less stupid kind of work. If you think I live like a prince, I am convinced that I live in a very stupid and obnoxious way.

This is leaving with a caravan, and won't reach you before the end of March. It is one of the pleasant aspects of this situation. It is even the worst of all.

Yours,

Rimbaud

To his family

Aden, 18 January 1882

Dear friends,

I have received your letter of December 27, 1881, containing a letter from Delahaye. You tell me you wrote twice about the receipt of that sum

d'argent. Comment se fait-il que vos lettres ne me soient pas arrivées? Et je viens de télégraphier d'Aden à Lyon, à la date du 5 janvier, sommant de payer cette somme! Vous ne me dites pas non plus quelle somme vous avez reçue, ce que je suis cependant pressé de savoir. Enfin, il est heureux que cela soit arrivé, après avoir été retenu pendant six mois! Je me demande aussi à quel change cela a pu vous être payé. A l'avenir, je choisirai un autre moyen pour mes envois d'argent, car la façon d'agir de ces gens est très désagréable. J'ai en ce moment environ 2.000 francs de libre, mais j'en aurai besoin prochainement.

Je suis sorti du Harar et rentré à Aden, où j'attends de rompre mon engagement avec la maison. Je trouverai facilement autre chose.

Quant à l'affaire du service militaire, vous trouverez ci-inclus une lettre du consul à mon adresse, vous montrant ce que j'ai fait et quelles pièces sont au ministère. Montrez cette lettre à l'autorité militaire, ça les tranquillisera. S'il est possible de m'envoyer un double de mon livret perdu, je vous serai obligé de le faire prochainement, car le consul me le demande. Enfin, avec ce que vous avez et ce que j'ai envoyé, je crois que l'affaire va pouvoir s'arranger.

Ci-joint une lettre pour Delahaye, prenez-en connaissance. S'il reste à Paris, cela fera bien mon affaire: j'ai besoin de faire acheter quelques instruments de précision. Car je vais faire un ouvrage pour la Société de géographie, avec des cartes et des gravures, sur le Harar et les pays Gallas. Je fais venir en ce moment de Lyon un appareil photographique; je le transporterai au Harar, et je rapporterai des vues de ces régions inconnues. C'est une très bonne affaire.

Il me faut aussi des instruments pour faire des levés topographiques et prendre des latitudes. Quand ce travail sera terminé et aura été reçu à la Société de géographie, je pourrai peut-être obtenir des fonds d'elle pour d'autres voyages. La chose est très facile.

Je vous prie donc de faire parvenir la commande ci-incluse à Delahaye, qui se chargera de ces achats, et vous n'aurez qu'à payer le tout. Il y en aura pour plusieurs milliers de francs, mais cela me fera un bon rapport. Je vous serai très reconnaissant de me faire parvenir le tout le plus tôt possible, *directement,* à Aden. Je vous conjure d'exécuter entièrement la commande; si vous me faisiez manquer quelque chose là-dedans, vous me mettriez dans un grand embarras.

Tout à vous,

Rimbaud

of money. How is it that your letters did not reach me? And I had just telegraphed from Aden to Lyon, on the date of January 5, insisting that the sum be paid! You do not tell me what amount you received, and I am anxious to know this. In short, it is fortunate it came, after being held back for six months! I also wonder at what rate of exchange you were paid. In the future, I will choose another means by which to send money, for the way those people carry on business is very disturbing. At this moment I have about 2000 francs in reserve, but I will soon need them.

I have left Harar and returned to Aden, where I expect to break off my contract with this business. I will easily find something else.

As concerns the problem of my military service, you will find inclosed a letter from the consul addressed to me, showing you what I did and what papers are at the ministry. Show this letter to the army authority and it will quiet them down. If it is possible to send me a copy of the lost booklet, I will be obliged if you do it very soon, because the consul is asking me for it. At any rate, with what you have and what I sent, I believe the matter will be taken care of.

Inclosed is a letter for Delahaye which you should look at. If he stays in Paris, that will suit me: I need someone to buy precision instruments for me. Because I am going to write a book for the Geography Society, with maps and engravings, on Harar and the Gallas country. At this moment I am having a camera sent me from Lyon. I will take it to Harar, and bring back views of those unfamiliar regions. This will be lucrative.

I also need instruments in order to make topographical sketches and measure latitudes. When this work is done and has been accepted by the Geographical Society, they will perhaps give me funds for other trips. This will be quite easy.

So, I beg you to send the inclosed order to Delahaye, who will take care of these purchases and all you will have to do is to pay for everything. It will come to several thousand francs, but it will bring me good returns. I will be very grateful if you send me everything as soon as possible, *directly,* to Aden. I implore you to carry out this order completely. If you made me miss something in this affair, it would be very embarrassing for me.

Sincerely

Rimbaud

À sa mère et à sa sœur

Mazeran, Viannay et Bardey,
Adresse télégraphique:
MAVIBA-MARSEILLE.

Aden, le 6 janvier 1883

Ma chère Maman,
Ma chère sœur,

J'ai reçu, il y a déjà huit jours, la lettre où vous me souhaitez la bonne année. Je vous rends mille fois vos souhaits, et j'espère qu'ils seront réalisés pour nous tous. Je pense toujours à Isabelle; c'est à elle que j'écris chaque fois, et je lui souhaite particulièrement tout à son souhait.

Je repars à la fin du mois de mars pour le Harar. Le dit bagage photographique m'arrive ici dans quinze jours, et je verrai vite à l'utiliser et à en repayer les frais, ce qui sera peu difficile, les reproductions de ces contrées ignorées et des types singuliers qu'elles renferment devant se vendre en France; et d'ailleurs, je retirerai là-bas même un bénéfice immédiat de toute la balançoire.

J'aime à compter que les frais sont terminés pour cette affaire; si cependant l'expédition nécessitait quelques nouvelles dépenses, faites-les encore, je vous prie, et terminez-en au plus tôt.

Envoyez-moi les livres également.

M. Dubar doit aussi m'envoyer un instrument scientifique nommé graphomètre.

Je compte faire quelques bénéfices à Harar cette année-ci, et je vous renverrai la balance de ce que je vous ai fait débourser. Pour longtemps, non plus, je ne vous troublerai avec mes commissions. Je vous demande bien pardon, si je vous ai dérangé[es]. C'est que la poste est si longue, aller et retour du Harar, que j'ai mieux aimé me pourvoir de suite pour longtemps.

Tout au mieux.

Rimbaud

To his mother and sister

Mazeran, Viannay and Bardey,
Telegraph address:
MAVIBA-MARSEILLES.

Aden, 6 January 1883

My dear Mother,
My dear sister,

A week ago I received the letter with your New Year's wishes. I return your wishes a thousand times over, and hope they will materialize for all of us. Isabelle is always in my thoughts. I write to her each time and I particularly hope all her wishes come true.

I am leaving again for Harar at the end of the month of March. The already mentioned photographic material will reach me in two weeks, and I will be able to use it immediately and pay for the cost, which will not be difficult since reproductions of those unknown regions and the unusual types they have will sell in France; and, moreover, I will receive even there an immediate benefit from the whole scheme.

I am hopeful that the expenses for this affair are at an end. If however the expedition demanded some further expenses, please pay them and end it as soon as possible.

And also send me the books.

M. Dubar is going to send me a scientific instrument called a graphometer.

I expect to bring in some money in Harar this year, and I will send you the balance of what I had you spend. For some time now I will not bother you with commissions. I am sorry if I have been a nuisance to you. Mail is so long coming from and going to Harar that I preferred to take care of everything immediately and for a long time.

My best to you.

Rimbaud

Mazeran, Viannay et Bardey,
  Lyon-Marseille-Aden.

Harar, le 6 mai 1883

Mes chers amis,

Le 30 avril, j'ai reçu au Harar votre lettre du 26 mars.

Vous dites m'avoir envoyé deux caisses de livres. J'ai reçu une seule caisse à Aden, celle pour laquelle Dubar disait avoir épargné vingt-cinq francs. L'autre est probablement arrivée à Aden, à présent, avec le graphomètre. Car je vous avais envoyé, avant de partir d'Aden, un chèque de 100 francs avec une autre liste de livres. Vous devez avoir touché ce chèque; et, les livres, vous les avez probab[leme]nt achetés. Enfin, à présent, je ne suis plus au courant des dates. Prochainement, je vous enverrai un autre chèque de 200 francs, car il faut que je fasse revenir des glaces pour la photographie.

Cette commission a été bien faite; et, si je le veux, je regagnerai vite les 2.000 francs que ça m'a coûté. Tout le monde veut se faire photographier ici; même on offre une guinée par photographie. Je ne suis pas encore bien installé, ni au courant; mais je le serai vite, et je vous enverrai des choses curieuses.

Ci-inclus deux photographies de moi-même par moi-même. Je suis toujours mieux ici qu'à Aden. Il y a moins de travail et bien plus d'air, de verdure, etc. . . .

J'ai renouvelé mon contrat pour trois ans ici, mais je crois que l'établissement fermera bientôt, les bénéfices ne couvrent pas les frais. Enfin, il est conclu que le jour qu'on me renverra, on me donnera trois mois d'appointements d'indemnité. A la fin de cette année-ci, j'aurai trois ans complets dans cette boîte.

Isabelle a bien tort de ne pas se marier si quelqu'un de sérieux et d'instruit se présente, quelqu'un avec un avenir. La vie est comme cela, et la solitude est une mauvaise chose ici-bas. Pour moi, je regrette de ne pas être marié et avoir une famille. Mais, à présent, je suis condamné à errer, attaché à une entreprise lointaine, et tous les jours je perds le goût pour le climat et les manières de vivre et même la langue de l' Europe. Hélas! à quoi servent ces allées et venues, et ces fatigues et ces aventures chez des races étranges, et ces langues dont on se remplit la mémoire, et ces peines sans nom, si je ne dois un jour, après quelques années, pouvior me reposer dans un endroit qui me plaise à peu près et trouver une famille, et avoir au moins un fils que je passe le reste de ma vie à élever à mon idée, à orner et à armer

To his family

Mazeran, Viannay and Bardey,
  Lyon-Marseilles-Aden.

Harar, 6 May 1883

My dear friends,

On April 30th, I received in Harar your letter of March 26th.

You say that you sent me two crates of books. I received a single crate in Aden, the one for which Dubar said he economized twenty-five francs. The other has probably reached Aden by now, with the graphometer. For I sent you, before leaving Aden, a check for 100 francs with another list of books. You must have cashed this check; and you have probably bought the books. But now I have lost track of dates. Very soon I will send you another check for 200 francs, because I have to have mirrors sent to me for the photography.

This commission was well carried out, and if I wish, I will quickly earn back the 2000 francs that this cost me. Here everyone wants to be photographed. They even offer one guinea a photograph. I am not yet well established, nor aware of things. But I will be soon, and I will send you some interesting things.

Inclosed are two photographs of me which I took. I am always better off here than in Aden. There is less work and much more air and vegetation, etc. . . .

I have renewed my contract for three years here, but I believe that the establishment will close down soon, since the profit does not cover the cost. In short, it is agreed that the day. I am dismissed I will be given three months salary indemnity. At the end of this year, I will have been in this place three full years.

Isabelle is wrong not to get married if some serious, well-educated fellow asks her, someone with a future. Such is life, and solitude is a bad thing down here. Personally I regret not being married and having a family. But now I am destined to wander about, associated with a very distant business, and each day I lost interest in the climate and the way of life and even the language of Europe. Alas, what is the point of these trips back and forth, the fatigue and the adventures with unfamiliar races, and the languages we memorize, and the endless discomforts, if I cannot one day, after a few years, settle down in one fairly pleasant place, and found a family and at least have a son whom I will spend the rest of my life raising in accordance with my views, forming and strengthening with the most complete education that can be found at that time, and whom I will see grow into a fa-

de l'instruction la plus complète qu'on puisse atteindre à cette époque, et que je voie devenir un ingénieur renommé, un homme puissant et riche par la science? Mais qui sait combien peuvent durer mes jours dans ces montagnes-ci? Et je puis disparaître, au milieu de ces peuplades, sans que la nouvelle en ressorte jamais.

Vous me parlez des nouvelles politiques. Si vous saviez comme ça m'est indifférent! Plus de deux ans que je n'ai pas touché un journal. Tous ces débats me sont incompréhensibles, à présent. Comme les musulmans, je sais que ce qui arrive arrive, et c'est tout.

La seule chose qui m'intéresse, [ce] sont les nouvelles de la maison et je suis toujours heureux à me reposer sur le tableau de votre travail pastoral. C'est dommage qu'il fasse si froid et lugubre chez vous, en hiver! Mais vous êtes au printemps, à présent, et votre climat, à ce temps-ci, correspond avec celui que j'ai ici, au Harar, à présent.

Ces photographies me représentent, l'une, debout sur une terrasse de la maison, l'autre, debout dans un jardin de café; une autre, les bras croisés dans un jardin de bananes. Tout cela est devenu blanc, à cause des mauvaises eaux qui me servent à laver. Mais je vais faire de meilleur travail dans la suite. Ceci est seulement pour rappeler ma figure, et vous donner une idée des paysages d'ici.

Au revoir,

Rimbaud
Maison Mazeran, Viannay et Bardey,
Aden.

Aux siens

Mazeran, Viannay et Bardey,
Lyon-Marseille-Aden.

Aden, le 5 mai 1884

Mes chers amis,

Comme vous le savez, notre société est entièrement liquidée, et l'agence du Harar, que je dirigeais, est supprimée; l'agence d'Aden aussi est fermée. Les pertes de la C[ompagn]ie en France sont, me dit-on, de près d'un million; pertes faites cependant dans des affaires distinctes de celles-ci, qui travaillaient assez satisfaisamment. Enfin, je me suis trouvé remercié fin avril, et, selon les termes de mon contrat, j'ai reçu une indemnité de trois mois d'appointements, jusque fin juillet. Je suis donc actuellement sans emploi,

mous engineer, a man made powerful and rich by science? But who knows
how many more days my life will have in these mountains? I could disap-
pear, in the midst of these tribes, without news of me ever getting out.

You write to me about political news. If you knew how indifferent I am
to all that. For more than two years I haven't touched a newspaper. All
those debates are for the present without meaning for me. Like the Mos-
lems, I know that what happens happens, and that is all.

The one thing that interests me is news from home, and I am always
happy to contemplate the picture of your pastoral work. It is too bad that
it is so cold and gloomy at Roche in winter time! But now you are in
spring, and your climate, at present, corresponds to what we have now in
Harar.

One of these photographs shows me standing on a terrace of the house;
another, standing in a café garden; another, with my arms crossed in a ba-
nana garden. All that has turned white because of the filthy water which I
use for washing. But I am going to work better in the future. This is only
to remind you of my face and give you some idea of the landscape here.

Au revoir,

Rimbaud
Offices of Mazeran, Viannay and Bardey,
Aden.

To his family

Mazeran, Viannay and Bardey,
  Lyon-Marseilles-Aden.

Aden 5 May 1884

My dear friends,

As you know, our Company is completely liquidated, and the agency at
Harar, which I directed, is closed; the agency at Aden also is closed. The
losses for the Company in France, I am told, are close to a million; losses
which however came about in deals distinct from ours which have been
transpiring satisfactorily. In short, I was dismissed at the end of April, and,
according to the terms of my contract, I received an indemnity of three
months' salary, until the end of July. So now I am without a job, although

quoique je sois toujours logé dans l'ancien immeuble de la C[ompagn]ie, lequel est loué jusqu'à fin juin. Monsieur Bardey est reparti pour Marseille, il y a une dizaine de jours, pour rechercher de nouveaux fonds pour continuer les affaires d'ici. Je lui souhaite de réussir, mais je crains fort le contraire. Il m'a dit de l'attendre ici; mais, à la fin de ce mois-ci, si les nouvelles ne sont pas satisfaisantes, je verrai à m'employer ailleurs et autrement.

Il n'y a pas de travail ici à présent, les grandes maisons fournissant les agences d'ici ayant toutes sauté à Marseille. D'un autre côté, pour qui n'est pas employé, la vie est hors de prix ici, et l'existence est intolérablement ennuyeuse, surtout l'été commencé; et vous savez qu'on a ici l'été le plus chaud du monde entier!

Je ne sais pas du tout où je pourrai me trouver dans un mois. J'ai de douze à treize mille francs avec moi et, comme on ne peut rien confier à personne ici, on est obligé de traîner son pécule avec soi et de le surveiller perpétuellement. Et cet argent, qui pourrait me donner une petite rente suffisante pour me faire vivre hors d'emploi, il ne me rapporte rien, que des embêtements continuels!

Quelle existence désolante je traîne sous ces climats absurdes et dans ces conditions insensées! J'aurais, avec ces économies, un petit revenu assuré; je pourrais me reposer un peu, après de longues années de souffrances; et non seulement je ne puis rester un jour sans travail, mais je ne puis jouir de mon gain. Le Trésor ici ne prend que des dépôts sans intérêts, et les maisons de commerce ne sont pas solides du tout!

Je ne puis pas vous donner une adresse en réponse à ceci, car j'ignore personnellement où je me serai trouvé entraîné prochainement, et par quelles routes, et pour où, et pour quoi, et comment!

Il est possible que les Anglais occupent prochainement le Harar; et il se peut que j'y retourne. On pourrait faire là un petit commerce; je pourrais peut-être y acheter des jardins et quelques plantations et essayer d'y vivre ainsi. Car les climats du Harar et de l'Abyssinie sont excellents, meilleurs que ceux de l'Europe, dont ils n'ont pas les hivers rigoureux; et la vie y est pour rien, la nourriture bonne et l'air délicieux; tandis que le séjour sur les côtes de la mer Rouge énerve les gens les plus robustes; et une année là vieillit les gens comme quatre ans ailleurs.

Ma vie ici est donc un réel cauchemar. Ne vous figurez pas que je la passe belle. Loin de là: j'ai même toujours vu qu'il est impossible de vivre plus péniblement que moi.

Si le travail peut reprendre ici à bref délai, cela va encore bien: je ne mangerai pas mon malheureux fonds en courant les aventures. Dans ce cas, je

I am still living in the former building of the Company, which is rented until the end of June. Monsieur Bardey left for Marseilles ten days ago, to try to get new funds in order to continue the business here. I hope he'll succeed, but I fear he won't. He told me to wait for him here, but at the end of this month, if the news is not satisfactory, I will see about getting another kind of job somewhere else.

There is no work here at present, since the large businesses which have agencies here have all collapsed in Marseilles. In addition, for the man out of work, living is very high here, and existence is unbearably boring, especially after summer has begun. You know that summer heat here is the worst in the world!

I have no idea where I will be in a month. I have on me between twelve and thirteen thousand francs, and since no one here can be trusted, I have to keep my savings on me and keep a constant eye on it. This money which could provide me with a sufficient small income, so that I could live without working, brings me nothing except continuous trouble!

What a miserable existence I am leading in this absurd climate and under these disagreeable conditions! With my savings, I would have a small assured income. I could rest a bit, after long years of suffering. Not only is it impossible for me to go one day without work, it is impossible for me to enjoy my earnings. The Treasury here accepts only deposits without interest, and business houses are not at all stable!

I cannot give you an address for an answer to this, because personally I do not know where I will be dragged to next, along which roads, toward what destination, for what reason, and by what means!

It is possible that the English will soon occupy Harar. And it is possible I will return there. I might set up a small business there. I might perhaps buy some gardens and plantations and try to make a living in that way. The climate of Harar and Abyssinia is excellent, better than that of Europe whose hard winters they don't have; and living is easy, the food good and the air delightful; whereas living on the coast of the Red Sea enervates the strongest; and one year there ages people as much as four years elsewhere.

So my life here is a real nightmare. Don't go thinking I am having a fine time. Far from it: I have always considered that it is impossible to live more painfully than I do.

If work starts up again here without much delay, all will be fine. I will not use up my wretched savings in looking for adventures. In that case, I would stay on as long as possible in this terrible hole of Aden; because personal enterprises are too dangerous in Africa, on the other side.

resterais encore le plus possible dans cet affreux trou d'Aden; car les entreprises personnelles sont trop dangereuses en Afrique, de l'autre côté.

Excusez-moi de vous détailler mes ennuis. Mais je vois que je vais atteindre les 30 ans (la moitié de la vie!) et je me suis fort fatigué à rouler le monde, sans résultat.

Pour vous, vous n'avez pas de ces mauvais rêves; et j'aime à me représenter votre vie tranquille et vos occupations paisibles. Qu'elles durent ainsi!

Quant à moi, je suis condamné à vivre longtemps encore, toujours peut-être, dans ces environs-ci, où je suis connu à présent, et où je trouverai toujours du travail; tandis qu'en France, je serais un étranger et je ne trouverais rien.

Enfin, espérons au mieux.

Salut prospère.

Arthur Rimbaud
Poste restante, Aden-Camp.
Arabie.

Aux siens

Aden, le 15 janvier 1885

Mes chers amis,

J'ai reçu votre lettre du 26 X^bre 84. Merci de vos bons souhaits. Que l'hiver vous soit court et l'année heureuse!

Je me porte toujours bien, dans ce sale pays.

J'ai rengagé pour un an, c'est-à-dire jusqu'à fin 85; mais il est possible que, cette fois encore, les affaires soient suspendues avant ce terme. Ces pays-ci sont devenus très mauvais, depuis les affaires d'Egypte. Je reste aux mêmes conditions. J'ai 300 francs net par mois, sans compter mes autres frais qui sont payés et qui représentent encore 300 autres francs par mois. Cet emploi est donc d'environ 7.000 francs par an, dont il me reste net environ 3.500 à 4.000 francs à la fin de l'année. Ne me croyez pas capitaliste: tout mon capital à présent est de 13.000 francs, et sera d'environ 17.000 fcs. à la fin de l'année. J'aurai travaillé cinq ans pour ramasser cette somme. Mais quoi faire ailleurs? J'ai mieux fait de patienter là où je pouvais vivre en travaillant; car quelles sont mes perspectives ailleurs? Mais, c'est égal, les années se passent, et je n'amasse rien. Je n'arriverai jamais à vivre de mes rentes dans ces pays.

Mon travail ici consiste à faire des achats de cafés. J'achéte environ deux cent mille francs par mois. En 1883, j'avais acheté plus de 3 millions dans

Excuse me for writing out all my troubles. But I see I am going to reach the age of thirty (half of my life!) and I am worn out with wandering over the globe, with no result.

You don't have these bad dreams. I like to imagine your quiet life and your peaceful occupations. May they continue!

But it is my fate to live for a long time still, for always perhaps, in this environment, where I am known now and where I will always find work; whereas in France, I would be a foreigner and would find nothing.

Anyway, let's hope for the best.

Be well and prosperous.

Arthur Rimbaud
P.O., Aden-Camp.
Arabia.

To his family

Aden, 15 January 1885

My dear friends,

I received your letter of December 26, 1884. Thanks for your good wishes. May your winter be brief and your new year happy!

I still feel pretty well in this filthy country.

I signed up again for one year, namely to the end of 1885; but it is possible that once again business will be suspended before that date. These countries are badly off since the trouble with Egypt. I am staying on with the same salary. I get 300 francs clear a month, without counting my other expenses which are paid and which come to 300 more francs a month. This position is therefore worth about 7,000 francs a year, out of which I clear between 3,500 and 4,000 francs by the end of the year. Don't think that I am a capitalist: my entire capital at present is 13,000 francs, and will be about 17,000 at the end of the year. I will have worked five years to make that sum. But what could I do elsewhere? I was wise to be patient there where I was able to live and work; for what chances do I have anywhere else? But it makes no difference. The years go by, and I save nothing. I will never succeed in living from my savings in this kind of country.

My work here consists in buying coffee. I buy about two hundred thousand francs a year. In 1883, I bought more than 3 million in the year, and

l'année, et mon bénéfice là-dessus n'est rien de plus que mes malheureux appointements, soit trois, quatre mille francs par an: vous voyez que les emplois sont mal payés partout. Il est vrai que l'ancienne maison a fait une faillite de neuf cent mille francs, mais non attribuable aux affaires d'Aden, qui, si elles ne laissaient pas de bénéfice, ne perdaient au moins rien. J'achète aussi beaucoup d'autres choses: des gommes, encens, plumes d'autruche, ivoire, cuirs secs, girofles, etc., etc.

Je ne vous envoie pas ma photographie; j'évite avec soin tous les frais inutiles. Je suis d'ailleurs toujours mal habillé; on ne peut se vêtir ici que de cotonnades très légères; les gens qui ont passé quelques années ici ne peuvent plus passer l'hiver en Europe, ils crèveraient de suite par quelque fluxion de poitrine. Si je reviens, ce ne sera donc jamais qu'en été; et je serai forcé de redescendre, en hiver au moins, vers la Méditerranée. En tous cas, ne comptez pas que mon humeur deviendrait moins vagabonde, au contraire, si j'avais le moyen de voyager sans être forcé de séjourner pour travailler et gagner l'existence, on ne me verrait pas deux mois à la même place. Le monde est très grand et plein de contrées magnifiques que l'existence de mille hommes ne suffirait pas à visiter. Mais, d'un autre côté, je ne voudrais pas vaga-bonder dans la misère, je voudrais avoir quelques milliers de francs de rentes et pouvoir passer l'année dans deux ou trois contrées différentes, en vivant modestement et en faisant quelques petits trafics pour payer mes frais. Mais pour vivre toujours au même lieu, je trouverai toujours cela très malheureux. Enfin, le plus probable, c'est qu'on va plutôt où l'on ne veut pas, et que l'on fait plutôt ce qu'on ne voudrait pas faire, et qu'on vit et décède tout autrement qu'on ne le voudrait jamais, sans espoir d'aucune espèce de compensation.

Pour les Corans, je les ai reçus il y a longtemps, il y a juste un an, au Harar même. Quant aux autres livres, ils ont en effet dû être vendus. Je voudrais bien vous faire envoyer quelques livres, mais j'ai déjà perdu de l'argent à cela. Pourtant, je n'ai aucune distraction, ici, où il n'y a ni journaux, ni bibliothèques, et où l'on vit-comme des sauvages.

Ecrivez cependant à la librairie Hachette, je crois, et demandez quelle est *la plus récente édition* du *Dictionnaire de Commerce et de Navigation,* de Guillaumin.—S'il y a une édition récente, d'après 1880, vous pouvez me l'envoyer: il y a deux gros volumes, ça coûte cent francs, mais on peut avoir cela au rabais chez Sauton. Mais s'il n'y a que de vieilles éditions, je n'en veux pas.—Attendez ma prochaine lettre pour cela.

Bien à vous,

Rimbaud

my profit from that is nothing more than my wretched salary, namely three, four thousand francs a year: you see that jobs are badly paid everywhere. It is true that the former company underwent a bankruptcy of nine hundred thousand francs, but not attributable to the Aden business, which, although it did not make a profit, at least lost nothing. I also buy many other things: gum, incense, ostrich plumes, ivory, dried leather, cloves, etc., etc.

I am not sending you my photograph; I carefully avoid all useless expenses. Moreover I am always badly dressed; all we can wear here is very light cotton; people who have lived a few years here can no longer stand the winter in Europe, they would die very soon from lung trouble. If I do go back, it will never be except in summer; and I will be obliged, at least in winter, to go toward the Mediterranean. In any case, don't count on my disposition growing less vagabond, on the contrary, if I had the means of traveling without being forced to settle down in order to work and earn my living, I wouldn't be seen two months in the same spot. The world is very big and full of magnificent places which it would take more than a thousand lives to visit. On the other hand, I wouldn't like to wander in misery, I wish I could have a few thousand francs income and be able to spend the year in two or three different places, living modestly and carrying on a few trade deals to pay for my expenses. But living always in the same place, I will always find wretched. But the most likely is that we go where we don't want to go, and do what we don't want to do, and live and die differently than we would like, without hope for any kind of compensation.

I received the Koran, long ago, just one year ago, right in Harar. The other books must have been sold. I would like to have you send me some books, but I have already lost money in doing that. Yet I have no distractions, here, where there are no newspapers and no libraries, and where people live like savages.

Please write to Hachette's, I believe, and ask which is the most recent edition of the *Dictionary of Commerce and Navigation* of Guillaumin.—If there is a recent edition, after 1880, you can send it to me: there are two big volumes and it costs one hundred francs, but you can get it marked down at Sauton's. But if there are only old editions, I don't want it.—Wait for my next letter for this.

Sincerely,

Rimbaud

Aux siens

Tadjourah, le 3 décembre 1885

Mes chers amis,

Je suis ici en train de former ma caravane pour le Choa. Ça ne va pas vite, comme c'est l'habitude; mais, enfin, je compte me lever d'ici vers la fin de janvier 1886.

Je vais bien.—Envoyez-moi le dictionnaire demandé, à l'adresse donnée. A cette même adresse, par la suite, toutes les communications pour moi. De là on me fera suivre.

Ce Tadjourah-ci est annexé depuis un an à la colonie française d'Obock. C'est un petit village Dankali avec quelques mosquées et quelques palmiers. Il y a un fort, construit jadis par les Egyptiens, et où dorment à présent six soldats français sous les ordres d'un sergent, commandant le poste. On a laissé au pays son petit sultan et son administration indigène. C'est un protectorat. Le commerce du lieu est le trafic des esclaves.

D'ici partent les caravanes des Européens pour le Choa, très peu de chose; et on ne passe qu'avec de grandes difficultés, les indigènes de toutes ces côtes étant devenus ennemis des Européens, depuis que l'amiral anglais Hewett a fait signer à l'empereur Jean du Tigré un traité abolissant la traite des esclaves, le seul commerce indigène un peu florissant. Cependant, sous le protectorat français, on ne cherche pas à gêner la traite, et cela vaut mieux.

N'allez pas croire que je sois devenu marchand d'esclaves. Les m[archand]ises que nous importons sont des fusils (vieux fusils à piston réformés depuis 40 ans), qui valent chez les marchands de vieilles armes, à Liège ou en France, 7 ou 8 francs la pièce. Au roi du Choa, Ménélik II, on les vend une quarantaine de francs. Mais il y a dessus des frais énormes, sans parler des dangers de la route, aller et retour. Les gens de la route sont les Dankalis, pasteurs bédouins, musulmans fanatiques: ils sont à craindre. Il est vrai que nous marchons avec des armes à feu et les bédouins n'ont que des lances: mais toutes les caravanes sont attaquées.

Une fois la rivière Hawache passée, on entre dans les domaines du puissant roi Ménélik. Là, ce sont des agriculteurs chrétiens; le pays est très élevé, jusqu'à 3.000 mètres au-dessus de la mer; le climat est excellent; la vie est absolument pour rien; tous les produits de l'Europe poussent; on est bien vu de la population. Il pleut là six mois de l'année, comme au Harar, qui est un des contreforts de ce grand massif éthiopien.

Je vous souhaite bonne santé et prospérité pour l'an 1886.

Bien à vous,

A. Rimbaud
Hôtel de l'univers, Aden.

To his family

Tadjourah, 3 December 1885

My dear friends,

I am here in the process of making up my caravan for Choa. It is slow work, as always; but I do hope to start off from here toward the end of January 1886.

I am well. — Send me the dictionary I asked for, to the address I gave. To this same address, henceforth, all communications for me. From there, letters will be forwarded.

This Tadjourah has been annexed for a year to the French colony of Obock. It is a small Dankali village with a few mosques and a few palm trees. There is a fort formerly built by the Egyptians, and where now sleep six French soldiers under the orders of a sergeant commanding the post. The country still has its little sultaned native government. It is a protectorate. The industry in this place is the selling of slaves.

The caravans of Europeans leave from here for Choa, which is not far; but it is extremely difficult to get through because the natives along the coast have become enemies of Europeans, since the English Admiral Hewett had Emperor Jean du Tigré sign a treaty abolishing slave traffic, the one somewhat flourishing native industry. However, under the French protectorate, there is no effort to impede this traffic, and that is well.

Don't think that I have become a slave merchant. The merchandise we import is rifles (old piston rifles, forty years out of date), which are worth 7 or 8 francs each, at dealers in old weapons in Liège or in France. To the king of Choa, Ménélik II, they are sold for about 40 francs. But there are huge expenses involved, not to mention dangers of the road going and coming. The people along the road are Dankalis, Bedouin shepherds, and fanatic Moslems: they are to be feared. It is true that we carry firearms and the Bedouins have only lances: but all caravans are attacked.

Once we cross the River Hawache, we enter the land of powerful King Ménélik. There, they are Christian farmers. The country is very high, up to 3,000 meters above sea level; the climate is excellent; living is very inexpensive; all the produce of Europe grows; we are liked by the population. It rains there six months in the year, as in Harar, which is one of the strongholds of this great Ethiopian plateau.

I wish you good health and prosperity for 1886.

Sincerely,

A. Rimbaud
Hôtel de l'univers, Aden.

Aux siens

Le Caire, 23 août 1887

Mes chers amis,

Mon voyage en Abyssinie s'est terminé.

Je vous ai déjà expliqué comme quoi, mon associé étant mort, j'ai eu de grandes difficultés au Choa, à propos de sa succession. On m'a fait payer deux fois ses dettes et j'ai eu une peine terrible à sauver ce que j'avais mis dans l'affaire. Si mon associé n'était pas mort, j'aurais gagné une trentaine de mille francs; tandis que je me retrouve avec les quinze mille que j'avais, après m'être fatigué d'une manière horrible pendant prés de deux ans. Je n'ai pas de chance!

Je suis venu ici parce que les chaleurs étaient épouvantables cette année, dans la mer Rouge: tout le temps 50 à 60 degrés; et, me trouvant très affaibli, après sept années de fatigues qu'on ne peut s'imaginer et des privations les plus abominables, j'ai pensé que deux ou trois mois ici me remettraient; mais c'est encore des frais, car je ne trouve rien à faire ici, et la vie est à l'européenne et assez chère.

Je me trouve tourmenté ces jours-ci par un rhumatisme dans les reins, qui me fait damner; j'en ai un autre dans la cuisse gauche qui me paralyse de temps à autre, une douleur articulaire dans le genou gauche, un rhumatisme (déjà ancien) dans l'épaule droit; j'ai les cheveux absolument gris. Je me figure que mon existence périclite.

Figurez-vous comment on doit se porter, après des exploits du genre des suivants: traversées de mer et voyages de terre à cheval, en barque, sans vêtements, sans vivres, sans eau, etc., etc.

Je suis excessivement fatigué. Je n'ai pas d'emploi à présent. J'ai peur de perdre le peu que j'ai. Figurez-vous que je porte continuellement dans ma ceinture seize mille et quelques cents francs d'or; ça pèse une huitaine de kilos et ça me flanque la dysenterie.

Pourtant, je ne puis aller en Europe, pour bien des raisons; d'abord, je mourrais en hiver; ensuite, je suis trop habitué à la vie errante et gratuite; enfin, je n'ai pas de position.

Je dois donc passer le reste de mes jours errant dans les fatigues et les privations, avec l'unique perspective de mourir à la peine.

Je ne resterai pas longtemps ici: je n'ai pas d'emploi et tout est trop cher. Par force, je devrai m'en retourner du côté du Soudan, de l'Abyssinie ou de l'Arabie. Peut-être irai-je à Zanzibar, d'où on peut faire de longs voyages en Afrique, et peut-être en Chine, au Japon, qui sait où?

To his family

My dear friends

My travels in Abyssinia are over.

I have already explained to you how, on the death of my associate, I had great difficulties in Choa, over his succession. They made me pay his debts twice, and I had a hard time salvaging what I had put into the business. If my associate had not died, I would have earned about thirty thousand francs; whereas I now have the fifteen thousand francs I had, after wearing myself out horribly for almost two years. I am not lucky!

I came here because the heat was terrible this year at the Red Sea: it was constantly between 50 and 60 degrees; and feeling very weakened, after seven years of fatigue you can't imagine and the most abominable privations, I thought that two or three months would put me back on my feet; but this involves more expense, because I find nothing to do here, and living is European style and quite expensive.

I am tormented these days by rheumatism in the back which makes me miserable. It is also in the left thigh which paralyzes me from time to time, an arthritic pain in the left knee, and rheumatism (I've had for some time) in the right shoulder; my hair is totally gray. I imagine that my existence is running out.

Try to imagine what a man's health is, after exploits such as the following: sea crossings and land journeys on horseback, in small boats, without clothes, without food, without water, etc., etc.

I am desperately tired. I have no job at present. I fear losing the little I have. Just think that I continually carry about in my belt sixteen thousand and a few hundred francs in gold; it weighs about eight kilos and gives me dysentery.

And yet I can't go to Europe, for many reasons. First, I would die in winter. Then, I am too accustomed to a wandering free existence; and finally, I have no position.

Therefore I have to spend the rest of my days wandering about in fatigue and privations, with the one prospect of dying in the saddle.

I won't stay here long: I have no work and everything is too expensive. I will probably be forced to return to the Soudan, or Abyssinia, or Arabia. Perhaps I will go to Zanzibar from where I could take long trips to Africa, and perhaps to China, Japan, God knows where?

Enfin, envoyez-moi de vos nouvelles. Je vous souhaite paix et bonheur.
Bien à vous,

Adresse: Arthur Rimbaud,
poste restante, au Caire (Egypte).

Aux siens

Harar, 4 août 1888

Mes chers amis,

Je reçois votre lettre du 27 juin. Il ne faut pas vous étonner du retard des correspondances, ce point étant séparé de la côte par des déserts que les courriers mettent huit jours à franchir; puis, le service qui relie Zeilah à Aden est très irrégulier, la poste ne part d'Aden pour l'Europe qu'une fois par semaine et elle n'arrive à Marseille qu'en quinze jours. Pour écrire en Europe et recevoir réponse, cela prend au moins trois mois. Il est impossible d'écrire directement d'Europe au Harar, puisqu'au-delà de Zeilah, qui est sous la protection anglaise, c'est le désert habité par des tribus errantes. Ici, c'est la montagne, la suite des plateaux abyssins: la température ne s'y élève jamais à plus de 25 degrés au-dessus de zéro, et elle ne descend jamais à moins de 5 degrés au-dessus de zéro. Donc pas de gelées, ni de sueurs.

Nous sommes maintenant dans la saison des pluies. C'est assez triste. Le gouvernement est le gouvernement abyssin du roi Ménélik, c'est-à-dire un gouvernement négro-chrétien; mais, somme toute, on est en paix et sûreté relatives, et, pour les affaires, elles vont tantôt bien, tantôt mal. On vit sans espoir de devenir tôt millionnaire. Enfin! puisque c'est mon sort de vivre dans ces pays ainsi! . . .

Il y a à peine une vingtaine d'Européens dans toute l'Abyssinie, y compris ces pays-ci. Or, vous voyez sur quels immenses espaces ils sont disséminés. A Harar, c'est encore l'endroit où il y en a le plus: environ une dizaine. J'y suis le seul de nationalité française. Il y a aussi une mission catholique avec trois pères, dont l'un Français comme moi, qui éduquent des négrillons.

Je m'ennuie beaucoup, toujours; je n'ai même jamais connu personne qui s'ennuyât autant que moi. Et puis, n'est-ce pas misérable, cette existence sans famille, sans occupation intellectuelle, perdu au milieu des nègres dont on voudrait améliorer le sort et qui, eux, cherchent à vous exploiter et vous mettent dans l'impossibilité de liquider des affaires à bref délai?

Well, send me news of yourselves. I wish you peace and happiness.
Sincerely,

Address: Arthur Rimbaud,
P.O., in Cairo (Egypt).

To his family

Harar, 4 August 1888

My dear friends,

I have received your letter of June 27. Don't be surprised at the delay in correspondence, since this spot is separated from the coast by deserts which it takes mail a week to cross. Then, the service between Zeilah and Aden is very irregular. Mail leaves Aden for Europe once a week and takes two weeks to reach Marseilles. To write to Europe and receive an answer takes at least three months. It is impossible to write directly from Europe to Harar, since beyond Zeilah, which is under English protection, is the desert inhabited by wandering tribes. Here there are mountains, the continuation of the Abyssinian plateaus: the temperature never goes higher than 25 degrees above zero, and never goes down lower than 5 degrees above zero.

We are now in the rainy season. It is quite desolate. The government is the Abyssinian government of King Menelik, namely a Negro-Christian government; but, all in all, we are in relative peace and safety, business is at times good and at times bad. We live without hope of becoming a millionaire soon. But anyway! since it is my fate to live in this country in this manner . . .

There are scarcely twenty Europeans in all of Abyssinia, including these countries. And you can see over what vast spaces they are scattered. Harar is still the place where there are the most: about ten. I am the only one of French nationality. There is also a Catholic mission with three Fathers, of whom one is French like myself, who are instructing Negro children.

I am still bored a great deal. I have never known anyone who is bored as much as I am. And then, how wretched my life is without a family, without intellectual occupation, lost in the midst of Negroes whose fate I would like to improve, but who try to exploit you and make it impossible for you to carry out your business swiftly. Obliged to speak their jargon, to eat

Obligé de parler leurs baragouins, de manger de leurs sales mets, de subir mille ennuis provenant de leur paresse, de leur trahison, de leur stupidité!

Le plus triste n'est pas encore là. Il est dans la crainte de devenir peu à peu abruti soi-même, isolé qu'on est et éloigné de toute société intelligente.

On importe des soieries, des cotonnades, des thalaris et quelques autres objets: on exporte du café, des gommes, des parfums, de l'ivoire, de l'or qui vient de très loin, etc., etc. Les affaires, quoique importantes, ne suffisent pas à mon activité et se répartissent, d'ailleurs, entre les quelques Européens égarés dans ces vastes contrées.

Je vous salue sincèrement. Ecrivez-moi.

Rimbaud

À sa mère

Harar, 10 août 1890

Il y a longtemps que je n'ai reçu de vos nouvelles. J'aime à vous croire en bonne santé, comme je le suis moi-même.

. . . .

Pourrais-je venir me marier chez vous, au printemps prochain? Mais je ne pourrai consentir à me fixer chez vous, ni à abandonner mes affaires ici. Croyez-vous que je puisse trouver quelqu'un qui consente à me suivre en voyage?

Je voudrais bien avoir une réponse à cette question, aussitôt que possible.

Tous mes souhaits.

Rimbaud

À sa mère

Harar, le 20 février 1891

Ma chère maman,

J'ai bien reçu ta lettre du 5 janvier.

Je vois que tout va bien chez vous, sauf le froid qui, d'après ce que je lis dans les journaux, est excessif par toute l'Europe.

Je vais mal à présent. Du moins, j'ai à la jambe droite des varices qui me font souffrir beaucoup. Voilà ce qu'on gagne à peiner dans ces tristes pays! Et ces varices sont compliquées de rhumatisme. Il ne fait pourtant pas

their filthy food, to accept endless discomforts coming from their laziness, their disloyalty, their stupidity!

This is not the saddest part. It is in the fear of gradually becoming an animal one's self, isolated as we are and cut off from every intelligent society.

We import silks, cottons, thalaris, and a few other objects. We export coffee, gum, perfumes, ivory, and gold which comes from far off, etc., etc. This business, although important, does not occupy my time and is divided, moreover, among the few Europeans who have strayed into these vast regions.

I send you sincere greetings. Write to me.

Rimbaud

To his mother

Harar, 10 August 1890

It is a long time since I heard from you. I like to believe you are in as good health as I am.

. . . .

Could I come home to you and get married next spring? But I couldn't agree on settling down there and giving up my occupation here. Do you think I could find someone who would consent to traveling with me?

I would like to have an answer to this question as soon as possible.

All good wishes.

Rimbaud

To his mother

Harar, 20 February 1891

My dear mother,

I received your letter of January 5.

I see that everything goes well at home, except the cold which, according to what I read in newspapers, is excessive throughout Europe.

I am not well at this moment. You see, varicose veins in my right leg are very painful. This is what you get by working hard in these sad regions! And these varicose veins are complicated by rheumatism. Yet it is not cold

froid ici; mais c'est le climat qui cause cela. Il y a aujourd'hui quinze nuits que je n'ai pas fermé l'œil une minute, à cause de ces douleurs dans cette maudite jambe. Je m'en irais bien, et je crois que la grande chaleur d'Aden me ferait du bien, mais on me doit beaucoup d'argent et je ne puis m'en aller, parce que je le perdrais. J'ai demandé à Aden un bas pour varices, mais je doute que cela se trouve.

Fais-moi donc ce plaisir: achète-moi un bas pour varices, pour une jambe longue et sèche—(le pied est n° 41 pour la chaussure). Il faut que ce bas monte par-dessus le genou, car il y a une varice au-dessus du jarret. Les bas pour varices sont en coton, ou en soie tissée avec des fils d'élastique qui maintiennent les veines gonflées. Ceux en soie sont les meilleurs, les plus solides. Cela ne coûte pas cher, je crois. D'ailleurs, je te rembourserai.

En attendant, je tiens la jambe bandée.

Adresser cela bien empaqueté, par la poste, à Monsieur Tian, à Aden, qui me fera parvenir à la première occasion.

Ces bas pour varices se trouvent peut-être à Vouziers. En tout cas, le médecin de la maison peut en faire venir un bon, de n'importe où.

Cette infirmité m'a été causée par de trop grands efforts à cheval, et aussi par des marches fatigantes. Car nous avons dans ces pays un dédale de montagnes abruptes, où l'on ne peut même se tenir à cheval. Tout cela sans routes et même sans sentiers.

Les varices n'ont rien de dangereux pour la santé, mais elles interdisent tout exercice violent. C'est un grand ennui, parce que les varices produisent des plaies, si l'on ne porte pas le bas pour varices; et encore! les jambes nerveuses ne supportent pas volontiers ce bas, surtout la nuit. Avec cela, j'ai une douleur rhumatismale dans ce maudit genou droit, qui me torture, me prenant souvent la nuit! Et il faut se figurer qu'en cette saison, qui est l'hiver de ce pays, nous n'avons jamais moins de 10 degrés au-dessus de zéro (non pas en dessous). Mais il règne des vents secs, qui sont très insalubres pour les blancs en général. Même des Européens, jeunes, de vingt-cinq à trente ans, sont atteints de rhumatismes, après 2 ou 3 ans de séjour.

La mauvaise nourriture, le logement malsain, le vêtement trop léger, les soucis de toutes sortes, l'ennui, la rage continuelle au milieu de nègres aussi bêtes que canailles, tout cela agit très profondément sur le moral et la santé, en très peu de temps. Une année ici en vaut cinq ailleurs. On vieillit très vite, ici, comme dans tout le Soudan.

Par votre réponse, fixez-moi donc sur ma situation par rapport au service militaire. Ai-je à faire quelque service? Assurez-vous-en, et répondez-moi.

Rimbaud

here. But it is the climate that causes this. For two weeks now I haven't closed my eyes a minute because of the pain in this accursed leg of mine. I would leave here, and believe that the intense heat of Aden would do me good, but I am owed a great deal of money, and I can't go away without losing it. I have sent to Aden for a stocking for varicose veins, but I doubt if it can be found.

So, will you be good enough to buy me a stocking for varicose veins, for a long thin leg (my foot takes a No. 41 shoe). The stocking must come above the knee, because there is a varicose vein above the bend of the knee. Stockings for varicose veins come in cotton, or in silk woven with elastic threads which support the swollen veins. The silk ones are better, and stronger. I believe it is not expensive. Moreover, I will reimburse you.

Meanwhile, I am keeping my leg bandaged.

Send it well wrapped by mail to Monsieur Tian, in Aden, and he will send it to me at the first opportunity.

These stockings for varicose veins can perhaps be found in Vouziers. In any case, the family doctor can get a good one, from any number of places.

This infirmity came about from too much strain on horseback, and from tiring marches. For in this region we have a labyrinth of mountains where you can't even stay on horseback. There are no roads or even paths there.

Varicose veins do not endanger one's health, but they prevent any violent exercise. It is troublesome because varicose veins produce sores unless the stocking is worn; and what is more, nervous people cannot easily stand wearing the stocking, especially at night. In addition, I have a rheumatic pain in this wretched right knee which tortures me, and which starts up only at night! And you must remember that in this season, which is winter here, we have never less than ten degrees above zero (not below). But there is frequent dry wind, very unhealthy for white people in general. Even young Europeans, between 25 and 30 years old, suffer from rheumatism, after living here 2 or 3 years!

Bad food, poor lodging, too light clothing, worries of all kinds, boredom, continual anger over Negroes who are both stupid and dishonest—all this has a deep influence on one's disposition and health, in a very short time. One year here is equal to five elsewhere. Men grow old here fast, as in all the Soudan.

In your answer tell me exactly what my position is with regard to military service. Do I have to give some time to it? Check on this and tell me.

Rimbaud

À sa mère

Ma chère maman,

J'ai bien reçu vos deux bas et votre lettre, et je les ai reçus dans de tristes circonstances. Voyant toujours augmenter l'enflure de mon genou droit et la douleur dans l'articulation, sans pouvoir trouver aucun remède ni aucun avis, puisqu'au Harar nous sommes au milieu des nègres et qu'il n'y a point là d'Européens, je me décidai à descendre. Il fallait abandonner les affaires: ce qui n'était pas très facile, car j'avais de l'argent dispersé de tous les côtés; mais enfin je réussis à liquider à peu près totalement. Depuis une vingtaine de jours, j'étais couché au Harar et dans l'impossibilité de faire un seul mouvement, souffrant des douleurs atroces et ne dormant jamais. Je louai seize nègres porteurs, à raison de 15 thalaris l'un, du Harar à Zeilah; je fis fabriquer une civière recouverte d'une toile, et c'est là dessus que je viens de faire, en douze jours, les 300 kilomètres de désert qui séparent les monts du Harar du port de Zeilah. Inutile de vous dire quelles souffrances j'ai subies en route. Je n'ai jamais pu faire un pas hors de ma civière; mon genou gonflait à vue d'œil, et la douleur augmentait continuellement.

Arrivé ici, je suis entré à l'hôpital européen. Il y a une seule chambre pour les malades payants: je l'occupe. Le docteur anglais, dès que je lui ai eu montré mon genou, a crié que c'est une *synovite arrivée à un point très dangereux,* par suite du manque de soins et des fatigues. Il parlait d'abord de couper la jambe; ensuite, il a décidé d'attendre quel-ques jours pour voir si le gonflement, diminuerait un peu avec les soins médicaux. Il y a six jours de cela, et aucune amélioration, sinon que, comme je suis au repos, la douleur a beaucoup diminué. Vous savez que la synovite est une maladie des liquides de l'articulation du genou, cela peut provenir d'hérédité, ou d'accidents, ou encore de bien des causes. Pour moi, cela a été certaine-ment causé par les fatigues des marches à pied et à cheval au Harar. Enfin, à l'état où je suis arrivé, il ne faut pas espérer que je guérisse avant au moins trois mois, sous les circonstances les plus favorables. Et je suis étendu, la jambe bandée, liée, reliée, enchaînée, de façon à ne pouvoir la mouvoir. Je suis devenu un squelette: je fais peur. Mon dos est tout écorché du lit; je ne dors pas une minute. Et ici la chaleur est devenue très forte. La nourri-ture de l'hôpital, que je paie pourtant assez cher, est très mauvaise. Je ne sais quoi faire. D'un autre côté, je n'ai pas encore terminé mes comptes avec mon associé, m[onsieu]r Tian. Cela ne finira pas avant la huitaine. Je sortirai de cette affaire avec 35.000 francs environ. J'aurais eu plus; mais, à cause de mon malheureux départ, je perds quelques milliers de francs. J'ai

Aden, 30 April 1891

My dear mother,

I received your two stockings and your letter, and I received them under sad circumstances. Since the swelling of my right knee continued getting worse, and the pain in the joints, and unable to find a remedy or advice, because in Harar we are in a Negro colony and there are no Europeans, I decided to go down to Aden. I had to give up the business, which was not easy, for my money was spread out in every direction; but finally I succeeded in liquidating almost everything. For twenty days, I was in bed in Harar, unable to move, suffering atrocious pain and never sleeping. I hired sixteen Negro porters, for 15 thalaris each, for the distance between Harar and Zeilah. I had a canvas-covered litter built, and it was on that that I have just covered in twelve days the 300 kilometers of desert separating the mountains of Harar from the harbor of Zeilah. No need to tell you the suffering I underwent on the way. I was never able to take one step outside my litter. You could almost see my knee swelling up and the pain increased continuously.

Once here, I went into the European hospital. There is only one room for patients who can pay. I am in it. The English doctor, as soon as I showed him my knee, exclaimed that it is a *synovitis which has reached a very dangerous point,* as the result of fatigue and lack of care. He spoke first of cutting the leg off. Then he decided to wait a few days to see if the swelling, would go down a bit, with medical care. There have been six days of this, with no change for the better, save that the pain has greatly diminished, since I am resting. You know that synovitis is a malady of the liquids in the joints of the knee, it can come from heredity, or an accident, or from many other causes. I believe it was caused by the fatigue of journeys on foot and horseback in Harar. At any rate, in the state I have reached, there is no hope I will be cured in less than three months, under the most favorable circumstances. And I am stretched out, my leg bandaged, tied and attached so that I cannot move it. I have become a skeleton. I frighten people. My skin is coming off my back because of the bed. I can't sleep one minute. And the heat has become very intense here. The hospital food, which is very expensive, is very bad. I don't know what to do. Another thing, I haven't concluded my accounting with my associate, Monsieur Tian. This will take another week. After the deal is closed I will have about 35 thousand francs. I would have had more, but because of my unfortunate departure I lost a few thousand francs. I want to be taken to a steamship

envie de me faire porter à un vapeur, et de venir me faire traiter en France, le voyage me ferait encore passer le temps. Et, en France, les soins médicaux et les remèdes sont bon marché, et l'air bon. Il est fort probable que je vais venir. Les vapeurs pour la France à présent sont malheureusement toujours combles, parce que tout le monde rentre des colonies à ce temps de l'année. Et je suis un pauvre infirme qu'il faut *transporter* très doucement! Enfin, je vais prendre mon parti dans la huitaine.

Ne vous effrayez pas de tout cela, cependant. De meilleurs jours viendront. Mais c'est une triste récompense de tant de travail, de privations et de peines! Hélas! que notre vie est donc misérable!

Je vous salue de cœur.

Rimbaud

P.S. — Quant aux bas, ils sont inutiles. Je les revendrai quelque part.

À sa mère et à sa sœur

Marseille, [jeudi 21 mai 1891]

Ma chère maman, ma chère sœur,

Après des souffrances terrible, ne pouvant me faire soigner à Aden, j'ai pris le bateau des Messageries pour rentrer en France.

Je suis arrivé hier, après treize jours de douleurs. Me trouvant trop faible à l'arrivée ici, et saisi par le froid, j'ai dû entrer à *l'hôpital de la Conception,* où je paie dix f[ran]cs par jour, docteur compris.

Je suis très mal, très mal, je suis réduit à l'état de squelette par cette maladie de ma jambe gauche[49] qui est devenue à présent énorme et ressemble à une énorme citrouille. C'est une synovite, une hydrarthrose, etc., une maladie de l'articulation et des os.

Cela doit durer très longtemps, si des complications n'obligent pas à couper la jambe. En tous cas, j'en resterai estropié. Mais je doute que j'attende. La vie m'est devenue impossible. Que je suis donc malheureux! Que je suis donc devenu malheureux!

J'ai à toucher ici une traite de f[ran]cs 36.800 sur le Comptoir national d'Escompte de Paris. Mais je n'ai personne pour s'occuper de placer cet argent. Pour moi, je ne puis faire un seul pas hors du lit. Je n'ai pas encore pu toucher l'argent. Que faire. Quelle triste vie! Ne pouvez-vous m'aider en rien?

Rimbaud.
Hôpital de la Conception.
Marseille.

and go to France for treatment, the trip would give me more time. And, in France, medical care and medicine are much cheaper, and the air is good. It is quite likely that I will go there. These days the steamships for France unfortunately are always filled, because everyone from the colonies is going home at this time of the year. And I am a poor cripple who has to be *carried* very gently! In short, I will make up my mind in a week.

Don't be upset by all this, however. Better days will come. But it is a sorry reward for so much work and privations and struggle! Alas! how wretched our life really is!

Warmest greetings

Rimbaud

P.S. — The stockings are useless. I will sell them somewhere.

To his mother and sister

Marseilles, [Thursday, 21 May 1891]

My dear mother, my dear sister,

After terrible suffering and unable to be cared for in Aden, I took the boat of the Messageries to return to France.

I arrived yesterday, after thirteen days of pain. Feeling too weak on my arrival here, and overcome with the cold, I had to enter the *Hospital of the Conception,* where I pay ten francs a day, doctor included.

I am very poorly, very poorly, I have shrunk to the state of a skeleton through this sickness of my left leg which now has become huge and looks like a huge pumpkin. It is a synovitis, hydrarthrosis, etc., a sickness of the joints and bones.

It will last a long time unless complications force them to cut off the leg. In any case, I will be crippled. But I doubt if I will wait. Life has become impossible for me. How wretched I am! How wretched I have become!

Here I have to cash a check of 36,800 francs at the Comptoir National d'Escompte de Paris. But I have no one to help me get this money. I can't take one step out of bed. I haven't yet been able to get my money. What can I do? What a sad life! Can't you help me in some way?

Rimbaud.
Hospital of the Conception.
Marseilles.

À sa sœur

Marseille, 23 juin 1891

Ma chère sœur,

Tu ne m'as pas écrit; que s'est-il passé? Ta lettre m'avait fait peur, j'aimerais avoir de tes nouvelles. Pourvu qu'il ne s'agisse pas de nouveaux ennuis, car, hélas, nous sommes trop éprouvés à la fois!

Pour moi, je ne fais que pleurer jour et nuit, je suis un homme mort, je suis estropié pour toute ma vie. Dans la quinzaine, je serai guéri, je pense; mais je ne pourrai marcher qu'avec des béquilles. Quant à une jambe artificielle, le médecin dit qu'il faudra attendre très longtemps, au moins six mois! Pendant ce temps que ferai-je, où resterai-je? Si j'allais chez vous, le froid me chasserait dans trois mois, et même en moins de temps; car, d'ici, je ne serai capable de me mouvoir que dans six semaines, le temps de m'exercer à béquiller! Je ne serais donc chez vous que fin juillet. Et il me faudrait repartir fin septembre.

Je ne sais pas du tout quoi faire. Tous ces soucis me rendent fou: je ne dors jamais une minute.

Enfin, notre vie est une misère, une misère sans fin! Pourquoi donc existons-nous?

Envoyez-moi de vos nouvelles.

Mes meilleurs souhaits.

Rimbaud.
Hôpital de la Conception.
Marseille.

Au Directeur des Messageries Maritimes

Marseille, 9 novembre 1891.[50]

UN LOT: UNE DENT SEULE.
UN LOT: DEUX DENTS.
UN LOT: TROIS DENTS.
UN LOT: QUATRE DENTS.
UN LOT: DEUX DENTS.

Monsieur le Directeur,

Je viens vous demander si je n'ai rien laissé à votre compte. Je désire changer aujourd'hui de ce service-ci, dont je ne connais même pas le nom, mais en tout cas que ce soit le service d'Aphinar. Tous ces services sont là

Marseilles, 23 June 1891

My dear sister,

You haven't written; what has happened? Your letter had frightened me. I wish I had news of you. I only hope there are no new troubles, because, alas, we are having too many trials at once!

All I do is weep day and night. I have ceased living. I am crippled for the rest of my life. In two weeks I will be cured, I think. But I will need crutches in order to walk. To have an artificial leg, the doctor says I will have to wait a long time, at least six months! What will I do during that time, where will I stay? If I went home to you, the cold would force me to leave in three months, and even in less time. From here I won't be able to move in less than six weeks, the time needed to practice using a crutch! So I wouldn't be home before the end of July. And I would have to leave again at the end of September.

I have no idea what to do. All these worries are driving me mad. I can't sleep for one minute.

Yes, our life is a misery, an endless misery! Why do we exist?
Send me the news.
Best wishes.

Rimbaud.
Hospital of the Conception.
Marseilles.

To the Director of the Messageries Maritimes

Marseilles, 9 November 1891.

ONE LOT: ONE SINGLE TUSK.
ONE LOT: TWO TUSKS.
ONE LOT: THREE TUSKS.
ONE LOT: FOUR TUSKS.
ONE LOT: TWO TUSKS.

Monsieur le Directeur,

I wish to know if I have left anything on your account. I would like to change from this service, whose name I don't even know, but in any case that it might be for the service of Aphinar. All the services there are every-

partout, et moi, impotent, malheureux, je ne peux rien trouver, le premier chien dans la rue vous dira cela.

Envoyez-moi donc le prix des services d'Aphinar à Suez. Je suis complètement paralysé: donc je désire me trouver de bonne heure à bord. Dites-moi à quelle heure je dois être transporté à bord.

where, and I, infirm, miserable, I cannot find anything, the first dog in the street will tell you so.

Please send me the price for services from Aphinar to Suez. I am completely paralyzed. I would therefore like to be on board well in advance. Tell me at what time I should be carried aboard.

Notes

1. An earlier version of this poem was sent, with the title *Credo in unam,* to Théodore de Banville on 24 May 1870. The present edition reproduces the final version, part of the "recueil Demeny." In the spirit of inclusiveness, it also retains between parentheses the thirty-five lines from the end of the third section that Rimbaud left out of the Demeny version. Throughout this edition, parentheses will be used to include lines of poetry omitted from the version chosen; see Murphy's multi-version edition for a thorough presentation and discussion of variants.

2. Variants (not including slight differences in punctuation and capitalization) in the "Recueil Demeny" version include: lines 16–17, "Et quand, pendant que minuit sonne, / Façonné, pétillant et jaune,"; line 29, "Au grillage, chantant des choses,"; and line 31, "Mais bien bas,— comme une prière . . ." In the "Recueil Verlaine": line 12, "Grogne un vieil air"; line 17, "Façonné comme une brioche"; line 26, "Les pauvres Jésus pleins de givre"; line 29, "Au treillage, grognant des choses"; lines 31–32, "Tout bêtes, faisant leurs prières / Et repliés vers ces lumières"; and line 35, "Et que leur chemise tremblotte."

3. Sarrebruck (Saarbrücken), August 2, 1870, was a major victory, whose importance was inflated by the emperor. Pitou: name for an unsophisticated soldier. Dumanet: name for a credulous trooper. Chassepot: name of the rifle's inventor. Boquillon: from a lampooning newspaper, *La lanterne de Boquillon.*

4. In line 12, the "Accomplice in spectacles" is Emile Ollivier, president of the Council of Ministers, who ordered the plebiscite of May 8th and declared war on Germany July 19th.

5. There are three versions of this poem. "Le cœur supplicié" ("The Tortured Heart") was sent to Georges Izambard on 13 May 1871, "Le cœur du pitre" ("The Fool's Heart") to Paul Demeny on 10 June of the same year. "Le cœur volé" ("The Stolen Heart") was recopied by Verlaine in late 1871 or early 1872.

6. line 4: *regard darne: darne* is a word of the Ardennes. It means "dazzled" or "dizzy." It is used especially for sheep, but sometimes for humans. *Darne* is also in *Les poètes de sept ans.*

7. In stanza 15, *Stryx* are night vampires, and the *Cariatides* are symbols of the greatness of antiquity.

8. In French, *vers* can mean either verses or worms.

9. The first twenty lines of this poem have been lost.

10. One aspect of this poem is a parody of the Parnassian poets who used such exotic plant names as: *Lotos, Hélianthes, Oçokas.* In the last stanza, Tréguier, birthplace of Renan, and Paramaribo, a city in Guyana, refer to Rimbaud's attack on both conventional French poetry and exotic poetry.

11. Rather than keep *desseins* (intentions), the word written in Rimbaud's hand, many editions change this word to *dessins* (drawings), thereby betraying the original manuscript. See Murphy, *Œuvres complètes*, vol. 1, 503.

12. In his note on the manuscript, Verlaine indicates "casseuses" (breakers) as a variant for "ployeuses."

13. A memory of Rimbaud's visits to the library in Charleville. Several neologisms: *boulus* (1.2) from *boulures; hargnosités* (1.3) from *hargneux; percaliser* (1.10) from *percale. Fécondés* (1.38), "made fertile," seems to refer to the love between the seated men and their chairs. The *petits amours de chaises* in the following line are the offspring. The spellings *emmaillottée* (1.15) and *gifflés* (1.22), often corrected by editors, are retained here, since dictionaries of the period accepted these spellings (see Murphy, *Œuvres complètes*, vol. 1, 521).

14. Since the manuscript for this poem was written in Verlaine's hand, nearly all editions have felt comfortable taking the liberty of changing the word from *vers* (worms or verse/verses; see "L'orgie parisienne" [Parisian Orgy] line 57) to *verts* (green). The present edition chooses to respect the manuscript, which clearly indicates *vers* (see Murphy, *Œuvres complètes*, vol. 4, 289), allowing for "a submersion precisely in the stuff of poetry" (Murphy, *Œuvres complètes*, vol. 1, 537; my translation).

15. A good example of Rimbaud's provocative-ironic style. *Je vis assis* (1.1) the poet scorns the active man. *une Gambier / Aux dents* (lines 3–4), cf. Manet's painting, *Le bon bock. Voilures* may mean clouds or smoke. *Le Seigneur du cèdre et des hysopes* (1.12) biblical (God reigns over the great and the small) for the violent contrast with line 13: which proves the irony of the sonnet's title. *Héliotropes:* a hieratic flower which honors the sun by turning toward it.

16. This album, of thirty pages, was first published in 1943. It contains humorous, obscene poems composed by friends of Verlaine who met together to recite poetry. They parodied one another. The name of the poet parodied usually appeared after the poem, followed by the initials of the real poet.

17. Paris in 1871: Alphonse Godillot: shoe merchant; Gambier: pipes; Wolff-Pleyel: pianos; Galopeau: frock coats; Meunier: chocolate; Le Perdriel: pharmacist; Veuillot: Catholic writer; Tropmann: criminal who was guillotined; Augier: playwright; Gill: artist; Mendès: writer; L'Hérissé: hatter; Enghiens chez soi: Enghiens mineral water tablets.

18. *Ibled* is chocolate made in Toulouse.

19. It would seem that Rimbaud chose to keep this misspelling; see Murphy *Œuvres complètes*, vol. 1, 705–6.

20. This poem is one of several from 1872 that reappear in *Délires II. Alchimie du verbe (Une saison en enfer)*.

21. The inclusion of "Patience," instead of the earlier version of the same poem (entitled "Bannières de mai" / "May Banners") reflects an editorial decision made possible by the inclusion of the manuscript in a recent exhibit at the Musée Condé in Chantilly (mentioned in the foreword to this edition). As Steve Murphy makes clear (*Œuvres complètes*, vol. 1 [Paris: Honoré Champion, 1999], 746–51), editions of Rimbaud's work should reprint "Patience," as it represents the last known version of the poem. See Emmanuelle Toulet, ed. *Livres du Cabi-*

net de Pierre Berès (Chantilly: Musée Condée, 2003) and Steve Murphy, "Trois manuscrits de Rimbaud," *Histoires littéraires* 17 (2004): 34–57, in particular 36–37.

22. On the back of "Patience," Rimbaud jotted down a line of poetry by Marceline Desbordes-Valmore: "Prends-y garde, ô ma vie absente!" ("Watch out, o my absent life!"); see Lucien Chovet, "Un *faux Rimbaud* encore non identifié ou Marceline Desbordes-Valmore plagiaire par anticipation de Rimbaud," *Histoires littéraires* 5 (2001): 61–66; this manuscript is reproduced in Murphy, "Trois manuscrits de Rimbaud," op. cit., between pp. 46 and 47.

23. Rimbaud clearly wrote "Nôtre" on the manuscript; see Murphy, *Œuvres complètes,* vol. 1, 770 (note) and Murphy, *Œuvres complètes,* vol. 4, 348.

24. The asterisk in line 15 sends the reader to this line, at the bottom of the manuscript. Whether it represents a correction or a variant of line 15 is not known; see Murphy, *Œuvres complètes,* vol. 1, 785.

25. For the reference to Enghien see the poem *Paris*. The last word in the poem, *Habitude,* would seem to be masturbation.

26. In May 2004, a previously unknown version of this poem went to auction. While its status as an earlier version does not change the choice of the current "Mémoire" as the version of reference (see Steve Murphy, *Histoires littéraires* 19 [2004]), it is notable for its title ("d'Edgar Poe. Famille maudite" ["by Edgar Poe. Damned Family"]), for the variants from the final version, and, perhaps most interestingly, for its provenance. Passed through the hands of Verlaine's ex-wife, Mathilde Mauté de Fleurville, this manuscript leaves hope that other previously unknown manuscripts are yet to come, and that Mathilde did not discard all documents from or relating to Rimbaud, as she claimed (see Ex-Madame Paul Verlaine, *Mémoires de ma vie* [Seyssel: Champ Vallon, 1992], 207–9).

27. The recently discovered manuscript shows clearly that this word is "avant," and not "ayant," as has long been thought.

28. Often corrected by editors, the spelling of "Boulevart" reflects not an error but an alternate spelling, accepted at the time; see Murphy *Œuvres complètes,* vol. 1, 861–62.

29. These nonsensical words are built around *sapristi,* which comes from *sacristi,* itself an exclamatory variant of *sacristie* (sacristy). Both *sapristi* and *sacristi* mean the rough equivalent of "Good heavens," but they appear in the French here because their usage is mostly onomatopoetic.

30. For this assignment—a translation of part of Lucretius's *De rerum natura*—Rimbaud handed in a corrected version of Sully-Prudhomme's recent (1869) translation of the same; this fact went unnoticed, as Rimbaud's assignment was chosen to be published in the *Bulletin de l'Académie de Douai* of 11 April 1870. For more on this poem, including the specific Sully-Prudhomme verses that Rimbaud corrected, see the Pléiade edition, 1028. Although in verse, this poem appears in the first part of *Proses* because it reflects, like the three other poems in this section, schoolboy pursuits more than serious attempts at poetry. In this respect, *Invocation à Vénus* is markedly different from its contemporary verse poems from *Poésies*.

31. For information on this school composition, including the numerous references to Villon throughout, see the notes in the Pléiade edition, 1028–30; the note to Olivier Basselin's work *Vaux-de-Vire (Valleys of the Vire),* popular satirical songs that inspired the English word *vaudeville,* is Rimbaud's.

32. Olivier Basselin, Vaux de Vire.

33. These prose poems were probably written in 1871.

34. The punctuation mark at the end of this poem is not clear on the ms.; while most editions have favored an exclamation point, the mark looks less like what is found at the end of

the previous line in this poem than the question mark at the end of the first part of "Vies" ("Lives"), on the other side of this folio. Given the undeniable curvature of the top of the symbol, the present edition breaks with tradition and opts for the question mark.

35. The order of the two poems entitled "Villes" ("Cities"), which appear on opposite sides of the same manuscript page, is not certain. Going against what has been editorial tradition since their first publication, Guyaux asserts that the discernible roman numerals *I* (below the title in "L'acropole officielle [. . .]") and *II* (covered by the title in "Ce sont des villes! [. . .]") are sufficient to place them in the order those numbers suggest. Murphy refutes this reasoning, reminding us that "Ce sont des villes! [. . .]" begins on ms. p. 15 and ends on p. 16, whereas "L'acropole officielle [. . .]" begins at the bottom of p. 16 (and continues on to p. 17). In the absence of a convincing argument to contradict almost all editions of *Illuminations,* the present edition maintains the traditional order for the "Villes" poems and refers to them not by roman numerals but by their first lines. For more on the order of these poems, see Guyaux *Poétique du fragment: Essai sur les* Illuminations *de Rimbaud* (1991), 251–52 and Murphy *Œuvres complètes,* vol. 4, 609–10.

36. It is unclear from the ms. if this word is *plans* or *plants.*

37. Born 20 October 1854, Rimbaud was fifteen on this date.

38. Following his signature, Rimbaud included early versions of "Sensation," "Ophélie" ("Ophelia"), and "Credo in unam," later entitled "Soleil et chair" ("Sun and Flesh").

39. *Anumphē,* the transliteration of the Greek, means unwedded. For more on this word and on Rimbaud's reading of Antigone and of female poets like Siefert, see Adrianna M. Paliyenko, "Re-reading *la femme poète:* Rimbaud and Louisa Siefert," *Nineteenth-Century French Studies* 26.1&2 (Fall 1997–Winter 1998): 146–58.

40. This translation—faithful to Verlaine's original line—keeps the caesura in the middle of the alexandrine to show the internal enjambment; that is, the break that divides the twelve beats into two equal six-syllable parts comes in the middle of a word, contrary to classical prosody. That Verlaine's poetry displays such breaks from traditional versification is the very point that Rimbaud is trying to make.

41. See the note about "Le cœur volé" ("The Stolen Heart") earlier in this edition.

42. Rimbaud's double negative is intentional.

43. Name of the group of young writers and artists, including Théophile Gautier, Gérard de Nerval, Pétrus Borel, and Arsène Houssaye, whose enthusiasm for Romanticism sparked the famous "bataille d'*Hernani*" in 1830. In 1833, Gautier published a collection of short stories with the title *Les Jeune-France,* ironically mocking his contemporaries.

44. *Comprachicos:* kidnappers of children who mutilate them in order to exhibit them as monsters.

45. Letter lost, quoted from memory by Verlaine's wife Mathilde. Ex-Madame Paul Verlaine, *Mémoires de ma vie* (Seyssel: Éditions Champ Vallon, 1992), 139.

46. Letter lost. This famous phrase is quoted in Ernest Delahaye, *Rimbaud, l'artiste et l'être moral,* (Messein, 1923), 39–40.

47. This word is a play on "carolopolitain," an adjective meaning "from Charleville."

48. Here Rimbaud is playing with one of the morphemes perceptible in the word "courage," "cou" (neck). Instead of spelling the word normally, Rimbaud substitutes "col," another word for neck (and from the same Latin root, *collum*), at the beginning of the word.

49. A mistake on Rimbaud's part; he meant his right leg.

50. Rimbaud dictated this, his last letter, to his sister. He died at 10 AM the next morning, 10 November 1891.

Index of Titles and First Lines